Models, Methods, Concepts & Applications

of the

Analytic Hierarchy Process

INTERNATIONAL SERIES IN OPERATIONS RESEARCH & MANAGEMENT SCIENCE

Frederick S. Hillier, Series Editor
Stanford University

Saigal, R. / *LINEAR PROGRAMMING: A Modern Integrated Analysis*

Nagurney, A. & Zhang, D. / *PROJECTED DYNAMICAL SYSTEMS AND VARIATIONAL INEQUALITIES WITH APPLICATIONS*

Padberg, M. & Rijal, M. / *LOCATION, SCHEDULING, DESIGN AND INTEGER PROGRAMMING*

Vanderbei, R. / *LINEAR PROGRAMMING: Foundations and Extensions*

Jaiswal, N.K. / *MILITARY OPERATIONS RESEARCH: Quantitative Decision Making*

Gal, T. & Greenberg, H. / *ADVANCES IN SENSITIVITY ANALYSIS AND PARAMETRIC PROGRAMMING*

Prabhu, N.U. / *FOUNDATIONS OF QUEUEING THEORY*

Fang, S.-C., Rajasekera, J.R. & Tsao, H.-S.J. / *ENTROPY OPTIMIZATION AND MATHEMATICAL PROGRAMMING*

Yu, G. / *OPERATIONS RESEARCH IN THE AIRLINE INDUSTRY*

Ho, T.-H. & Tang, C. S. / *PRODUCT VARIETY MANAGEMENT*

El-Taha, M. & Stidham , S. / *SAMPLE-PATH ANALYSIS OF QUEUEING SYSTEMS*

Miettinen, K. M. / *NONLINEAR MULTIOBJECTIVE OPTIMIZATION*

Chao, H. & Huntington, H. G. / *DESIGNING COMPETITIVE ELECTRICITY MARKETS*

Weglarz, J. / *PROJECT SCHEDULING: Recent Models, Algorithms & Applications*

Sahin, I. & Polatoglu, H. / *QUALITY, WARRANTY AND PREVENTIVE MAINTENANCE*

Tavares, L. V. / *ADVANCED MODELS FOR PROJECT MANAGEMENT*

Tayur, S., Ganeshan, R. & Magazine, M. / *QUANTITATIVE MODELING FOR SUPPLY CHAIN MANAGEMENT*

Weyant, J./ *ENERGY AND ENVIRONMENTAL POLICY MODELING*

Shanthikumar, J.G. & Sumita, U./*APPLIED PROBABILITY AND STOCHASTIC PROCESSES*

Liu, B. & Esogbue, A.O. / *DECISION CRITERIA AND OPTIMAL INVENTORY PROCESSES*

Gal, Stewart & Hanne/ *MULTICRITERIA DECISION MAKING: Advances in MCDM Models, Algorithms, Theory, and Applications*

Fox, B. L./ *STRATEGIES FOR QUASI-MONTE CARLO*

Hall, R.W. / *HANDBOOK OF TRANSPORTATION SCIENCE*

Grassman, W.K./ *COMPUTATIONAL PROBABILITY*

Pomerol & Barba-Romero / *MULTICRITERION DECISION IN MANAGEMENT*

Axsäter / *INVENTORY CONTROL*

Wolkowicz, Saigal & Vandenberghe/ *HANDBOOK OF SEMIDEFINITE PROGRAMMING: Theory, Algorithms, and Applications*

Hobbs, B. F. & Meier, P. / *ENERGY DECISIONS AND THE ENVIRONMENT: A Guide to the Use of Multicriteria Methods*

Dar-El/ *HUMAN LEARNING: From Learning Curves to Learning Organizations*

Armstrong/ *PRINCIPLES OF FORECASTING: A Handbook for Researchers and Practitioners*

Balsamo/ *ANALYSIS OF QUEUEING NETWORKS WITH BLOCKING*

Bouyssou et al/ *EVALUATION AND DECISION MODELS: A Critical Perspective*

Hanne, T./ *INTELLIGENT STRATEGIES FOR META MULTIPLE CRITERIA DECISION MAKING*

Models, Methods, Concepts & Applications of the Analytic Hierarchy Process

by

Thomas L. Saaty

and

Luis G. Vargas

University of Pittsburgh

Springer Science+Business Media, LLC

Library of Congress Cataloging-in-Publication

Saaty, Thomas L.
Models, methods, concepts & applications of the analytic hierarchy process / by Thomas L. Saaty and Luis G. Vargas.
p. cm. -- (International series in operations research & management science; 34)
Includes bibliographical references and index.
ISBN 978-1-4613-5667-7 ISBN 978-1-4615-1665-1 (eBook)
DOI 10.1007/978-1-4615-1665-1
1. Social sciences--Mathematical models. 2. Economics--Mathematical models. 3. Policy sciences--Mathematical models. 4. Decision making--Mathematical models. 5. Operations research--Mathematics. I. Vargas, Luis G. (Luis Gonzalez) II. Title. III. Series.

H61.25 .S2 2000
300'.1'5118--dc21

Originally published by Kluwer Academic Publishers in 2001
Softcover reprint of the hardcover 1st edition 2001

Printed on acid-free paper.

TABLE OF CONTENTS

PREFACE

This book is a collection of selected applications of the Analytic Hierarchy Process (AHP) in economic, social, political, and technological areas. This volume along with other volumes on decision making, planning, conflict resolution and forecasting, rounds out the diversity of application areas of the AHP.

We have been particularly interested in three themes: economics, the social sciences and the linking of measurement with human values. The AHP offers economists a substantially different approach to deal with economic problems through ratio scales. The main mathematical models on which economics has based its quantitative thinking up to now are utility theory which uses interval scales and linear programming. The axiomatic foundation of utility theory uses gambles or lotteries to elicit judgments about utilities from decision makers. Over the years, practitioners of utility theory have encountered paradoxes that contradict the basic axioms of their theory. Some of the developers of the paradoxes have even won Nobel prizes for their findings. We hope that the variety of examples included here can perhaps stimulate some readers to try applying this new approach.

The second theme is concerned with the social sciences. The AHP offers psychologists, sociologists and political scientists the methodology they have sought for some time to quantify and derive measurements for intangibles. We hope that the examples included in this book will induce them to study the theory. It should quickly become clear that the AHP is the kind of instrument they have been seeking.

The third theme is concerned with providing people in the physical and engineering sciences with a quantitative method to link hard measurement to human values. In such a process one needs to interpret what the measurements mean. A number is useless until someone understands what it means. It can have different meanings in different problems. Ten dollars are plenty to satisfy ones hunger but are useless by themselves in buying a new car. Such measurements are only indicators of the state of a system, but do not relate to the values of the human observers of that system.

Many of the applications in the book were sponsored, co-authored or supervised by the first author in his classes and in his research, and some by the second author. Our friendship has often brought us together to carry out a project that would otherwise be onerous for one person to do. We enjoy thinking of the topics, motivating the works and performing the task of collecting and bringing together what appears to us of potential interest to readers and users of the Analytic Hierarchy Process. Most of these studies have been edited and shortened but their essence preserved. We believe that the AHP is a general tool that is helpful in assisting the mind to organize its thoughts and experiences and to elicit judgments recorded in memory. Co-authorship of the papers and reports has been observed to be useful in debating judgments that may otherwise appear too subjective and idiosyncratic. Thus the reader will notice that many of the chapters are co-authored. The authors of these works often studied the literature to find out what the real actors in a problem thought and said and inferred judgments from their knowledge.

The variety combined in this book has been greatly enhanced with Expert Choice, the personal computer software implementation of the AHP, that is now used fairly widely by decision makers in industry and government, by consultants and by teachers and students in business and engineering schools. The first author has already put together another volume on applications with feedback and dependence using the network version of the AHP known as the Analytic Network Process (ANP). That topic is also studied by the first author in a chapter of his book "Fundamentals of Decision Making in Priority Theory with the Analytic Hierarchy Process" published in 1994 as the sixth volume of the AHP series and in a new book entitled "The Analytic Network Process" first published in 1996 and revised in 2001.

The following authors have contributed the chapters of this book:

Chapter 17: *The Case of the Spotted Owl versus the Logging Industry*
by Ronald J. Bucci and Steve Wagner

Chapter 18: *Selection of Recycling Goal Most Likely to Succeed*
by Annett Ahart, Lynn Ehrke, Chuck Fritz,
Ninamary Langsdale, Jack Oackey and Susan Sargut

Chapter 19: *To Drill or Not To Drill: A Synthesis of Expert Judgments*
by Hameed G. Nezad and Alan Baharlou

Chapter 20: *Modeling the Graduate Business School Admission Process*
by Thomas L. Saaty, J.W. France
and Kathy R. Valentine

Chapter 21: *Infertility Decision Making*
by Sudha Iyengar and Vijaya Ghandi

Chapter 22: *The Decision by the US Congress on China's Trade Status: A Multicriteria Analysis*
by Thomas L. Saaty and Yeonmin Cho

Chapter 23: *Deciding Between Angioplasty and Coronary Artery Bypass Surgery*
by Thomas A. Kasperski, John J. Umphred and
Andrew F. Firlik, MD

Some of the chapters in this volume were reports prepared for graduate courses taught by the first author (Chapters 4, 5, 6, 12, 14, 15, 16, 17 and 23) and by the second author (Chapters 11 and 18) while others, as indicated in the references of each chapter, are reproduced with permission of the authors after being appropriately edited and adapted. We are grateful to these authors for permission to include their edited materials in the book. The excellent collection of articles included here has been made possible because of their contributions.

CHAPTER 1

HOW TO MAKE A DECISION

1. INTRODUCTION

ιερά αρχή is the Greek word for hierarchy meaning holy origin or holy rule[1]. It is the ordering of parts or elements of a whole from the highest to the lowest. A hierarchy is the principle of control that secures the effective functioning of the organization[2].

"You can't compare apples and oranges," so the saying goes. But is this true? Consider a hungry person who likes both apples and oranges and is offered a choice between a large, red, pungent, juicy looking Washington State apple and an even larger, old and shrivelled, pale colored orange with a soft spot. Which one is that person more likely to choose? Let us reverse the situation and offer the same person on the next day a small, deformed, unripe apple with a couple of worm holes and a fresh colored navel orange from California. Which one is he or she more likely to choose now?

We have learned through experience to identify properties and establish selection criteria for apples and oranges and in fact we use that experience to make tradeoffs among the properties and reach a decision. We choose the apple or orange that yields, according to our preferences, the greater value across all the various attributes.

The Analytic Hierarchy Process (AHP) is a basic approach to decision making. It is designed to cope with both the rational and the intuitive to select the best from a number of alternatives evaluated with respect to several criteria. In this process, the decision maker carries out simple pairwise comparison judgments which are then used to develop overall priorities for ranking the alternatives. The AHP both allows for inconsistency in the judgments and provides a means to improve consistency.

The simplest form used to structure a decision problem is a hierarchy consisting of three levels: the goal of the decision at the top level, followed by a second level consisting of the criteria by which the alternatives, located in the third level, will be evaluated. Hierarchical decomposition of complex systems appears to be a basic device used by the human mind to cope with diversity. One organizes the factors affecting the decision in gradual steps from the general, in the upper

---

[1] Encyclopedia Catholica

[2] The Great Soviet Encyclopedia, Moscow 1970.

levels of the hierarchy, to the particular, in the lower levels. The purpose of the structure is to make it possible to judge the importance of the elements in a given level with respect to some or all of the elements in the adjacent level above. Once the structuring is completed, the AHP is surprisingly simple to apply.

In this chapter we show that there is a real and practical use for judgments and priorities in human affairs. This use is not contrived; we are led to them in a very natural way.

2. HOW TO STRUCTURE A DECISION PROBLEM

Perhaps the most creative task in making a decision is deciding what factors to include in the hierarchic structure. When constructing hierarchies one must include enough relevant detail to represent the problem as thoroughly as possible, but not so thoroughly as to lose sensitivity to change in the elements. Considering the environment surrounding the problem, identifying the issues or attributes that one feels should contribute to the solution, and who are the participants associated with the problem, are all important issues when constructing a hierarchy. Arranging the goals, attributes, issues, and stakeholders in a hierarchy serves two purposes: It provides an overall view of the complex relationships inherent in the situation and in the judgment process, and it also allows the decision maker to assess whether he or she is comparing issues of the same order of magnitude.

The elements being compared should be homogeneous. The hierarchy does not need to be complete; that is, an element in a given level does not have to function as a criterion for all the elements in the level below. Thus a hierarchy can be divided into subhierarchies sharing only a common topmost element. Further, a decision maker can insert or eliminate levels and elements as necessary to clarify the task of setting priorities or to sharpen the focus on one or more parts of the system. Elements that are of less immediate interest can be represented in general terms at the higher level of the hierarchy and elements of critical importance to the problem at hand can be developed in greater depth and specificity. The task of setting priorities requires that the criteria, the subcriteria, the properties or features of the alternatives be compared among themselves in relation to the elements of the next higher level.

Finally, after judgments have been made on the impact of all the elements, and priorities have been computed for the hierarchy as a whole, sometimes, and with care, the less important elements can be dropped from further consideration because of their relatively small impact on the overall objective.

3. PHILOSOPHY, PROCEDURE AND PRACTICE OF THE AHP

The Analytic Hierarchy Process is a general theory of measurement. It is used to derive ratio scales from both discrete and continuous paired comparisons in multilevel hierarchic structures. These comparisons may be taken from actual measurements or from a fundamental scale that reflects the relative strength of preferences and feelings. The AHP has a special concern with departure from consistency and the measurement of this departure, and with dependence within and between the groups of elements of its structure. It has found its widest applications in multicriteria decision making, in planning and resource allocation, and in conflict resolution [6, 8]. In its general form, the AHP is a nonlinear framework for carrying out both deductive and inductive thinking without use of the syllogism. This is made possible by taking several factors into consideration simultaneously, allowing for dependence and for feedback, and making numerical tradeoffs to arrive at a synthesis or conclusion (see Figures 1 and 2).

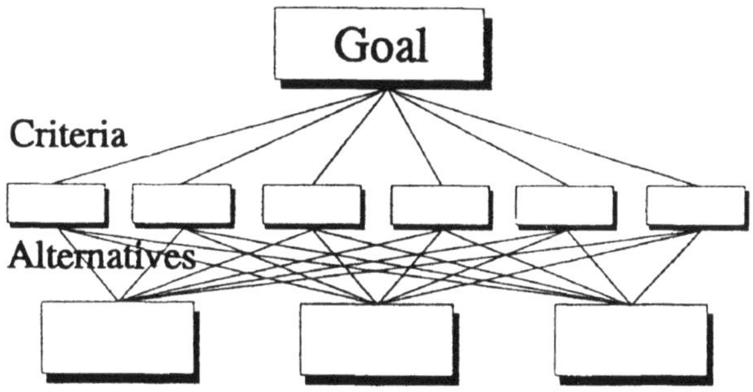

Figure 1. A three level hierarchy

For a long time people have been concerned with the measurement of both physical and psychological events. By physical we mean the realm of what is fashionably known as the tangibles in so far as they constitute some kind of objective reality outside the individual conducting the measurement. By contrast, the psychological is the realm of the intangibles, comprising the subjective ideas, feelings, and beliefs of the individual and of society as a whole. The question is whether there is a coherent theory that can deal with both these worlds of reality without compromising either. The AHP is a method that can be used to establish measures in both the physical and social domains.

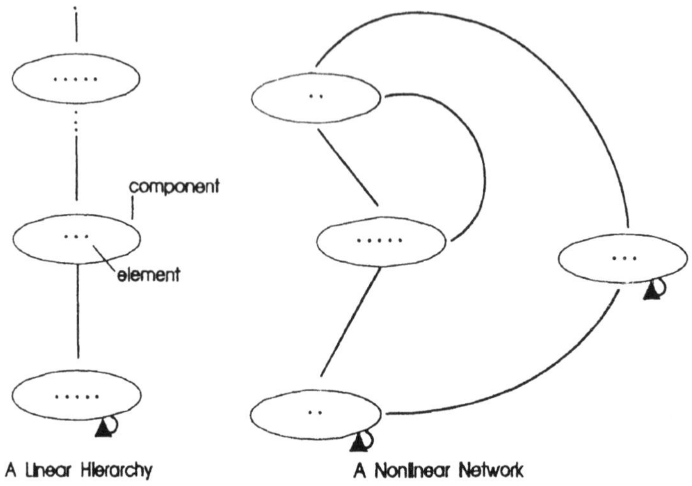

Figure 2. Structural Difference Between a Linear and a Nonlinear Network

In using the AHP to model a problem, one needs a hierarchic or a network structure to represent that problem, as well as pairwise comparisons to establish relations within the structure. In the discrete case these comparisons lead to dominance matrices and in the continuous case to kernels of Fredholm Operators [12], from which ratio scales are derived in the form of principal eigenvectors, or eigenfunctions, as the case may be. These matrices, or kernels, are positive and reciprocal, e.g., $a_{ij} = 1/a_{ji}$. In particular, special effort has been made to characterize these matrices [6, 16]. Because of the need for a variety of judgments, there has also been considerable work done to deal with the process of synthesizing group judgments [7].

For completeness we mention that there are four axioms in the AHP. Briefly and informally they are concerned with the reciprocal relation, comparison of homogeneous elements, hierarchic and systems dependence and with expectations about the validity of the rank and value of the outcome and their dependence on the structure and its extension [7].

4. ABSOLUTE AND RELATIVE MEASUREMENT AND STRUCTURAL INFORMATION

Cognitive psychologists have recognized for some time that there are two kinds of comparisons that humans make: absolute and relative. In absolute comparisons, alternatives are compared with a standard or baseline which exists in one's memory and has been developed through experience. In relative comparisons, alternatives are compared in pairs according to a common attribute. The AHP has been used with both types of comparisons to derive ratio scales of measurement. We call such scales absolute and relative measurement scales. Relative measurement w_i, i = 1, ..., n, of each of *n* elements is a ratio scale of values assigned to that element and derived by comparing it in pairs with the others. In paired comparisons two elements i and j are compared with respect to a property they have in common. The smaller i is used as the unit and the larger j is estimated as a multiple of that unit in the form $(w_i/w_j)/1$ where the ratio w_i/w_j is taken from a fundamental scale of absolute values.

Absolute measurement (sometimes called scoring) is applied to rank the alternatives in terms of either the criteria or the ratings (or intensities) of the criteria; for example: excellent, very good, good, average, below average, poor, and very poor; or A, B, C, D, E, F, and G. After setting priorities for the criteria (or subcriteria, if there are any), pairwise comparisons are also made between the ratings themselves to set priorities for them under each criterion and dividing each of their priorities by the largest rated intensity to get the ideal intensity. Finally, alternatives are scored by checking off their respective ratings under each criterion and summing these ratings for all the criteria. This produces a ratio scale score for the alternative. The scores thus obtained of the alternatives can in the end be normalized by dividing each one by their sum.

Absolute measurement has been used in a variety of applications. For example, it has been used to rank cities in the United States according to nine criteria as judged by six different people [13]. Another appropriate use for absolute measurement is in school admissions as in Chapter 20 [14]. Most schools set their criteria for admission independently of the performance of the current crop of students seeking admission. The school's priorities are then used to determine whether a given student meets the standard set for qualification. Generally, candidates are compared with previously set standard rather than with each other. In that case absolute measurement should be used to determine which students meet prior standards and qualify for admission.

5. THE FUNDAMENTAL SCALE

Paired comparison judgments in the AHP are applied to pairs of homogeneous elements. The fundamental scale of values to represent the intensities of judgments is shown in Table 1. This scale has been validated for effectiveness, not only in many applications by a number of people, but also through theoretical justification of what scale one must use in the comparison of homogeneous elements.

There are many situations where elements are equal or almost equal in measurement and the comparison must be made not to determine how many times one is larger than the other, but what fraction it is larger than the other. In other words there are comparisons to be made between 1 and 2, and what we want is to estimate verbally the values such as 1.1, 1.2, ..., 1.9. There is no problem in making the comparisons by directly estimating the numbers. Our proposal is to continue the verbal scale to make these distinctions so that 1.1 is a "tad", 1.3 indicates moderately more, 1.5 strongly more, 1.7 very strongly more and 1.9 extremely more. This type of refinement can be used in any of the intervals from 1 to 9 and for further refinements if one needs them, for example, between 1.1 and 1.2 and so on.

Table 1. The Fundamental Scale

Intensity of Importance	Definition	Explanation
1	**Equal Importance**	**Two activities contribute equally to the objective**
2	Weak	
3	**Moderate importance**	**Experience and judgment slightly favor one activity over another**
4	Moderate plus	
5	**Strong importance**	**Experience and judgment strongly favor one activity over another**
6	Strong plus	
7	**Very strong or demonstrated importance**	**An activity is favored very strongly over another; its dominance demonstrated in practice**
8	Very, very strong	
9	**Extreme importance**	**The evidence favoring one activity over another is of the highest possible order of affirmation**
Reciprocals of above	**If activity *i* has one of the above nonzero numbers assigned to it when compared with activity *j*, then *j* has the reciprocal value when compared with *i***	**A reasonable assumption**
Rationals	**Ratios arising from the scale**	**If consistency were to be forced by obtaining *n* numerical values to span the matrix**

The following two examples provide partial validation of the 1-9 scale used in the pairwise comparisons of homogeneous elements.

Which drink is consumed more in the US?

	A	B	C	D	E	F	G	Estimated	Actual
A:Coffee	1	9	5	2	1	1	1/2	0.177	0.18
B:Wine	1/9	1	1/3	1/9	1/9	1/9	1/9	0.019	0.01
C:Tea	1/5	3	1	1/3	1/4	1/3	1/9	0.042	0.04
D:Beer	1/2	9	3	1	1/2	1	1/3	0.116	0.12
E:Sodas	1	9	4	2	1	2	1/2	0.190	0.18
F:Milk	1	9	3	1	1/2	1	1/3	0.129	0.14
G:Water	2	9	9	3	2	3	1	0.327	0.33
							C.R.=	0.022	

Which food has more protein?

	A	B	C	D	E	F	G	Estimated	Actual
A:Steak	1	9	9	6	4	5	1	0.345	0.37
B:Potatoes	1/9	1	1	1/2	1/4	1/3	1/4	0.031	0.04
C:Apples	1/9	1	1	1/3	1/3	1/5	1/9	0.030	0.00
D:Soybeans	1/6	2	3	1	1/2	1	1/6	0.065	0.07
E:Whole Wheat Bread	1/4	4	3	2	1	3	1/3	0.124	0.11
F:Tasty Cake	1/5	3	5	1	1/3	1	1/5	0.078	0.09
G:Fish	1	4	9	6	3	5	1	0.328	0.32
							C.R.=	0.028	

6. COMMENTS ON BENEFIT/COST ANALYSIS

Often, the alternatives from which a choice must be made in a choice-making situation have both costs and benefits associated with them. In this case it is useful to construct separate costs and benefits hierarchies, with the same alternatives on the bottom level of each. Thus one obtains both a costs-priority vector and a benefit-priority vector. The benefit/cost vector is obtained by taking the ratio of the benefit priority to the costs priority for each alternative, with the highest such ratio indicating the preferred alternative. In the case where resources are allocated to several projects, such benefit-to-cost ratios or the corresponding marginal ratios prove to be very valuable.

For example, in evaluating three types of copying machines, the good attributes are represented in the benefits hierarchy and the costs hierarchy represents the pain and economic costs that one would incur by buying or maintaining each of the three types of machines. Note that the criteria for benefits and the criteria for costs need not be simply opposites of each other but instead may be partially or totally different. Also note that each criterion may be regarded at a different threshold of intensity and that such thresholds may themselves be prioritized according to desirability, with each alternative evaluated only in terms of its highest priority threshold level. Similarly, three hierarchies can be used to assess a benefit/(cost × risk) outcome.

7. THE EIGENVECTOR SOLUTION FOR WEIGHTS AND CONSISTENCY

There is an infinite number of ways to derive the vector of priorities from the matrix (a_{ij}). But emphasis on consistency leads to the eigenvalue formulation $Aw = nw$. To see this, assume that the priorities $w=(w_1, \ldots, w_n)$ with respect to a single criterion are known, such as the weights of stones, we can examine what we have to do to recover them. So we form the matrix of ratio comparisons and multiply it on the right by w to obtain nw as follows:

$$\begin{pmatrix} \frac{w_1}{w_1} & \frac{w_1}{w_2} & \cdots & \frac{w_1}{w_n} \\ \frac{w_2}{w_1} & \frac{w_2}{w_2} & \cdots & \frac{w_2}{w_n} \\ \vdots & \vdots & \ddots & \vdots \\ \frac{w_n}{w_1} & \frac{w_n}{w_2} & \cdots & \frac{w_n}{w_n} \end{pmatrix} \begin{pmatrix} w_1 \\ w_2 \\ \vdots \\ w_n \end{pmatrix} = n \begin{pmatrix} w_1 \\ w_2 \\ \vdots \\ w_n \end{pmatrix}$$

If a_{ij} represents the importance of alternative i over alternative j and a_{jk} represents the importance of alternative j over alternative k and a_{ik}, the importance of alternative i over alternative k, must equal $a_{ij}a_{jk}$ or $a_{ij}a_{jk} = a_{ik}$ for the judgments to be consistent. If we do not have a scale at all, or do not have it conveniently as in the case of some measuring devices, we cannot give the precise values of w_i/w_j but only an estimate. Our problem becomes $A'w' = \lambda_{max}w'$ where λ_{max} is the largest or principal eigenvalue of $A' = (a'_{ij})$ the perturbed value of $A = (a_{ij})$ with the reciprocal $a'_{ji} = 1/a'_{ij}$ forced. To simplify the notation we shall continue to write $Aw = \lambda_{max}w$ where A is the matrix of pairwise comparisons.

The solution is obtained by raising the matrix to a sufficiently large power, then summing over the rows and normalizing to obtain the priority vector $w = (w_1, \ldots, w_n)$. The process is stopped when the difference between components of the priority vector obtained at the kth power and at the $(k+1)$st power is less than some predetermined small value. The vector of priorities is the derived scale associated with the matrix of comparisons. We assign in this scale the value zero to an element that is not comparable with the elements considered.

An easy way to get an approximation to the priorities is to normalize the geometric means of the rows. This result coincides with the eigenvector for $n \leq 3$. A second way to obtain an approximation is by normalizing the elements in each column of the judgment matrix and then averaging over each row.

We would like to caution that for important applications one should use only the eigenvector derivation procedure because approximations can lead to rank reversal in spite of the closeness of the result to the eigenvector [10].

A simple way to obtain the exact value (or an estimate) of λ_{max} when the exact value (or an estimate) of w is available in normalized form is to add the columns of A and multiply the resulting vector by the priority vector w.

The problem now bcomes, how good is the principal eigenvector estimate w? Note that if we obtain $w = (w_1, ..., w_n)^T$, by solving this problem, the matrix whose entries are w_i/w_j is a consistent matrix which is our consistent estimate of the matrix A. The original matrix itself A, need not be consistent. In fact, the entries of A need not even be transitive; i.e., A_1 may be preferred to A_2 and A_2 to A_3 but A_3 may be preferred to A_1. What we would like is a measure of the error due to inconsistency. It turns out that A is consistent if and only if $\lambda_{max} = n$ and that we always have $\lambda_{max} \geq n$.

It is interesting to note that $(\lambda_{max}-n)/(n-1)$ is the variance of the error incurred in estimating a_{ij}. This can be shown by writing $a_{ij} = (w_i/w_j)\varepsilon_{ij}$, $\varepsilon_{ij} > 0$, $\varepsilon_{ij} = 1+\delta_{ij}$, $\delta_{ij} > -1$, and substituting in the expression for λ_{max}. It is δ_{ij} that concerns us as the error component and its value $|\delta_{ij}| < 1$ for an unbiased estimator. The measure of inconsistency can be used to successively improve the consistency of judgments. The consistency index of a matrix of comparisons is given by C.I. = $(\lambda_{max}-n)/(n-1)$. The consistency ratio (C.R.) is obtained by comparing the C.I. with the appropriate one of the following set of numbers (See Table 2) each of which is an average random consistency index derived from a sample of randomly generated reciprocal matrices using the scale 1/9, 1/8, ..., 1, ..., 8, 9. If it is not less than 0.10, study the problem and revise the judgments. The AHP includes a consistency index for an entire hierarchy. An inconsistency of 10 percent or less implies that the adjustment is small compared to the actual values of the eigenvector entries. A proof that the number of elements should be small to preserve consistency can be found in [6].

Table 2. Average Random Consistency Index (R.I.)

N	1	2	3	4	5	6	7	8	9	10
Random Consistency Index (R.I.)	0	0	.52	.89	1.11	1.25	1.35	1.40	1.45	1.49

8. HOW TO STRUCTURE A HIERARCHY

Perhaps the most creative and influential part of decision making is the structuring of the decision as a hierarchy. The basic principle to follow in creating this structure is always to see if one can answer the following question: "Can I compare the elements on a lower level in terms of some or all of the elements on the next higher level?"

A useful way to proceed is to work down from the goal as far as one can and then work up from the alternatives until the levels of the two processes are linked in such a way as to make comparison possible. Here are some suggestions for an elaborate design.

1. Identify overall goal. What are you trying to accomplish? What is the main question?
2. Identify subgoals of overall goal. If relevant, identify time horizons that affect the decision.
3. Identify criteria that must be satisfied in order to fulfill the subgoals of the overall goal.
4. Identify subcriteria under each criterion. Note that criteria or subcriteria may be specified in terms of ranges of values of parameters or in terms of verbal intensities such as high, medium, low.
5. Identify actors involved.
6. Identify actor goals.
7. Identify actor policies.
8. Identify options or outcomes.
9. Take the most preferred outcome and compare the ratio of benefits to costs of making the decision with those of not making it. Do the same when there are several alternatives from which to choose.
10. Do benefit/cost analysis using marginal values. Because we are dealing with dominance hierarchies, ask which alternative yields the greatest benefit; for costs, which alternative costs the most.

The software program Expert Choice [2] incorporates the AHP methodology and enables the analyst to structure the hierarchy and resolve the problem using relative or absolute measurements, as appropriate.

9. HIERARCHIC SYNTHESIS AND RANK

Hierarchic synthesis is obtained by a process of weighting and adding down the hierarchy leading to a multilinear form. The hierarchic composition principle is a theorem in the AHP that is a particular case of network composition which deals with the cycles and loops of a network.

What happens to the synthesized ranks of alternatives when new ones are added or old ones deleted? The ranks cannot change under any single criterion, but they can under several criteria depending on whether one wants the ranks to remain the same or allow them to change. Many examples are given in the literature showing that preference reversal and rank reversal are natural occurrences. In 1990 Tversky et. al. [18] concluded that the "primary cause" of preference reversal is the "failure of procedure invariance". In the AHP there is no such methodological constraint.

In the distributive mode of the AHP, the principal eigenvector is normalized to yield a unique estimate of a ratio scale underlying the judgments. This mode allows rank to change and is useful when there is dependence on the number of alternatives present or on dominant new alternatives which may affect preference among old alternatives thus causing rank reversals (see phantom alternatives [7]). In the ideal mode of the AHP the normalized values of the alternatives for each criterion are divided by the value of the highest rated alternative. In this manner a newly added alternative that is dominated everywhere cannot cause reversal in the ranks of the existing alternatives [6].

10. NORMATIVE - DESCRIPTIVE

All science is descriptive not normative. It is based on the notion that knowledge is incomplete. It uses language and mathematics to understand, describe and predict events with the object of testing the accuracy of the theory. Events involve two things: 1) controllable and uncontrollable conditions (e.g. laws) and 2) people or objects characterized by matter, energy and motion influenced by and sometimes influencing these conditions. A missile's path is subject to uncontrollable forces like gravity and controllable forces like the initial aim of the missile, its weight, perhaps the wind, and others. The conditions are not determined by the objects involved. The idea is to get the missile from A to B by ensuring that it follows its path with precision.

Economics is normative. It is based on expected utility theory and is predicated on the idea that the collective behavior of many individuals, each motivated by self interest, determines the market conditions which in turn influence or control each individual's behavior. In this case both the objects and the conditions are "up for grabs" because behavior is subject to rational influences that are thought to be understood. By optimizing individual behavior through rationality one can optimize the collective conditions and the resulting system, plus or minus some corrections in the conditions. But conditions are not all economic. Some are environmental, some social, some political and others cultural. We know little about their interactions. In attempting to include everything, normative theories treat intangible criteria as tangibles by postulating a convenient economic scale. It is hard to justify reducing all intangibles to economics in order to give the appearance of completeness. It is doubtful that economic theory can solve all human problems. To the contrary, some believe that it can create problems in other areas of human concern.

A normative theory is established by particular people external to the process of decision making. Experts often disagree on the criteria used to judge the excellence of a normative theory and the decision resulting from it. For example, a basic criterion of Utility Theory is the principle of rationality which says that if a person is offered more of that which he values, he should take it. In response to this dictum Herbert Simon [17] developed his idea of sufficiency (satisficing).

Whenever we are saturated even with a highly valued commodity, there is a cutoff point where the marginal increase in total value is less than or equal to zero. A theory constructed to satisfy such an assumption would undoubtedly encounter difficulties in its applications. Rank reversals would be appropriate to overcome the disadvantages of oversaturation.

The AHP is a descriptive theory in the sense of the physical sciences. It treats people separately from the conditions in which they find themselves, because so far no complete integrated theory of socio-economic-political-environmental-cultural factors exists that would enable us to deduce optimality principles for people's behavior. The AHP is an instrument used to construct a complete order through which optimum choice is derived.

In the AHP approach a particular decision is not considered wrong merely because it does not follow a prescribed set of procedures. The purpose of the AHP is to assist people in organizing their thoughts and judgments to make more effective decisions. Its structures are based on observations of how influences are transmitted and its arithmetic is derived from psychologists' observations of how people function in attempting to understand their behavior.

In its simplest form, the AHP begins with the traditional concept of ordinal ranking to stratify a hierarchy and advances further into numerical paired comparisons from which a ranking of the elements in each level is derived. By imposing a multiplicative structure on the numbers ($a_{ij} \cdot a_{jk} = a_{ik}$), the reciprocal condition is obtained. Thus, the AHP infers behavioral characteristics of judgments (inconsistency and intransitivity) from its basic framework of paired comparisons. It begins by taking situations with a known underlying ratio scale and hence known comparison ratios, and shows how its method of deriving a scale uniquely through the eigenvector gives back the original scale. Then, through perturbation the AHP shows that a derived scale should continue (through the eigenvector) to approximate the original scale providing that there is high consistency.

11. RATIONALITY

Rationality is defined in the AHP as:

- Focussing on the goal of solving the problem;
- Knowing enough about a problem to develop a thorough structure of relations and influences;
- Having enough knowledge and experience and access to knowledge and experience of others to assess the priority of influence and dominance (importance, preference or likelihood to the goal as appropriate) among the relations in the structure;
- Allowing for differences in opinion with an ability to develop a best compromise.

12. EXAMPLES

RELATIVE MEASUREMENT: CHOOSING THE BEST HOUSE

To illustrate the ideas discussed above regarding relative measurement, consider the following example; a family of average income wants to purchase a house. They must choose from three alternatives. The family identifies eight factors to look for in a house. These factors fall into three categories: economic, geographic, and physical. Although one might begin by examining the relative importance of these categories, the family feels they want to prioritize the relative importance of all the factors without working with the categories to which they belong. The problem is to select one of three candidate houses. In applying the AHP, the first step is *decomposition*, or the structuring of the problem into a hierarchy (see Figure 3). On the first (or top) level is the overall goal of *Satisfaction with House*. On the second level are the eight factors or criteria that contribute to the goal, and on the third (or bottom) level are the three candidate houses that are to be evaluated in terms of the criteria on the second level. The definitions of the factor and the pictorial representation of the hierarchy follow.

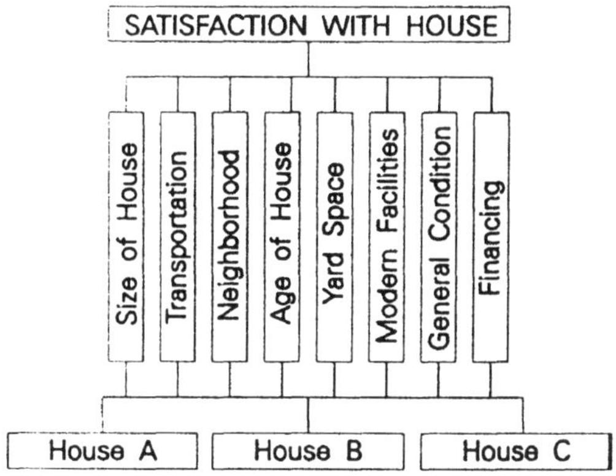

Figure 3. Decomposition of the problem into a hierarchy.

The factors important to the family are:

1. *Size of House:* Storage space; size of rooms; number of rooms; total area of house.
2. *Transportation:* Convenience and proximity of bus service.
3. *Neighborhood:* Degree of traffic, security, taxes, physical condition of surrounding buildings.
4. *Age of House:* Self-explanatory.

5. *Yard Space:* Includes front, back, and side space, and space shared with neighbors.
6. *Modern Facilities:* Dishwasher, garbage disposal, air conditioning, alarm system, and other such items.
7. *General Condition:* Extent to which repairs are needed; condition of walls, carpet, drapes, wiring; cleanliness.
8. *Financing:* Availability of assumable mortgage, seller financing, or bank financing.

The next step is *comparative judgment*. The elements on the second level are arranged into a matrix and the family buying the house makes judgments about the relative importance of the elements with respect to the overall goal, *Satisfaction with House*.

The questions to ask when comparing two criteria are of the following kind: of the two alternatives being compared, which is considered more important by the family and how much more important is it with respect to family satisfaction with the house, which is the overall goal?

The matrix of pairwise comparisons of the factors given by the home buyers in this case is shown in Table 3, along with the resulting vector of priorities. The judgments are entered using the Fundamental Scale, first verbally as indicated in the scale and then associating the corresponding number. The vector of priorities is the principal eigenvector of the matrix. This vector gives the relative priority of the factors measured on a ratio scale. That is, these priorities are unique to within multiplication by a positive constant. However, if one ensures that they sum to one they are always unique. In this case financing has the highest priority, with 33 percent of the influence.

In Table 3, instead of naming the criteria, we use the number previously associated with each.

Table 3. Pairwise Comparison Matrix for Level 1

	1	2	3	4	5	6	7	8	Priority Vector
1	1	5	3	7	6	6	1/3	1/4	.173
2	1/5	1	1/3	5	3	3	1/5	1/7	.054
3	1/3	3	1	6	3	4	6	1/5	.188
4	1/7	1/5	1/6	1	1/3	1/4	1/7	1/8	.018
5	1/6	1/3	1/3	3	1	1/2	1/5	1/6	.031
6	1/6	1/3	1/4	4	2	1	1/5	1/6	.036
7	3	5	1/6	7	5	5	1	1/2	.167
8	4	7	5	8	6	6	2	1	.333

$\lambda_{max} = 9.669$ C.R. = .169

Note for example that in comparing Size of House on the left with Size of House on top, a value of equal is assigned. However, when comparing it with Transportation it is strongly preferred and a 5 is entered in the (1,2) or first row, second column position. The reciprocal value 1/5 is automatically entered in the (2,1) position. Again when Size of House in the first row is compared with General Condition in the seventh column, it is not preferred but is moderately dominated by General Condition and a 1/3 value is entered in the (1,7) position. A 3 is then automatically entered in the (7,1) position. The consistency ration C.R. is equal to 0.169 and one needs to explore the inconsistencies in the matrix with the help of Expert Choice to locate the most inconsistent one and attempt to improve it if there is flexibility in the judgment. Otherwise, one looks at the second most inconsistent judgment and attempts to improve it and so on.

We now move to the pairwise comparisons of the houses on the bottom level, comparing them pairwise with respect to how much better one is than the other in satisfying each criterion on the second level. Thus there are eight 3×3 matrices of judgments since there are eight elements on level two, and three houses to be pairwise compared for each element. The matrices (Table 4) contain the judgments of the family involved. In order to facilitate understanding of the judgments, a brief description of the houses is given below.

House A: This house is the largest of them all. It is located in a good neighborhood with little traffic and low taxes. Its yard space is comparably larger than that of houses B and C. However, its general condition is not very good and it needs cleaning and painting. Also, the financing is unsatisfactory because it would have to be financed through a bank at a high interest.

House B: This house is a little smaller than House A and is not close to a bus route. The neighborhood gives one the feeling of insecurity because of traffic conditions. The yard space is fairly small and the house lacks the basic modern facilities. On the other hand, its general condition is very good. Also an assumable mortgage is obtainable, which means the financing is good with a rather low interest rate. There are several copies of B in the neighborhood.

House C: House C is very small and has few modern facilities. The neighborhood has high taxes, but is in good condition and seems secure. The yard space is bigger than that of House B, but is not comparable to House A's spacious surroundings. The general condition of the house is good, and it has a pretty carpet and drapes. The financing is better than for A but not better than for B.

Table 4 gives the matrices of the houses and their local priorities with respect to the elements on level two.

Table 4. Pairwise Comparison Matrices for Level 2

Size of House	A	B	C	Normalized Priorities	Idealized Priorities
A	1	6	8	.754	1.000
B	1/6	1	4	.181	0.240
C	1/8	1/4	1	.065	0.086

$\lambda_{max} = 3.136$ C.I. = .068 C.R. = .117

Yard Space	A	B	C	Normalized Priorities	Idealized Priorities
A	1	5	4	.674	1.000
B	1/5	1	1/3	.101	0.150
C	1/4	3	1	.226	0.335

$\lambda_{max} = 3.086$ C.I. = .043 C.R. = .074

Transportation	A	B	C	Normalized Priorities	Idealized Priorities
A	1	7	1/5	.233	0.327
B	1/7	1	1/8	.005	0.007
C	5	8	1	.713	1.000

$\lambda_{max} = 3.247$ C.I. = .124 C.R. = .213

Modern Facilities	A	B	C	Normalized Priorities	Idealized Priorities
A	1	8	6	.747	1.000
B	1/8	1	1/5	.060	0.080
C	1/6	5	1	.193	0.258

$\lambda_{max} = 3.197$ C.I. = .099 C.R. = .170

Neighborhood	A	B	C	Normalized Priorities	Idealized Priorities
A	1	8	6	.745	1.000
B	1/8	1	1/4	.065	0.086
C	1/6	4	1	.181	0.240

$\lambda_{max} = 3.130$ C.I. = .068 C.R. = .117

General Condition	A	B	C	Normalized Priorities	Idealized Priorities
A	1	1/2	1/2	.200	0.500
B	2	1	1	.400	1.000
C	2	1	1	.400	1.000

$\lambda_{max} = 3.000$ C.I. = .000 C.R. = .000

Age of House	A	B	C	Normalized Priorities	Idealized Priorities
A	1	1	1	.333	1.000
B	1	1	1	.333	1.000
C	1	1	1	.333	1.000

$\lambda_{max} = 3.000$ C.I. = .000 C.R. = .000

Financing	A	B	C	Normalized Priorities	Idealized Priorities
A	1	1/7	1/5	.072	0.111
B	7	1	3	.650	1.000
C	5	1/3	1	.278	0.428

$\lambda_{max} = 3.065$ C.I. = .032 C.R. = .056

The next step is to synthesize the priorities. There are two ways of doing that. One is the distributive mode. In order to establish the composite or global priorities of the houses we lay out in a matrix (Table 5) the local priorities of the houses with respect to each criterion and multiply each column of vectors by the priority of the corresponding criterion and add across each row, which results in the composite or global priority vector of the houses. The other way of synthesizing is the ideal mode. Here the priorities of the houses for each criterion are first divided by the largest value among them (Table 5). That alternative becomes the ideal and receives a value of 1. One then multiplies by the priority of the corresponding criterion and adds as before. House A is preferred if for example copies of B matter and hence the distributed mode is used. In a large number of situations with 10 criteria and 3 alternatives, the two modes gave the same best choice 92% of the time [7]. House B is the preferred house if the family wanted the best house regardless of other houses and how many copies of it there are in the neighborhood and hence the ideal mode is used.

Table 5. Synthesis

Distributive Mode										
	1 (.173)	2 (.054)	3 (.188)	4 (.018)	5 (.031)	6 (.036)	7 (.167)	8 (.333)		
A	.754	.233	.754	.333	.674	.747	.200	.072		.396
B	.181	.055	.065	.333	.101	.060	.400	.650	=	.341
C	.065	.713	.181	.333	.226	.193	.400	.278		.263
Ideal Mode										
A	1.00	.327	1.00	1.00	1.00	1.00	.500	.111		.584
B	.240	.007	.086	1.00	.150	.080	1.00	1.00	=	.782
C	.086	1.00	.240	1.00	.335	.258	1.00	.428		.461

ABSOLUTE MEASUREMENT

EVALUATING EMPLOYEES FOR RAISES

Employees are evaluated for raises. The criteria are Dependability, Education, Experience, and Quality, Each criterion is subdivided into intensities, standards, or subcriteria as shown in Figure 4. Priorities are set for the criteria by comparing them in pairs, and these priorities are then given in a matrix. The intensities are then pairwise compared according to priority with respect to their parent criterion (as in Table 6) and their priorities are divided by the largest intensity for each criterion (second column of priorities in Figure 4). Finally, each individual is rated in Table 7 by assigning the intensity rating that applies to him or her under each criterion. The scores of these subcriteria are weighted by the priority of that criterion and summed to derive a total ratio scale score for the individual. This approach can be used whenever it is possible to set priorities for intensities of criteria, which is usually possible when sufficient experience with a given operation has been accumulated.

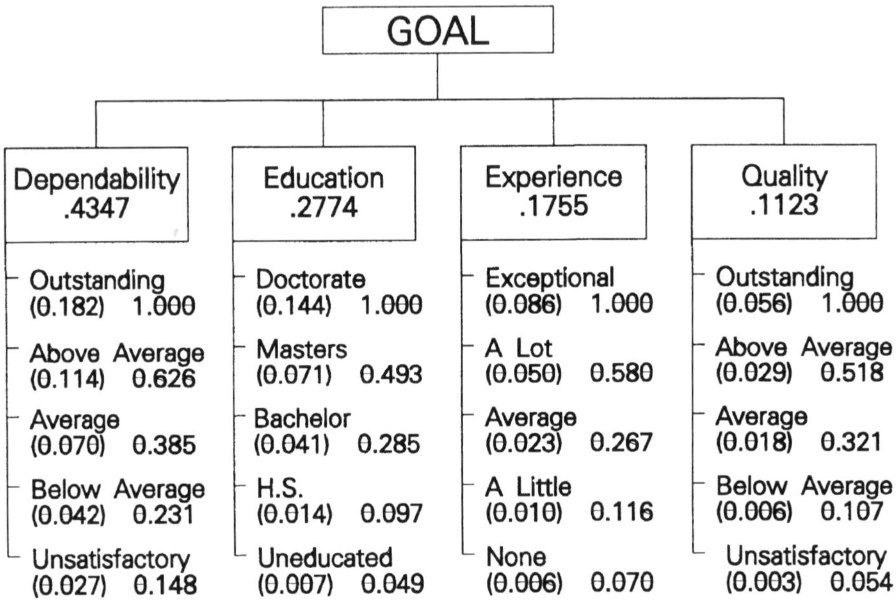

Figure 4. Employee evaluation hierarchy

Table 6. Ranking Intensities

	Outstanding	Above Average	Average	Below Average	Unsatisfactory	Priorities
Outstanding	1.0	2.0	3.0	4.0	5.0	0.419
Above Average	1/2	1.0	2.0	3.0	4.0	0.263
Average	1/3	1/2	1.0	2.0	3.0	0.630
Below Average	1/4	1/3	1/2	1.0	2.0	0.097
Unsatisfactory	1/5	1/4	1/3	1/2	1.0	0.062

Inconsistency Ratio = 0.015

Table 7. Ranking Alternatives

	Dependability .4347	Education .2774	Experience .1775	Quality .1123	Total
1. Adams, V	Outstanding	Bachelor	A Little	Outstanding	0.646
2. Becker, L	Average	Bachelor	A Little	Outstanding	0.379
3. Hayat, F	Average	Masters	A Lot	Below Average	0.418
4. Kesselman, S	Above Average	H.S.	None	Above Average	0.369
5. O'Shea, K	Average	Doctorate	A Lot	Above Average	0.605
6. Peters, T	Average	Doctorate	A Lot	Average	0.583
7. Tobias, K	Above Average	Bachelor	Average	Above Average	0.456

ORGAN TRANSPLANTATION

The City of Pittsburgh has become a leader in the world in organ transplantations. Because there are more patients who need livers, hearts and kidneys than there are available organs, it has become essential to assign priorities to the patients. The priorities shown in the figures are a result of several months of study by Alison R. Casciato and John P. O'Keefe in coordination with doctors and research scientists at a local hospital. Absolute measurement was used for this purpose and is shown in Figures 5, 5a, 5b, and 5c. The hierarchy of Figure 5 consists of the goal, the major criteria and subcriteria after which some of the subcriteria are further divided into yet smaller subcriteria or are divided into intensities for rating the patient. Figures 5a, 5b, and 5c give further subdivision into intensities for those subcriteria in Figure 5 that need to be further subdivided into intensities. In general, one would use the intensities to score a patient. When there is no intensity, either the full value of the criterion is assigned, or a zero value otherwise. For example, Criminal has .033 priority and that value is awarded to a patient with no criminal record. A patient with a criminal record would receive a zero. The goal is divided into: emotionally dependent and financially dependent patients: Both are divided into single, married, and divorced with and without dependent and financially dependent patients. Then each of them is further divided into: medical history (time on donor list, degree of disability), physical history (degree of ability to endure rehabilitation, willingness to cooperate, etc.), and social status (criminal record, volunteer work). The priorities are indicated next to each factor and sum to one for each level. A patient is ranked according to the intensities under each criterion. The higher the total score the better the opportunity to receive a transplant.

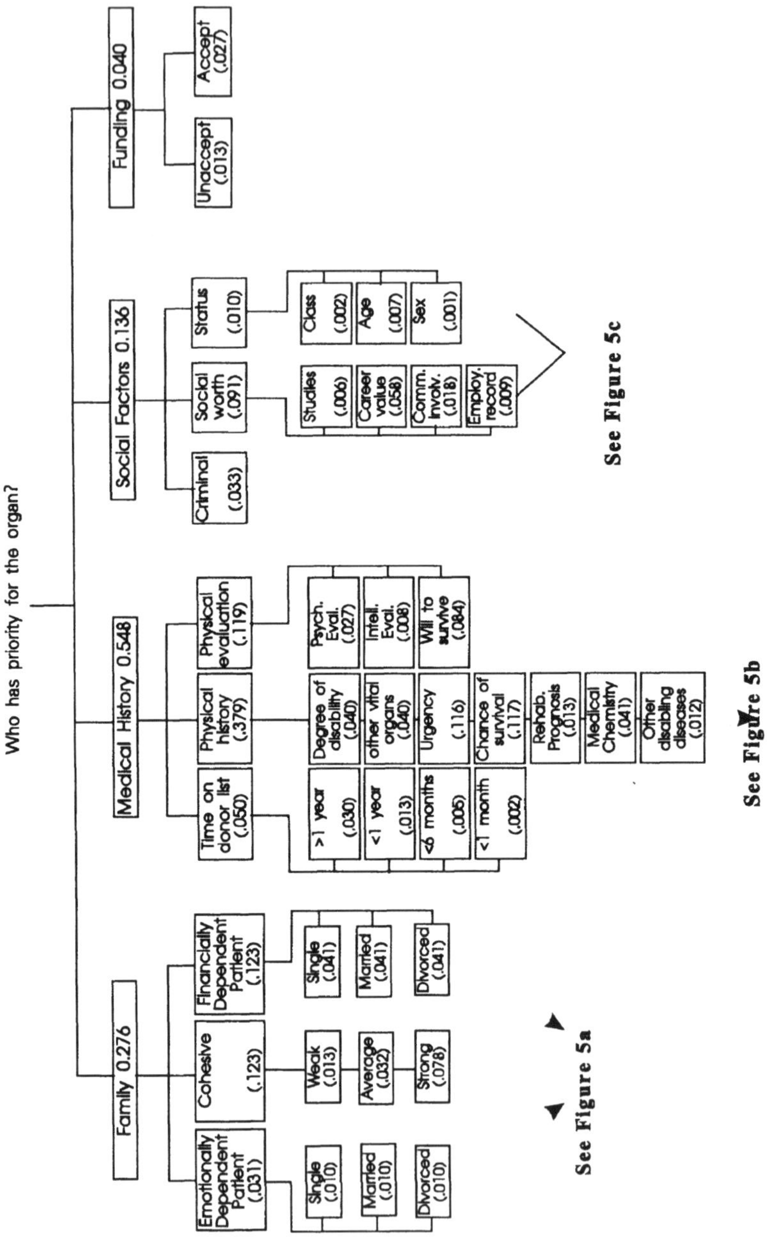
Who has priority for the organ?
Family 0.276
Medical History 0.548
Social Factors 0.136
Funding 0.040
Emotionally Dependent Patient (.031)
Cohesive (.123)
Financially Dependent Patient (.123)
Single (.010)
Married (.010)
Divorced (.010)
Weak (.013)
Average (.032)
Strong (.078)
Single (.041)
Married (.041)
Divorced (.041)
Time on donor list (.050)
Physical history (.379)
Physical evaluation (.119)
>1 year (.030)
<1 year (.013)
<6 months (.005)
<1 month (.002)
Degree of disability (.040)
other vital organs (.040)
Urgency (.116)
Chance of survival (.117)
Rehab. Prognosis (.013)
Medical Chemistry (.041)
Other disabling diseases (.012)
Psych. Eval. (.027)
Intell. Eval. (.008)
Will to survive (.084)
Criminal (.033)
Social worth (.091)
Status (.010)
Studies (.006)
Career value (.058)
Comm. involv. (.018)
Employ. record (.009)
Class (.002)
Age (.007)
Sex (.001)
Unaccept (.013)
Accept (.027)
See Figure 5a
See Figure 5b
See Figure 5c

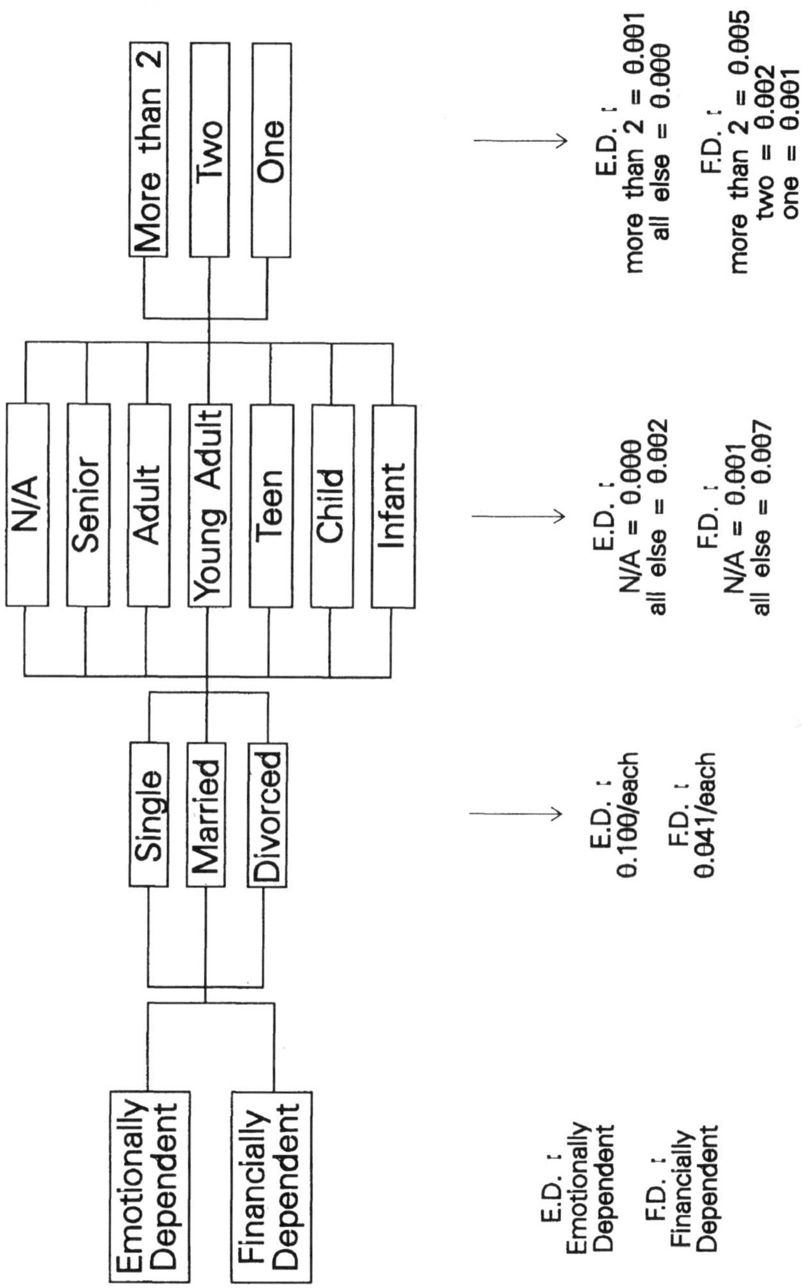

Figure 5a. Organ Transplantation - Family Factors

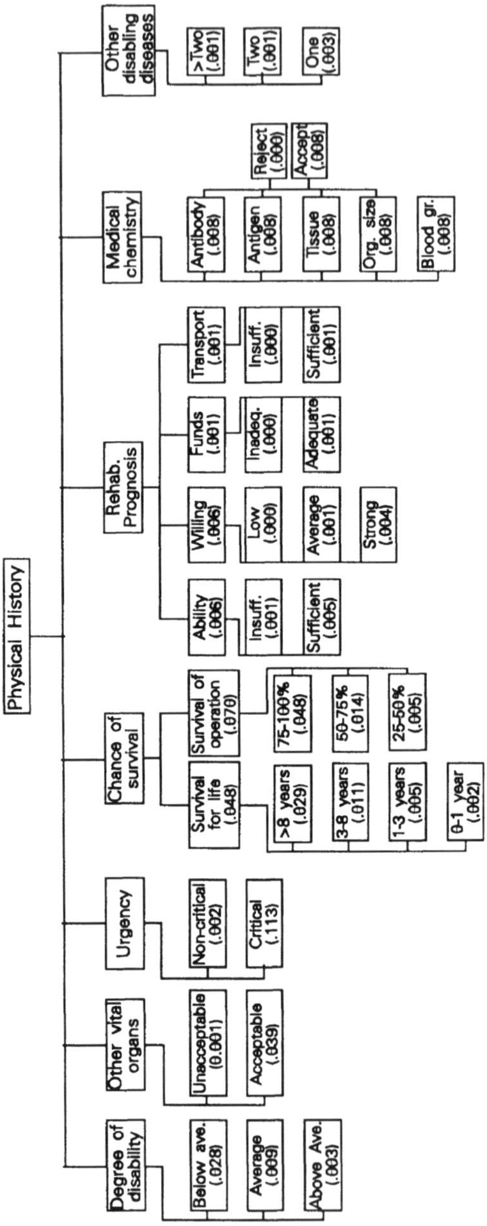

Figure 5b. Organ Transplantation - Medical History Factors

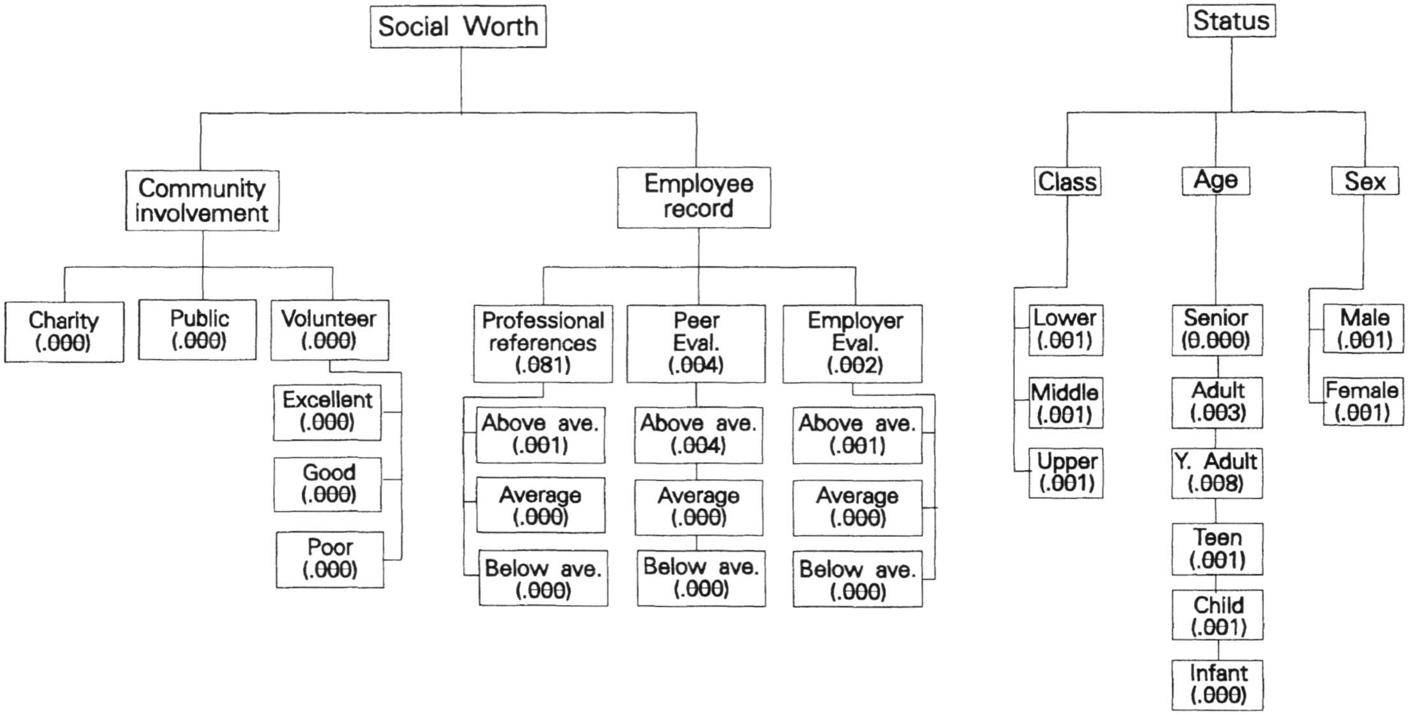

Figure 5c. Organ Transplantation - Social Factors

13. APPLICATIONS IN INDUSTRY AND GOVERNMENT

In addition to the many illustrations given in this book, the AHP has been used in the economics/management area in subjects including auditing, database selection, design, architecture, finance, macro-economic forecasting, marketing (consumer choice, product design and development, strategy), planning, portfolio selection, facility location, forecasting, resource allocation (budget, energy, health, project), sequential decisions, policy/strategy, transportation, water research, and performance analysis. In political problems, the AHP is used in such areas as arms control, conflicts and negotiation, political candidacy, security assessments, war games, and world influence. For social concerns, it is applied in education, behavior in competition, environmental issues, health, law, medicine (drug effectiveness, therapy selection), population dynamics (interregional migration patterns, population size), and public sector. Some technological applications include market selection, portfolio selection, and technology transfer. Additional applications are discussed in Golden et. al. [3] and R.F. Dyer and E.H. Forman [1]. For a complete set of references see the bibliography at the end of reference [7].

REFERENCES

1. Dyer, R.F. and E.H. Forman, *An Analytic Framework for Marketing Decisions: Text and Cases*, Prentice-Hall, Englewood Cliffs, NJ., 1989.
2. Expert Choice Software, Expert Choice, Inc., 4922 Ellsworth Ave., Pittsburgh, PA 15213, 1994.
3. Golden, B.L., P.T. Harker and E.A. Wasil, *Applications of the Analytic Hierarchy Process*, Springer-Verlag, Berlin, 1989.
4. Kinoshita, E., *The AHP Method and Application*, Sumisho Publishing Company, Tokyo, 1993.
5. Saaty, T.L., *Decision Making for Leaders*, RWS Publications, 4922 Ellsworth Ave. Pittsburgh. First appeared 1982 Wadsworth, Belmont, CA., 1990.
6. Saaty, T.L., *The Analytic Hierarchy Process*, paperback edition, RWS Publications, Pittsburgh, PA. First appeared 1980, McGraw Hill, New York., 1990.
7. Saaty, T.L., *Fundamentals of Decision Making and Priority Theory*, RWS Publications, 4922 Ellworth Ave., Pittsburgh, PA., 1994.
8. Saaty, T.L. and J. Alexander, *Conflict Resolution*, Praeger, New York., 1989.
9. Saaty, T.L. and K.P. Kearns, *Analytical Planning - The Organization of Systems*, International Series in Modern Applied Mathematics and Computer Science 7, Oxford, England, Pergamon Press., 1985.
10. Saaty, T.L. and L.G. Vargas, *The Logic of Priorities, Applications in Business, Energy, Health, Transportation*, Kluwer-Nijhoff Publishing, Boston., 1982.
11. Saaty, T.L. and L.G. Vargas, *Prediction, Projection and Forecasting*, Kluwer Academic, Boston., 1991.

12. Saaty, T.L. and L.G. Vargas, "A Model of Neural Impulse Firing and Synthesis", *Journal of Mathematical Psychology* 37 (1993) 200-219.
13. Saaty, T.L., "Absolute and Relative Measurement with the AHP: The Most Livable Cities in the United States", *Socio-Economic Planning Sciences* 20/6 (1986) 327-331.
14. Saaty, T.L., J.W. France and K.R. Valentine, "Modeling the Graduate Business School Admissions Process", *Socio-Economic Planning Sciences* 25/2 (1991) 155-162.
15. Saaty, T.L., "Axiomatic Foundation of the Analytic Hierarchy Process", *Management Science* 32/7 (1986) 841-855.
16. Saaty, T.L., "What is Relative Measurement? The Ratio Scale Phantom", *Mathematical and Computer Modelling* 17/4-5 (1993) 1-12.
17. Simon, Herbert A., "A Behavioral Model of Rational Choice", *Quarterly Journal of Economics* 69 (1955) 99-118.
18. Tversky, A., P. Slovic and D. Kahneman, "The Causes of Preference Reversal", *The American Economic Review* 80/1 (1990) 204-215.

CHAPTER 2

THE SEVEN PILLARS OF THE ANALYTIC HIERARCHY PROCESS

1. INTRODUCTION

The Analytic Hierarchy Process (AHP) provides the objective mathematics to process the inescapably subjective and personal preferences of an individual or a group in making a decision. With the AHP and its generalization, the Analytic Network Process (ANP), one constructs hierarchies or feedback networks, then makes judgments or performs measurements on pairs of elements with respect to a controlling element to derive ratio scales that are then synthesized throughout the structure to select the best alternative.

Fundamentally, the AHP works by developing priorities for alternatives and the criteria used to judge the alternatives. Usually the criteria, whose choice is at the mercy of the understanding of the decision-maker (irrelevant criteria are those that are not included in the hierarchy), are measured on different scales, such as weight and length, or are even intangible for which no scales yet exist. Measurements on different scales, of course, cannot be directly combined. First, priorities are derived for the criteria in terms of their importance to achieve the goal, then priorities are derived for the performance of the alternatives on each criterion. These priorities are derived based on pairwise assessments using judgment, or ratios of measurements from a scale if one exists. The process of prioritization solves the problem of having to deal with different types of scales, by interpreting their significance to the values of the user or users. Finally, a weighting and adding process is used to obtain overall priorities for the alternatives as to how they contribute to the goal. This weighting and adding parallels what one would have done arithmetically prior to the AHP to combine alternatives measured under several criteria having the *same* scale (a scale that is often common to several criteria is money) to obtain an overall result. With the AHP a multidimensional scaling problem is thus transformed to a unidimensional scaling problem.

The seven pillars of the AHP are: 1) **Ratio scales, proportionality, and normalized ratio scales** are central to the generation and synthesis of priorities, whether in the AHP or in any multicriteria method that needs to integrate existing ratio scale measurements with its own derived scales; in addition, ratio scales are the only way to generalize a decision theory to the case of dependence and feedback because ratio scales can be both multiplied, and added - when they belong to the same scale such as a priority scale; when two judges arrive at two different ratio scales for the same problem one needs to test the compatibility of their answers and accept or reject their closeness. The AHP has a non-statistical index for doing this. Ratio scales can also be used to make decisions within an even more general framework involving several hierarchies for benefits, costs, opportunities and risks, and using a common criterion such as *economic* to ensure commensurability; ratio scales are essential in proportionate resource allocation as in linear programming, recently generalized to deal with relative measurement for both the objective function and the constraints obtaining a ratio scale solution vector form which it is possible to decide on the relative values of the allocated resources; one can associate with each alternative a vector of benefits, costs, time of completion, etc., to determine the best alternative subject to all these general concerns; 2) **Reciprocal paired comparisons** are used to express judgments semantically automatically linking them to a numerical fundamental scale of absolute numbers (derived from stimulus-response relations) from which the principal eigenvector of priorities is then derived; the eigenvector shows the dominance of each element with respect to the other elements; an element that does not have a particular property is automatically assigned the value zero in the eigenvector without including it in the comparisons; dominance along all possible paths is obtained by raising the matrix to powers and normalizing the sum of the rows; inconsistency in judgment is allowed and a measure for it is provided which can direct the decision maker in both improving judgment and arriving at a better understanding of the problem; scientific procedures for giving less than the full set of n(n-1)/2 judgments in a matrix have been developed; using interval judgments eventually leading to the use of optimization and statistical procedures is a complex process which is often replaced by comparing ranges of values of the criteria, performing sensitivity analysis, and relying on conditions for the insensitivity of the eigenvector to perturbations in the judgments; the judgments may be considered as random variables with probability distributions; the AHP has at least three modes for arriving at a ranking of the alternatives: a) ***Relative***, which *ranks* a few alternatives by comparing them in pairs and is particularly useful in new and exploratory decisions, b) ***Absolute***, which *rates* an unlimited number of alternatives one at a time on intensity scales constructed separately for each covering criterion and is particularly useful in decisions where there is considerable knowledge to judge the relative importance of the intensities and develop priorities for them; if desired, a few of the top rated alternatives can then be compared against each other using the relative mode to obtain further refinement of the priorities; c) ***Benchmarking***, which ranks alternatives by including a known alternative in the group and comparing the other against it; 3) **Sensitivity of the principal right eigenvector** to perturbation in judgments limits the number of elements in each set of comparisons to a few and requires that they be homogeneous; the left eigenvector is only meaningful as reciprocal; due to the choice of a unit as one of the two elements in each paired comparison to determine the relative dominance of the second element, it is not possible to derive the principal left eigenvector directly from paired comparisons as the dominant element cannot be decomposed a priori ; as a result, to ask for how much less one element is than another we must take the reciprocal of what we get by asking how much more the larger element is; 4) **Homogeneity and clustering** are used to extend the fundamental scale gradually from cluster to adjacent cluster, eventually enlarging the scale from 1-9 to 1-∞; 5) **Synthesis that can be extended to dependence and feedback** is applied to the derived ratio scales to create a uni-dimensional ratio scale for representing the overall outcome. Synthesis of the scales derived in the decision structure can only be made to yield correct outcomes on known scales by additive weighting. It should be carefully noted that additive weighting in a hierarchical structure leads to a multilinear form and hence is nonlinear. It is known that under very general conditions such multilinear forms are dense in general function spaces (discrete or continuous), and thus linear combinations of them can be used to approximate arbitrarily close to any nonlinear element in that space. Multiplicative weighting, by raising the priorities of the alternatives to the power of the priorities of the criteria (which it determines through additive weighting!) then multiplying the results, has four major flaws: a) It does not give back weights of existing same ratio scale measurements on several criteria as it should; b) It assumes that the matrix of judgments is always consistent, thus sacrificing the idea of inconsistency and how to deal with it, and not allowing redundancy of judgments to improve validity about the real world; c) Most critically, it does not generalize to the case of interdependence and feedback, as the AHP generalizes to the Analytic Network Process (ANP), so essential for the many decision problems in which the criteria and alternatives depend on each other; d) It always preserves rank which leads to unreasonable outcomes and contradicts the many counterexamples that show rank reversals should be allowed; 6) **Rank preservation and reversal** can be shown to occur without adding or deleting criteria, such as by simply introducing enough copies of an alternative or for numerous other reasons; this leaves no doubt that rank reversal is as intrinsic to decision making as rank preservation also is; it follows that any decision theory must have at least two modes of synthesis; in the AHP they are called the distributive and ideal modes, with guidelines for which mode to use; rank can always be preserved by using the ideal mode in both absolute measurement and relative measurement; 7) **Group judgments** must be integrated one at a time carefully and mathematically, taking into consideration when desired the experience, knowledge, and power of each person involved in the decision, without the need to force consensus, or to use majority or other ordinal ways of voting; the theorem regarding the *impossibility* of constructing a social utility function from individual utilities that satisfies four reasonable conditions which found their validity with *ordinal* preferences is *no longer true* when *cardinal* ratio scale preferences are used as in the AHP. Instead, one has the *possibility* of constructing such a function. To deal with a large group requires the use of questionnaires and statistical procedures for large samples.

2. RATIO SCALES

A *ratio* is the relative value or quotient a/b of two quantities a and b *of the same kind*; it is called commensurate if it is a rational number, otherwise it is incommensurate. A statement of the equality of two ratios a/b and c/d is called *proportionality*. A ratio scale is a set of numbers that is invariant under a similarity transformation (multiplication by a positive constant). The constant cancels when the ratio of any two numbers is formed. Either pounds or kilograms can be used to measure weight, but the ratio of the weight of two objects is the same for both scales. An extension of this idea is that the weights of an entire set of objects whether in pounds or in kilograms can be standardized to read the same by normalizing. In general if the readings from a ratio scale are aw_i^*, i=1,...,n, the standard form is given by $w_i = aw_i^* / aw_i^* = w_i^* / w_i^*$ as a result of which we have w_i = 1, and the w_i, i=1,...,n, are said to be normalized. We no longer need to specify whether weight for example is given in pounds or in kilograms or in another kind of unit. The weights (2.21, 4.42) in pounds and (1, 2) in kilograms, are both given by (1/3, 2/3) in the standard ratio scale form.

The relative ratio scale derived from a pairwise comparison reciprocal matrix of judgments is derived by solving:

$$\sum_{j=1}^{n} a_{ij}\, w_j = \lambda_{\max}\, w_i \tag{1}$$

$$\sum_{i=1}^{n} w_i = 1 \tag{2}$$

with $a_{ji}=1/a_{ij}$ or $a_{ij}\, a_{ji}=1$ (the reciprocal property), $a_{ij} > 0$ (thus A is known as a positive matrix) whose solution, known as the principal right eigenvector, is normalized as in (2). A relative ratio scale does not need a unit of measurement.

When $a_{ij}\, a_{jk} = a_{ik}$, the matrix $A=(a_{ij})$ is said to be consistent and its principal eigenvalue is equal to n. Otherwise, it is simply reciprocal. The general eigenvalue formulation given in (1) is obtained by perturbation of the following consistent formulation:

$$Aw = \begin{array}{c} \\ A_1 \\ \vdots \\ A_n \end{array}\!\!\begin{array}{c} \begin{array}{ccc} A_1 & \cdots & A_n \end{array} \\ \begin{bmatrix} \dfrac{w_1}{w_1} & \cdots & \dfrac{w_1}{w_n} \\ \vdots & \ddots & \vdots \\ \dfrac{w_n}{w_1} & \cdots & \dfrac{w_n}{w_n} \end{bmatrix} \end{array} \begin{bmatrix} w_1 \\ \vdots \\ w_n \end{bmatrix} = n \begin{bmatrix} w_1 \\ \vdots \\ w_n \end{bmatrix} = nw.$$

where A has been multiplied on the right by the transpose of the vector of weights $w = (w_1,\dots, w_n)$. The result of this multiplication is nw. Thus, to recover the scale from the matrix of ratios, one must solve the problem $Aw = nw$ or $(A - n\mathrm{I})w = 0$. This is a system of homogeneous linear equations. It has a nontrivial solution if and only if the determinant of A-nI vanishes, that is, n is an eigenvalue of A. Now A has unit rank since every row is a constant multiple of the first row. Thus all its eigenvalues except one are zero. The sum of the eigenvalues of a matrix is equal to its trace, that is, the sum of its diagonal elements. In this case the trace of A is equal to n. Thus n is an eigenvalue of A, and one has a nontrivial solution. The solution consists of positive entries and is unique to within a multiplicative constant.

The discrete formulation given in (1) and (2) above generalizes to the continuous case through Fredholm's integral equation of the second kind and is given by:

$$\int_a^b K(s,t)\, w(t)\, dt = \lambda_{\max}\, w(s) \tag{3}$$

$$\lambda \int_a^b K(s,t) w(t) dt = w(s) \tag{4}$$

$$\int_a^b w(s) ds = 1 \tag{5}$$

where instead of the matrix A we have as a positive kernel, $K(s,t) > 0$. Note that the entries in a matrix depend on the two variables i and j which assume discrete values. Thus the matrix itself depends on these discrete variables, and its generalization, the kernel function also depends on two (continuous) variables. The reason for calling it kernel is the role it plays in the integral, where without knowing it we cannot determine the exact form of the solution. The standard way in which (3) is written is to move the eigenvalue to the left hand side which gives it the reciprocal form. In general, by abuse of notation, one continues to use the symbol λ to represent the reciprocal value. Our equation for response to a stimulus is now written in the standard form (4) with the normalization condition (5). Here also, we have the reciprocal property (6) and as in the finite case, the kernel $K(s,t)$ is consistent if it satisfies the relation (7):

$$K(s,t)\, K(t,s) = 1 \tag{6}$$

$$K(s,t)\, K(t,u) = K(s,u), \text{ for all } s,\ t, \text{ and } u \tag{7}$$

An example of this type of kernel is $K(s,t) = e^{s-t} = e^s / e^t$. It follows by putting $s=t=u$, that $K(s,s)=1$ for all s which is analogous to having ones down the diagonal of the matrix in the discrete case. A value of λ for which Fredholm□s equation has a nonzero solution $w(t)$ is called a characteristic value (or its reciprocal is called an eigenvalue) and the corresponding solution is called an eigenfunction. An eigenfunction is determined to within a multiplicative constant. If $w(t)$ is an eigenfunction corresponding to the charateristic value λ and if C is an arbitrary constant, we can easily see by substituting in the equation that $Cw(t)$ is also an eigenfunction corresponding to the same λ. The value λ=0 is not a characteristic value because we have the corresponding solution $w(t)=0$ for every value of t, which is the trivial case, excluded in our discussion.

It may be useful to recount a little of the history of how Fredholm's equation came about in the ratio scale formulation of the AHP. My student Hasan Ait-Kaci and I first recognized the connection between Fredholm's equation and the AHP in a paper we wrote in the late 1970's. In the early 1980's, I and my friend and colleague, Professor Luis Vargas, used this formulation in the framework of neural firing and published several papers on the subject. In December of 1996, I had the nagging idea that the ratio scale relation for electrical firing was not reflected in our solution, and that periodicity had to be involved in the solution with which I began. Many researchers on the brain had considered neural firing in the framework of a damped periodic oscillator. It was my friend Janos Aczel, the leading functional equation mathematician in the world, who provided me with a variety of solutions for the functional equation ($w(as) = bw(s)$). I had proved in the theorem given below that this equation characterizes the solution of Fredholm's equation and its solution is an eigenfunction of that equation. My work is an extension of the work I had done earlier with Vargas. The solution has the form of a damped periodic oscillator of period one. It has an additional logarithmic property that corresponds to Fechner's law discussed later in this paper.

A matrix is consistent if and only if it has the form $A=(w_i/w_j)$ which is equivalent to multiplying a column vector that is the transpose of $(w_1, ..., w_n)$ by the row vector $(1/w_1, ..., 1/w_n)$. As we see below, the kernel $K(s,t)$ is separable and can be written as

$$K(s,t)= k_1(s)\, k_2(t).$$

Theorem: *$K(s,t)$ is consistent if and only if it is separable of the form:*

$$K(s,t)=k(s)/k(t).(8)$$

Theorem: *If $K(s,t)$ is consistent, the solution of (4) is given by*

$$w(s) = \frac{k(s)}{\int_S k(s)ds} .(9)$$

In the discrete case, the normalized eigenvector was independent of whether all the elements of the pairwise comparison matrix A are multiplied by the same constant a or not, and thus we can replace A by aA and obtain the same eigenvector. Generalizing this result we have:

$$K(as, at)=aK(s,t)=k(as)/k(at)=a\, k(s)/k(t)$$

which means that K is a homogeneous function of order one. In general, when $f(ax_1, ..., ax_n)=a^n f(x_1, ..., x_n)$ holds, f is said to be homogeneous of order n. Because K is a degenerate kernel, we can replace $k(s)$ above by $k(as)$ and obtain $w(as)$. We have now derived from considerations of ratio scales the following condition to be satisfied by a ratio scale:

Theorem: *A necessary and sufficient condition for w(s) to be an eigenfunction solution of Fredholm's equation of the second kind, with a consistent kernel that is homogeneous of order one, is that it satisfy the functional equation*

$$w(as)=bw(s)$$

where $b=\alpha a$.

We have for the general damped periodic response function $w(s)$,

$$w(s) = Ce^{\log b \frac{\log s}{\log a}} P\left(\frac{\log s}{\log a}\right)$$

where P is periodic of period 1 and $P(0)=1$.

We can write this solution as

$$v(u)=C_1\, e^{-\beta u} P(u)$$

where $P(u)$ is periodic of period 1, $u=\log s/\log a$ and $\log ab/{-\beta}$, $\beta>0$. It is interesting to observe the logarithmic function appear as part of the solution. It gives greater confirmation to the Weber-Fechner law developed in the next section.

3. PAIRED COMPARISONS AND THE FUNDAMENTAL SCALE

Instead of assigning two numbers w_i and w_j and forming the ratio w_i/w_j we assign a single number drawn from the fundamental 1-9 scale of absolute numbers to represent the ratio $(w_i/w_j)/1$. It is a nearest integer approximation to the ratio w_i/w_j. The derived scale will reveal what the w_i and w_j are. This is a central fact about the relative measurement approach of the AHP and the need for a fundamental scale.

In 1846 Weber found, for example, that people while holding in their hand different weights, could distinguish between a weight of 20 g and a weight of 21 g, but could not if the second weight is only 20.5 g. On the other hand, while they could not distinguish between 40 g and 41 g, they could between 40g and 42g, and so on at higher levels. We need to increase a stimulus s by a minimum amount $\Delta\Delta s$ to reach a point where our senses can first discriminate between s and $s + \Delta s$. Δs is called the just noticeable difference (jnd). The ratio $r = \Delta s/s$ does not depend on s. Weber's law states that change in sensation is noticed when the stimulus is increased by a constant percentage of the stimulus itself. This law holds in ranges where Δs is small when compared with s, and hence in practice it fails to hold when s is either too small or too large. Aggregating or decomposing stimuli as needed into clusters or hierarchy levels is an effective way for extending the uses of this law.

In 1860 Fechner considered a sequence of just noticeable increasing stimuli. He denotes the first one by s_0. The next just noticeable stimulus is given by

$$s_1 = s_1 + \Delta s_0 = s_0 + \frac{\Delta s_0}{s_0} s_0 = s_0(1 + r)$$

based on Weber's law.

Similarly $s_2 = s_1 + \Delta s_1 = s_1(1 + r) = s_0(1 + r)^2 \equiv s_0 \alpha^2$. In general $s_n = s_{n-1}\alpha = s_0\alpha^n \ (n = 0, 1, 2, \ldots)$.

Thus stimuli of noticeable differences follow sequentially in a geometric progression. Fechner noted that the corresponding sensations should follow each other in an arithmetic sequence at the discrete points at which just noticeable differences occur. But the latter are obtained when we solve for n. We have

$n = \dfrac{(\log s_n - \log s_0)}{\log \alpha}$ and sensation is a linear function of the logarithm of the stimulus. Thus if M denotes the sensation and s the stimulus, the psychophysical law of Weber-Fechner is given by

$$M = a \log s + b, \quad a \neq 0 .$$

We assume that the stimuli arise in making pairwise comparisons of relatively comparable activities. We are interested in responses whose numerical values are in the form of ratios. Thus $b = 0$, from which we must have $\log s_0 = 0$ or $s_0 = 1$, which is possible by calibrating a unit stimulus. Here the unit stimulus is s_0. The next noticeable stimulus is $s_1 = s_0\alpha = \alpha$ which yields the second noticeable response $a \log \alpha$. The third noticeable stimulus is $s_2 = s_0\alpha^2$ which yields a response of $2a \log \alpha$. Thus we have for the different responses:

$M_0 = a \log s_0$, $M_1 = a \log \alpha$, $M_2 = 2a \log \alpha, \ldots$, $M_n = na \log \alpha$.

While the noticeable ratio stimulus increases geometrically, the response to that stimulus increases arithmetically. Note that $M_0 = 0$ and there is no response. By dividing each M_i by M_1 we obtain the sequence of absolute numbers 1, 2, 3, ... of the fundamental 1-9 scale. Paired comparisons are made by identifying the less dominant of two elements and using it as the unit of measurement. One then determines, using the scale 1-9 or its verbal equivalent, how many times more the dominant member of the pair is than this unit. In making paired comparisons, we use the nearest integer approximation from the scale, relying on the insensitivity of the eigenvector to small perturbations (discussed below). The reciprocal value is then automatically used for the comparison of the less dominant element with the more dominant one. Despite the foregoing derivation of the scale in the form of integers, someone might think that other scale values would be better, for example using 1.3

in the place of 2. Imagine comparing the magnitude of two people with respect to the magnitude of one person and using 1.3 for how many there are instead of 2.

We note that there may be elements that are closer than 2 on the 1-9 scale, and we need a variant of the foregoing. Among the elements that are close, we select the smallest. Observe the incremental increases between that smallest one and the rest of the elements in the close group. We now consider these increments to be new elements and pairwise compare them on the scale 1-9. If two of the increments are themselves closer than 2 we treat them as identical, assigning a 1 (we could carry this on ad infinitum – but we will not). In the end each component of the eigenvector of comparisons of the increments is added to unity to yield the unnormalized priorities of the close elements for that criterion. Note that only the least of these close elements is used in comparisons with the other elements that can be compared directly using the normal 1-9 scale. Its priority is used to multiply the priorities of these close elements and finally the priorities of all the elements are renormalized.

How large should the upper value of the scale be? Qualitatively, people have a capacity to divide their response to stimuli into three categories: high, medium and low. They also have the capacity to refine this division by further subdividing each of these intensities of responses into high, medium and low, thus yielding in all nine subdivisions. It turns out, from the requirement of homogeneity developed below, that to maintain stability, our minds work with a few elements at a time. Using a large number of elements in one matrix leads to greater inconsistency.

4. SENSITIVITY OF THE PRINCIPAL EIGENVECTOR PLACES A LIMIT ON THE NUMBER OF ELEMENTS AND THEIR HOMOGENEITY

To a first order approximation, perturbation Δw_1 in the principal eigenvector w_1 due to a perturbation ΔA in the matrix A where A is consistent is given by:

$$\Delta w_1 = \sum_{j=2}^{n} (v_j^T \Delta A\, w_1 / (\lambda_1 - \lambda_j) v_j^T w_j) w_j .$$

The eigenvector w_1 is insensitive to perturbation in A, if the principal eigenvalue λ_1 is separated from the other eigenvalues λj, here assumed to be distinct, and none of the products $v_j^T w_j$ of left and right eigenvectors is small. We should recall that the nonprincipal eigenvectors need not be positive in all components, and they may be complex. One can show that all the $v_j^T w_j$ are of the same order, and that $v_1^T w_1$, the product of the normalized left and right principal eigenvectors is equal to n. If n is relatively small and the elements being compared are homogeneous, none of the components of w_1 is arbitrarily small and correspondingly, none of the components of v_1^T is arbitrarily small. Their product cannot be arbitrarily small, and thus w is insensitive to small perturbations of the consistent matrix A. The conclusion is that n must be small, and one must compare homogeneous elements. Later we discuss placing a limit on the value of n.

5. CLUSTERING AND USING PIVOTS TO EXTEND THE SCALE FROM 1-9 TO 1- ∞

In Figure 1, an unripe cherry tomato is eventually and indirectly compared with a large watermelon by first comparing it with a small tomato and a lime, the lime is then used again in a second cluster with a grapefruit and a honey dew where we then divide by the weight of the lime and then multiply by its weight in the first cluster, and then use the honey dew again in a third cluster and so on. In the end we have a comparison of the unripe cherry tomato with the large watermelon and would accordingly extended the scale from 1-9 to 1-721.

Such clustering is essential, and must be done separately for each criterion. We should note that in most decision problems, there may be one or two levels of clusters and conceivably it may go up to three or four adjacent ranges of homogeneous elements (Maslow put them in seven groupings). Very roughly we have in decreasing order of importance: 1) Survival, health, family, friends and basic religious beliefs some people were known to die for; 2) Career, education, productivity and lifestyle; 3) Political and social beliefs and contributions; 4) Beliefs, ideas, and things that are flexible and it does not matter exactly how one advocates or uses them. Nevertheless one needs them, such as learning to eat with a fork or a chopstick or with the fingers as many people do interchangeably. These categories can be generalized to a group, a corporation, or a government. For very important decisions, two categories may need to be considered. Note that the priorities in two adjacent categories would be sufficiently different, one being an order of magnitude smaller than the other, that in the synthesis, the priorities of the elements in the smaller set have little effect on the decision. We do not have space to show how some *undesirable* elements can be compared among themselves and gradually extended to compare them with *desirable* ones as above. Thus one can go from negatives to positives but keep the measurement of the two types positive, by eventually clustering them separately.

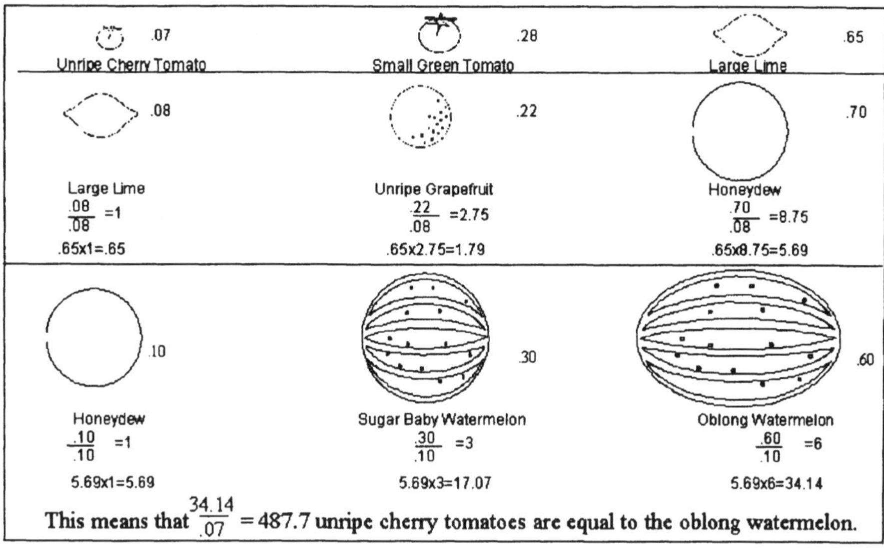

Figure 1: Clustering

6. SYNTHESIS: HOW TO COMBINE TANGIBLES WITH INTANGIBLES – ADDITIVE VS MULTIPLICATIVE

Let H be a complete hierarchy with h levels. Let B_k be the priority matrix of the kth level, $k = 2, ..., h$. If W' is the global priority vector of the pth level with respect to some element z in the (p-1)st level, then the priority vector W of the qth level ($p < q$) with respect to z is given by the multilinear (and thus nonlinear) form,

$$W = B_q B_{q-1} \cdots B_{p+1} W'.$$

The global priority vector of the lowest level with respect to the goal is given by,

$$W = B_h B_{h-1} \cdots B_2 W'.$$

In general, $W' = 1$. The sensitivity of the bottom level alternatives with respect to changes in the weights of elements in any level can be studied by means of this multilinear form.

Assume that a family is considering buying a house and there are three houses to consider A, B, and C. Four factors dominate their thinking: the price of the house, the remodeling costs, the size of the house as reflected by its footage and the style of the house which is an intangible. They have looked at three houses with numerical data shown below on the quantifiables (Figure 2):

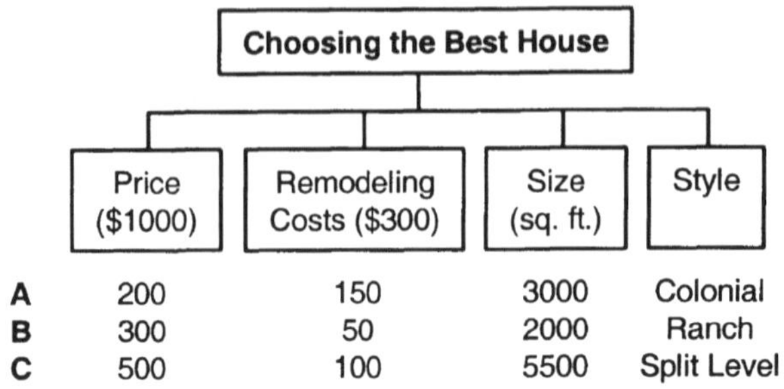

Figure 2. Ranking Houses on Four Criteria

If we add the costs on price and modeling and normalize we obtain respectively (A,B,C) = (.269,.269,.462). Now let us see what is needed for normalization to yield the same result.

First we normalize for each of the quantifiable factors. Then we must normalize the factors measured with respect to a single scale (Figure 3).

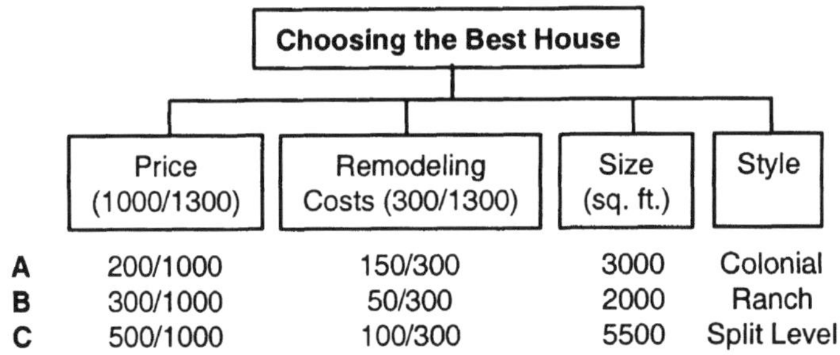

Figure 3. Normalization of the Measurements

Here we learn two important lessons to be used in the general approach. Normalizing the alternatives for the two criteria involving money in terms of the money involved on both criteria leads to relative weights of importance for the criteria. Here for example Price is in the ratio of about three to one when compared with Remodeling Cost and when compared with the latter with respect to the goal of choosing the best house, it is likely to be assigned the value "moderate" which is nearly three times more as indicated by the measurements. Here the criteria Price and Remodeling Cost derive their priorities only from the alternatives because they are equally important factors, although they can also acquire priorities from higher level criteria as to their functional importance with respect to the ease and availability of different amounts of money. We now combine the two factors with a common scale by weighting and adding. We have (Figure 4):

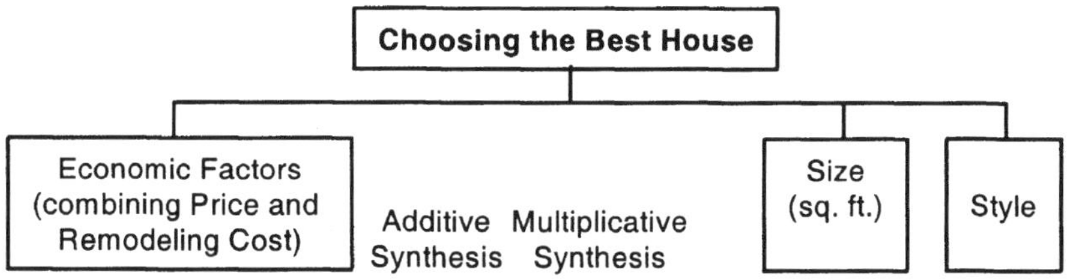

	Economic Factors		Additive Synthesis	Multiplicative Synthesis	Size (sq. ft.)	Style
A	350/1300	=	.269	.256	3000/10500	Colonial
B	350/1300	=	.269	.272	2000/10500	Ranch
C	600/1300	=	.462	.472	5500/10500	Split Level

Figure 4. Combining the Two Costs through Additive or Multiplicative Syntheses

The left column and its decimal values in the second column give the exact value of the normalized dollars spent on each house obtained by additive synthesis (weighting and adding). By aggregating the two factor measured with dollars into a single factor, one then makes the decision as to which house to buy by comparing the three criteria as to their importance with respect to the goal.

The second lesson is that ***when the criteria have different measurements, their importance cannot be determined from the bottom up through measurement of the alternatives, but from the top down, in terms of the goal. The same process of comparison of the criteria with respect to the goal is applied to all criteria if, despite the presence of a physical scale, they are assumed to be measurable on different scales as they might when actual values are unavailable or when it is thought that such measurement does not reflect the relative importance of the alternatives with respect to the given criterion. Imagine that no physical scale of any kind is known!*** We might note in passing that the outcome of this process of comparison with respect to higher level criteria yields meaningful (not arbitrary) results as noted by two distinguished proponents of multi-attribute value theory (MAVT) Buede and Maxwell [1], who wrote about their own experiments in decision making:

> *These experiments demonstrated that the MAVT and AHP techniques, when provided with the same decision outcome data, very often identify the same alternatives as 'best'. The other techniques are noticeably less consistent with MAVT, the Fuzzy algorithm being the least consistent.*

Multiplicative synthesis, as in the third column of numbers above, done by raising each number in the two columns in the previous table to the power of its criterion measured in the relative total dollars under it, multiplying the two outcomes for each alternative and normalizing, *does not* yield the *exact answer* obtained by adding dollars! In addition, A and B should have the same value, but they do not with multiplicative synthesis. The multiplicative "solution" devised for the fallacy of always preserving rank and avoiding inconsistency fails, because it violates the most basic of several requirements mentioned in the introduction to this paper.

Multiplicative and additive syntheses are related analytically through approximation. If we denote by a_i the priority of the ith criterion, i = 1,...,n, and by x_i, the priority of alternative x with respect to the ith criterion, then

$$\prod x_i^{a_i} = \exp\log\prod x_i^{a_i} = \exp(\sum\log x_i^{a_i}) = \exp(\sum a_i \log x_i)$$
$$\approx 1 + \sum a_i \log x_i \approx 1 + \sum(a_i x_i - a_i) = \sum a_i x_i$$

If desired, one can include a remainder term to estimate the error. With regard to additive and multiplicative syntheses being close, one may think that in the end it does not matter which one is used, but it does. Saaty and Hu [7] have shown that despite such closeness on every matrix of consistent judgments in a decision, the synthesized outcomes by the two methods not only lead to different final priorities (which can cause a faulty allocation of resources) but more significantly to *different rankings* of the alternatives. For all these problems, but more significantly because it does not generalize to dependence and feedback even with consistency guaranteed, and because of the additive nature of matrix multiplication needed to compute feedback in network circuits to extend the AHP to the ANP, I do not recommend ever using multiplicative synthesis. It can lead to an undesirable ranking of the alternatives of a decision.

7. RANK PRESERVATION AND REVERSAL

Given the assumption that the alternatives of a decision are completely independent of one another, can and should the introduction (deletion) of new (old) alternatives change the rank of some alternatives without introducing new (deleting old) criteria, so that a less preferred alternative becomes most preferred? Incidentally, how one prioritizes the criteria and subcriteria is even more important than how one does the alternatives which are themselves composites of criteria. Can rank reverse among the criteria themselves if new criteria are introduced? Why should that not be as critical a concern? The answer is simple. In its original form utility theory assumed that criteria could not be weighted and the only important elements in a decision were the alternatives and their utilities under the various criteria. Today utility theorists imitate the AHP by rating, and some even by comparing the criteria, somehow. There was no concern then about what would happen to the ranks of the alternatives should the criteria weights themselves change as there were none. The tendency, even today, is to be unconcerned about the theory of rank preservation and reversal among the criteria themselves.

The house example of the previous section teaches us an important lesson.

If we add a fourth house to the collection, the priority weights of the criteria Price and Remodeling Cost would change accordingly. Thus the measurements of the alternatives and their number, which we call structural factors, always affect the importance of the criteria. When the criteria are incommensurate and their functional priorities are determined in terms of yet higher level criteria or goals, one must still weight such functional importance of the criteria by the structural effect of the alternatives. What is significant in all this is that the importance of the criteria always depends on the measurements of the alternatives. If we assume that the alternatives are measured on a different scale for each criterion, it becomes obvious that normalization is the instrument that provides the structural effect to update the importance of the criteria in terms of what alternatives there are. Finally, the priorities of the alternatives are weighted by the priorities of the criteria that depend on the measurements of the alternatives. This implies that the overall ranking of any alternative depends on the measurement and number of all the alternatives. To always preserve rank means that the priorities of the criteria should not depend on the measurements of the alternatives but should only derive from their own functional importance with respect to higher goals. This implies that the alternatives should not depend on the measurements of other alternatives. Thus one way to always preserve rank is to rate the alternatives one at a time. In the AHP this is done through absolute measurement with respect to a complete set of intensity ranges with the largest value intensity value equal to one. It is also possible to preserve rank in relative measurement by using an ideal alternative with full value of one for each criterion.

The logic about what can or should happen to rank when the alternatives *depend* on each other has always been that *anything* can happen. Thus, when the criteria functionally depend on the alternatives, which implies that the alternatives, which of course depend on the criteria, would then depend on the alternatives themselves, rank may be allowed to reverse. The Analytic Network Process (ANP) is the generalization of the AHP to deal with ranking alternatives when there is functional dependence and feedback of any kind. Even here, one can have a decision problem with dependence among the criteria, but with no dependence of criteria on alternatives and rank may still need to be preserved. The ANP takes care of functional dependence, but if the criteria do not depend on the alternatives, the latter are kept out of the supermatrix and ranked precisely as they are dealt with in a hierarchy [8].

Examples of rank reversal abound in practice, and they do not occur because new criteria are introduced. The requirement that rank always be preserved or that it should be preserved with respect to irrelevant alternatives. To every rule or generalization that one may wish to set down about rank, it is possible to find a counterexample that violates that rule. Here is the last and most extreme form of four variants of an attempt to qualify what should happen to rank given by Luce and Raiffa, each of which is followed by a counterexample. They state it but and then reject it. *The addition of new acts to a decision problem under uncertainty never changes old, originally non-optimal acts into optimal ones. The all-or-none feature of the last form may seem a bit too stringent ... a severe criticism is that it yields unreasonable results.* The AHP has a theory and implementation procedures and guidelines for when to preserve rank and when to allow it to reverse. One mode of the AHP allows an irrelevant alternative to cause reversal among the ranks of the original alternatives.

Guidelines for Selecting the Distributive or Ideal Mode

The distributive mode of the AHP produces preference scores by normalizing the performance scores; it takes the performance score received by each alternative and divides it by the sum of performance scores of all alternatives under that criterion. This means that with the Distributive mode the preference for any given alternative would go up if we reduce the performance score of another alternative or remove some alternatives.

The Ideal mode compares each performance score to a fixed benchmark such as the performance of the best alternative under that criterion. This means that with the Ideal mode the preference for any given alternative is independent of the performance of other alternatives, except for the alternative selected as a benchmark. Saaty and Vargas [11] have shown by using simulation, that there are only minor differences produced by the two synthesis modes. This means that the decision should select one or the other if the results diverge beyond a given set of acceptable data.

The following guidelines were developed by Millet and Saaty [3] to reflect the core differences in translating performance measures to preference measures of alternatives. ***The Distributive (dominance) synthesis mode should be used when the decision maker is concerned with the extent to which each alternative dominates all other alternatives under the criterion. The Ideal (performance) synthesis mode should be used when the decision maker is concerned with how well each alternative performs relative to a fixed benchmark.*** In order for dominance to be an issue the decision-maker should regard inferior alternatives as relevant even after the ranking process is completed. This suggests a simple test for the use of the Distributive mode: ***if the decision maker indicates that the preference for a top ranked alternative under a given criterion would improve if the performance of any lower ranked alternative was adjusted downward, then one should use the Distributive synthesis mode.*** To make this test more actionable we can ask the decision maker to imagine the amount of money he or she would be willing to pay for the top ranked alternative. If the decision maker would be willing to pay more for a top ranked alternative after learning that the performance of one of the lower-ranked alternatives was adjusted downward, then the Distributive mode should be used.

Consider selecting a car: Two different decision makers may approach the same problem from two different points of views even if the criteria and standards are the same. The one who is interested in "getting a well performing car" should use the Ideal mode. The one who is interested in "getting a car that stands out" among the alternatives purchased by co-workers or neighbors, should use the Distributive mode.

8. GROUP DECISION MAKING

Here we consider two issues in group decision making. The first is how to aggregate individual judgments, and the second is how to construct a group choice from individual choices.

How to Aggregate Individual Judgments

Let the function $f(x_1, x_2, ..., x_n)$ for synthesizing the judgments given by n judges, satisfy the

(i) Separability condition (S): $f(x_1, x_2,...,x_n)= g(x_1)g(x_2)... g(x_n)$ for all $x_1, x_2,...,x_n$ in an interval P of positive numbers, where g is a function mapping P onto a proper interval J and is a continuous, associative and cancellative operation.[(S) means that the influences of the individual judgments can be separated as above.]

(ii) *Unanimity condition* (U): $f(x, x,...,x) = x$ for all x in P. [(U) means that if all individuals give the same judgment x, that judgment should also be the synthesized judgment.]

(iii) *Homogeneity condition* (H): $f(ux_1, ux_2,...,ux_n) = uf(x_1, x_2,...,x_n)$ where $u > 0$ and x_k, ux_k (k=1,2,...,n) are all in P. [For ratio judgments (H) means that if all individuals judge a ratio u times as large as another ratio, then the synthesized judgment should also be u times as large.]

(iv) *Power conditions* (P_p) : $f(x_1^p, x_2^p,...,x_n^p) = f^p(x_1, x_2,...,x_n)$. [($P_2$) for example means that if the kth individual judges the length of a side of a square to be x_k, the synthesized judgment on the area of that square will be given by the square of the synthesized judgment on the length of its side.]

Special case ($R=P_{-1}$): $f(1/x_1, 1/x_2,...,1/x_n) = 1/f(x_1, x_2,...,x_n)$. [(R) is of particular importance in ratio judgments. It means that the synthesized value of the reciprocal of the individual judgments should be the reciprocal of the synthesized value of the original judgments.]

Aczel and Saaty (see[9] and [10]) proved the following theorem:

Theorem *The general separable (S) synthesizing functions satisfying the unanimity (U) and homogeneity (H) conditions are the geometric mean and the root-mean-*

power. If moreover the reciprocal property (R) is assumed even for a single n-tuple $(x_1, x_2,...,x_n)$ of the judgments of n individuals, where not all x_k are equal, then only the geometric mean satisfies all the above conditions.

In any rational consensus, those who know more should, accordingly, influence the consensus more strongly than those who are less knowledgeable. Some people are clearly wiser and more sensible in such matters than others, others may be more powerful and their opinions should be given appropriately greater weight. For such unequal importance of voters not all g's in (S) are the same function. In place of (S), the weighted separability property (WS) is now: $f(x_1, x_2,...,x_n)= g_1(x_1)g_2(x_2)... g_n(x_n)$. [(WS) implies that not all judging individuals have the same weight when the judgments are synthesized and the different influences are reflected in the different functions $(g_1, g_2,...,g_n)$.]

In this situation, Aczel and Alsina (see [9]) proved the following theorem:

Theorem *The general weighted-separable (WS) synthesizing functions with the unanimity (U) and homogeneity (H) properties are the weighted geometric mean* $f(x_1, x_2, \ldots, x_n) = x_1^{q_1} x_2^{q_2} \cdots x_n^{q_n}$ *and the weighted root-mean-powers* $f(x_1, x_2, \ldots, x_n) = \sqrt[\gamma]{q_1 x_1^{\gamma} + q_2 x_2^{\gamma} \cdots + q_n x_n^{\gamma}}$, *where* $q_1+q_2+\ldots+q_n=1$, $q_k>0$ $(k=1,2,\ldots,n)$, $\gamma > 0$, *but otherwise* $q_1, q_2, \ldots, q_n, \gamma$ *are arbitrary constants.*

If f also has the reciprocal property (R) and for a single set of entries $(x_1,x_2,...,x_n)$ of judgments of n individuals, where not all x_k are equal, then *only the weighted geometric mean* applies. We give the following theorem which is an explicit statement of the synthesis problem that follows from the previous results, and applies to the second and third cases of the deterministic approach:

Theorem *If* $x_1^{(i)}, \ldots, x_n^{(i)}$ $i=1, \ldots, m$ *are rankings of n alternatives by m independent judges and if* a_i *is the importance of judge i developed from a hierarchy for evaluating the judges, and hence* $\sum_{i=1}^{m} a_i = 1$, *then*

$$\left(\prod_{i=1}^{m} x_1^{a_i} \right), \ldots, \left(\prod_{i=1}^{m} x_n^{a_i} \right)$$

are the combined ranks of the alternatives for the m judges.

The power or priority of judge *i* is simply a replication of the judgment of that judge (as if there are as many other judges as indicated by his/her power a_i), which implies multiplying his/her ratio by itself a_i times, and the result follows.

The first requires knowledge of the functions which the particular alternative performs and how well it compares with a standard or benchmark. The second requires comparison with the other alternatives to determine its importance.

On the Construction of Group Choice from Individual Choices

Given a group of individuals, a set of alternatives (with cardinality greater than 2), and individual ordinal preferences for the alternatives, Arrow proved with his Impossibility Theorem that it is impossible to derive a rational group choice (construct a social choice function that aggregates individual preferences) from ordinal preferences of the individuals that satisfy the following four conditions, i.e., at least one of them is violated:

Decisiveness: the aggregation procedure must generally produce a group order.

Unanimity: if all individuals prefer alternative A to alternative B, then the aggregation procedure must produce a group order indicating that the group prefers A to B.

Independence of irrelevant alternatives: given two sets of alternatives which both include A and B, if all individuals prefer A to B in both sets, then the aggregation procedure must produce a group order indicating that the group, given any of the two sets of alternatives, prefers A to B.

No dictator: no single individual preferences determine the group order.

Using the ratio scale approach of the AHP, it can be shown that because now the individual preferences are cardinal rather than ordinal, it is possible to derive a rational group choice satisfying the above four conditions. It is possible because: a) Individual priority scales can always be derived from a set of pairwise cardinal preference judgments as long as they form at least a minimal spanning tree in the completely connected graph of the elements being compared; and b) The cardinal preference judgments associated with group choice belong to a ratio scale that represents the relative intensity of the group preferences.

REFERENCES

1. Buede, D. and D.T. Maxwell, (1995),"Rank Disagreement: A Comparison of Multi-criteria Methodologies", *Journal of Multi-Criteria Decision Analysis*, Vol. 4, 1-21.
2. Luce, R. D. and H. Raiffa, (1957), *Games and Decisions*, Wiley, New York.
3. Millet,I. And T.L. Saaty, (1999), "On the Relativity of Relative Measures--Accommodating Both Rank Preservation and Rank Reversal in the AHP". *European Journal of Operational Research.*
4. Peniwati, K., (1996), "The Analytic Hierarchy Process: The Possibility for Group Decision Making", pp. 202-214, *Proceedings of the Fourth Inter-*

national Symposium on the Analytic Hierarchy Process, Vancouver, Canada. (Obtainable from RWS Publications, 4922 Ellsworth Avenue, Pittsburgh, PA 15213.)

5. Saaty, T. L., (1999-2000 ed.), *Decision Making For Leaders*. RWS Publications, 4922 Ellsworth Avenue, Pittsburgh, PA 15213.
6. Saaty, T. L., (2000), *The Brain, Unraveling the Mystery of How It Works: The Neural Network Process*, RWS Publications, 4922 Ellsworth Avenue, Pittsburgh, PA 15213.
7. Saaty, T. L. and G. Hu, (1998), "Ranking by Eigenvector Versus Other Methods in the Analytic Hierarchy Process", *Appl. Math. Letters*, Vol. 11, No. 4, pp. 121-125.
8. Saaty, T. L., (1996), *Decision Making with Dependence and Feedback: The Analytic Network Process*, RWS Publications, 4922 Ellsworth Avenue, Pittsburgh, PA 15213.
9. Saaty, T. L., (1994), *Fundamentals of Decision Making and Priority Theory*, RWS Publications, 4922 Ellsworth Avenue, Pittsburgh, PA 15213.
10. Saaty, T. L., (1990), *Multicriteria Decision Making: The Analytic Hierarchy Process*, RWS Publications, 4922 Ellsworth Avenue, Pittsburgh, PA.
11. Saaty, T.L. and L. G. Vargas, (1993), "Experiments on Rank Preservation and Reversal in Relative Measurement," *Mathematical and Computer Modeling*, 17, No. 4/5, pp. 13-18.
12. Vargas, L. G., (1994), "Reply to Schenkerman's Avoiding Rank Reversal in AHP Decision Support Models", *European Journal of Operational Research*, 74, pp. 420-425.

CHAPTER 3

ARCHITECTURAL DESIGN

1. INTRODUCTION

This chapter illustrates the use of the Analytic Hierarchy Process in determining the amount and location of space assigned to each room, according to its function, in the design of a house [1].

We develop the plan of a house to satisfy a family's needs by considering the size of the lot, the size and shape of the different architectural spaces, their priorities, and their overall contiguity. We begin by identifying needs and then integrating them with the final plan by relating shape, size, geometric design and location to our mental criteria and personal needs. This approach also permits one to treat all these needs and their relation to the environment in a coherent framework.

We study design by addressing six basic factors: 1) architectural needs; 2) Budget allocation; 3) allocation of areas to satisfy needs; 4) size and shape of the areas; 5) clustering spaces according to general needs; 6) identifying and locating individual spaces in each cluster.

We assume that in this hypothetical example we are dealing with the needs of a family of three, the husband (H), the wife (W), and their child (CH). They already own a fully paid lot, on which they wish to build a custom designed house (see Figure 1). The husband and wife have a maximum total disposable budget of \$70,000 to cover construction and landscaping improvement costs. Other costs such as legal fees, architectural fees, permits, etc. are not included. The cost of construction is assumed to be \$30 per square foot and that of landscaping \$1.20 per square foot. (The matrices of judgments are included for completeness.)

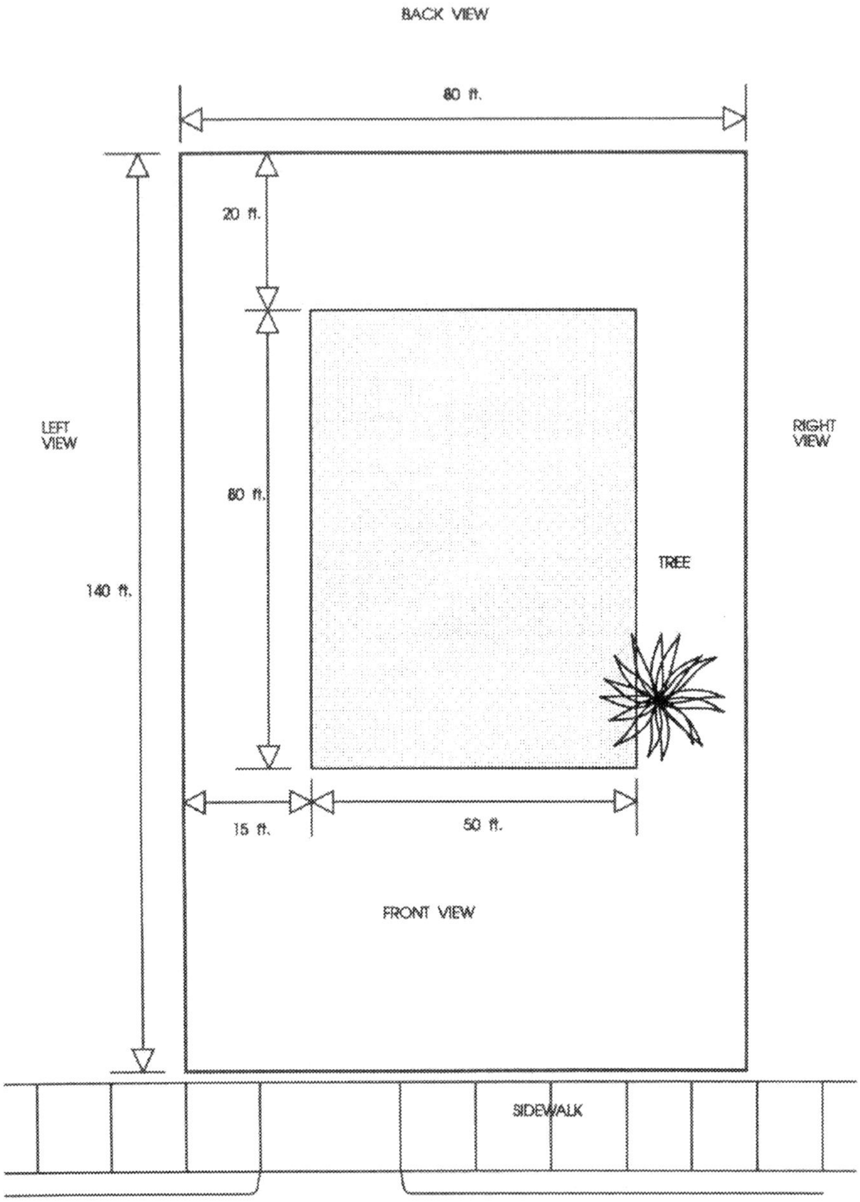

Figure 1. The Lot

2. ARCHITECTURAL NEEDS

The members of the family are considered to be the actors or decision makers. The parents will exercise far greater influence than the child on the design process. Since each of them will be seeking to satisfy similar human needs expressed through architectural design, we will consider their objectives to be the same, the difference being that each party may assign a different weight to each objective. These objectives are: 1) The need to eat (M); 2) The need to rest (R); 3) The need to entertain (E); 4) The need to clean (K); 5) The need to store (S); 6)The need to communicate, e.g., through halls and entrance, within the house (C).

First we develop a set of priorities indicating the relative power of the parties in determining the outcome for the above architectural needs (see Table 1). Table 1 consists of calculations done for the parties. The table shows that the child will not influence decisions greatly, even if the husband were to enter a full coalition with him. In our estimate in this hypothetical example, combining both parties would only increase their joint power slightly (0.453), but they would still be unable to surpass the power of the wife (0.547). Because of this fact, we eliminate the child from further consideration of influence, and focus on the husband (H) and wife (W) as the sole representatives of the family needs.

Table 1. Power of the Parties

	W	H	CH	Eigenvector	Revised Power
W	1	2	4	.547	.613
H	1/2	1	4	.387	.387
CH	1/4	1/4	1	.109	.000

$\lambda_{max} = 3.054$, C.R. = 0.05

Next, we prioritize the importance of the objectives from the standpoints of W and H (Table 2). We then weight each outcome by the power of the corresponding party (see the last column of Table 2), and take the sum of the composite outcomes (see Table 2a and Figure 2). This sum will be used to allocate square footage to each architectural space for each objective.

Next, a predetermined array of architectural spaces are assigned to each party, arranged in such a way as to satisfy one or more of the above objectives. For example, the family room can be placed in such a way as to satisfy entertainment and resting needs (see Figure 2). The parties will be allowed to change or modify their estimate of the importance of these functions. We then pairwise compare these spaces with respect to the six objectives listed above, to determine what each party's preference is to satisfy its particular objectives. This yields weights or priorities for the space assigned. This prioritization can be revised after later negotiations among the parties, in order to reach an acceptable compromise solution. The results are shown in Tables 3 and 4. We note from these comparisons, that H and W have widely differing preferences for the space assigned within each objective. This is reflected in their priorities for the spaces also shown in the tables. These preferences are then weighted by the priority of the objective for that party and by the power of the party, i.e., we use the last column of Table 2 to obtain the last columns of Tables 3 and 4. Table 5 gives the sum of the priorities of the spaces for H and W.

Table 2. Strength of Objectives

Party: Wife (Power of Party .613)

	R	M	E	K	S	C	Eigenvector	Objectives Adjusted for Power
R	1	.50	.33	4	6	6	.198	.121
M	2	1	.33	3	4	4	.206	.127
E	3	3	1	6	7	7	.424	.260
R	.25	.33	.17	1	4	5	.096	.059
M	.17	.25	.14	.25	1	1	.038	.023
E	.17	.25	.14	.20	1	1	.037	.023

λ_{max} = 6.456, C.R. = .07

Party: Husband (Power of Party .387)

	R	M	E	K	S	C	Eigenvector	Objectives Adjusted for Power
R	1	2	.33	5	6	6	.247	.096
M	.50	1	.33	4	5	5	.176	.068
E	3	3	1	6	8	8	.440	.170
R	.20	.25	.17	1	1	1	.049	.019
M	.17	.20	.13	1	1	1	.044	.017
E	.17	.20	.13	1	1	1	.044	.017

λ_{max} = 6.141, C.R. = .02

Table 2a. Combined Weight of Objectives

	Wife	Husband	Combined Weight
R	.121	.096	.217
M	.127	.068	.195
E	.260	.170	.430
D	.059	.019	.078
S	.023	.017	.040
C	.023	.017	.040

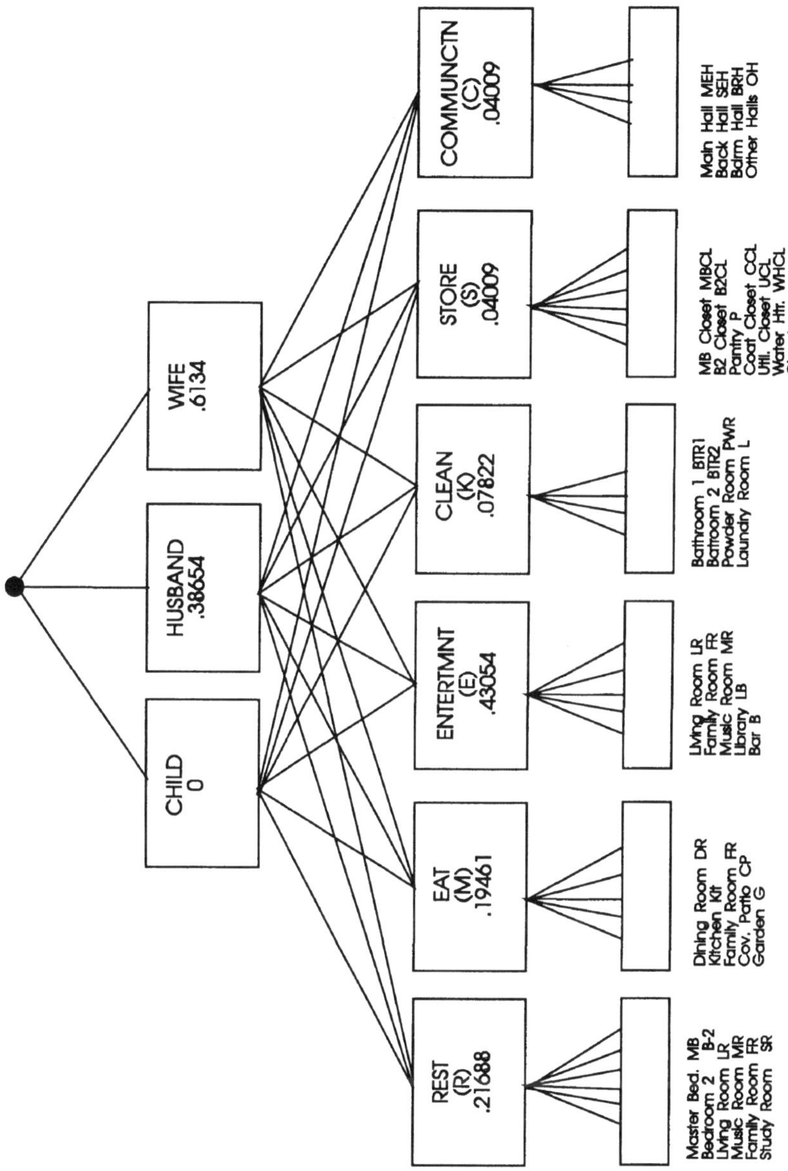

Figure 2. Space Prioritization Hierarchy

Table 3. Wife's Priorities of Architectural Spaces

Objective: Rest (Weight of Objective - Wife: .121)

	MB	B-2	LR	SR	MR	FR	Eigenvector	Adjusted for Power
MB	1	3	6	5	5	7	.428	.052
B-2	.33	1	7	8	8	6	.337	.041
LR	.17	.14	1	2	2	1	.072	.009
SR	.20	.13	.50	1	1	3	.065	.008
MR	.20	.13	.50	1	1	1	.050	.006
FR	.14	.17	1	.33	1	1	.048	.006

λ_{max} = 6.499, C.R. = .08

Objective: Eat (Weight of Objective - Wife: .127)

	DR	FR	KIT	CP	G	Eigenvector	Adjusted for Power
DR	1	4	6	4	5	.511	.065
FR	.25	1	5	1	2	.179	.023
KIT	.17	.20	1	.33	.25	.046	.006
CP	.25	1	3	1	.50	.120	.015
G	.20	.50	4	2	1	.144	.018

λ_{max} = 5.286, C.R. = .07

Objective: Entertainment (Weight of Objective - Wife: .260)

	LR	FR	MR	LB	B	Eigenvector	Adjusted for Power
LR	1	4	5	5	4	.495	.129
FR	.25	1	4	5	5	.273	.071
MR	.20	.25	1	1	2	.089	.023
LB	.20	.20	1	1	.50	.064	.017
B	.25	.20	.50	2	1	.080	.021

λ_{max} = 5.398, C.R. = .09

Objective: Clean (Weight of Objective - Wife: .059)

	BTR1	BTR2	PWR	L	Eigenvector	Adjusted for Power
BTR1	1	4	5	6	.589	.035
BTR2	.25	1	3	4	.233	.014
PWR	.20	.33	1	3	.118	.007
L	.17	.25	.33	1	.061	.004

λ_{max} = 4.205, C.R. = .08

Table 3 (cont.)

Objective: Store (Weight of Objective - Wife: .023)

	MBCL	B2CL	P	CCL	UCL	WHCL	Eigenvector	Adjusted for Power
MBCL	1	3	3	5	2	6	.371	.009
B2CL	.33	1	4	5	1	3	.228	.005
P	.33	.25	1	4	1	3	.131	.003
CCL	.20	.20	.25	1	.25	1	.047	.001
UCL	.50	1	1	4	1	3	.168	.004
WHCL	.17	.33	.33	1	.33	1	.054	.001

λ_{max} = 6.309, C.R. = .05

Objective: Communicate (Weight of Objective - Wife: .023)

	MEH	SEH	BRH	OH	Eigenvector	Adjusted for Power
MEH	1	5	4	6	.591	.014
SEH	.20	1	.33	.50	.076	.002
BRH	.25	3	1	4	.236	.005
OH	.17	2	.25	1	.096	.002

λ_{max} = 4.220, C.R. = .08

Table 4. Husband's Priority of Architectural Spaces

Objective: Rest (Weight of Objective - Husband: .096)

	MB	B-2	LR	SR	MR	FR	Eigenvector	Adjusted for Power
MB	1	3	.33	.25	.25	1	.084	.008
B-2	.33	1	.25	.20	.20	.25	.041	.004
LR	3	4	1	2	2	1	.274	.026
SR	4	5	.50	1	1	3	.238	.023
MR	4	5	.50	1	1	3	.238	.023
FR	1	4	1	.33	.33	1	.125	.012

λ_{max} = 6.440, C.R. = .07

Objective: Eat (Weight of Objective - Husband: .068)

	DR	FR	KIT	CP	G	Eigenvector	Adjusted for Power
DR	1	1	5	1	1	.250	.017
FR	1	1	4	2	2	.309	.021
KIT	.20	.25	1	.33	.50	.069	.005
CP	1	.50	3	1	1	.193	.013
G	1	.50	2	1	1	.179	.012

λ_{max} = 5.098, C.R. = .02

Table 4. (cont.)

Objective: Entertainment (Weight of Objective - Husband: .260)

	LR	FR	MR	LB	B	Eigenvector	Adjusted for Power
LR	1	5	.33	.33	2	.184	.031
FR	.20	1	.50	.33	1	.087	.015
MR	3	2	1	1	4	.312	.053
LB	3	3	1	1	5	.342	.058
B	.50	1	.25	.20	1	.074	.013

$\lambda_{max} = 5.373$, C.R. = .09

Objective: Clean (Weight of Objective - Husband: .019)

	BTR1	BTR2	PWR	L	Eigenvector	Adjusted for Power
BTR1	1	5	6	7	.645	.012
BTR2	.20	1	2	4	.193	.004
PWR	.17	.50	1	1	.089	.002
L	.14	.25	1	1	.073	.001

$\lambda_{max} = 4.119$, C.R. = .05

Objective: Store (Weight of Objective - Husband: .017)

	MBCL	B2CL	P	CCL	UCL	WHCL	Eigenvector	Adjusted for Power
MBCL	1	3	4	5	3	2	.368	.006
B2CL	.33	1	3	3	2	1	.186	.003
P	.25	.33	1	2	.50	.33	.075	.001
CCL	.20	.33	.50	1	.33	.25	.051	.001
UCL	.33	.50	2	.33	1	1	.137	.002
WHCL	.50	.1	.33	.25	1	1	.183	.003

$\lambda_{max} = 6.141$, C.R. = .02

Objective: Communicate (Weight of Objective - Husband: .017)

	MEH	SEH	BRH	OH	Eigenvector	Adjusted for Power
MEH	1	5	4	6	.591	.010
SEH	.20	1	.33	.50	.076	.001
BRH	.25	3	1	4	.236	.004
OH	.17	2	.25	1	.096	.002

$\lambda_{max} = 4.220$, C.R. = .08

Table 5. H & W Combined Priorities of Architectural Spaces

Objective		Architectural Space	Weight
E	LR	Living Room (from R & E)	.195
	FR	Family Room (from R,M & E)	.147
	MR	Music Room (from R & E)	.105
	LB	Library	.075
	B	Bar	.033
M	DR	Dining Room	.082
	KIT	Kitchen	.010
	CP	Covered Patio	.028
R	MB	Master Bedroom	.060
	B-2	Bedroom 2	.080
	SR	Study Room	.030
K	BTR1	Bathroom 1	.047
	BTR2	Bathroom 2	.017
	PWR	Powder Room	.008
	L	Laundry Room	.005
S	MBCL	Master Bedroom Closet	.015
	B2CL	Bedroom 2 Closet	.009
	P	Pantry	.004
	CCL	Coat Closet	.002
	UCL	Utility Closet	.006
	WHCL	Water Heater Closet	.004
C	MEH	Main Entrance Hall	.023
	SEH	Secondary Entrance Hall	.003
	BRH	Bedroom Hall Closet	.009
	OH	Other Halls	.004

3. ALLOCATION OF THE BUDGET, PROPERTY AND ARCHITECTURAL SPACES

From the total budget of $70,000, H and W must decide on the proportion they would like to allocate to construction and to exterior improvement. With the assistance of an architect, they both agree to allocate 85% or nearly $60,000 to Construction and the remainder to Landscaping.

We now proceed to allocating a proportion of the area to each objective. With the $60,000 budget and construction cost of $30 per sq. ft., we calculate that the house would have a maximum area of 2000 sq. ft. Table 2a gives the parties' joint preference priorities of the importance of each objective. These priorities are now used to proportionately allocate the 2000 sq. ft. among the objectives, as shown in Table 6 below.

Table 6. Allocation of Areas

Total Area to Allocate			2000 Sq. Ft.			
Objective	R	M	E	K	S	C
Strength of Objective	.22	.19	.43	.08	.04	.04
Area per Objective (sq. ft.)	433.7	389.2	861.0	156.4	80.0	80.0

Next, we use each party's preferences to assess the size of the architectural space associated with each objective (determined previously in Table 5). Here the question we answer through pairwise comparisons is as follows: How does a party evaluate the size of a particular space, as compared with the size of other spaces within the same objective, in order to obtain a fair split of spaces for that objective? The preferences are shown in Tables 7 and 8. There, we also weight the resulting priorities by the power of each party (see last columns of Tables 7 and 8).

Table 7. Wife's Preferences

Objective: Rest (Power of Wife: .613)

	MB	BR-2	SR	Eigenvector	Adjusted for Power
MB	1	5	4	.683	.419
B-2	.20	1	.50	.117	.072
SR	.25	2	1	.200	.123

λ_{max} = 3.025, C.R. = .02

Objective: Eating (Power of Wife: .613)

	DR	FR	KIT	CP	Eigenvector	Adjusted for Power
DR	1	6	4	6	.602	.369
FR	.17	1	.33	3	.111	.068
KIT	.25	3	1	4	.139	.139
CP	.17	.33	.25	1	.060	.037

λ_{max} = 4.211, C.R. = .03

Objective: Entertainment (Power of Wife: .613)

	LR	FR	MR	LB	B	Eigenvector	Adjusted for Power
LR	1	4	5	4	9	.522	.320
FR	.25	1	2	1	7	.174	.107
MR	.20	.50	1	.50	4	.098	.060
LB	.25	1	2	1	7	.174	.107
B	.11	.14	.25	.14	1	.032	.020

λ_{max} = 5.152, C.R. = .04

Table 7. (cont.)

Objective: Cleaning (Power of Wife: .613)

	BTR1	BTR2	PWR	L	Eigenvector	Adjusted for Power
BTR1	1	4	6	4	.570	.350
BTR2	.25	1	5	3	.249	.153
PWR	.17	.20	1	.33	.058	.035
L	.25	.33	3	1	.124	.076

$\lambda_{max} = 4.223$, C.R. = .08

Objective: Store (Power of Wife: .613)

	MBCL	B2CL	P	CCL	UCL	WHCL	Eigenvector	Adjusted for Power
MBCL	1	1	3	3	3	3	.314	.193
B2CL	1	1	2	2	2	2	.240	.147
P	.33	.50	1	1	1	1	.111	.068
CCL	.33	.50	1	1	1	1	.111	.068
UCL	.33	.50	1	1	1	1	.111	.068
WHCL	.33	.50	1	1	1	1	.111	.068

$\lambda_{max} = 6.018$, C.R. = .003

Objective: Communicate (Power of Wife: .613)

	MEH	SEH	BRH	OH	Eigenvector	Adjusted for Power
MEH	1	4	.33	.20	.121	.074
SEH	.25	1	.14	.13	.044	.027
BRH	3	7	1	.33	.272	.167
OH	5	8	3	1	.563	.345

$\lambda_{max} = 4.153$, C.R. = .06

Table 8. Husband's Preferences

Objective: Rest (Power of Husband: .387)

	MB	BR-2	SR	Eigenvector	Adjusted for Power
MB	1	4	3	.634	.245
B-2	.25	1	1	.174	.067
SR	.33	1	1	.192	.074

$\lambda_{max} = 3.009$, C.R. = .009

Objective: Eating (Power of Husband: .387)

	DR	FR	KIT	CP	Eigenvector	Adjusted for Power
DR	1	3	4	5	.549	.212
FR	.33	1	1	3	.193	.075
KIT	.25	1	1	3	.182	.070
CP	.25	.33	.33	1	.076	.030

$\lambda_{max} = 4.076$, C.R. = .03

Table 8. (cont.)

Objective: Entertainment (Power of Husband: .387)

	LR	FR	MR	LB	B	Eigenvector	Adjusted for Power
LR	1	4	5	4	9	.522	.202
FR	.25	1	2	1	7	.174	.067
MR	.20	.50	1	.50	4	.098	.038
LB	.25	1	2	1	7	.174	.067
B	.11	.14	.25	.14	1	.032	.012

$\lambda_{max} = 5.152$, C.R. = .03

Objective: Cleaning (Power of Husband: .387)

	BTR1	BTR2	PWR	L	Eigenvector	Adjusted for Power
BTR1	1	4	6	4	.570	.220
BTR2	.25	1	5	3	.249	.096
PWR	.17	.20	1	.33	.058	.022
L	.25	.33	3	1	.124	.124

$\lambda_{max} = 4.223$, C.R. = .08

Objective: Store (Power of Husband: .387)

	MBCL	B2CL	P	CCL	UCL	WHCL	Eigenvector	Adjusted for Power
MBCL	1	1	3	4	4	3	.340	.131
B2CL	1	1	2	2	2	2	.236	.091
P	.33	.50	1	1	1	1	.108	.042
CCL	.25	.50	1	1	1	1	.104	.040
UCL	.25	.50	1	1	1	1	.104	.040
WHCL	.33	.50	1	1	1	1	.108	.042

$\lambda_{max} = 6.046$, C.R. = .007

Objective: Communicate (Power of Husband: .387)

	MEH	SEH	BRH	OH	Eigenvector	Adjusted for Power
MEH	1	4	.33	.20	.121	.047
SEH	.25	1	.14	.13	.044	.017
BRH	3	7	1	.33	.272	.105
OH	5	8	3	1	.563	.218

$\lambda_{max} = 4.153$, C.R. = .06

The combined overall weight for each space in each objective is the sum of these for each party, as shown in Table 9. The last column of Table 9 gives the space allocated to each architectural space within each objective, by multiplying the previous column entries by the total square footage allotted to each objective from Table 6.

4. DIMENSIONS

The choice of dimensions for the rooms (measured in feet) can be made by hierarchical analysis if we have no idea of what is wanted. However, in general people formulate notions about these needs from the environment in which they live. They would make adjustments on what they already know and have experienced. To unfold that complexity of feelings in a hierarchy would be superfluous. Thus, the shape and dimensions of the rooms given in this chapter is an expression of our feelings as what a family of three would require and how each choice would fit with the dimensions of other rooms, whose dimensions are known, to obtain efficient use of each space and proper balance in functionality and aesthetics. For example, a very large living room and very small bedrooms or dining room would probably be considered to be misproportioned.

As an illustration we take the "Rest" objective which is allotted 433 square feet. Three types of spaces or rooms are associated with it. They and their comparisons according to relative contribution to "Rest" are shown in Tables 7, 8 and 9. The priorities and resulting proportion of the total area are given by:

	Architectural Space	Objective's Area	Weight	Area Allocated to Space (Sq. Ft.)
MB	Master Bedroom	433	.664	288
B-2	Bedroom 2	433	.139	60.3
SR	Study Room	433	.197	85.3

Our goal now is to let both H and W determine the shape of different "Rest" areas, check for optimum size, and revise inconsistencies such as the one above, where B-2 should presumably have a higher weight than the SR. For each objective, we proceed according to the priority of the spaces within it by selecting the higher one, then the next higher and so on.

Table 9. Allocation of Areas to Architectural Spaces

Objective	Area of Objective (sq. ft.)	Architectural Space	Party's Preferences		Combined Weight	Area Allocated
			W	H		
R	433.7	MB	.419	.245	.664	288.0
		B-2	.072	.067	.139	60.3
		SR	.123	.074	.197	85.3
M	389.2	DR	.369	.212	.582	226.4
		FR	.068	.075	.143	55.6
		KIT	.139	.070	.209	81.3
		CP	.037	.030	.067	25.9
E	861.0	LR	.320	.202	.522	449.6
		FR	.107	.067	.174	149.9
		MR	.060	.038	.098	84.1
		LB	.107	.067	.174	149.9
		B	.020	.012	.032	27.4
K	156.4	BTR1	.350	.220	.570	89.1
		BTR2	.153	.096	.249	38.9
		PWR	.035	.022	.058	9.0
		L	.076	.048	.124	19.3
S	80.0	MBCL	.193	.131	.324	25.94
		B2CL	.147	.091	.238	19.07
		P	.068	.042	.110	8.82
		CCL	.068	.040	.108	8.67
		UCL	.068	.040	.108	8.67
		WHCL	.068	.042	.110	8.82
C	80.0	MEH	.074	.047	.121	9.64
		SEH	.027	.017	.044	3.53
		BRH	.167	.105	.272	21.79
		OH	.345	.218	.563	45.01

The first pairwise comparison was done on the Master Bedroom (see Table 10), given that this space is the most important with respect to the "Rest" objective. The dimensions developed through prioritization were 14' by 20' yielding 280 sq. ft. (less than the 288 sq. ft. allotted to this space). We must show how this is done. In the following pairwise comparisons, we assume that the parties had previously determined a set of dimensions to be ranked. To determine this set, H and W could use, as a reference point, their experience with currently known and used spaces, whose dimensions could accurately be measured. They could then make judgments accordingly. For example, suppose that H and W presently use a Master Bedroom whose dimensions are 14' by 14'. Moreover, let us suppose that they feel comfortable with a width of 14' but not with a 14' length. They would then vary the length to make the comparisons as shown in Table 10.

It is clear that their preferred dimensions may not fit harmoniously with the total area for each objective. In this case adjustments must be made to produce a good fit and by reducing or increasing the area allotted to that space. They would then examine whether this allocation is compatible with the priorities of the next space within the objective and the availability of remaining space to allocate to it. For example, MB is 14' x 20' and B-2 is 14' x 14', exceeding the area allotted to R (i.e., 433 sq. ft.). Thus SR could not be included. Later we also make adjustments in the areas allotted to the objectives, to remedy such violations. For example, this can be achieved in a second iteration, where the parties H and W change their preferences to a MB of 16' x 16' which yields a total area of 256 sq. ft., and a B-2 of 14' x 14' which when combined with the MB yield a total area of 424 sq. ft. assigned to the R objectives. This leaves 9 sq. ft. (433 sq. ft. - 424 sq. ft.) as a residual area in the R objective.

Table 10. Dimensions of Architectural Space
Parties: H and W
Objective : Rest

Master Bedroom

Dim.	Area	14x14	14x16	16x16	14x20	Eigenvector
14x14	196	1	.33	.20	.17	.061
14x16	224	3	1	.33	.20	.124
16x16	256	5	3	1	.50	.302
14x20	280	6	5	2	1	.514

$\lambda_{max} = 4.094$ C.R. = .04

Bedroom 2

Dim.	Area	12x10	12x12	12x14	12x16	14x14	Eigenvector
12x10	120	1	.33	.25	.20	.17	.045
12x12	144	3	1	.33	.25	.20	.080
12x14	168	4	3	1	.33	.33	.154
12x16	192	5	4	3	1	.33	.269
14x14	196	6	5	3	3	1	.451

$\lambda_{max} = 5.300$ C.R. = .07

This process can be continued for each of the remaining objectives, until a final list containing the dimensions of all spaces is achieved, as shown in Table 11. The last column of this table gives the surplus (or deficit) so far produced for each objective. The total area must be no more than 2000 sq. ft. This is attained by adjusting the dimensions of some spaces and by revising the priorities when it is clear that a serious judgment error has been committed and that the comparison made is unacceptable to each of the parties. People usually start out with high aspirations and end up making compromises.

Some of the inconsistencies are a result of disagreements between the parties as to what should be valued most. The comparisons are sometimes unrealistic and are adjusted in terms of what is needed apart from high ideals for variety. In the final analysis, the dimensions of each of the spaces are slightly adjusted to absorb a deficit and to yield a surplus to meet the overall constraint of space availability.

Table 11. Dimensions of Architectural Spaces

Architectural Space	Revised Weight	Area	Dimens.	Surplus Area
Master Bedroom (MB)	.590	256	16'x16'	9
Bedroom 2 (B-2)	.387	138	2'x14'	
Dining Room (DR)	.576	224	4'x16'	5
Kitchen (KIT)	.411	160	0'x16'	
Living Room (LR)	.558	480	0'x24'	37
Family Room (FR)	.260	224	4'x16'	
Library (LB)	.139	120	0'x12'	
Bathroom 1 (BTR1)	.518	81	9'x 9'	(9)
Bathroom 2 (BTR2)	.230	36	9'x 4'	
Powder Room (PWR)	.102	16	4'x 4'	
Laundry Room (L)	.205	32	8'x 4'	
Master Bedroom Closet (MBCL)	.375	30	10'x 3'	(1)
Bedroom 2 Closet (B-2CL)	.263	21	7'x 3'	
Pantry (P)	.113	9	3'x 3'	
Coat Closet (CCL)	.075	6	3'x 2'	
Utility Closet (UCL)	.075	6	3'x 2'	
Water Heater Closet (WHCL)	.112	9	3'x 3'	
Main Entrance Hall (MEH)	.375	30	5'x 6'	(24)
Secondary Entrance Hall(SEH)	.250	20	4'x 5'	
Bedroom Hall (BRH)	.338	27	9'x 3'	
Other Halls (OH)	.338	27	9'x 3'	
Totals (sq. ft.)		1982		18

5. CONTIGUITY OF ARCHITECTURAL SPACES

To determine the location and contiguity of the architectural spaces, we first set down criteria for location. We note that the front view of a house usually faces the street and may be separated from it by a garden. The other three sides separate the house from neighbors with spaces of varying size, which may be used for different purposes, e.g., driveway, garden or the like. For the house under consideration, the dimensions are shown in Figure 1, where the surrounding space is an open grassy area with a tree on the right hand side of the house. Note that the construction site must fall within the 4000 square foot rectangle in Figure 1. Our task is to indicate the location of the objectives and then the spaces within this area.

We do not insist that there should be straight rectangular walls surrounding the construction site. Thus, the contiguity of the rooms and hence the general layout of the house is our next task, and is the most difficult. We focus on the three highest priority objectives: E,R and M. They have 84.2% of the weight. We divide the priority of each by their total, so that the three sum to unity.

	Prior Weight	Cumulative Weight	Adjusted Weight
E	.430	.647	.511
R	.217	.000	.258
M	.195	.842	.231

Next we identify the location criteria used to determine the relative importance of the different locations in this single level house (see Figure 3). They are: Front View (FV) (facing yard and street); Back View (BV) (facing yard); Left Side View (LV); and Right Side View (RV) (with a tree).

We then develop priorities for the relative importance of these locations with respect to the objectives E, R and M. The parties may perform the following types of pairwise comparisons shown in Table 12 below, which answer the following question: Which location is most desirable for E or R or M?

Graphically, these priorities are illustrated in Figure 4. Now we turn our attention to locating the highest priority room, the Living Room, in the highest priority location for Entertainment needs, which is in the Front View. To accomplish this task, the building area is divided into quadrants of 4'x4' as shown in Figure 5, and the Husband and Wife may jointly (or separately if desired) attempt to position LR. This prioritization process shows which quadrants are chosen for the Living Room. Table 13 shows these calculations.

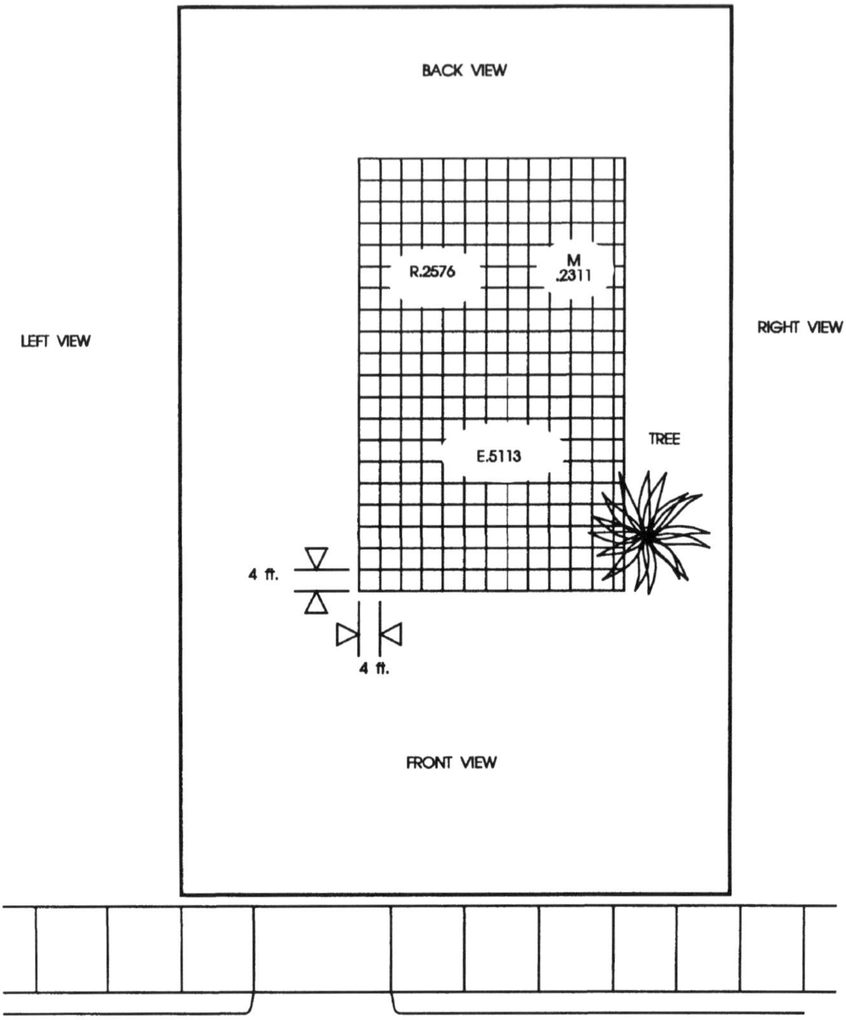

Figure 3. Plot Locations

Table 12. Prioritization of Locations

Objective: Rest (Power of Objective: .258)

	FV	BV	LV	RV	Eigenvector	Adjusted for Power
FV	1	.25	.33	.50	.095	.025
BV	4	1	2	3	.467	.120
LV	3	.50	1	2	.277	.071
RV	2	.33	.50	1	.160	.041

λ_{max} = 4.031, C.R. = .01

Objective: Entertainment (Power of Obj.: .511)

	FV	BV	LV	RV	Eigenvector	Adjusted for Power
FV	1	5	2	3	.486	.249
BV	.20	1	.33	.33	.080	.041
LV	.50	3	1	1	.227	.116
RV	.33	3	1	1	.207	.106

λ_{max} = 4.034, C.R. = .01

Objective: Eat (Power of Obj.: .231)

	FV	BV	LV	RV	Eigenvector	Adjusted for Power
FV	1	2	2	.33	.220	.051
BV	.50	1	1	.25	.121	.028
LV	.50	1	1	.25	.121	.028
RV	3	4	4	1	.539	.124

λ_{max} = 4.021, C.R. = .008

Objective:	FV	BV	LV	RV	Total
R	.025	.120	.071	.041	.258
E	.249	.041	.116	.106	.511
M	.051	.028	.028	.124	.231

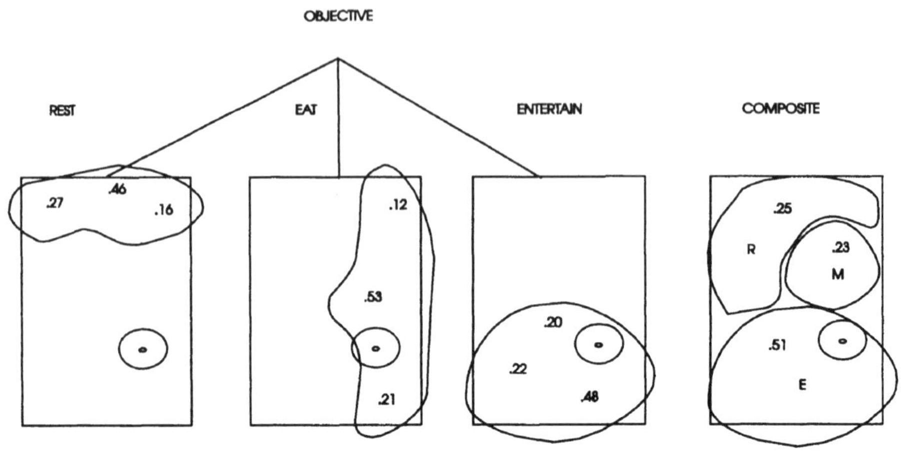

Figure 4. Location of Objectives

Table 13. Positioning of the Living Room

	$A_{6-12}E_{6-12}$	$C_{6-10}H_{6-10}$	$A_{1-6}F_{1-6}$	$C_{1-5}H_{1-5}$	Eigenvector
$A_{6-12}E_{6-12}$	1	1/2	4	3	.321
$C_{6-10}H_{6-10}$	2	1	4	3	.455
$A_{1-6}F_{1-6}$	1/4	1/4	1	1/2	.086
$C_{1-5}H_{1-5}$	1/3	1/3	2	1	.139

λ_{max} = 4.081, C.R. = .03

As we observe from this pairwise comparison, quadrant $C_{6-10}H_{6-10}$ was selected for the LR. Therefore, we proceed to lay it out in the lot as shown in Figure 6.

Next, the parties position the second highest priority space in the house, the FR. Because this space satisfies E needs, it would also have to be positioned towards the front part of the lot as previously determined. Table 14 shows the calculations for the FR.

Table 14. Positioning of the Family Room

	$C_{1-4}F_{1-4}$	$E_{1-4}H_{1-4}$	$G_{1-4}J_{1-4}$	Eigenvector
$C_{1-4}F_{1-4}$	1	.25	.20	.094
$E_{1-4}H_{1-4}$	4	1	.33	.280
$G_{1-4}J_{1-4}$	5	3	1	.626

λ_{max} = 3.086, C.R. = .08

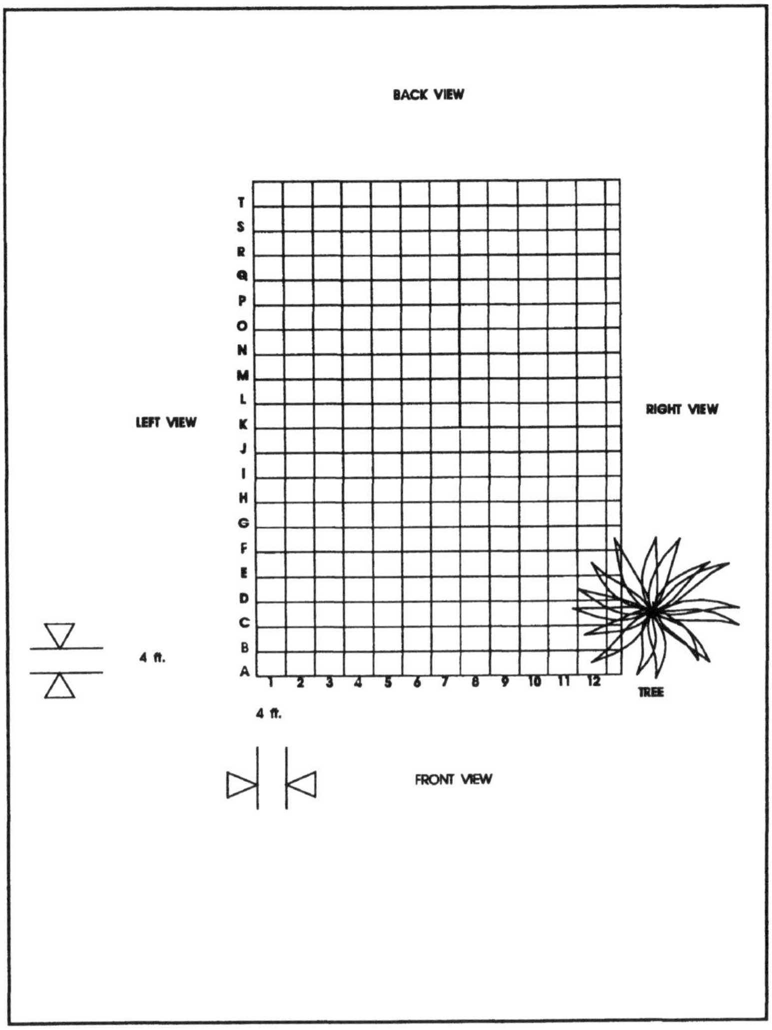

Figure 5. 4'x4' Plot Divisions

The third highest priority space is the LB, which is also the last space we must place within the E objective. Following the same procedure explained above, the parties determine its position by pairwise comparisons, as shown in Table 15.

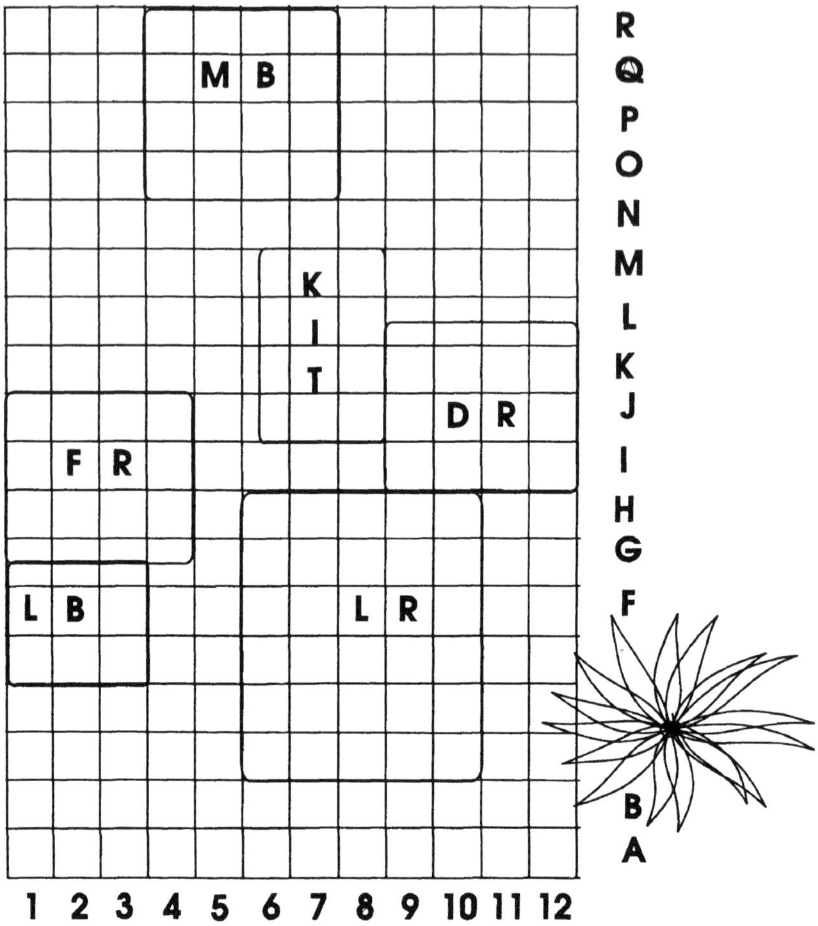

Figure 6. Priority-based room locations

Table 15. Positioning of the Library Room

	$E_{1-3}G_{1-3}$	$D_{1-2}G_{1-2}$	$C_{1-3}E_{1-3}$	Eigenvector
$E_{1-3}G_{1-3}$	1	4	6	.682
$D_{1-2}G_{1-2}$	.25	1	4	.236
$C_{1-3}E_{1-3}$	.17	.25	1	.082

λ_{max} = 3.108, C.R. = .10

The fourth ranking space was the DR, which now satisfies M needs. The parties now use the right hand side of the construction site to position this particular space. The same procedure will be applied to the next space in ranking, which happens to be the Master Bedroom, but this space will be placed towards the back part of the lot since it satisfies R needs. The positioning of this space is shown in Table 16 below and in Figure 6.

Table 16. MB and DR Positioning

Positioning of the Dining Room

	$I_{7-10}K_{7-10}$	$I_{9-12}K_{9-12}$	$I_{9-10}M_{9-10}$	Eigenvector
$I_{7-10}K_{7-10}$	1	.20	.25	.090
$I_{9-12}K_{9-12}$	5	1	4	.665
$I_{9-10}M_{9-10}$	4	.25	1	.245

λ_{max} = 3.152, C.R. = .15

Positioning of the Master Bedroom

	$P_{1-4}S_{1-4}$	$O_{1-4}R_{1-4}$	$O_{4-7}R_{4-7}$	$K_{1-4}N_{1-4}$	Eigenvector
$P_{1-4}S_{1-4}$	1	.33	.25	.50	.093
$O_{1-4}R_{1-4}$	3	1	.50	3	.305
$O_{1-7}R_{1-7}$	4	2	1	3	.459
$K_{1-4}N_{1-4}$	2	.33	.33	1	.143

λ_{max} = 4.081, C.R. = .03

This process can be continued in a systematic way, by positioning each remaining space, always working in the next highest priority space, until all the spaces have been placed. Figure 7 shows one of the possible solutions for the layout.

Having located the spaces of the three main objectives, the remaining spaces for storage, communication and cleaning are carefully placed within the remaining spaces. The closets are appropriately located in the rooms and halls, the dimension of which may be altered by reshaping the dimensions of adjacent rooms. Alternative positions for bathrooms and closets, for example, can be similarly analyzed and located with respect to their bedrooms.

The readjustments involve iterations of the process to obtain a coherent architectural design. If the problem of locating rooms in a single level dwelling seems complicated, more than that of a two or more story house, it is even more complicated for a split-level house. The main reason for this is that one must not only locate rooms in the two levels, but must also match the levels at the boundary where they meet to obtain aesthetic, efficient and practical transition from one to the other. Split-level houses are known to provide the opportunity for greater efficiency and variety in using space that a two story house. Inclined ground is better suited to split-level housing than flat ground.

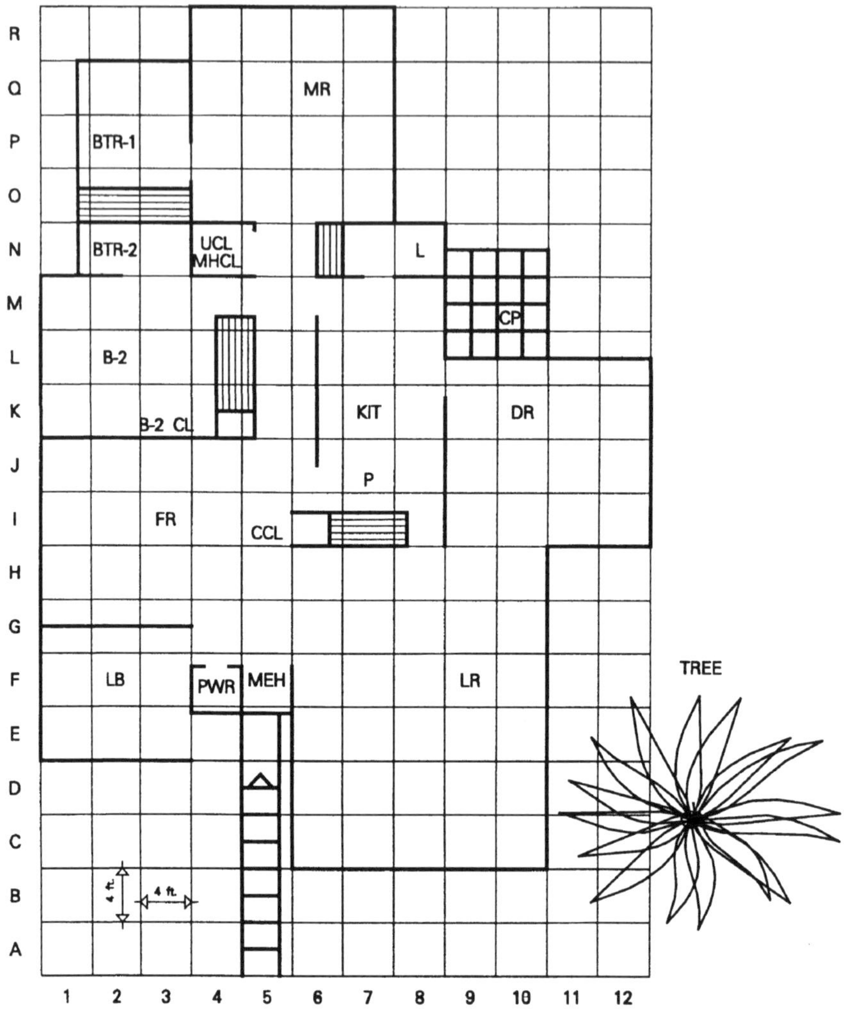

Figure 7. The Final Layout - A Possible Solution

6. CONCLUSION

We have illustrated the use of a new method that can be used as an aid to formalize some of the intuitive aspects of architectural design. Through its use, the architect and the builder can enable owner participation (at the desired level) in the process.

REFERENCES

1. Saaty, T.L. and M.H. Beltran, "The Analytic Hierarchy Process: A New Approach to Deal with Fuzziness in Architecture," *Architectural Science Review* 25 (1982) 64-69.

CHAPTER 4

DESIGNING A MOUSETRAP

1. INTRODUCTION

This chapter illustrates the sequential use of hierarchies in the selection, design and marketing of a mouse trap. The project described in this chapter is not so much about building a better mousetrap as it is about a person's hope to reach a higher state by engulfing oneself in the project. Not a higher state in the classical sense that is indicative of a great mind expanding, but a state that helps a person to grow through doing, always reminding one that there are numerous ways to see a problem. By reminding the student to be open and sensitive to new ideas and new creative processes, the professor can foster positive growth. Emphasizing that you never reach a state where you are all that there is, and your ways are the best, can lead to a healthy respect for continued growth buttressed by a positive attitude, and a striving for a more fulfilling life.

A better mousetrap was not the goal of the assignment. To develop a person through the use of reasoning and agonizing can lead to a sense of accomplishment that comes only when the inputs come from within the person. The project has raised my self-esteem, while helping to humble me so that I can use my unique gifts while respecting the gifts of others in the healthiest of manners. A very fine line exists between self-confidence and arrogance when a person is elevated in this way, however, the sense of humility that comes from respecting the ideas of others can hold a check over the entire process.

2. EFFECTIVENESS CRITERIA

To design a new mousetrap, initial thinking centered around how today's mousetraps function and what makes them effective. Brainstorming revealed various methods of exterminating a rodent's life (Figure 1).

To evaluate the various methods of execution, criteria had to be identified for judging the effectiveness of the trap and the neatness of the kill to distinguish one method from another. Other criteria included were low cost, reusability and ease of use. The alternative methods to kill a mouse were electric shock, gas, poison, hanging, smashing and trapping. Based on the evaluation of the six criteria, it was determined that electric shock was the most desirable method (Table 1).

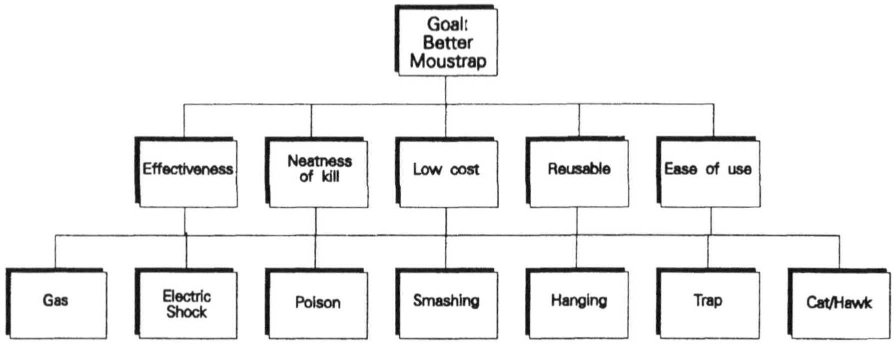

Figure 1. Methods of Extermination

Table 1. Priorities of Alternative Methods of Extermination

	Goal = Better mousetrap Criteria					
	Effectiveness	Neatness of kill	Low cost	Reusable	Ease of use	Composite priorities
Alternatives	0.564	0.220	0.137	0.039	0.039	
Gas	0.208	0.228	0.040	0.216	0.161	0.188
Electric Shock	0.208	0.403	0.090	0.210	0.161	0.223
Poison	0.208	0.091	0.052	0.032	0.161	0.152
Smashing	0.208	0.164	0.141	0.210	0.161	0.187
Hanging	0.093	0.057	0.247	0.045	0.161	0.107
Trap	0.055	0.037	0.405	0.210	0.161	0.109
Cat/Hawk	0.022	0.021	0.025	0.077	0.032	0.025

The next step was to determine where to aim the shock (Level 2 in Figure 2). The results of the hierarchy (Table 2) led to the legs and feet being evaluated at .497, the head of the mouse coming in second at .216 and an inconsistency ratio of .077.

The findings from the second model led to the development of a third model (Level 3 in Figure 2). In it the alternatives of the second model were used to evaluate various methods for delivering the electric shock. This third model, the optimal shock delivery system had, as its alternatives, a floating wire system, a wire griding system, a full chamber shock system using a side to side delivery wave of electricity and a polarized shock pattern which would run from end to end on the trap (Table 3).

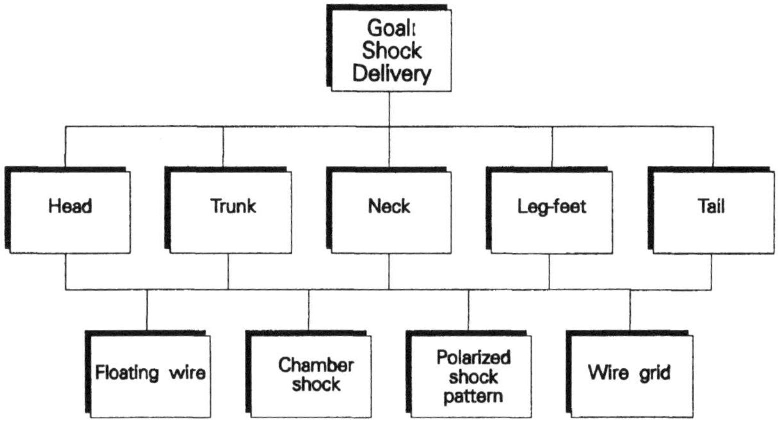

Figure 2. Shock Delivery Methods

Table 2. Judgements and priorities with respect to goal for optimal shock delivery

	HEAD	TRUNK	NECK	LEG-FEET	TAIL
HEAD		3.0	2.0	1/4	5.0
TRUNK			1/2	1/5	4.0
NECK				1/4	4.0
LEG-FEET					5.0
TAIL					

0.216	
HEAD	XXXXXXXXXXXXXXX
0.099	
TRUNK	XXXXXXX
0.142	
NECK	XXXXXXXXXX
0.497	
LEG-FEET	XXXXXXXXXXXXXXXXXXXXXXXXXXXXXXXXXXXXXX
0.047	
TAIL	XXXXXX

Once the synthesis was completed it was clear that given the weights assigned to the criteria, a wire grid design would provide the best means of delivering the shock to the mouse's legs and feet (and even any other body parts). As can be seen from the first three models, the decisions made in each model drive those made in the subsequent model. With that in mind it was clear how to kill the rodent, what area should receive the shock and the optimal means to do it.

Table 3. Alternative Methods for Delivering the Shock

	Goal = Shock delivery Criteria					
	Head	Trunk	Neck	Leg/Feet	Tail	Composite parts
Alternatives	0.216	0.099	0.142	0.497	0.047	
Floating Wire	0.173	0.095	0.077	0.055	0.05	0.090
Chamber Shock	0.377	0.594	0.294	0.148	0.408	0.274
Polarized Shock Pattern	0.377	0.246	0.572	0.135	0.424	0.273
Wire Grid	0.073	0.064	0.056	0.662	0.063	0.362

3. ATTRACTING THE MOUSE

The next issue was how to attract the mouse to the trap. For this a fourth model was developed whose goal was to identify the best luring device (Figure 3). Criteria included cost, with a set of sub-criteria; ease of use, also with sub-criteria; appeal (attracting power), with its own sub-criteria; and reusability. The alternative means of attracting a mouse were developed and evaluated under each set of criteria and sub-criteria.

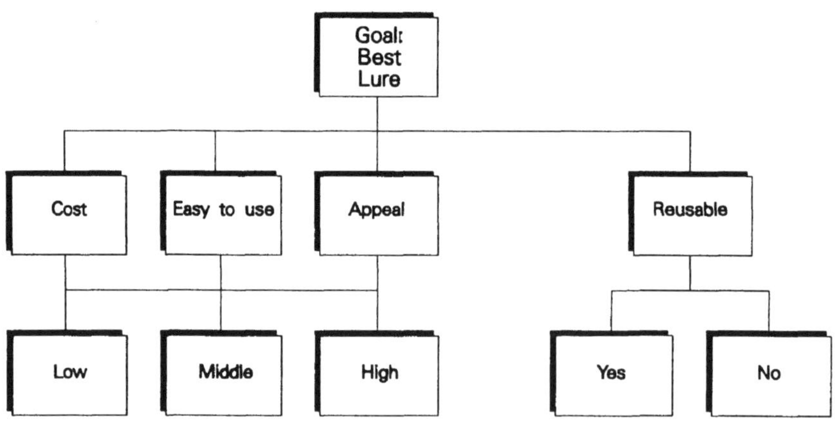

Figure 3. Best Lure

The synthesis concluded that the alternatives of food scent and sex scent were within .001 of each other. For this reason it was decided to include both lures in the mousetrap. Combining food scent and sex scent would be much more powerful than attracting the rodent by means of any type of real food or dim lighting system (Table 4).

Table 4. Alternative Lures

	Goal = Best lure Criteria			
	Cost	Easy to use	Appeal	Reusable
Alternatives	0.062	0.126	0.594	0.218
Low	0.637	0.075	0.073	N/A
Middle	0.258	0.229	0.226	N/A
High	0.105	0.696	0.700	N/A
Yes	N/A	N/A	N/A	0.615
No	N/A	N/A	N/A	0.385

4. THE TRAP SHAPE

The fifth model was used to decide on the optimal shape of the trap given that the trap was to perform electrically (Figure 4).

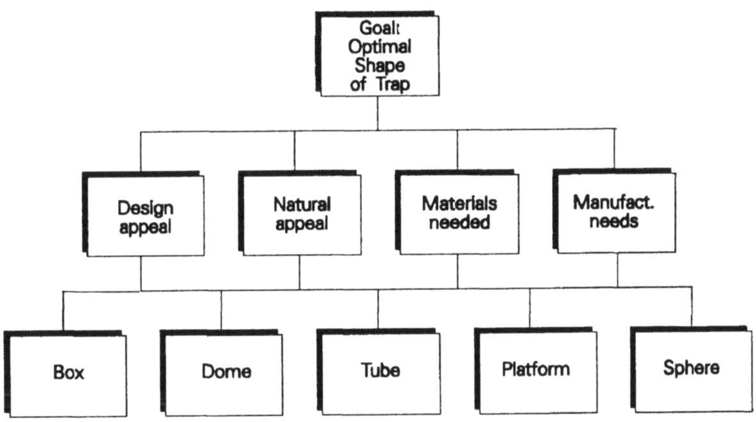

Figure 4. Shape of the Trap

The alternatives generated included a sphere, a tube, a platform, a box and a dome. Each alternative was evaluated for its design appeal based on the presumed human need for an attractive trap. From the rodent's perspective, the trap needed natural appeal which focused on the mouse's curious nature. Other criteria were materials needed in construction and the various considerations about ease of manufacture (Table 5).

Table 5. Alternative Shapes

	Criteria				
	Design appeal	Natural appeal	Materials needed	Manufact. needs	Composite priorities
Alternatives	0.226	0.590	0.092	0.092	
Box	0.158	0.156	0.166	0.230	0.164
Dome	0.205	0.143	0.084	0.107	0.148
Tube	0.465	0.534	0.425	0.215	0.479
Platform	0.075	0.067	0.259	0.364	0.114
Sphere	0.097	0.100	0.066	0.083	0.095

5. THE COST AND BENEFITS OF THE TRAP

Once the synthesis was completed, with an inconsistency ratio of .05, the obvious clear shape of choice was a tube design with a composite priority of 0.479. Up to this point it has been clear how each previous model drove the subsequent model's creation. Now, with all the elements in place, an idea born of the AHP could begin to take form. Before entering the actual design phase, however, it was important to evaluate the costs and benefits of actual mousetraps. Two models were developed; one for the costs (Figure 5) of the trap and the other for the benefits (Figure 6). The mousetrap costs model looked at both using a trap and not using it. Under not using a trap further considerations included health issues, property damage, lower property value and the potential embarrassment of having rodents in the house. Sub-criteria under using a trap were the purchasing cost, the operating cost, trap maintenance time, the visibility of the trap in the house. Under the sub-criteria of not using the trap (i.e., health issue and property damage) were food damage, mouse's excrement in the house, the bite factor and damage considerations to clothes and furniture.

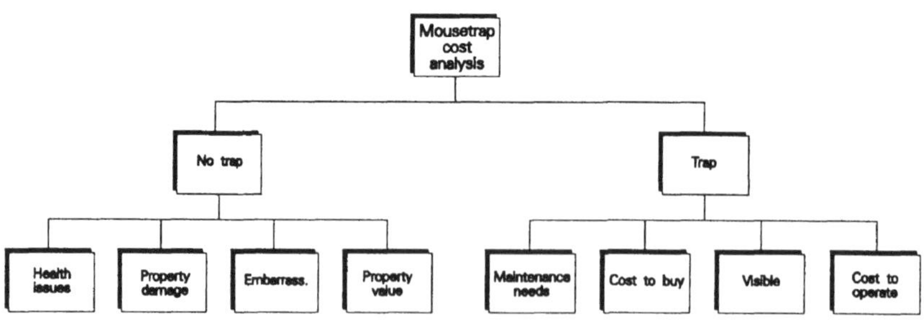

Figure 5. Costs of the Trap

With the synthesis completed it became clear that the costs of having the trap outweighed those of not having the trap. Attention now focused on the benefits of using the trap given the findings of the last model. (Table 6)

Table 6. Mousetrap Cost Analysis

	No trap		Trap
	0.385		0.615
Health Issues	0.606	Maintenance needs	0.495
Property Damage	0.166	Cost to buy	0.128
Embarrassment	0.063	Visible	0.290
Property Value	0.166	Cost to Operate	0.088

The benefits model, similar to the costs model, looked at both using and not using the mousetrap. Under using the trap, the issues included a clean home environment, maintaining current property value, no damage to food/clothes or property, a rodent free environment and no embarrassment due to the lack of a mouse. Considered under not using the trap were the opportunity to earn money by breeding and selling them, development of mouse races and the chance to obtain low cost pets. The mousetrap benefits model showed that the benefits of using a trap outweighed those of not using one and a subjective judgment followed that the benefits did outweigh the costs. (Table 7)

Table 7. Mousetrap benefits analysis

	No Trap		Trap
	0.417		0.583
Pets	0.504	Health	0.483
Race Them	0.279	Maintain Property Value	0.228
Make Profit	0.217	No Damage	0.131
(Sell Them)		Rodent Free Environment	0.106
		No Embarrassment	0.053

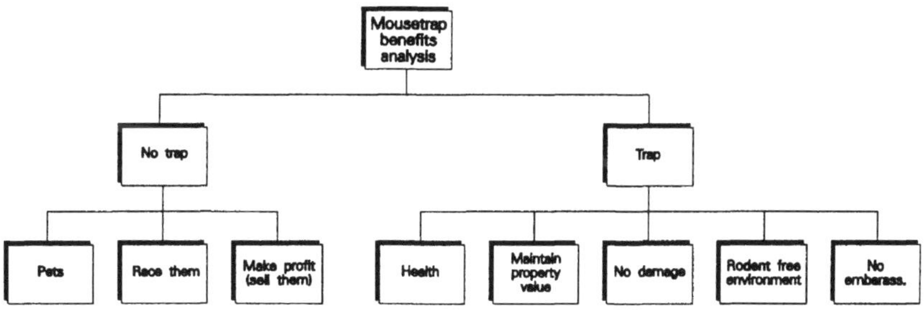

Figure 6. Benefits of the Trap

6. A MARKETING MODEL

At this point it seemed that only the trap design itself was left to be developed, but a question arose as to whether this trap, once developed, could prosper monetarily. Our concern now focussed on profits and on the development of a model (Figures 7 and 8) that would assist in deciding which markets should be entered once the trap took physical form. Criteria included the trap's profit potential, customer need and geographic location. Both profit potential and customer need used sub-criteria of high, medium and low with greatest weight going to high. Geographic location had sub-criteria of sections of the country (i.e., Eastern, Midwest, Central, Mountain and Western). Under these were the alternatives of metro cities, metro suburbs and rural areas. Once the synthesis was completed the first choice of a market to enter was found to be metro suburbs at 0.549, followed by metro cities at 0.266 and rural at 0.185 (Tables 8 and 9).

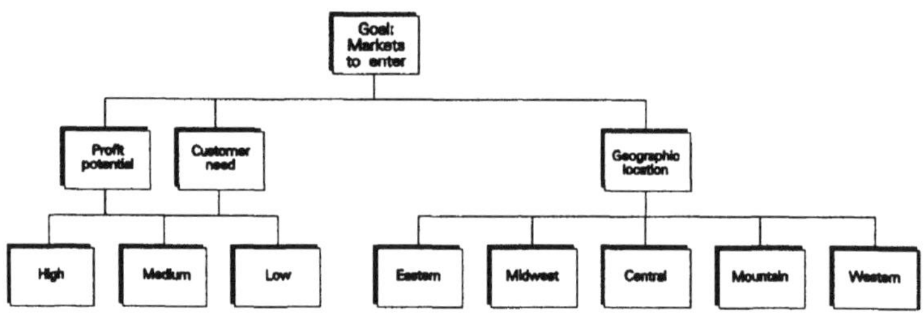

Figure 7. Alternative Regional Markets

Table 8. Priorities of Alternative Regional Markets

Goal = Markets to enter			
Criteria:	Profit potential	Customer need	Geographic location
Alternatives	.660	.211	.129
High	0.938	0.738	N/A
Medium	0.196	0.196	N/A
Low	0.065	0.065	N/A
Eastern	N/A	N/A	0.362
Midwest	N/A	N/A	0.251
Central	N/A	N/A	0.148
Mountain	N/A	N/A	0.100
Western	N/A	N/A	0.138

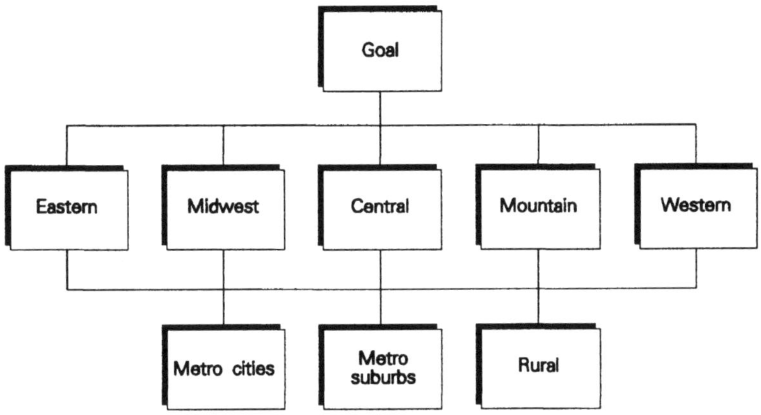

Figure 8. Alternative Marketing Locations

Table 9. Priorities of Alternative Marketing Locations

	Eastern	Midwest	Central	Mountain	Western
Alternatives	.302	0.251	.148	0.100	0.138
Metro Cities	0.249	0.249	0.249	0.249	0.249
Metro Suburbs	0.594	0.594	0.594	0.594	0.594
Rural	0.157	0.157	0.157	0.157	0.157

7. THE DESIGN

With regard to the actual trap, some of the design questions included the shape of the entrance to the trap, how long should the trap be, where to place wire griding, how to make it reusable and a number of other questions. Figure 9 contains the preliminary drawings of the front and back of the trap and one complete sideview. Also, a picture of the front and back with the wire grid floor is included to aid in understanding the design.

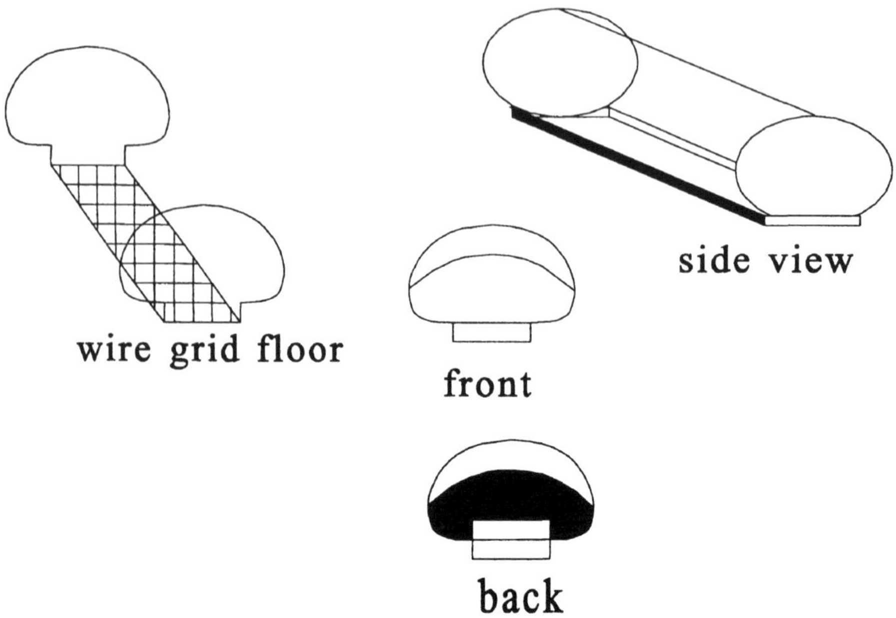

Figure 9. Preliminary Drawing of the Trap

Figures 10 through 13 contain the formal design plans. Figure 10 gives an overview of the trap. The 3 1/4" section outlines the inner chamber while the 4 1/4" section shows the outlays of the chamber. All solid lines depict the outer layer of steel and the inner dashed line depicts the thickness of the materials used. This convention is adhered to for all the following exhibits.

Figure 10. Overview

Figure 11 contains views of the front and rear ends. If the trap was "electrified" at all times, it was unlikely that a mouse would enter. A means of detecting entry was needed to send a signal to the delay mechanism housing assembly. At 1.2 seconds after the beam is broken, the four corners of the wire griding receive an electrical charge of one hundred and ten volts. The trap chamber is the section that the mouse enters while the electrical components enclosure opens to dispose of the dead rodent with a twist of the wrist. This is why a seven inch piano hinge, and the magnetic closure are included. Remember the first hierarchy.

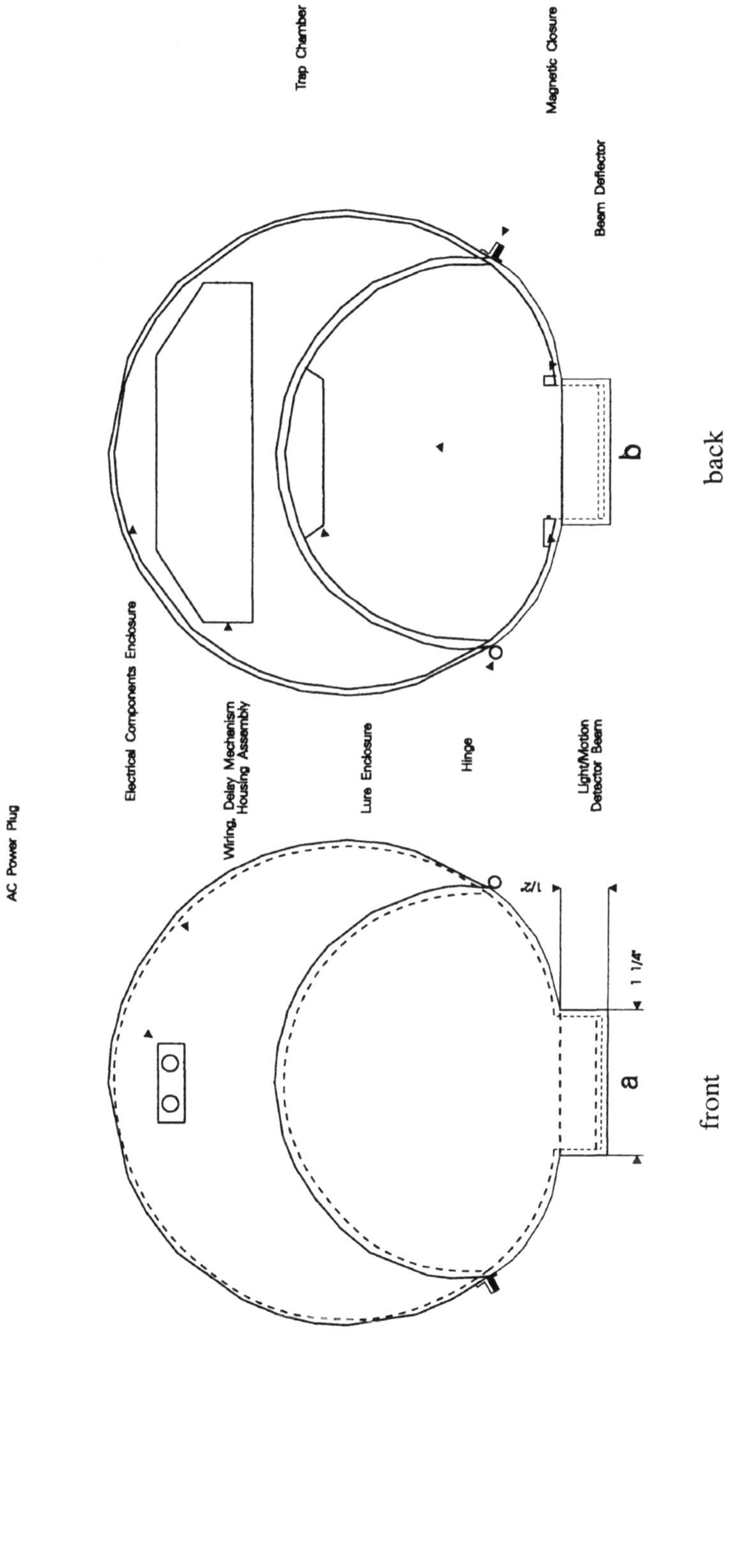

Figure 11. End Views

Reusability and ease of use were indeed among the initial criteria. The lure was located on the top section of the trap chamber to make replacement easy and to force the mouse's weight downward on the wire grid as it pushed up to get toward the lure.

Figure 12 is the rear elevation, the view of the trap from its magnetic closure side.

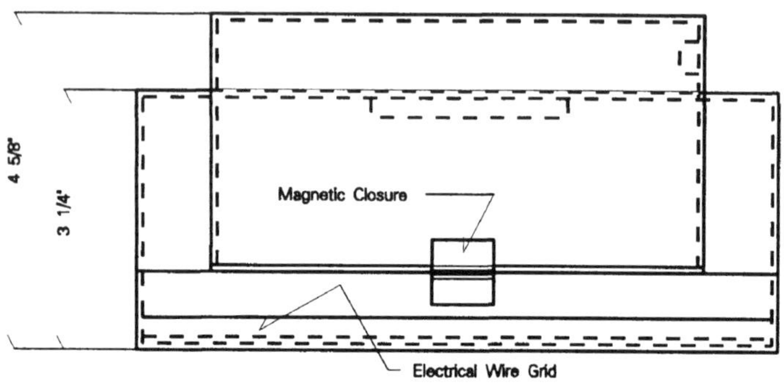

Figure 12. Rear Elevation

Figure 13 contains two views, a front elevation and Section A-A.

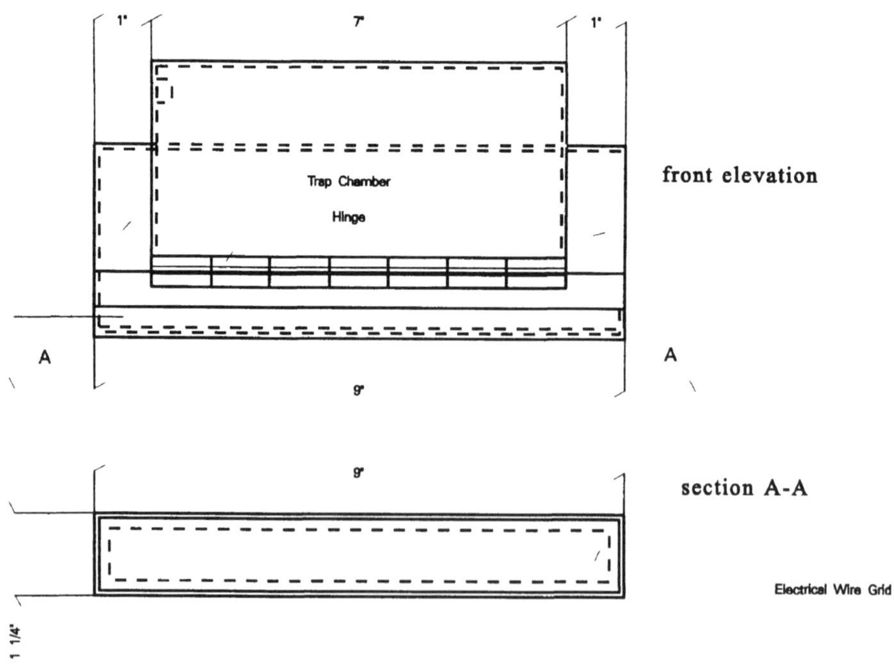

Figure 13. Front and Section Elevations

The front elevation is the hinge side. The overall length of the complete trap is 9" long while the section that opens is 7" long. While observing the front elevation, note the two downward pointing arrows labeled "A". This represents a cross-section of this area and a top down view can be seen in section A-A. This is the complete 9" electrical wire grid that is located in the channel of the trap chamber.

It is important to note that this type of thinking and design can come only when you ask not only how it has been done, but how you might do it differently.

8. CONCLUSIONS

The AHP was used to model the stages of designing a new mouse trap. The model helps elucidate the thinking process. Without the beginning models as stepping stones, the later models would be meaningless separate entities with no tie to the overall goal of building a better mousetrap.

Table 10 contains an overall view of the reconstituted master hierarchy. Note that this exhibit displays only the first three levels of the total picture. To understand the complete model, it is useful to examine the previous tables and visualize where each component part fits.

This exercise (the overall model) demonstrates how decisions in one model lead to the creation of another model and affect choices made for each model thereafter. The cost/benefit analysis and the decision about what markets to enter were driven by the preceding models but not to the same extent that the first five models were. Although the master hierarchy model was created after the completion of the project, it serves to demonstrate the sequence of events followed and the relative importance of each with respect to those models they affected.

Table 10. Master Hierarchy

			GOAL *1.000*			
TYPE *0.430*	SHK-AREA *0.223*	SHK-DEL *0.123*	OPT-LURE *0.073*	OPT-SHAP *0.060*	CTS-BENE *0.050*	MARKETS *0.041*
-L-COST *0.092*	-HEAD *0.198*	-FLT-WIRE *0.056*	-COST *0.062*	-DSGN-APP *0.280*	-COST *0.500*	PROFPOT *0.640*
-EFFECTI *0.426*	-TRUNK *0.067*	-WIREGRID *0.612*	-EASY USE *0.151*	-NTL APPL *0.614*	-BENEFITS *0.500*	CUST-ND *0.288*
-NEAT *0.315*	-NECK *0.132*	-CHMB-SHK *0.160*	-APPEAL *0.635*	-MAT-NEED *0.053*		GEO-LOC *0.073*
-REUSABLE *0.095*	-LEG-FEET *0.552*	-POLZ-SHK *0.173*	-REUSABLE *0.151*	-MFG-NEED *0.053*		
-EASY USE *0.072*	-TAIL *0.051*					

REFERENCES

1. Dobias, A.P., "Designing a Mousetrap Using the Analytic Hierarchy Process and Expert Choice", *European Journal of Operational Research* 48, 1 (1990) 57-65.

2. Saaty, Thomas L., *Decision Making for Leaders.* Pittsburgh, PA: RWS Publications, 1988.

CHAPTER 5

DESIGNING THE BEST CATAMARAN

1. INTRODUCTION

This chapter illustrates use of the Analytic Hierarchy Process in the selection and design of a sailboat. How does one bring together one's ideas when designing a versatile sailing machine? Imagination plays an important role but is full of disconnected thoughts. The AHP was used to first choose the overall sailboat design, and then to select some fundamental hydrodynamic features of the newly designed boat.

There are four basic sailboat designs: sloop, ketch, catamaran and trimaran. The sloop has one hull and one mast. The ketch has one hull with one large mast located at the centerpoint of the yacht's deck, and a smaller mast (mizzenmast) that is usually located behind the helm (where the captain steers). Each vessel uses one mainsail and one jib (triangular shaped foresail), except for the ketch which also uses a mizzensail (mainsail on the mizzenmast).

A catamaran and a trimaran differ in only one major feature. The catamaran is made of two pontoons that are attached by a variety of spar configurations. Usually a tarp stretches between the two pontoons. The trimaran has three pontoons, with the center one being the main body of the vessel. These pontoons are usually connected by a reinforced fiberglass structure. Both the catamaran and the trimaran have one mast, that is located around the centerpoint.

By thoroughly evaluating each type of vessel, the AHP led to the development of a design comprising the best features of both the sloop and the catamaran. This new vessel design is called a Main-Hull-Mono-maran (MHM-maran). The MHM-maran broadly resembles a catamaran. It has two pontoons, but one is much larger than the other. The larger pontoon (major pontoon) is similar to a sloop in both size and appearance. The smaller pontoon (minor pontoon), is approximately 1/3 the length and 1/4 the width of the major pontoon. The minor pontoon is for added sailing performance while the major pontoon provides all living and storage facilities.

2. BASIC DESIGN

Four criteria were used (see Figure 1) to evaluate the four alternative designs: catamaran, ketch, sloop and trimaran. With respect to sailing performance, both the sloop and the ketch have a greater ability to sail close to the wind (close-hauled position). But the marans are far lighter than their counterparts, thus they sail faster in most "points" of sailing. By points of sailing we mean the direction from which the wind is blowing: a run is with the wind blowing from behind, a reach is with the wind blowing from either side and close-to-the-wind (close-hauled) is with the wind blowing 30 to 35 degrees off the bow.

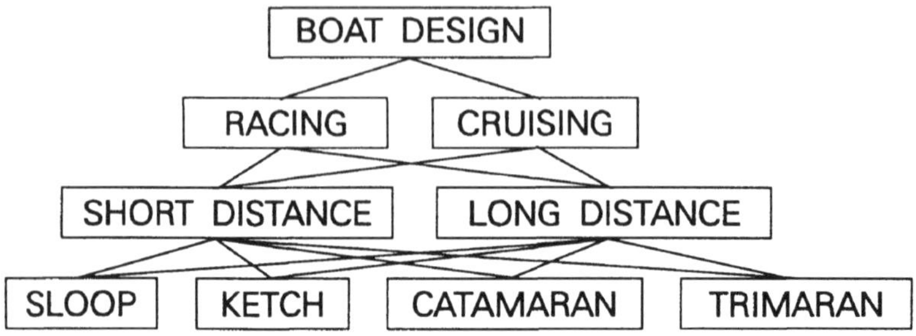

Figure 1. Hierarchy of Boat Types

The criteria were separated into two distinct categories: cruising and racing. With respect to personal design preferences, long-distance racing was the criterion that carried the greatest weight. Following it was short-distance racing, long-distance cruising and short-distance cruising, in that order. The goal was to design some sort of racing yacht.

CRITERIA	WEIGHTS
1. Short Dist. Racing	.231
2. Long Dist. Racing	.623
3. Short Dist. Cruising	.052
4. Long Dist. Cruising	.094

Until recently, the marans did not receive much respect when it came to structural integrity. They were not considered very seaworthy, and in storms the pontoons tended to break apart. But with the development of expensive and strong plastics, vast improvements have been made. Still, many sailors prefer the traditional structural strength of both the sloop and the ketch.

Evaluating each alternative with the above criteria revealed some interesting results. The catamaran, as almost every sailor knows, is superior to all other yachts when it comes to short-distance racing. It is very light and fast but it does not have adequate storage or living facilities, so it is not suitable for long-distance racing. Instead, the sloop was determined to be the best yacht for long-distance racing. It really did not matter which yacht was best for short or long-distance cruising, because neither of these criteria had significant weight to greatly affect the overall outcome. The overall weights of the alternatives are given by:

ALTERNATIVES	WEIGHTS
1. Sloop	.379
2. Catamaran	.348
3. Ketch	.138
4. Trimaran	.134

Notice how close the weights of both the sloop and the catamaran are. Up to this point, the results from each hierarchy were used without question, mainly because the final weights clearly marked which was the superior alternative. Before beginning this evaluation it was assumed that the conclusion would be the sloop. But this did not turn out to be the case. It was the catamaran. The catamaran ended up following the sloop by only 0.031. This led to an entirely new conclusion - the development of a sailboat that takes advantage of the distinct characteristics of both the sloop and the catamaran.

3. THE BEST COMBINATION OF CATAMARAN AND SLOOP: *A New Alternative*

Since a sloop consists of one large hull, and a catamaran consists of two pontoons, a yacht that combines both characteristics will have to be somewhere in between. Two options are possible - a yacht with one main hull and a single fixed pontoon or a yacht with a variable pontoon. This is where the concept of the Main Hull Mono-maran enters. It is a distinct yacht that has one large hull (main hull) that is shaped much like a sloop's hull. It also has an attached pontoon which provides the vessel with characteristics typically associated with a catamaran. When the sea is rough, one has the option to have the pontoon trail the vessel.

There are only two alternatives in this hierarchy, Yacht A and Yacht B. The only difference between them is that A has a fixed pontoon whereas B has a variable one which can move from the port to the starboard side and vice-versa. There are three criteria: Agility (0.558), Stability (0.122) and Anchorability (0.320).

AGILITY is the ability of a design to quickly maneuver under sail. STABILITY is the ability to keep the yacht heeled as upright as possible. Finally, ANCHORABILITY refers to how easy it is to, or not to, anchor or dock the yacht. A fixed pontoon limits docking ability because the dock (slip) needs to be sufficiently wide to accommodate the vessel. The final weights for the two designs are given by:

ALTERNATIVES	WEIGHTS
Yacht B	.696
Yacht A	.304

Thus, in this hierarchy, Yacht B, the model with variable pontoon, is decidedly preferred.

Now that a basic yacht concept has been derived through the process provided by the AHP, the specifics of the MHM-maran, namely, the keel, the rudder, and the sails were designed.

4. THE KEEL

The keel is the most important hydrodynamic feature of any sailboat. A keel is responsible for a boat's stability and prevents it from sliding across the water on certain points of sailing (close-hauled & reach position). Once a keel is chosen, the rudder is relatively easy to design. As the hydrodynamics of the rudder are dependent upon those of the keel: there is a close relationship between keel and rudder.

Since the Australians introduced a winged keel in the 1983 America's Cup, there has been a tremendous amount of research in this area. Many of the keel test results are not available to the public, since it is mainly the very competitive yachting syndicates that perform and sponsor these activities.

When selecting a keel, performance and practicality were considered (see Figure 2). The criteria were: mud, rock, sand and the degree of heel of the yacht. The mud, rock and sand elements were selected, because these are the substances that sailors most often hit when they go aground. A keel provides stability and many other performance factors, but in this case only the degree of heel (leaning to one side) was taken into consideration. The two criteria (performance and practicality) were considered equally important, and within practicality, the three substances the keel can come in contact with are also considered equally relevant.

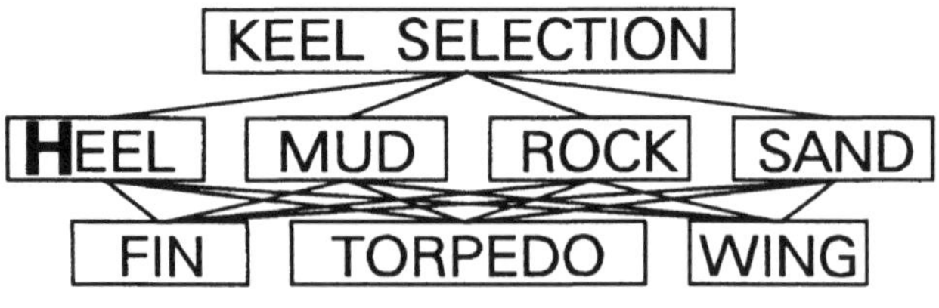

Figure 2. Keel selection

Thus, we have:

CRITERIA	WEIGHTS
Heel	1/2
Mud	1/6
Rock	1/6
Sand	1/6

Keels are classified into three basic types - winged, torpedo and fin. A deep keel was not considered because such keels have been outdated and are poor performers. Generally speaking, a winged keel provides the least amount of heel because of the lift action that each wing creates as it glides through the water. The wings actually serve as a vertical stabilizer. As the yacht heels (leans on its side), the wings keep the boat a few more degrees upright. The benefit of such a feature is that it allows the vessel to catch as much wind as possible, while minimizing the amount spilled. However, a winged keel is unsuitable for the MHM-maran, because the minor pontoon will serve the same purpose. When the minor pontoon is correctly positioned on the leeward side of the vessel, it will effectively reduce the vessel's degree of heel. When evaluating the criteria, the wing was the least favored.

The torpedo keel outperforms the fin keel with the respect to heeling because the torpedo limits the amount of heel. The torpedo keel is given that name because it is a standard fin keel with a torpedo shaped bulb on the bottom (Figure 3a). It is no longer a common type of keel, but at one time it was thought that having much of the lead weight at the base of the keel would act as a stabilizer. Some designers have combined the features of both the winged and torpedo keels.

The most common keel is the fin keel (Figure 3b). It goes straight down deep and tends to draw much water. Variations of the fin keel exist, such as a shoal draft keel which draws less water, but is thicker and longer. The shoal draft keel was not considered because it is not a good hydrodynamic performer. The fin keel was favored and after placing it on the major pontoon, it was found to be an excellent choice. When sailing in a close-hauled or reach position, the fin keel would reduce the MHM-marans sliding effect across the water.

The winged keel presents a problem in mud (Figure 3c). If one runs into mud, there is a good chance of getting stuck. The wings tend to anchor themselves into the mud, making it difficult to break away. The torpedo keel is no worse than the fin keel, but the bulb base can also stick into the mud.

(a) Torpedo keel (b) Fin keel. (c) Medium oft-sweeping wing keel

Figure 3. Types of Keels

Rocks are a problem for all keels. Sailing in shallow waters with a rocky bottom is hazardous. A winged keel does not fare well when it hits rock - structurally it can crack, or a wing can break off if the impact is sufficiently strong. A torpedo keel is better in rock than a winged keel but no better than a fin keel. A fin keel usually receives the least damage when its base hits rock. If the forward middle part of a keel is hit by rock, it could suffer chips and cracks.

When a boat hits sand, it goes "thump, thump", a sensation sometimes associated with engine problems. Fin and torpedo keels do about the same thing when hitting sand, causing the boat to skid across. With a winged keel, one needs to be concerned as to whether or not enough thump is due to one of the wings, which could break off. We have:

ALTERNATIVES	WEIGHTS
Fin	.391
Torpedo	.352
Wing	.257

We determined that the fin keel is the best suited for our purposes. Earlier, we spoke of its hydrodynamic advantages. With respect to the environment, the fin keel is the least affected by different bottom surfaces. It is relatively easy to get out of the mud, and it is least damaged when coming into contact with hard surfaces.

5. THE RUDDER

There is a definite relationship between a keel and a rudder and once the keel type is selected, the rudder more or less falls into place. What had to be considered was the rudder work coefficient (CWR) and the angle of deflection. These became the criteria. There are three basic alternatives - an attached rudder, a skeg type and a spade rudder (see Figure 4).

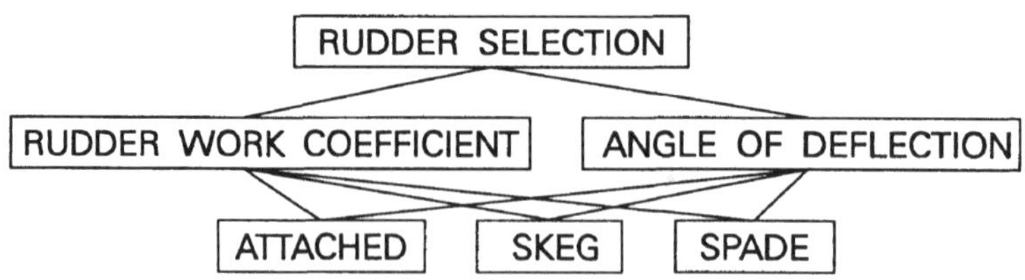

Figure 4. Rudder Selection

The attached rudder is connected to the keel with hinges (Figure 5a). At one time, this type of rudder was widely used, especially when the yacht had a deep keel (a keel that began shortly after the bow and went all the way back to the aft). Neither deep keels nor attached rudders are in much use nowadays.

The skeg rudder is made in a variety of shapes and sizes (Figure 5b). It is not attached to the keel. Rather, it is attached to a skeg that extends from the base of the hull. The theory behind such a design is that it is more streamlined and allows water to pass slightly faster by the rudder, thus making the rudder's movements more effective.

The spade rudder is the sailing industry's most commonly used rudder (Figure 5c). It is attached to a rudder post which in turn is connected to the helm (steering wheel) by a pulley assembly mechanism. It is also made in a variety of shapes and sizes. Some go deep, but never deeper than the deepest point of the keel, while others tend to be less rectangular. This type tends to be the number one choice among yacht manufacturers today, mostly because it is easy to configure hydrodynamically with specific keel characteristics. Thus, it was not surprising that the spade rudder was the most favored. Spade rudders are commonly used in conjunction with fin keels.

CRITERIA	WEIGHTS	ALTERNATIVES	WEIGHTS
Rudder work coefficient	.556	Spade	.470
		Skeg	.319
Angle of deflection	.444	Attached	.211

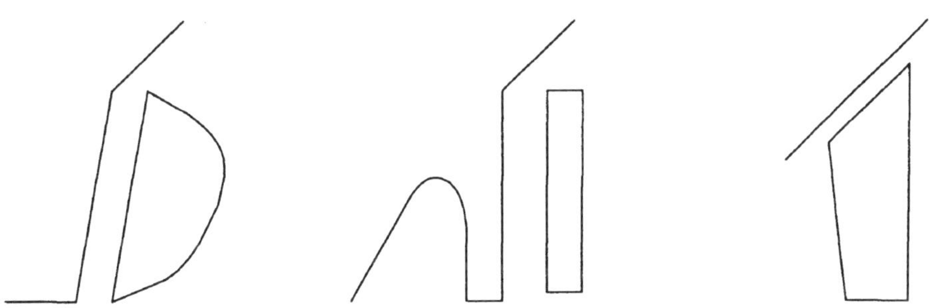

(a) Deep keel with an attached rudder. (b) Skeg type rudder. (c) Spade rudder.

Figure 5. Types of Rudders

6. THE OVERALL MHM-MARAN STRUCTURE

So far we have selected the major underwater hydrodynamic features and the basic overall design (see Figure 6). Now it is time to take a closer look. The big design problem is connecting the pontoons together. There are only two choices at this stage: one solid piece, or two poles (see Figure 7).

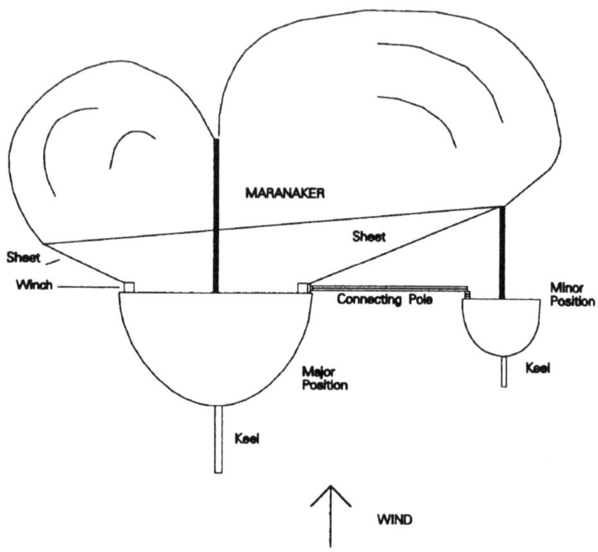

Figure 6. MHM-Maran on a run position.

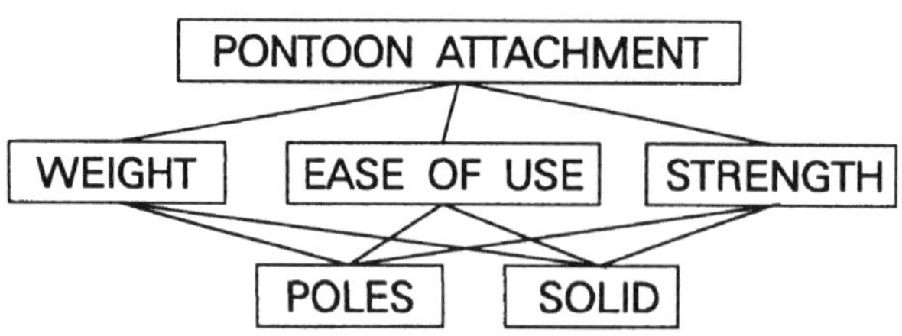

Figure 7. Pontoon Attachment

Each choice had to be flexible enough, so that it would move with the pontoon to the other side of the vessel. A solid connection, that leaves no visible gap between both pontoons, raises the question of seaworthiness. Such a structure could get swamped by a wave and break. Also, a solid structure would weigh more than two poles, thus adding to the overall weight of the vessel.

By comparing both alternatives with respect to the criteria: the poles were most favored except on strength. Using poles is not only less expensive, but easier to design. On the main pontoon, a dual track assembly would follow the rear perimeter on which the ends of the poles would be attached. On the minor pontoon, two curved tracks would travel along the centerline where the poles would also connect (Figure 8).

CRITERIA	WEIGHTS	ALTERNATIVES	WEIGHTS
Ease	.637	Poles	.528
Strength	.258	Solid	.472
Weight	.105		

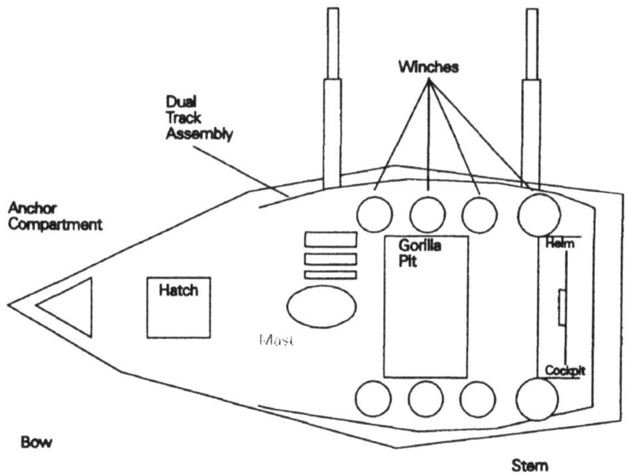

Figure 8. Main hull.

This design connects the two poles, and the tracks serve to provide the poles with movement, allowing the minor pontoon to swing around the main hull (Figures 9 and 10).

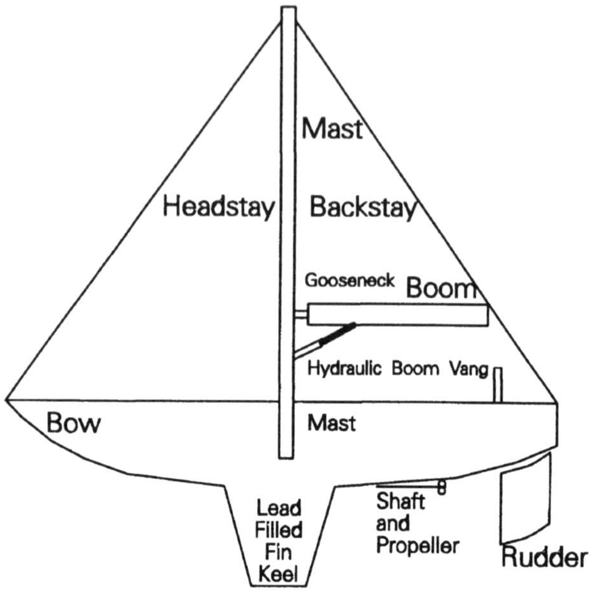

Figure 9. Main hull side view.

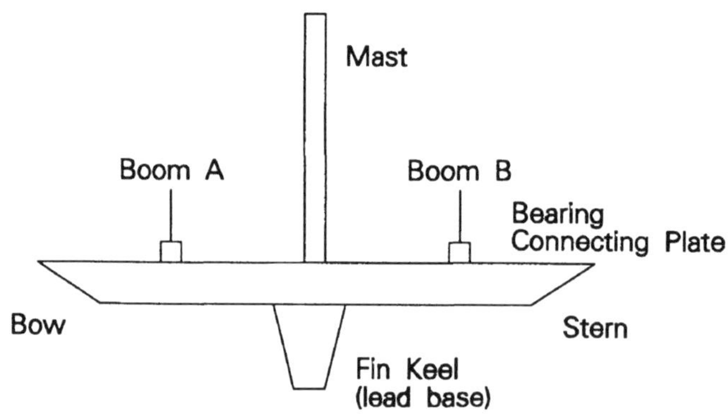

Figure 10. Pontoon side view.

The poles are strong, present no problem with respect to seaworthiness, and would be much lighter than a solid structure. Poles can also extend and retract, thus they are most suitable for the necessary pontoon swings.

Next we selected the material from which the pontoons would be built (see Figure 11). The possibilities are fiberglass, aluminum, titanium and stainless steel. These materials happened to be the most resistant to rust. Titanium is light, strong but also very expensive and difficult to work with. Yet, it is a popular metal among the yacht racing community, because of its lightness and strength. Aluminum alloys are much cheaper than titanium and are sufficiently strong for most yachting needs.

Aluminum is light, but much heavier than titanium. Fiberglass is good for salt water, but it is also heavy. It cannot undergo much direct stress. Stainless steel is relatively expensive and heavy, yet it is very strong.

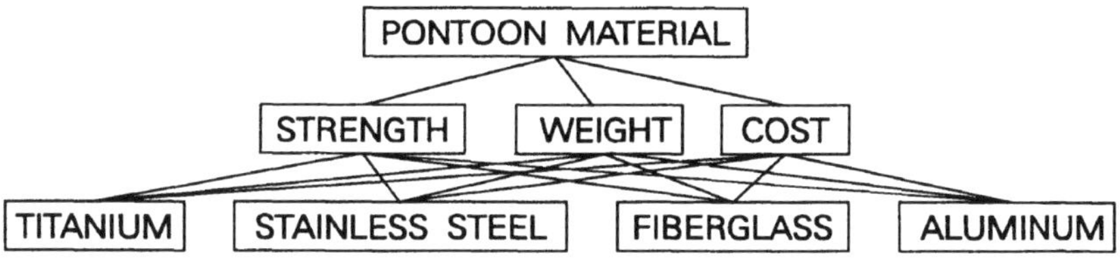

Figure 11. Pontoon Material Selection.

By having a dual track assembly follow the aft half of the major pontoon's toerail (see Figure 12) the minor pontoon would be mobile. It would be able to swing around to the leeward side (the side where the wind exits the surface of the boat) to minimize the MHM-maran degree of heel. On the run position, it would not matter which side the minor pontoon is positioned, since the wind is blowing from behind. The evaluation of all materials with respect to strength, cost and weight gave rise to titanium as the most favored. This guarantees that a strong, and flexible connection would be made between both pontoons.

CRITERIA	WEIGHTS	ALTERNATIVES	WEIGHTS
Strength	.648	Titanium	.564
Weight	.230	Stainless Steel	.161
Cost	.122	Fiberglass	.063
		Aluminum	.212

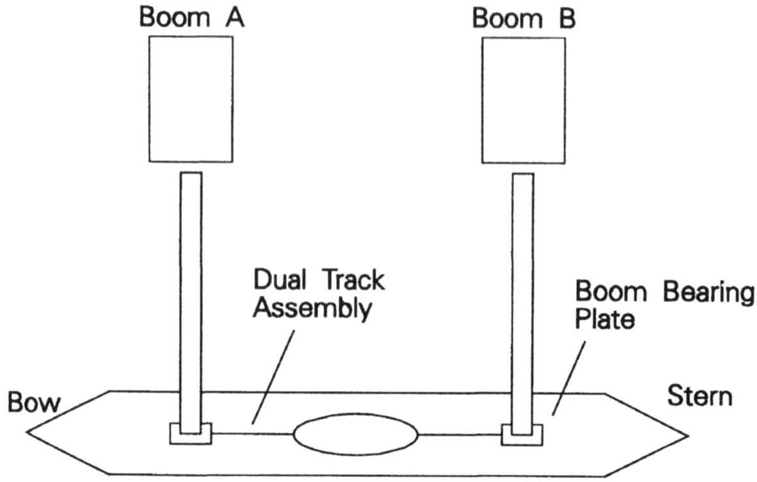

Figure 4.12. Pontoon top view.

7. CONCLUSION

The hierarchic conceptualization of sailboat design yielded the unique MHM-maran structure. With one large and one small pontoon (connected by two poles made of titanium), a fin keel, spade rudder and a never before seen sail (maranaker), it offers many performance benefits to the sailor and it is being considered by a contemporary sailboat manufacturer. However, it may be expensive for the average sailor.

REFERENCES

1. American Institute of Aeronautics & Astronautics, *Symposium on AER/Hydronautics of Sailing*, vols. 8-10, 15, 19, and 23. Western Periodicals Publishing Co., North Hollywood, CA 91605.
2. Florence, R., *The Optimum Sailboat*, Harper & Row Publishing Co., NY, 1986.
3. Heaton, P., *Make Sail*, Pelham Books, London, England, 1972.
4. Kelly, A., *Strong Solids*, Clarendon Press, Oxford, England, 1986.
5. Karlson, G.L., "Designing the Best Catamaran", *Mathematical and Computer Modelling* 17, 4-5 (1993) 179-186.
6. Street, D.M., *The Ocean Sailing Yacht*, Norton Publishing Co., NY, 1973.

CHAPTER 6

THE SELECTION OF A BRIDGE

1. INTRODUCTION

This chapter illustrates the use of the AHP for selecting the most appropriate bridge design in two different applications. The one recommended in the second application coincides with the decision that was actually made, demonstrating that the exclusion of an important, but hard to perceive actor, can alter the final decision. In this example we learn that decision making is not simply including multiple criteria in the decision, but more importantly the diverse people or groups who influence the outcome because of their own purposes.

By the close of the 1990's, the Golden Triangle Area in the City of Pittsburgh will once again be under construction to improve the flow of traffic into, out of, and through the city. The Mon Warf will be reconstructed, and the Fort Pitt Bridge will undergo rehabilitation. The Commonwealth Bridge Project is an effort by federal, state and local agencies to construct an alternative route across the Monongahela River to alleviate traffic congestion between the central business district of downtown Pittsburgh and Pittsburgh International Airport (Figure 1). A new bridge, and a high occupancy vehicle (HOV) busway will be built to the Wabash Tunnel [4]. The bridge will consist of three HOV lanes and a lane for pedestrian traffic. The Port Authority and PennDOT want to begin construction by 1997, so that the new bridge will be open for use when the Fort Pitt Bridge is closed for rehabilitation. The cost of the entire busway project is estimated at $300 million, and estimates for the new bridge range from $30 to $40 million.

At the time of the writing of the two reports[1] on which this chapter is based, the bridge type had not been decided, although the second paper (a follow up on the first) did point to the bridge type that was chosen a few weeks later. The difference between the two approaches is the shift in emphasis among the stakeholders from the Public to the Coast Guard because of concern with safety and with the economic impact that the bridge would have on the area.

The bridge types considered by The Port Authority of Allegheny County (PAT) were: a Cable-stayed bridge, a Truss bridge, and a Tied-arch bridge.

---

[1] See acknowledgments in the Preface.

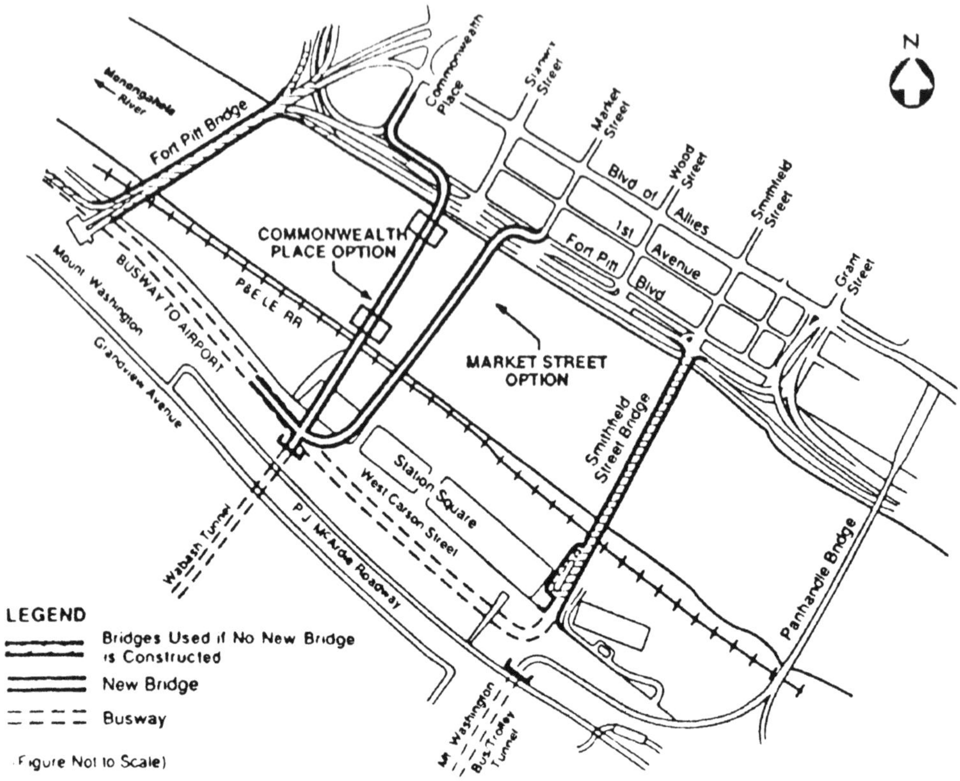

Figure 1. Proposed Commonwealth Bridge location

2. THREE ALTERNATIVE BRIDGE TYPES

CABLE-STAYED BRIDGES

Although the original concept of cable-stays dates back to Egyptian sailing ships, on which inclined ropes hanging from a mast were used to support a beam [1], it was not until the 19th century that the first cable-stayed bridge, the Roeblings bridge, at Niagara Falls New York, was constructed [2]. Built in 1855, it spanned 807 feet across a river gorge (Figure 2).

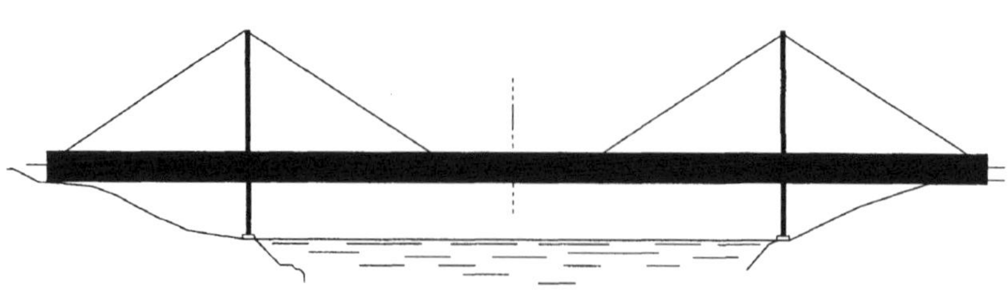

Figure 2. The Cable-Stayed Bridge

Despite the fulfillment of this engineering feat, modern cable-stayed bridges were not considered feasible until shortly after World War II, when German engineers pioneered their development. The main hurdles were technology-based; the limitation of high strength materials, structural analysis and construction methods [3].

To overcome design limitations, only cables with very high tensile strength are used. This minimizes beam deflection which becomes increasingly important as the span increases. Moreover, adding several stay cables allows the use of more slender deck beams (Figure 3a) which require less flexural stiffness. By decreasing the cable spacing supports (Figure 3b), local bending moments in the girders are also reduced.

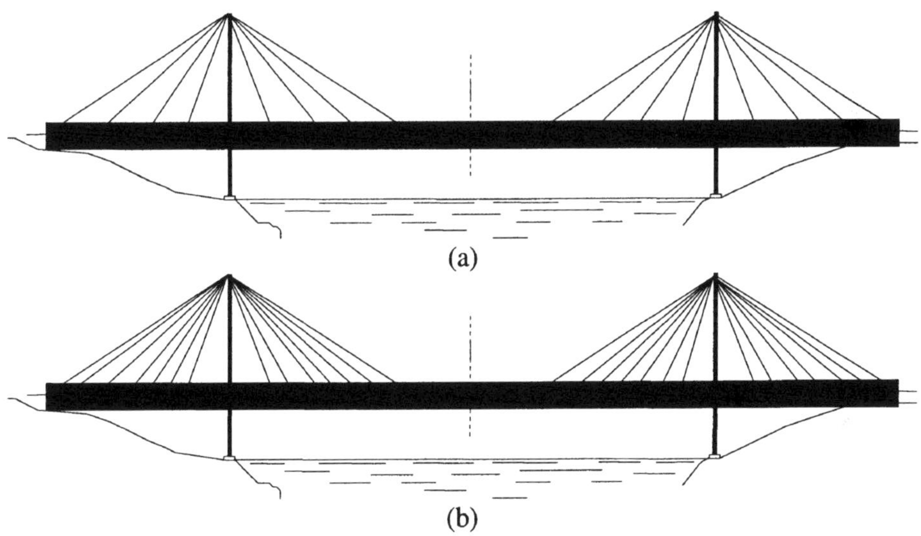

Figure 3. a) Cable-stay bridge with several cables; b) Cable-stay bridge with cable separation reduced.

The second presupposition for the success of cable-stayed bridge types is the simplification of the deck cross-section. Simple double-edge girders supporting transverse floor beams and top slabs provide a synergistic reinforcing action. As a result, the deck structure acts as a unit over intermediate supports.

Because of their aesthetically pleasing form, cable-stayed bridges can be found in almost all modern cities. The early cable-stayed bridges in North America were mostly constructed from steel because that was the traditional method at the time. However, due to the high cost of material and labor the all-steel bridge has been losing competitiveness. To address this decline, modern designers have developed an orthotopic composite deck, a concrete deck slab supported by steel framing. Today, virtually all cable-stayed bridges contain an orthotopic deck.

The economic viability and aesthetic appeal of the cable-stayed bridge make it the most popular bridge type for spans ranging between 650 and 1650 feet. In North America there were 25 cable-stayed bridges constructed or under development in the 20 years between 1971 and 1993.

TRUSS BRIDGES

Truss bridges have been used in North America for decades. A truss may be described as a triangulated assembly of straight members. The design of the truss structure [3] allows applied loads to be resisted primarily by axial forces in its straight truss members; the truss proper is loaded only at the nodes or intersection of straight members. It is a very efficient and sturdy design.

Figure 4 shows five main types of trusses, each providing a slight variation in load distribution. Also included in this figure is a general illustration of the Warren Truss bridge. The two most common are the Pratt and the Warren designs. Bridge design is typically performed on a case-by-case basis considering variables such as traffic, durability, and dependability.

A truss bridge has two major structural advantages [3]: a) The primary member forces are axial loaded; (b) the open web system permits the use of a greater overall depth than for an equivalent solid web girder. Both factors lead to economy in material and a reduced dead weight. Increased depth results in reduced deflections, and a more rigid structure. These advantages are achieved at increased fabrication and maintenance costs.

The conventional truss bridge is typically most economical for medium spans (500-1500 ft). Traditionally it has been used for spans intermediate between the plate girder and the stiffened suspension bridge designs. Modern construction techniques have tended to increase the economical span of both steel and concrete girders. Thus the steel truss bridge is a direct competitor to the cable-stayed for intermediate spans. The relative lightness of a truss bridge is advantageous because it can be assembled part-by-part using lifting equipment of small capacity. Alternatively, the number of field connections may be supplanted by pre-assembly.

From an architectural perspective the truss bridge rarely possesses aesthetic beauty. This is partly due to the complexity of the intersection of its load bearing component. In bridges of moderate span, it appears best to provide a simple and regular structure. For this reason, the Warren truss usually looks better than other forms.

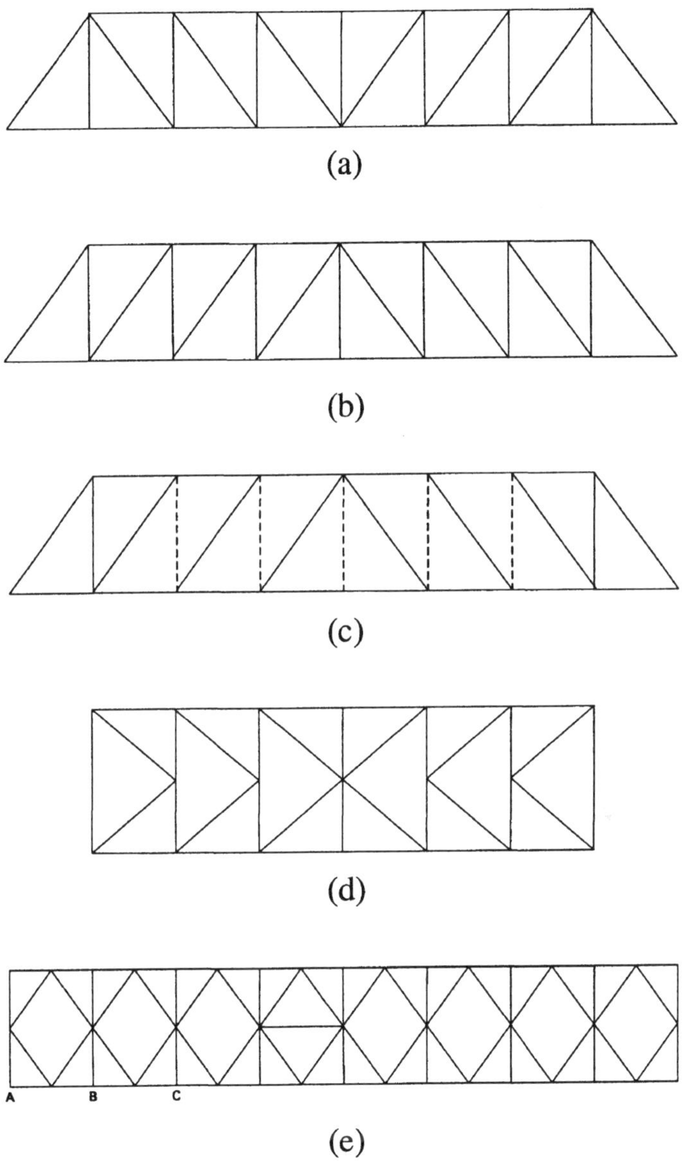

Figure 4. Five of the most common Truss type bridges a) Pratt Truss; b) Howe Truss; c) Warren Truss; d) K-bracing system; e) Diamond bracing system.

TIED-ARCH BRIDGES

The structural form of the arch has been used for its architectural beauty and outstanding strength for centuries. Because of the manner in which it distributes the applied load [3], with the aid of inward-acting horizontal components, the arch is capable of distributing loads both above and below its structure. In a tied arch design, the horizontal reactions to the arch rib are supplied by a tie at deck level. Figure 5 illustrates common tied- arch bridge types.

Some of the distinguishable features of the tied-arch are that it reduces bending moments in the superstructure and is fairly economical to construct relative to an equivalent straight, simple supported girder or truss [3].

Aesthetically, the arch has been the most appealing of all bridge types. Its appearance is familiar and expressive. The curved shape is always pleasing to view.

The disadvantages of the tied-arch are probably its high relative fabrication and building costs. The conventional curved arch rib usually entails the highest expense. Building problems vary with structure type, with the least problematic structure being the cantilever-arch and the tied-arch possibly being the most difficult. The difficulty with the latter arises from the fact that the horizontal reactions are not available until the deck is completed.

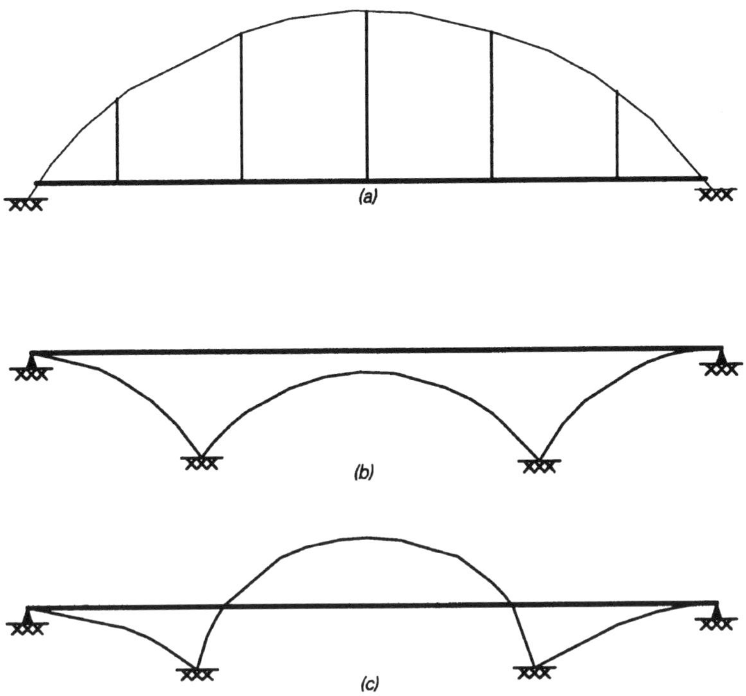

Figure 5. Three common Tied-Arch bridge types.

3. THE DECISION MAKING PROCESS

The most desirable bridge type would conceivably be the one which brings the most satisfaction to the greatest number of stakeholders. Using this goal, a hierarchy (see Figure 6) was developed with major stakeholders at the second level, the driving criteria at the third level and the three alternative bridge types at the fourth level.

STAKEHOLDERS

Published reports have estimated the number of stakeholders involved in this project to be in the hundreds. The most important stakeholders were aggregated into seven broad groups. Commonality within the groups was maintained. The identifiable groups are: a federal agency, the commercial business district, the public, state agencies, the Port Authority Transit, the designers, and special interest groups such as concrete suppliers, steel manufacturers, environmentalists and others.

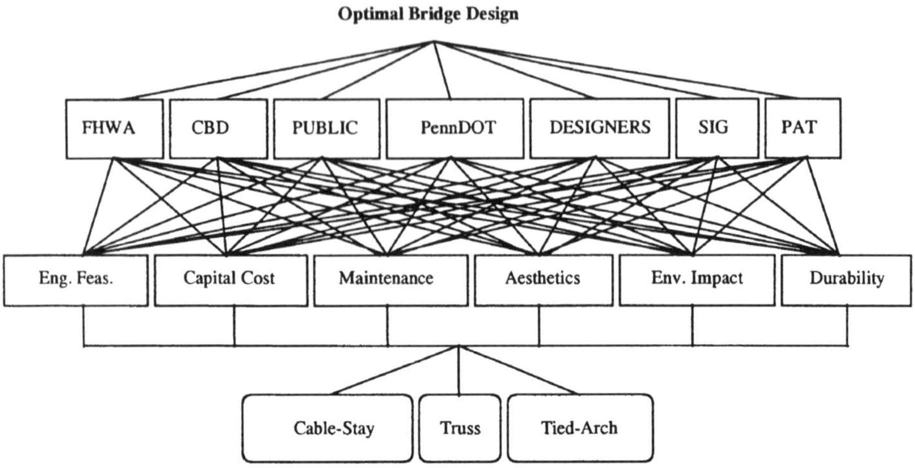

Figure 6. Bridge Selection Hierarchy

A FEDERAL AGENCY (FHWA) represents an array of federal departments. They are a key financier of the project and will have dictates with respect to the engineering integrity of any bridge type.

THE COMMERCIAL BUSINESS DISTRICT (CBD) broadly represents the businesses in downtown Pittsburgh. However, with respect to bridge type it is suggested that Station Square is the dominant entity because of the interest in maintaining the historical appearance of the site.

The PUBLIC represents the population of Pittsburgh which would use the new service (and the bridge itself).

The PENNSYLVANIA DEPARTMENT OF TRANSPORTATION (PennDOT) represents the complex interest of the state. These interests are financial (as the state provides part of the capital), political, technical and environmental.

THE DESIGNERS represent engineers, architects and planners and their representative professional organizations. It is recognized that designers provide crucial technical input and, as such, are strategically positioned to influence the decision making process.

THE PORT AUTHORITY TRANSIT (PAT) is the ultimate project owner. They are responsible for all management issues from conception to construction, as well as subsequent maintenance. This makes them a premier stakeholder.

SPECIAL INTEREST GROUPS (SIG) is a very broad category with diverse and possibly conflicting interests. With regard to the bridge type the three most significant special interest groups are likely to be: concrete suppliers, steel manufacturers and environmentalists. The indigenous steel industry of Pittsburgh has declined in size and influence in recent times; however, the concrete industry remains strong. Environmentalists are active and sometimes vocal.

CRITERIA

In the level below the stakeholders are the criteria. which drive the decision making process. The most important criteria are:

Engineering Feasibility (EF): The technical knowledge and experience of both the designers and contractors in regard to the bridge type.

Capital Cost (CC): Necessary funding.[2] Because the costs were committed, low costs are included in the overall benefits hierarchy as one the criteria.

Maintenance (MA): General cleaning, painting and inspection vary dramatically with bridge type.

Aesthetics (AE): Architectural attractiveness.

Environmental Impact (EI): The ecological and historical adjustments that must be compromised.

Durability (DU): The life of the bridge and the potential major repairs over and above routine maintenance.

4. JUDGEMENTS AND DECISIONS

To find the most desirable bridge design, the actors were compared to determine their relative influence (Table 1). The stakeholder ranking, as suggested by the authors in order of importance, is PAT (0.337), CBD (0.221), Federal Agency (0.136), State Agencies (0.136), Designers (0.085), Special Interests (0.056) and the Public (0.029). The criteria were then compared according to each actor and the composite relative priorities calculated (Table 2). Finally, the

[2]The cable-stayed bridge type is very efficient in terms of section sizes and material used. However, there is limited experience with their use in the State of Pennsylvania. As a result, the capital costs would vary greatly depending on the tender procedure used (statewide, nationwide or international).

alternatives were compared according to the criteria and the final priorities computed.

This information was synthesized to yield the most desirable bridge type which was determined to be the Truss type bridge.

The priorities of the three alternatives are:

Truss bridge	0.371
Tied-arch bridge	0.320
Cable-stayed bridge	0.309

Table 1. Actors' Comparisons

	FHWA	CBD	PUBLIC	PennDOT	Designers	SIG	PAT
FHWA	1	2	1/5	1	1/2	1/3	3
CBD	1/2	1	1/6	1/2	1/3	1/4	2
PUBLIC	5	6	1	5	4	3	7
PennDOT	1	2	1/5	1	1/2	1/3	3
Designers	2	3	1/4	2	1	1/2	4
SIG	3	4	1/3	3	2	1	5
PAT	1/3	1/2	1/7	1/3	1/4	1/5	1

Table 2. Priorities of the Criteria

	(0.135	0.221	0.029	0.136	0.085	0.056	0.337)	
	FHWA	CBD	PUBLIC	PennDOT	Designers	SIG	PAT	Priorities
EF	0.117	0.048	0.037	0.216	0.313	0.033	0.260	0.173
CC	0.340	0.048	0.297	0.082	0.197	0.357	0.100	0.147
MA	0.069	0.116	0.297	0.052	0.118	0.097	0.260	0.154
AE	0.069	0.401	0.074	0.216	0.136	0.224	0.061	0.174
EI	0.202	0.270	0.114	0.352	0.117	0.224	0.061	0.181
DU	0.202	0.116	0.182	0.082	0.118	0.064	0.260	0.171

5. BRIDGE SELECTION REVISITED

The analysis just presented was prepared by MBA students. Several months following the foregoing analysis another MBA student revisited the decision and sought validation with two individuals closely involved in the bridge selection process. The hierarchy developed in this second approach is given in Figure 7 and the results are provided in Table 3. Note that the hierarchy used is similar to the one given in Figure 6. However, the elements in the levels are not identical to the ones in the first approach. The major difference between the two approaches is the addition of a new stakeholder, the U.S. Coast Guard, and the deletion of The Public.

UNITED STATES COAST GUARD (USCG): River transportation has a significant impact on the economy of Pittsburgh and the surrounding area in Western Pennsylvania. Since there will be three bridges in close proximity to one another (Smithfield Street, Monongahela River, and Fort Pitt), ample room must be maintained for river traffic. The Coast Guard will also want to minimize the impact of the bridge construction on river traffic.

Table 3. Priorities of the Criteria for the Revisited Bridge Decision

	(0.173	0.087	0.118	0.173	0.036	0.051	0.361)	
	FHWA	CBD	USCG	PennDOT	Designers	SIG	PAT	Priorities
EF	0.218	0.048	0.214	0.220	0.346	0.228	0.230	0.212
CC	0.354	0.137	0.043	0.344	0.248	0.100	0.121	0.195
MA	0.053	0.083	0.161	0.053	0.070	0.046	0.230	0.132
AE	0.073	0.400	0.067	0.114	0.155	0.432	0.121	0.146
EI	0.189	0.249	0.383	0.191	0.129	0.148	0.070	0.170
DU	0.112	0.083	0.123	0.078	0.052	0.046	0.230	0.142

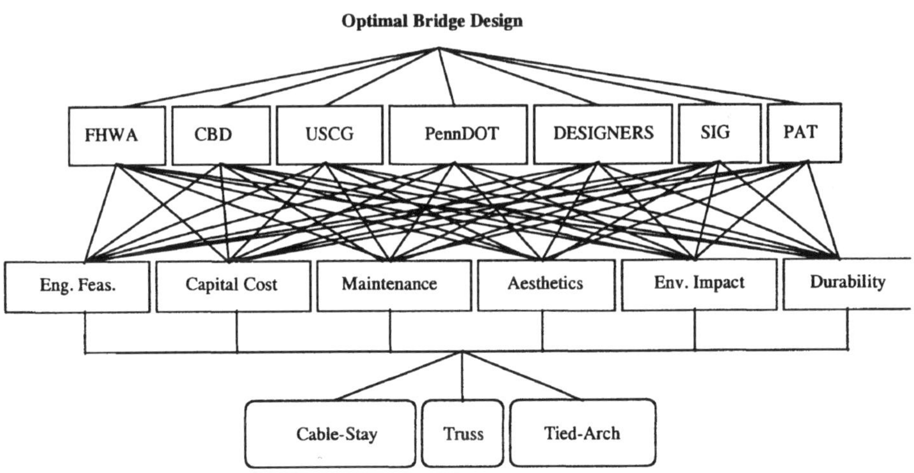

Figure 7. Hierarchy for the Revised Bridge Decision

The priorities of the three alternatives are now:

Tied-arch bridge:	0.471
Cable-stayed bridge:	0.328
Truss bridge:	0.201

It must be noted that another important difference between the two approaches, in addition to the ones mentioned above, is the group of decision makers providing the judgments. Although in both occasions judgments were provided by people with good information on the project, the second time the judgments were given by the two individuals close to the committee that made the final recommendation of the tied-arch type bridge.

5. CONCLUSION

The AHP was used to select the best alternative (the Tied-arch type bridge) from among closely competing alternatives. It also facilitated the learning process and gave users a more thorough understanding of the competing factors in a complex decision making environment. It illustrates the sensitivity of the outcome to what factors one chooses to include. It is certain that so far major public works divisions have not been as thorough and comprehensive as may be needed to ensure the success and longevity of an important project. More examples of such applications need to be brought to the attention of authorities for better value and longer lasting performance.

REFERENCES

1. Leonhardt, F. and W. Zelbner, "Past, Present & Future of Cable-Stayed Bridges," chapter in *Cable-Stayed Bridges, Recent Development and Their Future*, M. Ito et al (Editors) Elsevier Science Publishers, 1991.

2. Tang, M.C., "Cable-Stayed Bridges in North America," chapter in *Cable-Stayed Bridges, Recent Development and Their Future*, M. Ito et al (Editors) Elsevier Science Publishers, 1991.

3. O'Connor, *C., Design of Bridge Superstructures*, Wiley-Interscience, John Wiley & Sons, Inc., 1971.

4. *Phase I: Airport busway/Wabash HOV Alternative Analysis Draft Environmental Impact Statement Allegheny County, Pennsylvania.* Prepared by U.S. Department of Transportation Federal Transit Administration in

cooperation with Federal Highway Administration, United States Coast Guard, Pennsylvania Department of Transportation and Port Authority of Allegheny County, September 1992.

CHAPTER 7

MEASURING DEPENDENCE BETWEEN ACTIVITIES: INPUT-OUTPUT APPLICATION TO THE SUDAN

1. INTRODUCTION

In this chapter we illustrate how to deal with dependence among the elements of the same level of a hierarchy (inner dependence) with an application we made in the design of the Transportation System for the Sudan (see [2]). The outcome of this analysis was an input-output table which parallels the work of econometricians. This application was done a few years after the Sudan Transport Study was finished.

Input-output matrices in economics are generally obtained as follows. Let $A_1, A_2, \ldots, A_N$ denote N sectors of an economy and let S be a matrix whose s_{ij} entry indicates the output from sector i which becomes an input to sector j. Let Y_j be the net contribution from sector i to the final (consumer) demand. We have:

$\sum_{i=1}^{N} s_{ij} = S_j$ total intermediate output of sector j (domestic needs from other sectors)

$S_j + Y_j = O_j$ total output of sector j

The technological coefficients are obtained as follows

$\dfrac{s_{ij}}{S_j + Y_j} = w_{ij}$ (contribution of sector i to produce a unit of output j)

$$\frac{s_{ij}}{S_j + Y_j} = \left(\frac{s_{ij}}{S_j}\right)\left(\frac{S_j}{S_j + Y_j}\right) = \frac{s_{ij}\,S_j}{S_j O_j}$$

To obtain the matrix of technological coefficients by the AHP we must estimate s_{ij}/S_j and S_j/O_j. Let us see what these represent. $S_j/(S_j + Y_j)$ represents the proportion of the total output of sector j allocated to domestic consumption. The total output is estimated, for $j = 1, \ldots, N$, by means of the AHP by asking the following question: How strong is one sector compared to another when allocating outputs to domestic needs? If this question cannot be answered directly, domestic needs may be hierarchically decomposed into production, demand, labor, capital, and cost. These sectors are prioritized separately with respect to each criterion. After prioritizing these criteria according to their impact on production, composition is used to obtain an overall measure of importance for the sectors. Let us denote the estimates of (S_j/O_j) by x_j.

Again s_{ij}/S_j represents the proportion of the total intermediate output from sector i allocated to sector j. We have

$$\sum_{i=1}^{N} s_{ij} / S_j = 1$$

We construct a matrix of pairwise comparisons among the sectors as they relate to sector i. We answer the following question. How strong is the dependence of one sector in comparison with another in receiving output from sector j? The result is a matrix of pairwise comparisons which yields a column eigenvector of weights. When this is done for each sector we obtain a matrix W whose columns are these eigenvectors.

Finally, we take the elementwise product of each column of the matrix W with the column vector $x = (x_1, x_2, ..., x_N)$ to obtain the estimates of the technological coefficients, i.e., the input-output matrix.

The most important fact we have to take into consideration when the matrix of technological coefficients is estimated using the AHP is the proportion of total intermediate outputs for each sector in relation to the total output. This proportion was estimated in this example by extensive study of the literature on the Sudanese economy available at the time (Saaty and Vargas, 1979).

2. APPLICATION

The Sudan is considered to be mainly an agricultural country. At the time the econometric models were constructed (1973) and the input-output analysis was done, the data used were from the year 1961. At this time, the major problem of the Sudan was the lack of an adequate transport system.

We considered the following six sectors.

(1) Agriculture (AGR)
(2) Public utilities (PU)
(3) Manufacturing and mining (M&M)
(4) Transportation and distribution (T&D)
(5) Construction (CONS)
(6) Services (SERV)

To make the same order of magnitude comparison with Agriculture and Transportation (another major activity), the other sectors were grouped into an aggregate. We have

The question to be asked to form the matrices of pairwise comparisons is: Given two sectors, i and j, which sector allocates more of its outputs to satisfy domestic needs (total intermediate outputs)? We first compare the elements in the aggregate, then separately compare the aggregate with agriculture and transport and use the resulting weight of the aggregate to compose the relevant weights from the four sectors in the aggregate itself. To save space we have not written out justifications of the judgments, which are available in a separate study.

	Satisfaction of domestic needs	PU	M&M	CONS	SERV	Eigenvector
AGG:	PU	1	1/2	1/2	1/3	0.1272
	M&M	2	1	1	1	0.2804
	CONS	2	1	1	1	0.2804
	SERV	3	1	1	1	0.3120

$\lambda_{max} = 4.02$, C.I. = 0.007, C.R. = 0.007

Satisfaction of domestic needs	AGR	T&D	AGG	Eigenvector
AGR	1	1/2	2	0.3108
T&D	2	1	2	0.4934
AGG	1/2	1/2	1	0.1948

$\lambda_{max} = 3.05$, C.I. = 0.025, C.R. = 0.04

For the relative importance of the sectors we have:

Sectors	Final Weights $S_i/(S_i+Y_i)$	Estimates of $Y_i/(S_i+Y_i)$
1	0.3108	0.6892
2	0.0248	0.9752
3	0.0546	0.9454
4	0.4934	0.5066
5	0.0546	0.9454
6	0.0608	0.9392

Now we identify the relationships among the sectors. They are given by the rows of the following table.

I.O.	AGR	PU	M&M	T&D	CONS	SERV
AGR	X		X	X	X	
PU	X		X	X		X
M&M	X			X	X	X
T&D	X	X	X		X	X
CONS						X
SERV		X	X	X	X	X

Given a certain sector i we ask: for any two sectors, h and k, to which sector are more products from sector i allocated? The following treatments answer this question for each sector.

Agriculture

The main crop in the Sudan is cotton. Cotton is exported and also allocated to the manufacturing sector. Thus agriculture, transportation and distribution, and construction do not receive a large amount of agricultural products. A new aggregate is formed. (Note that only four sectors are considered under agriculture.)

$$\begin{array}{c} \textit{Aggregate} \\ \textit{(AGG)} \end{array} \begin{cases} \textit{Agriculture} \\ \textit{Transport and Distribution} \\ \textit{Construction} \end{cases}$$

As we pointed out above, the Sudan lacks adequate transportation. We aggregated the two sectors which do not consume substantial quantities from agriculture, AGR and T&D, because, although the main crop after cotton is wheat, the agricultural sector allocates most of its output (i.e., wood) to construction. Transportation is developed by means of loans from Arab oil countries and the World Bank. Thus, we also aggregated agriculture and transportation to form a subaggregate.

	Input from agriculture	AGR	T&D	Eigenvector
SUBAGG:	AGR	1	9	0.9000
	T&D	1/9	1	0.1000

$\lambda_{max} = 2.0$, C.I. = 0.0, C.R. = 0.0

	Input from agriculture	SUBAGG	CONS	Eigenvector
AGG:	SUBAGG	1	1/9	0.1000
	CONS	9	1	0.9000

$\lambda_{max} = 2.0$, C.I. = 0.0, C.R. = 0.0

Input from agriculture	AGG	M&M	Eigenvector
AGG	1	1/3	0.25
M&M	3	1	0.75

$\lambda_{max} = 2.0$, C.I. = 0.0, C.R. = 0.0

Sectors	Final weights
AGR	0.0225
PU	0.0000
M&M	0.7500
T&D	0.0025
CONS	0.2250
SERV	0.0000

Note: The weights of AGR and T&D are obtained as follows.

$$\begin{matrix} AGR \\ T\&D \end{matrix} \begin{bmatrix} 0.9 \\ 0.1 \end{bmatrix} x(0.1)\,x(0.25) = \begin{bmatrix} 0.0225 \\ 0.0025 \end{bmatrix}$$

The weight of construction is obtained by multiplying (0.9) by (0.25) = 0.225.

Public Utilities

Input from PU	AGR	M&M	T&D	SERV	Eigenvector
AGR	1	1/9	1/7	1/5	0.0410
M&M	9	1	2	5	0.5242
T&D	7	1/2	1	3	0.3030
SERV	5	1/5	1/3	1	0.1318

$\lambda_{max} = 4.12$, C.I. = 0.04, C.R. = 0.04

Manufacturing and Mining

Input from M&M	AGR	T&D	CONS	SERV	Eigenvector
AGR	1	1/2	1/9	1	0.0758
T&D	2	1	1/5	3	0.1628
CONS	9	5	1	9	0.6941
SERV	1	1/3	1/9	1	0.0681

$\lambda_{max} = 4.03$, C.I. = 0.01, C.R. = 0.01

Transportation and Distribution

Input from T&D	AGR	PU	M&M	CONS	SERV	Eigenvector
AGR	1	1/3	1/2	1/2	7	0.1400
PU	3	1	1	2	9	0.3434
M&M	2	1	1	1	7	0.2596
CONS	2	1/2	1	1	7	0.2260
SERV	1/7	1/9	1/7	1/7	1	0.0310

$\lambda_{max} = 5.11$, C.I. = 0.03, C.R. = 0.03

Construction

Construction only gives its products to services. Thus we associate the value 1 with services.

Services in the Sudan are very poor. We have assumed that the allocation of service outputs to services, and to construction, are so negligible that these two could be aggregated. We have

$$Aggregate(AGG)\begin{cases} Construction \\ Services \end{cases}$$

	Input from services	CONS	SERV	Eigenvector
AGG:	CONS	1	9	0.9000
	SERV	1/9	1	0.1000

$\lambda_{max} = 2.0$, C.I. = 0.0, C.R. = 0.0

Services

Input from Services	PU	M&M	T&D	AGG	Eigenvector
PU	1	1/2	1/2	3	0.1930
M&M	2	1	1	5	0.3680
T&D	2	1	1	5	0.3680
AGG	1/3	1/5	1/5	1	0.0704

$\lambda_{max} = 4.004$, C.I. = 0.001, C.R. = 0.001

The weights of construction and services are obtained by multiplying 0.0704, the weight of the aggregate, by 0.9 and 0.1, respectively.

Sectors	Final weights
AGR	0.0000
PU	0.1930
M&M	0.3680
T&D	0.3680
CONS	0.0634
SERV	0.0070

The matrix whose rows are the foregoing eigenvectors gives the distribution of total intermediate outputs to the sectors. It is given by the following table.

Shares → of the total intermediate outputs	Producers ↓	AGR	PU	M&M	T&D	CONS	SERV
	AGR	0.0225	0	0.7500	0.0025	0.2250	0
	PU	0.0410	0	0.5242	0.3030	0	0.1318
	M&M	0.0750	0	0	0.1628	0.6841	0.0681
	T&D	0.1400	0.3434	0.2596	0	0.2260	0.0310
	CONS	0	0	0	0	0	1
	SERV	0	0.1939	0.3683	0.3683	0.0634	0.0070

At the beginning we computed how strongly the sectors allocate outputs to domestic needs. The vector of weights was:

AGR	*PU*	*M & M*	*T & D*	*CONS*	*SERV*
0.3108	*0.0248*	*0.0546*	*0.4934*	*0.0546*	*0.0608*

Thus we multiply each column of the above matrix by this vector (element-wise multiplication), e.g., for the first column we have

$$\begin{bmatrix} 0.0225 \times 0.3108 \\ 0.0410 \times 0.0248 \\ 0.0750 \times 0.0546 \\ 0.1400 \times 0.0546 \\ 0 \quad \times 0.0546 \\ 0 \quad \times 0.0608 \end{bmatrix} = \begin{bmatrix} 0.0070 \\ 0.0009 \\ 0.0041 \\ 0.0691 \\ 0 \\ 0 \end{bmatrix}$$

The weighted matrix is then given by:

	AGR	*PU*	*M & M*	*T & D*	*CONS*	*SERV*
AGR	0.0070	0	0.2331	0.0008	0.0699	0
PU	0.0009	0	0.0130	0.0075	0	0.0033
M & M	0.0041	0	0	0.0089	0.0379	0.0037
T & D	0.0691	0.1694	0.1281	0	0.1115	0.0153
CONS	0	0	0	0	0	0.0546
SERV	0	*0.0117*	0.0117	0.0224	0.0039	0.0004

If we compare this matrix with the following input-output matrix obtained by traditional methods, we see that there are very minor differences.

	AGR	*PU*	*M & M*	*T & D*	*CONS*	*SERV*
AGR	0.00737	0	0.21953	0.00042	0.06721	0
PU	0.00024	0	0.01159	0.00618	0	0.00283
M & M	0.00393	0	0	0.00857	0.04216	0.00322
T & D	0.06993	0.14536	0.12574	0	0.09879	0.00641
CONS	0	0	0	0	0	0.05402
SERV	0	*0.01*03	0.02549	0.02422	0.0052	0.00021

The factors considered in this problem were purely economic. This suggests that this type of analysis can be extended to study social systems and particularly to introduce social factors in the resource allocation problem when the activities are interrelated (a problem briefly mentioned by V. Leontief, the founder of input-output analysis).

REFERENCES

1. Saaty, T.L. and L.G. Vargas, "Estimation of Input-Output Technological Coefficients," *Socioeconomic Planning Sciences* 13 (1979) 333-336.

2. Saaty, T.L., "The Sudan Transport Study," *Interfaces* 20, 3 (1977) 147-157.

CHAPTER 8

TECHNOLOGICAL CHOICE IN LESS DEVELOPED COUNTRIES

1. INTRODUCTION

It is widely believed that the economic situation of less developed countries (LDCs) can be greatly improved by conscious and judicious application of science and technology to the solution of their many problems. This belief is well supported by evidence attributing the rapid economic growth achieved by industrially advanced countries to the technology factor ([1], [13]). Early economic theorists noted that the level of savings and investment in the LDCs was low. They recommended transfusion of capital to spur investment and capital formation; but beginning with the late fifties the emphasis shifted to transfusion of technology rather than capital. However, the collective experience of the LDCs with imported technology over the past three decades has been far from encouraging, as is apparent from the growing discontent voiced by the "Group of 77."

A substantial body of literature attempts to grapple with the problem of transferring technology effectively to the LDCs (for example, [4], [10], [13] and [15]). This literature represents a significant part of the scholarly output in the broader area of technology transfer and technological innovation. We make no attempt here to survey the literature on technology transfer in general, or even international technology transfer in particular, but will merely note that the problem has been approached from a number of different perspectives, with contributions from economists, sociologists, anthropologists, political scientists, and technical professionals. Some are concerned with the "how to" of technology transfer; that is, with the mechanisms and methods of transfer. Some describe the process of technology transfer and diffusion. Yet others critically assess the consequences of transferring advanced technology to less developed countries and appear to be voicing concern about a rather fundamental question: the "why" of technology transfer. These varied disciplinary approaches indicate the complexity of factors impinging on technological choice in the LDCs.

The field is rich in conceptualizations and historical accounts of the ways in which technology has been transferred among today's advanced countries. With respect to theories, one can mention the notion of the "technology gap" ([5]); the product life cycle hypothesis ([16]); and the depiction of the diffusion process as a logistic or S-shaped curve [9]), which has stood empirical validation in economic studies ([3], [6]). These theories have yet to be integrated into an overall framework that would provide guidance to planners involved in technology transfer. All are vulnerable to the criticism of being limited in scope. A recent body of literature views technology transfer as a bargaining process between economically unmatched participants in an imperfect market. Prescriptions for the LDCs range from moving toward an alternative model of development that emphasizes the small and the human ([12]) to a more "pragmatic" emphasis on developing integrated science and technology policies based on needs and goals, building up local research and development capabilities to better assimilate imported technologies as well as develop indigenous ones, and exploring avenues for regional economic and technological cooperation with other LDCs.

Two dominant and somewhat opposing themes emerge from a survey of the literature on international transfers. One focuses on the process of imitation, while the other considers technological change as predicated on sociocultural change. The latter asserts that unless a revolution occurs whereby social attitudes and values are rapidly transformed, externally introduced technologies cannot operate optimally in the social environment of the LDCs. It is possible to take a balanced approach, one that acknowledges the importance of imitation as well as the sociocultural barriers, and because of their obvious interdependence, allows for them to proceed simultaneously.

Most discussions of technology transfer have paid little attention to methodologies for the assessment of technology. The available ones ([7]) do not appear well suited to the needs of LDCs because most have as their aim the prediction of technological futures. Here we present an integrated approach to technological assessment, choice, and transfer and analyze its possible impacts on the sectors of the economy of LDCs. After the potentially most useful technologies are identified, a benefit/cost framework is developed to also consider nontechnological factors that may influence economic development.

2. APPLICATIONS TO TECHNOLOGY TRANSFER

In dealing with the problem of technology transfer, the AHP can be applied at several levels. At a global level, one might be interested in predicting, in general terms, the future course of technology transfers to the LDCs. A hierarchical representation of this problem is depicted in Figure 1. At the first level of the hierarchy, we list the following actors who might be expected to play a role in determining the future course of technology transfers: the governments of the developed nations, the governments of the LDCs, "neutral" third parties such as the many United Nations organizations involved in technology transfer issues, the USSR and Eastern bloc nations, multinational corporations, the private sector as represented by big and small businesses, and labor unions. Each actor pursues a set of objectives such as technological leadership, trade, balance of payments, employment generation, economic expansion, and so on, vis-à-vis technology transfer. These objectives, spelled out in greater detail in Figure 1, constitute the second level of the hierarchy. At the third level we indicate the future scenarios: an optimistic scenario that envisages increased flow of technology to the LDCs and among world nations in general, a scenario that is merely the extension of the status quo into the future, and a pessimistic scenario that foresees substantial reduction in the overall volume of trade in technology. Increased flow of technology could occur if, for instance, the much debated code of conduct for technology transfer and

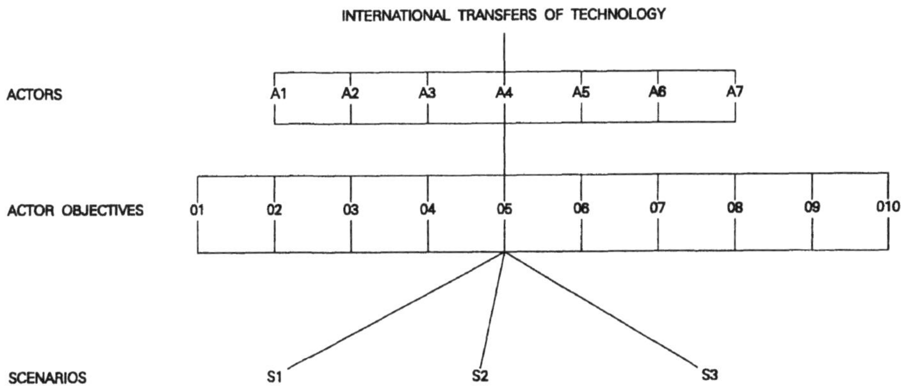

ACTORS

A1 = Governments of the developed countries
A2 = LDC governments
A3 = UN agencies (UNDP, UNCTAD, etc.)
A4 = USSR and Eastern Bloc Nations
A5 = Multinational Corporations
A6 = Small and big businesses in the LDCs
A7 = Labor unions

ACTOR OBJECTIVES

01 = Technological Leadership
02 = Trade in Goods and Services
03 = Balance of Payments
04 = Employment Generation
05 = Nationalism, Regionalism
06 = Expansion, Growth, Profits
07 = Political Leverage
08 = Preservation of own Culture, Environment
09 = Social Justice
010 = Protection of Domestic Enterprises

SCENARIOS

S1 = "Optimistic": Increased technological dependence and exchange
S2 = "Status Quo"
S3 = "Pessimistic": Concentration, localized integration, 'Closed door' policies in technology transfer

Figure 1. Technology Transfer Hierarchy

the international economic order should become realities. The pressures of the different actors and the strength with which they pursue current policies could result in indefinite extension of the status quo, or the continued impasse regarding technology transfer issues could deflect the LDCs toward policies of self-reliance and regional cooperation, thereby reducing the flow of technology from the advanced to the less developed countries.

To estimate the likelihood of the three scenarios, we first make a pairwise comparison of the relative influence of the different actors, which yields a set of weights for this factor. Next the objectives of each actor are compared in pairwise fashion in terms of their importance to the concerned actor. We pose questions such as: "How important is objective O1 relative to objectives O2, O3, and so on, for actor A1?" Having prioritized the objectives of each actor in this way, we apply the weights of actor influence to these objectives to obtain a set of weighted objectives. The process is continued by comparing the scenarios with respect to their relative contribution to the achievement of each objective and by weighting the scenario priorities by the weighted objectives. This results in an index of the overall likelihood or importance of each scenario.

For the purpose of illustration, we have limited the hierarchy to only three levels. The richness of the hierarchy can be extended as necessary by adding more levels and more elements within each level. For instance, a level of actor policies could be interposed between the objectives and scenarios, which might relate to taxation, imports and exports, degree of encouragement given to foreign ownership of capital, preferential treatments accorded to countries as sources of supply of goods and technologies, and so on.

Let us now see how this approach can be used to enable planners of an LDC to make technological choices. A survey of the literature suggests that the following criteria are paramount in technology transfer:

1. *Need:* Technology has to be tailored to the needs of the country. Need can be defined in terms of *suitability* and *urgency*. A technology might be considered suitable if it is proven to meet similar needs in other contexts. Needs will be influenced by overall national sectoral priorities.

2. *Adaptability:* It must be possible to adapt the technology to the local environment. Two considerations determining adaptability are the *ability* and the *willingness* to adapt. The lack of a sufficient science and technology base in terms of the availability of skilled manpower, maintenance facilities, materials in sufficient quantity and quality, presence of facilitating institutions and change agents, and the like, affects the ability to adapt. The willingness to adapt depends on the strength of custom, tradition, power relationships within the society, and similar social, cultural, and political considerations.

3. *Relative freedom from the risk of obsolescence:* Here our attention is focused on what may be termed "mass" technologies – technologies whose interface with the eventual user is close and extensive. Many of these technologies are certain to involve substantial investment. In the context of an LDC, the technology transferred must be capable of being supported throughout its useful life; that is, some insulation from the risk of obsolescence must be available. The most modern technology may be difficult to adapt, while a currently obsolete technology may at a later date leave the LDC without adequate support. Thus a careful tradeoff has to be made as to the nature of the technology to acquire.

4. *No undesirable second-order consequences:* If the LDCs have any advantage as late comers in the process of technological development, it is the opportunity to profit from the lessons learned by the advanced countries as to the negative effects of certain types of technology. Impact analysis must be an integral part of any attempt to evaluate technologies for importation.

In general the needs for technology are influenced by sectoral priorities. Also, each of the preliminary assessment criteria listed above will be emphasized differently in the various economic sectors. For example, adaptability might be stressed in agriculture, which is a more traditional sector than manufacturing in most LDCs, whereas obsolescence risk might be underscored in manufacturing (see [11]).

Sectoral priorities may be taken as "given" if they are based on planning exercises done outside the context of technology assessment, a likely situation in many LDCs. However, the sectoral priorities themselves can be hierarchically determined. Two approaches are possible: a forward approach that starts with a level of national objectives and works down toward the desired sectoral priorities, and a backward approach that begins with constraints in both the internal and external environment of the LDC and converges on the feasible sectoral priorities, given the constraints (see [2]). Figure 2 illustrates the backward approach.

Returning to the problem of technology assessment (Figure 3), we then have sector priorities at level 1, assessment criteria at level 2, and candidate technologies at level 3. Two assumptions are made in this particular construction of the hierarchy. First, technologies may or may not be sector-specific; some can be of general applicability, impacting many or all of the sectors - for example, transportation or communication technologies. Second, the importance of the assessment criteria varies across sectors, as mentioned earlier. Hence we prioritize the criteria by sector and weight the priorities of the criteria by sector weights to generate composite weighted criteria that can be applied uniformly to candidate technologies, after the technologies have been prioritized by criteria. A centralized technology evaluation organization would find this approach attractive from an administrative point of view and in the preparation of suitable guidelines.

To generate the criteria weights by sector, we pose, as before, a series of questions of the following type: for agricultural technologies (or manufacturing technologies, and so on), what is the relative importance of "need," adaptability," "freedom from obsolescence risk," and "no undesirable second-order consequences"? This procedure entails pairwise comparison of each of the criteria with the others within a given sector.

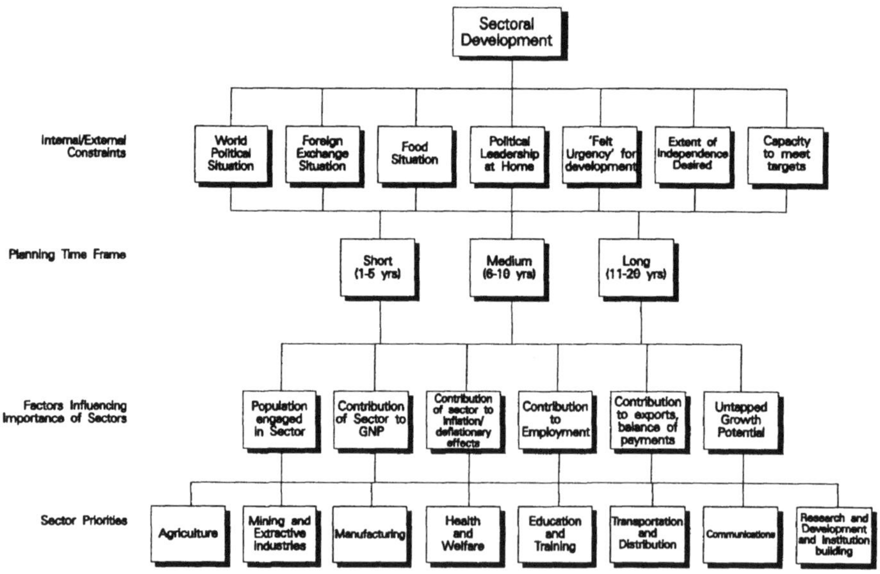

Figure 2. Backward Process Hierarchy in Technology Assessment

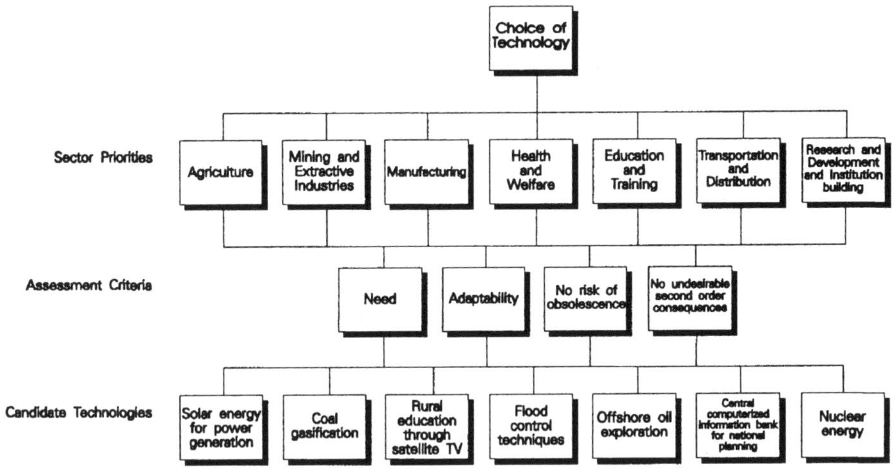

Figure 3. Technology Assessment Hierarchy

It is thus possible to do a preliminary screening of many candidate technologies on the basis of the four key criteria and the sector weights of the country. This would result in a subset of the original list of candidate technologies that can be taken up for more detailed analysis.

3. AN EXAMPLE: TECHNOLOGY TRANSFER USING THE AHP

In this example, which illustrates the approach described above, the sectoral priorities are taken as given and assumed to have been determined exogenously. In the context of a particular LDC, let us say the following are the sector priority weights:

Agriculture	0.25
Mining and extractive industries	0.08
Health	0.12
Industry	0.15
Education and training	0.12
Communications	0.15
Transportation and distribution	0.06
Research and development	0.07

Prioritizing the Assessment Criteria With Sectors

As already discussed, the assessment criteria do not play the same role in all the sectors. They are prioritized within each sector in pairwise comparison matrices:

AGRICULTURE

	(N)	(A)	(R)	(S)	Weight
Need (N)	1	1/3	7	5	0.292
Ease of Adaptability (A)	3	1	9	7	0.587
No Risk of Obsolescence (R)	1/7	1/9	1	1	0.056
No Undesirable Second-Order Consequences (S)	1/5	1/7	1	1	0.065

Consistency Index (C.I.) = 0.031

This matrix emphasizes that in the agricultural sector, the prime consideration for introducing an imported technology is adaptability. Risk of obsolescence and undesirable second-order consequences play relatively less important roles. These judgments, of course, are those of a particular analyst who provided the pairwise ratings shown in the matrix. Typically the entries of the matrix would be obtained after considerable debate and ultimate convergence by consensus among the members concerned.

MINING AND EXTRACTIVE INDUSTRIES

	N	A	R	S	Weight
N	1	3	3	1	0.395
A	1/3	1	1	1/3	0.132
R	1/3	1	1	1	0.173
S	1	3	1	1	0.300

C.I. = 0.052

In the mining sector, in contrast to agriculture, need for the particular technology is felt to be the dominant criterion. "No undesirable second-order consequences" ranks second. Adaptability and risk of obsolescence are relatively less important, presumably owing to the state of development of this sector in the particular LDC.

HEALTH

	N	A	R	S	Weight
N	1	1	3	7	0.402
A	1	1	3	7	0.402
R	1/3	1/3	1	3	0.143
S	1/7	1/7	1/3	1	0.057

C.I. = 0.002

The health needs of LDCs are widely different from those of the more advanced nations. Hence need and adaptability dominate here.

INDUSTRY

	N	A	R	S	Weights
N	1	1/3	1	1/3	0.132
A	3	1	3	1	0.395
R	1	1/3	1	1	0.173
S	3	1	1	1	0.300

C.I. = 0.050

The high weight assigned to adaptability and second-order consequences is self-explanatory in this sector. Whereas in agriculture the problem of adaptability may be related to the ability or willingness to adapt, in manufacturing there may be infrastructural barriers to adaptation, such as lack of skilled manpower, local suppliers of spare parts, repair facilities, and the like. The size of the market might dictate scaled-down plants, which could create operating problems.

EDUCATION AND TRAINING

	N	A	R	S	Weight
N	1	5	9	3	0.587
A	1/5	1	5	1	0.172
R	1/9	1/5	1	1/5	0.044
S	1/3	1	5	1	0.196

C.I. = 0.033

The need for the particular type of educational technology is important, but education that raises levels of aspiration can be dysfunctional if there are no simultaneous increases in available opportunities. Hence a high score is obtained on undesirable consequences of rapid education.

COMMUNICATIONS

	N	A	R	S	Weight
N	1	5	1/5	1	0.169
A	1/5	1	1/7	1	0.047
R	5	7	1	5	0.615
S	1	1	1/5	1	0.169

C.I. = 0.070

Modern communications technologies are characterized by high obsolescence risk. LDC concern with obsolescence risk is reflected by the high weight attached to that factor in this sector. Criteria weights in the remaining sectors are obtained similarly.

TRANSPORTATION AND DISTRIBUTION

	N	A	R	S	Weight
N	1	1/3	1/5	1	0.096
A	3	1	1/3	3	0.249
R	5	3	1	5	0.558
S	1	1/3	1/5	1	0.096
					C.I. = 0.020

R&D AND INSTITUTION BUILDING

	N	A	R	S	Weight
N	1	5	1	3	0.397
A	1/5	1	1/5	1	0.090
R	1	5	1	3	0.397
S	1/3	1	1/3	1	0.116
					C.I. = 0.010

Now these sector-based criteria weights are adjusted by the sector priorities to get the overall criteria weights for the particular LDC:

Need 0.302
Ease of adaptability 0.314
No risk of obsolescence 0.230
No undesirable second-order consequences 0.154

ASSESSMENT OF CANDIDATE TECHNOLOGIES

It is now possible to apply these overall weights to candidate technologies. Let us assume that this LDC is considering adapting the following seven candidate technologies (all "mass" technologies, some of which have direct and potential impacts in many sectors):

1. Solar energy development (SOL) for rural power and irrigation;
2. Coal gasification plants (CG) to utilize an abundantly available natural mineral resource;
3. Satellite television for extending primary and secondary education to the rural areas (RUR);
4. Flood control techniques (FC) to avoid massive national losses due to floods;
5. Offshore oil exploration (OIL) to minimize dependence on foreign oil;
6. A computerized national information bank (COMP) to facilitate national and state-level planning;
7. Nuclear energy (NUCL) for electricity generation.

These technologies are now compared to each other with respect to each of the assessment criteria. Application of the pairwise comparison procedure yields the following weights with regard to *need* for the different candidate technologies:

NEED

	SOL	CG	RUR	FC	OIL	COMP	NUCL
Weight:	.112	.027	.341	.179	.258	.058	.024

C.I. = 0.18

In the opinion of the analyst who provided the judgments in this matrix, rural education (a long-term, low-risk project) and oil exploration (a short-to-medium term, high-risk project) are the major national needs. Flood control and solar energy are believed to be the next most important technologies from the point of view of addressing national needs most directly. The consistency index of 0.18 is rather high, even for a 7×7 judgment matrix. To some extent this happens because of the broad types of comparison involved. In real life, one would be more specific by clustering technologies so that they are more comparable.

Next, with respect to *ease of adaptability*, the relative standing of the candidate technologies is as follows:

EASE OF ADAPTABILITY

	SOL	CG	RUR	FC	OIL	COMP	NUCL
Weight:	.381	.054	.263	.158	.034	.021	.090

C.I. = 0.13

Solar energy technology is believed by the analyst to be most easily adaptable, followed by rural education through satellite television, and then by flood control. Nuclear energy, being more automated, scores higher on adaptability, whereas the need for trained and skilled personnel is higher for both coal gasification and oil exploration technologies, which makes them more difficult to adapt.

With respect to no risk of obsolescence, the relative standing of the candidate technologies is as follows:

NO RISK OF OBSOLECENCE

	SOL	CG	RUR	FC	OIL	COMP	NUCL
Weight:	.155	.030	.135	.357	.058	.097	.168

C.I. = 0.20

Finally, the criterion of *no undesirable second-order consequences* led to the following prioritization:

NO UNDESIRABLE 2ND ORDER CONSEQUENCES

	SOL	CG	RUR	FC	OIL	COMP	NUCL
Weight:	.457	.043	.172	.167	.043	.099	.018

C.I. = 0.11

The weights obtained for each technology under each criterion are then weighted by the criteria weights and summed to get the overall technology weights:

Solar energy 0.259
Coal gasification 0.039
Rural education 0.243
Flood control 0.211
Oil exploration 0.109
Computerized information bank 0.062
Nuclear energy 0.077

The overall weighted priorities suggest that solar energy should receive maximum emphasis, followed by satellite television, flood control, oil exploration, nuclear energy, computerized information bank, and coal gasification, in that order. The high weight for solar energy is principally due to the high weight it obtains with respect to ease of adaptability to a rural economy and the absence of any conceivable second-order consequences associated with this technology.

Despite the high need for satellite television for rural education, it is perceived by the analyst to be a potentially dysfunctional technology in the sense of distracting the masses rather than really educating them. Similarly the high need score for oil exploration is counterbalanced by problems in adapting the technology to local situations, obsolescence risk, and possible second-order consequences like pollution of the coastal area. Nuclear energy gains on account of its relatively easy adaptability and the fact that the technology is a rather stable one less prone to obsolescence.

It is clear from this example that the AHP permits quantification of the relative priorities of various technological options. The rankings obtained here reflect the values, opinions, and judgments of a particular rater. But if the prioritization is done in a group setting, then debate can be generated and judgments made on the basis of consensus. The purpose of the example is to illustrate the application of the AHP rather than to suggest any particular prioritization of technologies for any particular LDC.

After the potentially most useful or desirable technologies are identified on the basis of the four key criteria, conventional approaches such as cost/benefit analysis can then be used to select from among the candidate technologies.

Figure 4 suggests a cost/benefit approach using the AHP. We construct separate cost and benefit hierarchies and use the final cost and benefit weights to derive cost/benefit ratios for the technologies under consideration. Thus we obtain an ordering of the technologies in terms of their cost/benefit ratios.

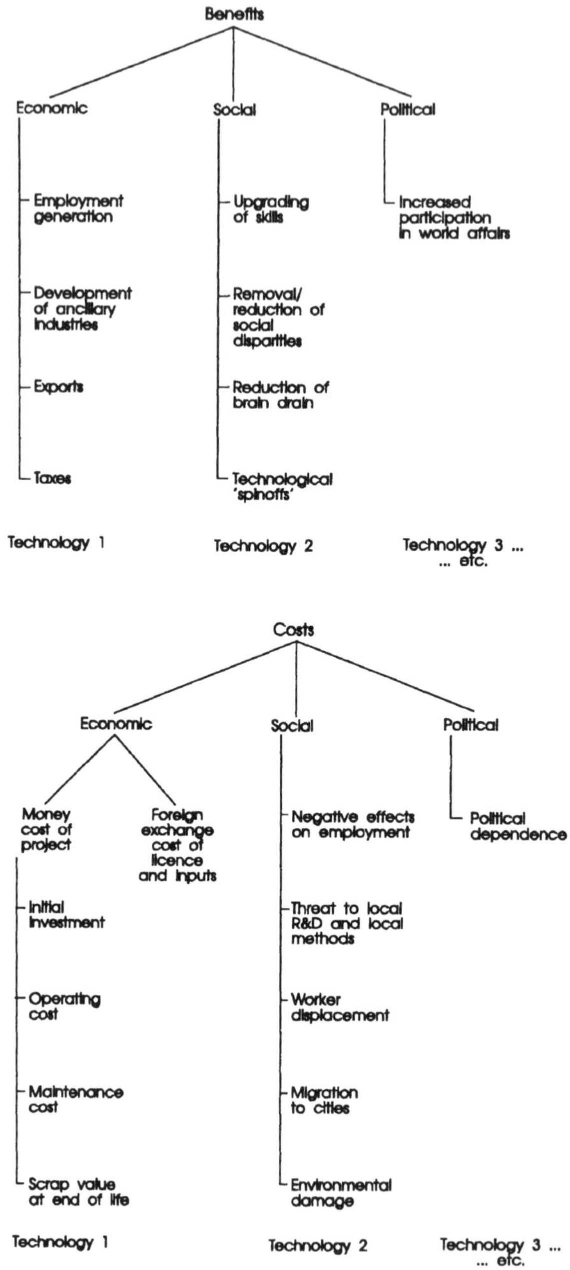

Figure 4. Benefits and Costs Hierarchies

REFERENCES

1. Denison, E.F., "Accounting for United States Economic Growth, 1929-1969," *Brookings Institution*, Washington, D.C., 1974.
2. Emshoff, J.R. and T.L. Saaty, "Applications of the Analytic Hierarchy Process to Long Range Planning Processes", *European Journal of Operational Research* 10, 2 (1982) 131-143.
3. Grilliches, Z., "Hybrid Corn and the Economics of Innovation", *Science* 29 (1960) 275-280.
4. Jones, G., "The Role of Science and Technology in Developing Countries," *Oxford University Press,* Oxford, 1971.
5. Kimenta, J., "Economic Theory and Transfer of Technology", In: D.L. Spenser and A. Woroniak, eds., The Transfer of Technology to Developing Countries, Praeger, New York, 1967.
6. Mansfield, E.I., , "Technical Change and the Rate of Imitation", Econometrika 29 (1961) 741-66.
7. Organization for Economic Cooperation and Development (OECD), *Analytical Methods in Government Science Policy*, Paris, 1972.
8. Ramanujam, V. and T.L. Saaty, "Technological Choices in Less Developed Countries," *Technological Forecasting and Social Choice* 19 (1981) 81-98.
9. Rogers, E.M., *The Diffusion of Innovations*, Free Press, New York, 1962.
10. Rosenberg, N., *Technological Change and Economic Growth*, Harper & Row, New York, 1972.
11. Saaty, T.L. and L.G. Vargas, "Estimating Technological Coefficients by the Analytic Hierarchy Process", *Socioeconomic Planning Sciences* 13 (1979) 333-336.
12. Schumacher, E.F., *Small is Beautiful*, Harper & Row, New York, 1975.
13. Solo, R.A. and E.M. Rogers, eds., *Inducing Technological Change for Economic Growth and Development*, Michigan State University Press, East Lansing, 1971.
14. Solow, R.M., "Technical Change and the Aggregate Production Function", *Review of Economics and Statistics* 39 (1957) 312-320.
15. Spencer, D.L. and A. Woroniak, eds., *The Transfer of Technology to Developing Countries*, Praeger, New York, 1967.
16. Vernon, R., "International Investment and International Trade in the Product Life Cycle", *Quarterly Journal of Economics* 80 (1966) 190-207.

CHAPTER 9

MARKET ATTRACTIVENESS OF DEVELOPING COUNTRIES

1. INTRODUCTION

Companies operating in international markets need to evaluate the potential market attractiveness of developing countries with which they may want to do business. These companies have access to substantial amounts of information from specialized sources and from statistical data supplied by international institutions. Such vast and diverse information is rarely used in a systematic way in the management decision process. When it is used, the entire process is most often inadequately formalized. The available information generally deals with economic factors, while in the present international arena, judgment about politics must also be taken into account. This chapter illustrates the applicability and advantages of the Analytic Hierarchy Process to this decision problem, and uses it to create maps of joint economic progress and political stability in a number of countries for two time periods 1990-1991 and 1995-1997.

A salient business phenomenon in the past ten years has been the "globalization" of economic and industrial activity. Production is spreading throughout the world in pursuit of economic and labor advantages. These advantages offer greater flexibility in maintaining quality, lowering costs and improving competitiveness. In addition, the type of government running a country and its political outlook affect the internal administration and the international image of that country which could encourage or deter companies from seeking business there.

Companies operating in the international environment, who analyze the market of developing countries to determine their own actions, often only consider specific factors such as the supply of raw materials, infrastructure requirements, demand on the goods, and the exploitation of attractive production factors. Nowadays they must consider the international situation as a macroenvironment in which economic, financial and political factors create new conditions. These conditions, directly and indirectly, could represent threats or opportunities to business. The need for a thorough analysis of the macroenvironment is stressed in the Strategic Management literature which is growing in importance with its own approaches. Such names as "External Audit" and "External Factor Evaluation" [2] are being used to classify the environment. To model the discontinuity in the present situation, the scenario approach has been used [7].

The authors' company, Iritecna, has manufacturing activities in the general engineering industry which include steel and non-ferrous metallurgy, logistic activities for industrial plants and transport systems, and various involvements in public utility infrastructures. It has locations in Latin America, North Africa, Eastern Europe, the Middle and Far East. Its relationship to the world market is not a simple transaction oriented buying-selling relationship. Rather, the relationship with partners places emphasis on: 1) the quantity of money involved (about $1,000,000 U.S.) and the significance of the length of a contract (preferably more than one year); 2) the complexity of the rules of payment; and 3) the presence of the company as a shareholder in some business activity.

The broad spectrum of industry segments in which the company operates as well as its close involvement with the host country required by the particular way of doing each type of business has suggested to the Planning Department the need for an ongoing activity to monitor prevalent political and economic-financial trends in the countries where it operates. In order of decreasing importance, the goals of this undertaking are to create a process through a study and resulting report that:

- incorporates and correctly addresses the use of information, standard scale data, ratings, and subjective judgments arising from different sources,
- supports and enhances the process of resource allocation for promotional and commercial purposes,
- suggests new opportunities not well perceived by the company because of its strong involvement in existing business activities,
- develops a final report containing a graded map with (cartographic) characteristics, a kind of tactical board which portrays activity countries positioned according to their socio-economic and political movements that influence the macro-factors,
- makes possible learning about the future of the macroenvironment in which the company operates,
- stimulates team discussion about the problem of where to go and when to go, and utilizes expert knowledge and judgment for that purpose.

The last three goals clarify the intention to start a "macroenvironment modelling activity" that enables involvement and utilization of the creativity and judgment of both analysts and managers. Reports usually do not conform with an ongoing modelling process, but must be examined item by item. The specialized literature [2] suggests the use of weighted scoring methods to summarize and evaluate information relating to "macroenvironmental analysis." Multicriteria methodologies such as Electre [9] specify a process to scale data and evaluate a final alternative to follow for each decision. But these methods do not satisfy the need for a flexible framework to represent an ongoing process of decision making. Multivariate statistical methods, used as geometric representations supporting Multiple Criteria Decision Making processes [3], were tested. It was difficult to interpret the final outcome as a map of the environment because of its dependence on the measurable statistical properties of the data rather than on the perception of the problem with its social and political ramifications as they apply to each country.

The AHP [11] appeared to be well suited mainly for the richness of its frame (hierarchical arrangement of the factors) which permits one to give evidence of how the problem is perceived. It also allows for the use of intangible factors side by side with tangible ones. It uses a simple procedure of paired comparisons to elicit judgments from which it derives ratio scales. It then combines these ratio scales to derive an overall ratio scale for the decision. Guided by a number of applications of the AHP in the socio-economic planning field, it was decided to use it in making this type of decision to: a) structure and map the problem in the economic and political dimensions; b) interpret and use the results for decision purposes.

2. REPRESENTATION OF THE PROBLEM

The market attractiveness of a country is perceived to be related to two sets of factors deriving from two points of view: economic and financial, and political. Explicit mention of politics stems from the need for specifying factors that are in general included but not completely measured, by some of the financial indicators of risk. The economic-financial factors considered here are:

a) *Growth rate of Gross Domestic Product (GDP),* to give evidence about the economic forces of the country.

b) *GDP per Person*, to monitor the present richness of the country. The assumption "per" person is a cover up for concentrated isles of richness in a developing country.

c) *Inflation rate*, is an indicator of stability in managing exchange rate leverage and of potential future development.

d) *Current account over GDP*, is an indicator of a country's proneness to invest.

e) *Risk of direct investment*, is a way to monitor the credit worthiness of a country.

The political factors are:

f) *Turmoil*, relating to the level of sociopolitical conflict within the country.

g) *Strategic Relevance*, is an indicator of a country's geographic and historical importance.

Following the AHP approach, this portion of the problem is modelled as shown in the top portion of Figure 1. Two important comments need to be made regarding the structure of the model.

First, the "economic-financial" node of the first level could be further subdivided into "economic" and "financial" and placed at the second level of the hierarchy. The five factors described above would then be positioned in the third level of the hierarchy and linked to the parent node to which they belong.

Second, the "strategic relevance" node could be decomposed into four sibling nodes; underground resources, geographic position, historical importance, and power sharing.

These nodes have not been included in the present version because our aim has been to remain "simple" and relevant. We would also have encountered the difficulty of finding more specific data on them.

The third level of the model contains rating intensities by which the second level criteria are measured: High, Medium High, Medium, Medium Low, and Low.

Where quantitative information is available, a relationship between rating intensities and measurement data is used to make the evaluation (See Table 1). All evaluations are ordered to give less desirable traits a lower rating. For example, heavy turmoil, significant inflation and considerable risk for investment are all given low ratings.

A country is evaluated for its "performance" with respect to each second level criterion using the most appropriate rating grade to describe it. These results are weighted and combined to yield weights with respect to the two major criteria. A map of market potential displaying the synthesized results is the output sought.

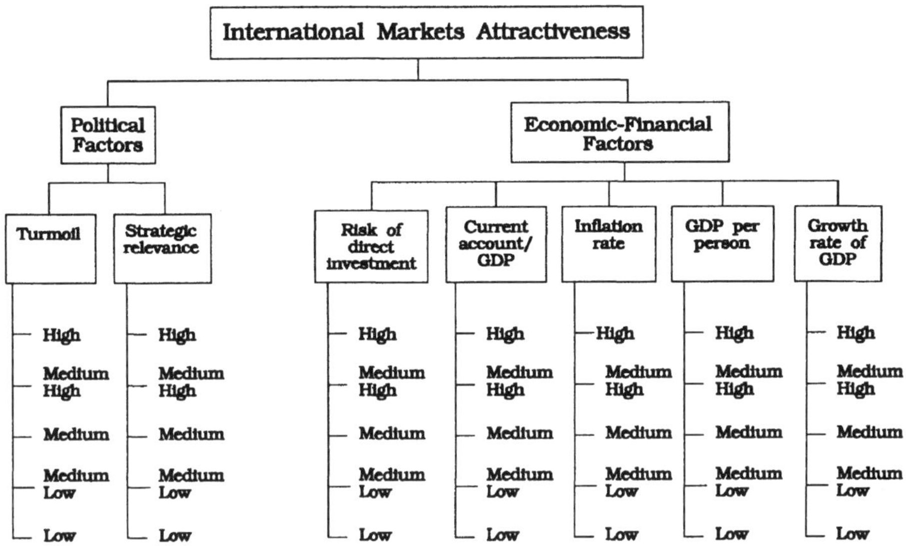

Figure 1. Hierarchical Structure

3. PRIORITIES

The AHP methodology requires priorities for each level of criteria and for each rating intensity. These priorities are always determined in terms of their parent node in the hierarchy. Relative value is derived from pairwise comparisons. Judgments can be made directly with numerical scales or with a semantic scale translated to numbers. For example, within the "Political" factors, the "Turmoil" subcriterion is strongly more important than "Strategic relevance" (scale value 5). This strength of dominance is assigned for two reasons.

Table 1. Relation Between Rating Grades and Measurement Data

SUB-CRITERIA	HIGH	MEDIUM-HIGH	MEDIUM	MEDIUM-LOW	LOW
Turmoil	Consolidated and stable democracy or stable dictatorship. Absence of social tension.	Democracy not fully consolidated or dictatorship with initial signs of opposition and of social tension.	Very recent democracy with political power not consolidated. Spreading social conflict.	Strong opposition outside the democratic process. Presence of guerillas. Bad social conditions.	Political anarchy and ugly social conditions.
Strategic Performance	Richness of raw materials. Key role for power sharing in the area. Bridge between two different areas. Historical relevance in the area.		Presence of some raw materials. Partnership in regional alliances. Active role in international negotiation processes.		Absence of raw materials. Marginal role (political, ideological and historical) in the area.
Risk of Direct Investment	Time reference 1990-1991: (ref. Institutional Investors) in the top list of Credit Country ratings 1991. Time reference 1995-1997: (ref. Planning Review) Risk Rating for direct investment A+, A	Time reference 1995-1997: (ref. Planning Review) Risk Rating of direct Investment A-, B+, B	Time reference 1990-1991: (ref. Institutional Investors) In median position of the list of Credit Country rating 1991. Time reference 1995-1997: (ref. Planning Review) Risk rating for direct investment B-, C+, C	Time reference 1995-1997: (ref. Planning Review) Risk Rating for direct investment C-, D+	Time reference 1990-1991: (ref. Institutional Investors) At the bottom of the list of Credit Country rating 1991. Time reference 1995-1997: (ref. Planning Review) Risk for direct investment D, D-
Current Account/GDP	> 3%	3% > > 1%	1% > > 0%	0% > > -2%	-2% >
Inflation Rate	< 2%	2% < < 4%	4% < < 7%	7% < < 10%	10% <
GDP per capita	> 5000$	5000$ > > 3000$	3000$ > > 1500$	1500$ > > 500$	500$ >
Growth rate of GDP	> 4%	4% > > 3%	3% > > 2%	2% > > 1%	1% >

First present conditions are more relevant and pressing than long term and uncertain evidence, and secondly, for "Turmoil" there is a significant amount of information supplied by the specialized press and/or ratings institutes, while the importance of "Strategic relevance" requires expert knowledge.

Evaluation of the elements under "Economic and financial" factors appears in Table 2.

The resulting priorities show that:

- "Risk of Direct Investment" and "GDP Growth" are equally important and together these two criteria dominate the remaining criteria.
- "Inflation Rate" and "GDP per Person" are next in priority and are significantly less important than the previous two.
- "Balance Account/GDP" has the lowest priority.

These results mean that in order for a country to be attractive it should be in the expansion phase and present low risk.

The AHP proved useful in creating intensity ratings for the next stage because for most of the criteria there were no data for rating the alternatives and one had to resort to the use of judgments. The resulting priorities are related to the relevance given to the scale. For example, "Risk of Direct Investment" had no economic indicator to evaluate the countries. Therefore, we had to create a scale of relative intensities for the criteria and then used that to rate the countries. Here we did not have the means to conduct and combine diverse analyses and to produce a numerical outcome to be used in the model.

The pairwise comparison matrices for the five rating grades under each second level criterion appear in Tables 3a-g. The local priorities represent the relative importance of a particular rating with respect to the parent criterion. It should be noted that the differences in priorities decrease as one moves from the two highest rating grades (High and Medium High) to the two lowest ones (Medium Low and Low) for nearly all seven second level criteria. Exceptions are "Risk of Direct Investment" and "Inflation Rate" for which it appears more correct that there should be significant change from Medium High to Medium.

Two axes were chosen to represent "Political" and "Economic and Financial" criteria. The five rating intensities are positioned along each axis in increasing priority order. In synthesizing the local priorities established above, the rating scales can be grouped into four segments with respect to each of the two major criteria (see Table 4). The result is that the intersection of the two groupings leads to a division of each segment of one into four subsegments.

Table 2. Pairwise Comparison Matrix Components of the Financial Economic Criteria

	Risk of Direct Investment	Current Account / GDP	Inflation rate	GDP per person	Growth rate of GDP	priorities
Risk of Direct Investment	1	6	3	3	1	0.353
Current Account/ GDP		1	1/2	1/1	1/6	0.058
Inflation Rate			1	1	1/3	0.118
GDP pro capite				1	1/3	0.118
Growth rate of GDP					1	0.353

Table 3-a. Pairwise Comparison Matrix for the Rating Grades of "Turmoil"

	HIGH	MEDIUM HIGH	MEDIUM	MEDIUM LOW	LOW	priorities
HIGH	1	1.5	3	5	7	0.429
MEDIUM-HIGH		1	1.5	3	5	0.268
MEDIUM			1	1.5	3	0.156
MEDIUM-LOW				1	1.5	0.091
LOW					1	0.057

Table 3-b. Pairwise Comparison Matrix for the Rating Grades of "Strategic Relevance"

	HIGH	MEDIUM HIGH	MEDIUM	MEDIUM LOW	LOW	priorities
HIGH	1	1.5	3	5	7	0.429
MEDIUM-HIGH		1	1.5	3	5	0.268
MEDIUM			1	1.5	3	0.156
MEDIUM-LOW				1	1.5	0.091
LOW					1	0.057

Table 3-c. Pairwise Comparison Matrix for the Rating Grades of "Risk of Direct Investment"

	HIGH	MEDIUM HIGH	MEDIUM	MEDIUM LOW	LOW	priorities
HIGH	1	1.5	3	5	9	0.409
MEDIUM-HIGH		1	1.8	4	9	0.295
MEDIUM			1	2.5	7	0.117
MEDIUM-LOW				1	5	0.09
LOW					1	0.029

Table 3-d. Pairwise Comparison Matrix for the Rating Grades of "Balance Account/GDP"

	> 3% H	3% > > 1% M H	1% > > 0% M	0% > > -2% M L	-2% > L	priorities
> 3% H	1	2	4	7	9	0.460
3% > > 1% M H		1	3	5	8	0.299
1% > > 0% M			1	3	6	0.144
0% > > -2% M L				1	3	0.065
-2% > L					1	0.032

Table 3-e. Pairwise Comparison Matrix for the Rating Grades of "Inflation Rate"

	< 2% H	2% < < 4% M H	4% < < 7% M	7% < < 10% M L	10% < L	priorities
< 2% H	1	1.5	3	6	9	0.409
2% < < 4% M H		1	3	5	7	0.324
4% < < 7% M			1	3	6	0.159
7% < < 10% M L				1	4	0.076
10% < L					1	0.033

Table 3-f. Pairwise Comparison Matrix for the Rating Grades of "GDP per person"

	> 5000$ H	5000$ > > 3000 M H	3000$ > > 1500 M	1500$ > > 500% M L	500$ > L	priorities
> 5000$ H	1	2	4	7	9	0.460
5000$ > > 3000 M H		1	3	5	8	0.299
3000$ > > 1500 M			1	3	6	0.144
1500$ > > 500 M L				1	3	0.065
500$ > L					1	0.032

Table 3-g. Pairwise Comparison Matrix for the Rating Grades of "Growth Rate of GDP"

	> 4% H	4% > > 3% M H	3% > > 2% M	2% > > 1% M L	1% > L	priorities
> 4% H	1	1.5	2.5	5	9	0.460
4% > > 3% M H		1	1.5	3	9	0.299
3% > > 2% M			1	2	7	0.144
2% > > 1% M L				1	7	0.065
1% > L					1	0.032

Table 4. Basic Map for Countries Positioning

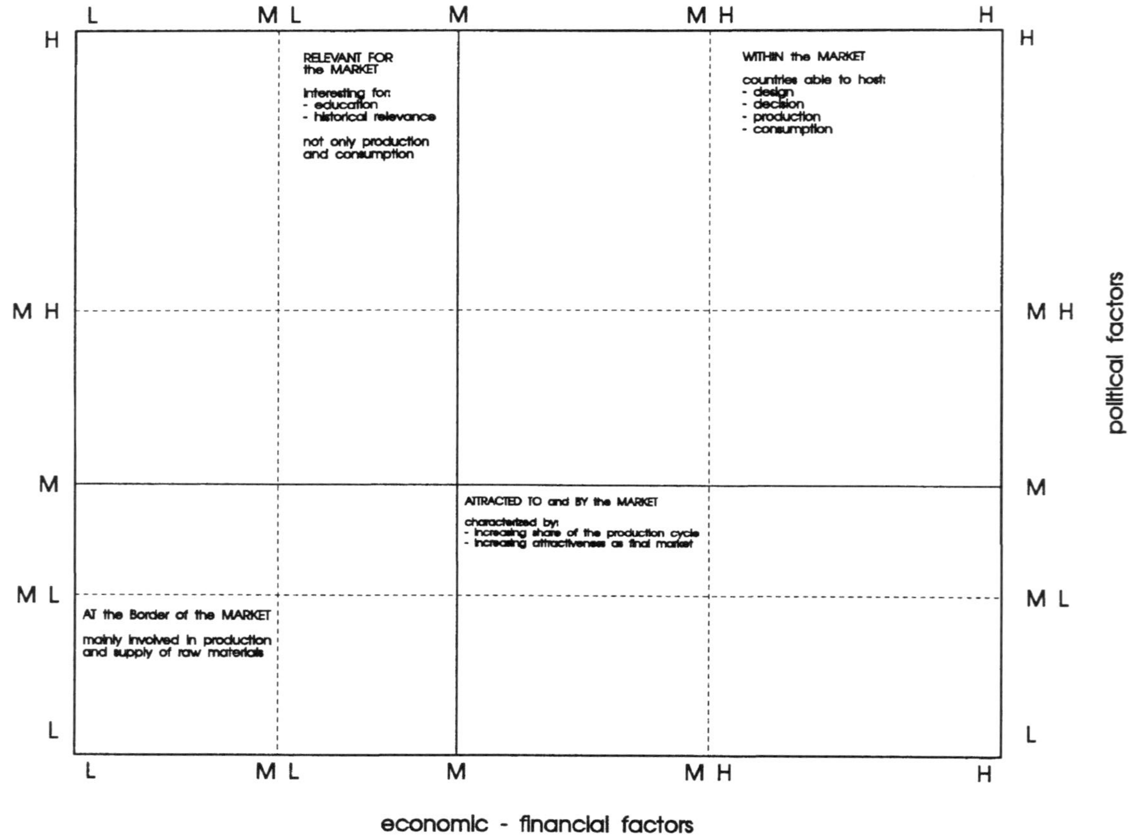

Each of the segments and subsegments has a unique size. Here the AHP analysis offers a different approach than the commonly used procedure called the Boston Consulting Group matrix representation. Segment uniqueness is a feature provided by the AHP to more accurately set the values of the five rating intensities which is not possible in other methods known to us. Table 4 portrays an interpretation of the four major segments in terms of overall market attractiveness.

4. COUNTRY RATINGS

Countries examined in the study fall in six geographical regions:

- Latin America
- Mediterranean Africa
- Middle East
- Eastern Europe
- Indian Subcontinent, and
- Far East

For historical reasons, the first four regions represent the reference market for Italian companies exporting industrial plants and infrastructures. The last two are included because in the last decade they have come to represent growing opportunities for Italian exports. There are also other reasons than historical ones that necessitate tracing countries according to recent trends, to attract some of them into influence zones, whose leaders are:

- U.S.A.;
- E.E.C.;
- Japan.

The countries included in this analysis (see Table 5) are the more important ones in each region. They belong to the well known category of Developing or Newly Industrialized Countries. Some relevant countries which one might expect to find in Table 10.5, are missing mostly because of lack of complete data and/or because they are in the process of splitting into sovereign states. South Africa and Nigeria, which do not belong to the geographical regions mentioned above, are included for their relevance to Italian companies. The country list reflects the fact that the company originating the study is based in Italy and is dependent on its government's political and cultural relationship with other nations. Had the company been French instead of Italian, the list could have been different, including some countries in Central Africa.

The model evaluates each country under each of the seven second level criteria. The evaluation is made by assigning the most appropriate rating intensity to a country's "performance" in each of the "performance" categories. The most appropriate rating intensity is determined by the best available quantitative and qualitative information. The study considers two time reference periods: 1990 to 1991 and 1995 to 1997.

The sources of financial and economic information for each of the reference periods are the following:

Period 1990-1991

- "Risk of Direct Investment" is based on rating data [1];
- "Current Account/GDP" is based on data from the "World Bank Annual Report";
- "Inflation Rate" is based on the annual report on risk forecast published by Planning Review;
- "GDP per Person" was derived using data relating GDP and Population [12];
- "GDP Growth" is based on data from the annual report of Planning Review.

Period 1995-1997

- "Risk of Direct Investment" is based on rating data of the annual report of Planning Review;
- "Current Account/GDP" is derived from the annual report of Planning Review (Current Account) and on World Bank Report data (forecast of GDP value);
- "Inflation Rate" is based on the annual report on risk forecast published by Planning Review;
- "GDP per Person" was derived using data relating GDP and Population of the World Bank Annual Report;
- "GDP Growth" is based on data of the annual report of Planning Review.

For the two reference periods, the country ratings for the two subcriteria of the political criterion are based on the annual report of Planning Review for "Turmoil" and on subjective judgments for "Strategic Relevance".

5. POSITIONS OF COUNTRIES

Based on the rating data of the countries, a market attractiveness map is developed in Table 4. The priority distribution of countries for the 1990-1991 time period appears in Table 7. Table 8 represents the change in priorities of the countries from the first to the second time period according to region. Table 9 shows the priority distribution of the countries for the 1995-1997 time period. The final maps suggest the following ideas:

- Most countries fall along a diagonal starting from the lowest point (L-L) to the highest one (H-H) on both main criteria. This indicates that there is a possible correlation between the economic-financial and the political factors;

- The highest subquadrant (MH-MH, H-H) contains the Far Eastern Countries. The accuracy of this outcome is commonly supported by reports made in literature specializing in political and economic trends [6]. The Far East could be the one area in which newcomer countries are entering in a continental area market. This fact is perceived by commentators to be one of the major competitive advantages of Japan who is succeeding (where Europe and the USA have problems) in creating a market development area. The position of Malaysia and Hong Kong is worsening due to a decrease in their rating on Risk of Direct Investment. China is moving toward this subquadrant slowly but very significantly. Saudi Arabia is also included in this subquadrant, but its uniqueness (no other significant country of the area is as close a position on the map) indicates a possible long term instability.

Table 5. Country Ratings 1990-1991

Time reference 1990/91	POLITICAL FACTORS		ECONOMIC FINANCIAL FACTORS						
	Turmoil	Strategic relevance	Risk of direct investment	Current account / G.D.P.	Inflation rate	G.D.P. per person	Growth rate G.D.P.	Political evaluation	Economic financial evaluation
Local priorities	83%	17%	35%	8%	12%	12%	35%		
algeria	M	MH	M	L	L	M	M	40.8	35.8
argentina	M	M	M	ML	L	H	M	36.5	32.8
bangladesh	M	ML	L	L	M	L	L	33.8	11.0
bolivia	ML	L	L	L	L	ML	M	18.8	21.5
brazil	M	M	ML	M	L	M	L	36.5	16.8
bulgaria	M	L	L	ML	L	ML	L	32.4	8.8
chile	M	L	M	L	L	MH	H	32.8	57.8
china	MH	MH	MH	ML	ML	L	H	82.5	63.2
colombia	ML	ML	ML	M	L	ML	H	21.2	46.8
cuba	H	MH	L	ML	ML	ML	ML	93.8	17.0
ecuador	ML	ML	L	L	L	ML	ML	21.2	15.3
egypt	M	MH	ML	L	L	ML	H	40.8	45.2
hong kong	H	MH	H	ML	ML	H	H	93.8	85.1
hungary	M	M	MH	L	L	MH	L	36.5	36.1
india	M	M	MH	L	ML	L	H	36.5	62.7
indonesia	ML	M	MH	ML	ML	ML	H	23.7	64.1
iran	M	MH	ML	ML	ML	L	MH	40.8	34.8
iraq	ML	MH	M	ML	M	M	ML	28.1	30.1
malaysia	H	M	H	ML	MH	M	H	89.4	82.8
mexico	MH	M	M	L	L	MH	M	58.2	38.3
morocco	M	M	ML	L	M	ML	MH	36.5	37.7
nigeria	ML	M	L	ML	L	L	H	23.7	38.6
pakistan	ML	M	ML	L	ML	L	H	23.7	45.5
peru	ML	ML	L	MH	M	ML	L	21.2	15.8
philippines	ML	M	ML	L	ML	ML	H	23.7	46.4
poland	M	M	ML	L	L	M	L	36.5	15.4
russia	M	MH	M	ML	L	ML	L	40.8	21.3
saudi arabia	H	H	H	L	MH	H	MH	100.0	80.5
singapore	MH	M	H	H	MH	H	H	58.2	97.8
south africa	MH	H	M	MH	L	MH	ML	68.8	36.8
south korea	MH	MH	H	MH	M	H	H	82.5	90.7
syria	MH	MH	L	M	L	ML	H	82.5	41.8
taiwan	H	M	H	H	MH	H	H	89.4	97.8
thailand	M	MH	H	L	M	M	H	40.8	77.5
turkey	M	H	MH	M	L	M	H	47.1	65.8
venezuela	M	M	M	H	L	M	MH	36.5	48.3
vietnam	H	M	L	ML	L	L	MH	89.4	28.5

Table 6. Country Ratings 1995-1997

Time reference 1995/97	POLITICAL FACTORS		ECONOMIC FINANCIAL FACTORS						
	Turmoil	Strategic relevance	Risk of direct investment	Current account / G.D.P.	Inflation rate	G.D.P. per person	Growth rate G.D.P.	Political evaluation	Economic financial evaluation
Local priorities	83%	17%	35%	6%	12%	12%	35%		
algeria	ML	M	ML	L	L	M	H	23.7	47.1
argentina	M	M	M	ML	L	H	H	36.5	84.3
bangladesh	M	ML	L	L	M	L	ML	33.8	18.0
bolivia	ML	L	L	L	L	ML	M	19.8	21.5
brazil	M	M	ML	M	L	M	M	38.5	30.1
bulgaria	M	L	ML	ML	ML	ML	ML	32.8	22.1
chile	M	L	M	L	L	MH	H	32.8	57.8
china	MH	MH	MH	M	ML	L	H	82.5	84.3
colombia	ML	ML	L	M	L	ML	H	21.2	41.8
cuba	MH	M	ML	ML	M	ML	ML	58.2	24.5
ecuador	ML	ML	L	L	L	ML	M	21.2	21.5
egypt	M	M	L	ML	L	ML	M	38.5	21.9
hong kong	MH	H	MH	MH	ML	H	H	68.8	78.7
hungary	MH	ML	MH	MH	L	MH	M	55.8	53.0
india	M	MH	M	L	ML	L	H	40.8	52.8
indonesia	ML	M	M	ML	ML	ML	H	23.7	54.2
iran	M	MH	ML	M	L	ML	H	40.8	46.8
iraq	M	M	L	ML	L	M	ML	38.5	17.7
malaysia	H	M	MH	L	M	MH	H	89.4	71.4
mexico	MH	M	MH	L	L	MH	H	58.2	67.8
morocco	M	M	ML	L	M	ML	MH	38.5	37.7
nigeria	ML	M	L	M	L	L	MH	23.7	28.6
pakistan	ML	M	L	L	L	L	H	23.7	39.2
peru	ML	ML	L	L	L	ML	ML	21.2	15.3
philippines	ML	M	L	L	L	ML	MH	23.7	29.0
poland	M	M	M	ML	L	M	ML	36.5	30.1
russia	M	H	M	ML	L	ML	ML	47.1	28.3
saudi arabia	H	H	MH	L	M	H	H	100.0	77.3
singapore	H	M	H	MH	MH	H	H	89.4	95.3
south africa	M	H	L	M	L	MH	MH	47.1	35.9
south korea	MH	M	H	MH	ML	H	H	58.2	85.1
syria	MH	MH	L	M	L	ML	M	62.5	23.0
taiwan	H	M	H	H	MH	H	H	89.4	97.8
thailand	MH	MH	H	L	M	M	H	82.5	77.5
turkey	M	MH	MH	M	L	M	H	40.8	65.9
venezuela	M	M	M	H	L	MH	H	36.5	63.9
vietnam	H	M	L	ML	L	L	H	89.4	39.6

Table 7. Map - Reference Period 1990-1991

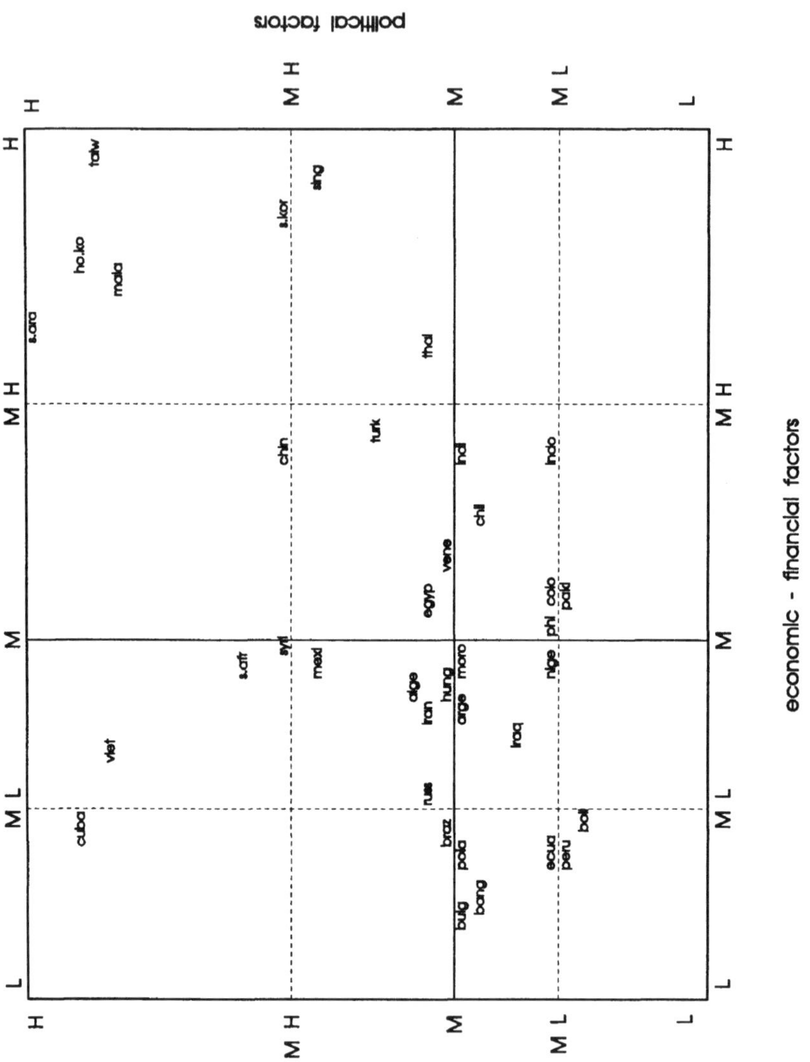

Table 8. Shifting in Countries Map Position Reference Time Period 1990-1991

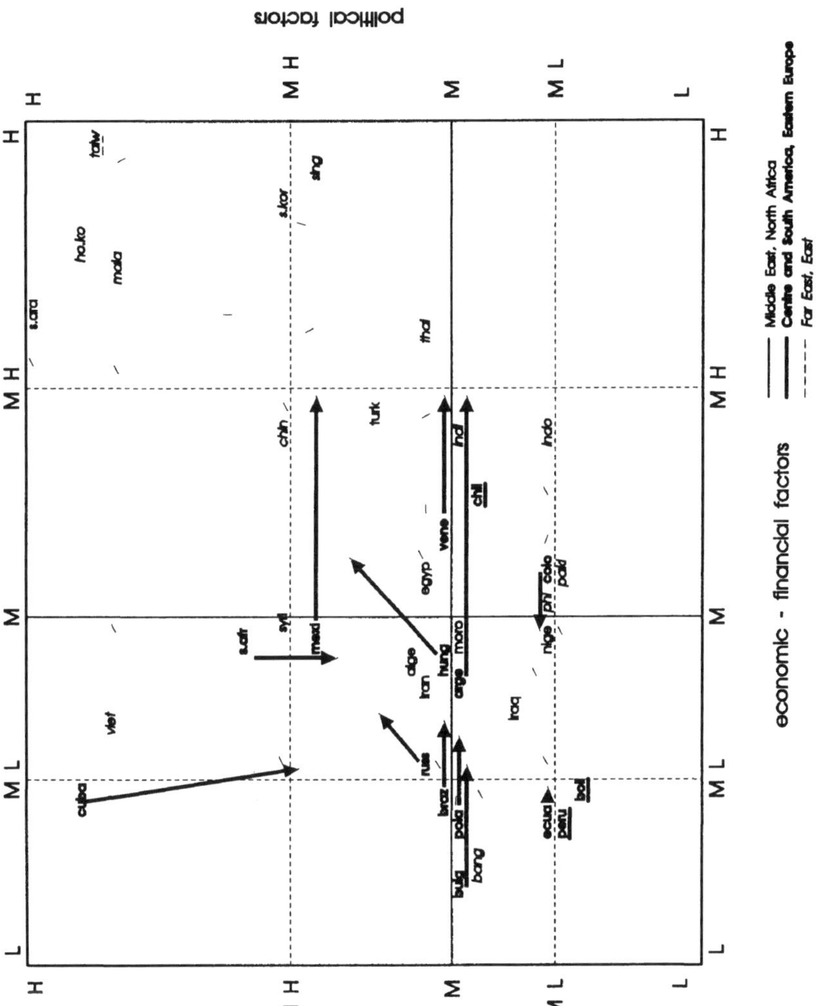

Table 9. Map - Reference Period 1995-1997

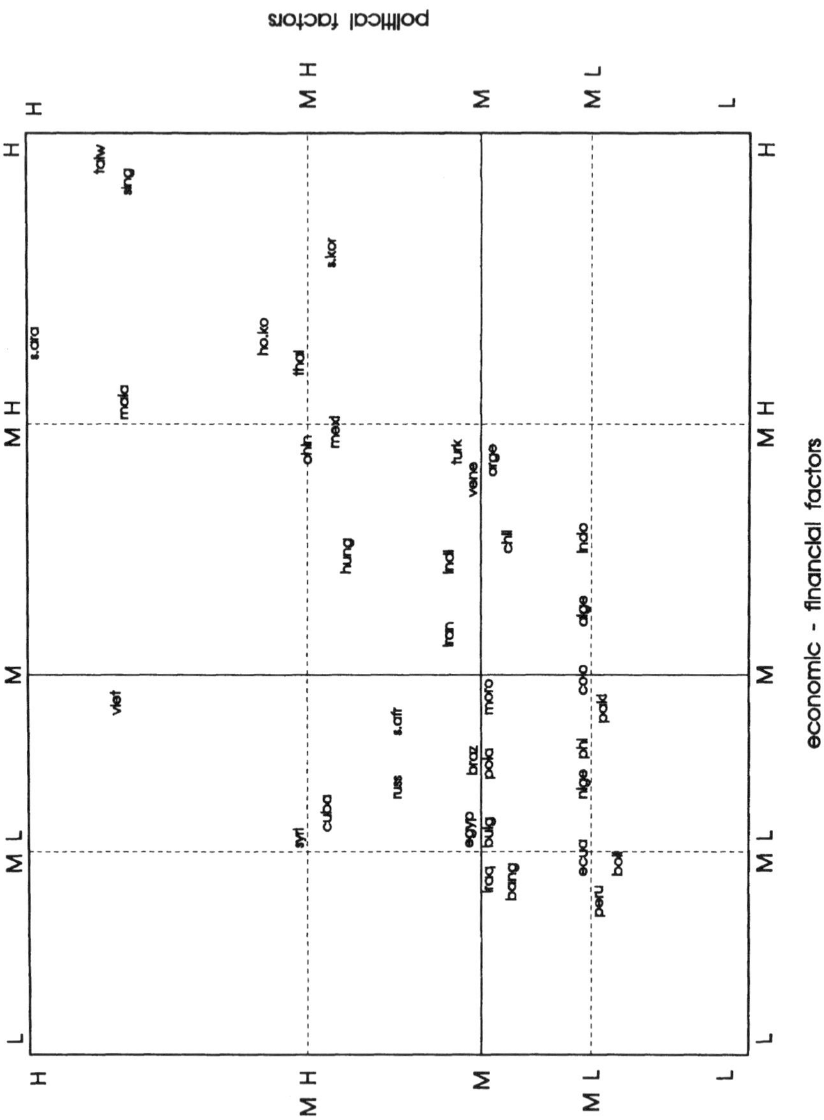

- In the second highest subquadrant (M-M, MH-MH), there are countries that appear to shift their position on the map between the two reference periods. Turkey, perceived to be an interesting newcomer [10], shows a stable economic-financial position. It is a country moving west by requesting EEC membership, and east toward the ex-USSR republics with Turkish languages. Hungary and Mexico are entering this subquadrant, both being close to other continental markets (the European and the North American). Mexico and other Latin American countries (notably Argentina) are also moving close to this subquadrant. This is an indication of significant movements in the American continent whose central core is NAFTA (North American Free Trade Agreement), represented in the literature [4] as a possible strategic initiative to counter the EEC. India is also moving to this subquadrant and is reported to be the western reference of the far eastern continental area market.

- To the left of the above mentioned subquadrants is the ML-M corner where one finds Russia and Poland. The position of Russia especially in the 1995-1997 reference frame is worthy of a short observation. It is positioned in that grouping in Table 4 because it is "relevant for the market for its educational and historical relevance - not just for production and consumption." It is interesting to note that the specialized press [5] has described Russia as "very attractive because high-tech companies could hire the best Russian experts at low cost in the fields of fiber optics, nuclear physics and satellite technology".

- At the top left side of the map one finds two countries, Cuba and Vietnam. These two countries are expected to have a transition phase with less political and economic troubles than Eastern Europe. Vietnam is considered by the specialized press [5] to be very interesting because of its skilled, disciplined and cheap labor force.

- Below the main diagonal there is a set of countries (Indonesia, Colombia, Pakistan, Philippines, Nigeria) that have a medium economic-financial position but a poor political position. Within this group there are two countries, Columbia and Pakistan, which because of drug trade and investment in the nuclear sector may become a serious cause of instability in the North-South relationship.

- At the end of the main diagonal there are three Latin American countries (Ecuador, Peru, Bolivia) which even without a negative environment in Latin America do not show clear signs of progress.

6. CONCLUSION

The observations made above on the countries' positions, show the effectiveness of the AHP in discriminating between different situations. But there also remain a number of countries in the center of the map that may need further separation, perhaps by expanding the second level criteria. Such work is in progress. It requires user interface modification of software implementation, combining the hierarchic composition and its resulting map. The decision maker is given the opportunity to add criteria, modify their weights and note the resulting map. This modification could allow a fine tuning of the model which would facilitate sensitivity analysis. Sensitivity analysis is particularly needed to deal with political change. It is believed that in the current environment, "Turmoil" is more important than "Strategic relevance". It seems important to explore changes in countries' positions by shifting emphasis from the present situation ("Turmoil") to the long term trend ("Strategic Relevance"). Similarly, by scrutinizing the economic-financial side of the model, it appears promising to assign higher priority to indicators of richness and to the competitive position (GDP per Person, Balance Account/GDP) to obtain greater resolution at the center of the map.

The outcome of this study has been well received within the company with interest being shown by managers through their participation. They began with the final map and worked backwards to the structure of the model making suggestions for further improvements. The map provides evidence for the validity of the impact of macroenvironmental changes on international business and it is a valid support for establishing a connection between scanning the macroenvironment and perceptions of strategic issues [8].

REFERENCES

1. "Credit Country Rating", *Institutional Investor*, 1991
2. David, R.F., *Concepts of Strategic Management*, Maxwell McMillan International Edition, 1991.
3. Marescal B. and J.P. Brans, "Geometrical representation for MCDM", *European Journal of Operational Research* 54, 6 (1991) October.
4. *Le Monde Diplomatique*, no. 486, March 1993.
5. *Le Monde Diplomatique*, no. 469, April 1993.
6. *Le Monde Diplomatique*, no. 169, April 1993.
7. aa.vv., Monografic issues on Scenarios, *Planning Review*, March-April, April June 1992.
8. Morecroft, J.D.W., "Executive Knowledge, Models and Learning", *European Journal of Operational Research* 56, 1 (1992) May.

9. Roy, B., "The Outranking Approach and the Foundations of Electre Methods", in Carlos A. Bana e Costa (ed.), *Readings in Multiple Criteria Decision Aid*, Springer-Verlag, 1990.
10. Rullani, E., "due problemi irrisolti per il capialsimo industriale negli anni novanta", *Economia e Politica Industriale* 74, 76 (1992).
11. Saaty, T.L., *Multicriteria Decision Making: The Analytic Hierarchy Process*, RWS Publications, 4922 Ellsworth Avenue, Pittsburgh, PA, 1990.
12. *World Bank Annual Report*, 1993.

CHAPTER 10

AN ANALYTIC HIERARCHY PROCESS BASED APPROACH TO THE DESIGN AND EVALUATION OF A MARKETING DRIVEN BUSINESS AND CORPORATE STRATEGY

1. INTRODUCTION

The dramatic changes in the business environment, as highlighted in Table 1, suggest that the old and proven ways of doing business may not suffice in assuring survival and growth in the 1990s and beyond. Heightened environmental uncertainty and complexity calls for increased attention to creativity in generating strategic directions for the firm, rigor in evaluating the strategic options on multiple and independent objectives, and vision and focus to assure effective utilization of resources. Most managers could greatly benefit from a framework and methodology which would allow them to accomplish these tasks while at the same time assuring that the strategy is driven by the critical *marketing considerations*. The Analytic Hierarchy Process (AHP) provides such a framework and methodology.

2. THE BUILDING BLOCKS OF STRATEGY

A marketing driven strategic business plan requires the generation, evaluation and choice of eight interrelated components:

(1) Mission

The mission should offer an explicit, visionary, and unique direction for the entire planning process. It offers a first cut at the determination of the business boundaries of the firm. It also serves to mobilize the firm to act and differentiate it from the others.

(2) Planning horizon

Planning should accommodate both the short- and long-term needs of the firm. Explicit tradeoffs between the two time horizons should be identified.

(3) Environmental scenarios

Planning should explicitly take into account the expected environment. A clear understanding of the environmental forces facing the firm would aid in generating creative strategic options for turning environmental threats into opportunities. Such scenarios could also provide the basis for the development of contingency plans. While the various environmental forces are often conveniently summarized into one of three scenarios, pessimistic, optimistic, and status quo, a detailed environmental analysis focusing on the market, competition, technology, and other environmental forces is essential if one wants to identify the key threats and opportunities facing the firm. This analysis of the environment can include the identification of likely external and internal problems that might prevent achieving the objectives of the strategic business unit (SBU) and the firm, key internal strengths and external opportunities facing the SBUs and the firm, complete competitive analysis encompassing all the critical success factors facing the firm, and the likely trend in the various external and internal forces, their key interdependencies and expected impact.

Table 1. The changing business environment

- More intensified and sophisticated competition (from domestic and international firms) and changes in the competitive environment due to the formation of strategic alliances.
- Revolutionary technological developments.
- Increased integration of customer and resource markets.
- Highly volatile economic conditions.
- Changing political/regulatory environment.
- Introduction of innovative marketing and distribution practices and organizations.
- Expanding internationalism of business.
- Changing and more sophisticated consumer markets.
- Heightened awareness of ethical/moral considerations.
- A climate of more litigations (product liability) leading to increased cost and risk of doing business and of introducing innovative new products.

(4) Objectives

It is imperative that management develop operational definitions of their objectives. The objective - whether it is a desired level of growth in profit and sales, a reduction in downside risk, or some other idiosyncratic management objective - should facilitate the accomplishment of the mission and provide the criteria for evaluating any strategic options.

(5) Criteria

The focus of any marketing driven strategy should be the target *market segments*. Since it is often difficult to directly evaluate the impact of market segments on the firm's objectives, an intermediate set of criteria is suggested. These criteria focus on: (a) the attractiveness of the market segment (a composite measure of market attractiveness including variables such as size, growth etc.), (b) the firm's strength in the segment (also a composite score which includes measures of the firm's competitive strengths such as technology, distribution, its market share etc.), and (c) synergy - a dimension recognizing the interdependency among activities which, if not included explicitly as part of the strength dimension, should be used as a separate dimension.

(6) Market/product portfolio

Identification of the current, potential, and desired market/product portfolio is the focal point of the planning process. The desired market/product portfolio includes current markets/products and new ones developed either internally or externally (via marketing and advertising). The market/product portfolio is the core marketing dimension of the process. It is this focus on the selection of a portfolio of market segments which differentiates a marketing driven from a non-marketing oriented business or corporate strategy. The portfolio of segments and their associated products define the business boundaries of the firm and to the extent that the firm employs a global perspective, it would also incorporate the portfolio of *countries* by mode of operation. This step often involves three interrelated processes: (a) identification of new market segments (for target product by country); (b) evaluation of the current and new segments on the criteria and objectives specified in points (4) and (5); and (c) the generation of and evaluation of a *portfolio* of products/segments which reflects portfolio considerations such as diversification versus focus or, in the international context, the desired levels of integration and coordination of product/segments across countries.

(7) Strategic options

Creative options should be generated to meet the needs of the market segments and offer the firm a unique competitive advantage. These options should identify the major leverage points the firm has (e.g. research and development, manufacturing, marketing, finance etc.) and the strategic thrust most likely to meet three interrelated criteria: (a) meeting the segment needs; (b) differentiating the firm from its competitors; and (c) accomplishing the firm's own objectives. The identification of strategic options should also include determining whether the strategy can be accomplished internally or requires a merger, acquisition, or other forms of strategic alliances. Since the generation and evaluation of strategic options is the primary outcome of any strategy process, it is especially important to assure that before making the final selection, the participating managers examine whether better strategies can be developed by increasing, reducing, eliminating, or adding activities (products, segments, countries, distribution systems etc.) or reallocating resources among the various options.

(8) Functional and resource requirements

Once the strategic options are identified, the functional requirements (from each operating department) for meeting the needs of the strategic options should be identified and evaluated.

3. AN AHP FORMULATION OF A MARKETING DRIVEN BUSINESS AND CORPORATE STRATEGY

The selected methodology for implementing this approach is the AHP [2, 3]. Following this approach, the entire process can be summarized in a single hierarchy in which the lowest three levels present the desired business and corporate strategies. The evaluation of the strategies must reflect the relative importance of all the considerations at the higher levels of the hierarchy. Thus, in the hierarchy illustrated in Figure 1, the priorities for allocating resources among the functional requirements are weighted (sum of the weights of each row is always 100) by their contribution to the achievement of the strategic options (new acquisitions, new markets to enter etc.). These options are in turn evaluated with respect to their ability to achieve the desired product/market portfolio of the firm. The selected portfolio is in turn evaluated on its market attractiveness, business strengths, and synergy. These composite criteria are then weighted according to their importance to the achievement of the objectives of the firm, which in turn are weighted on their importance under (a) the expected scenarios and their likelihood of occurrence in the short and long term and (b) management tradeoff between short and long term horizons in accomplishing its overall mission.

An AHP-based approach for the development of a marketing driven business and corporate strategy provides:

1. A marketing-oriented approach to strategic planning - this is done primarily through the focus on the market segments, and the design of effective positioning and associated marketing strategies which meet both the segments' needs and management's own objectives.

2. Planning by top management and the management of the strategic business units rather than by a planning staff.

3. A process which encourages and enhances

- thoroughness in analyzing the situation,
- creativity in generating strategic options,
- rigor in evaluating the options.

4. A group process which allows the integration of diverse management perspectives and data. The approach helps top management reach consensus while

at the same time identifying important areas of disagreement which require further examination and study.

5. Short operational planning documents (focusing on the selected hierarchy), rather than lengthy reports.

6. A vehicle for coordinating the efforts of the various functional areas and assuring their cooperation in the implementation of an integrated business and corporate strategy.

7. A procedure which encourages sensitivity analysis and experimentation.

8. A continuous *process* which allows for update and modification as needed.

Mission:	Achieve Leadership Position in the XYZ Market			
Planning Horizon:	Short Term	Long Term		
Scenarios:	Optimistic	Status Quo	Pessimistic	
Objectives:	Profit	Growth	Downside	Risks
Criteria:	Market Attractiveness	Business Strengths	Synergy	
Market/ Product Portfolio:	M. Segment 1 Product 1	M. Segment 2 Product 2	M. Segment 3 Product 2	
Strategic Options (SO) to Meet the Needs of the Segments:	SO1 SO 2	SO 3	SO 4 SO 5	
Functional Requirements:	R&D Manufacturing	Marketing		

Figure 1. The basic marketing driven planning hierarchy.

The hierarchy presented in Figure 1 provides the framework for the planning process and a presentation of overall results. The complete results can often be provided in a short report organized along the eight key levels of the hierarchy. Each of the strategy sections (Levels 6, 7, and 8 of the hierarchy) should include the selected strategies and identify:

- specific programs required to implement the strategy;
- required resources;
- expected results;
- individuals responsible for implementation.

4. APPLICATIONS

The marketing driven planning process described in the previous section and outlined in the hierarchy of Figure 1 has been applied in a number of cases ranging from the selection of a portfolio of segments and products to the design of an overall SBU and corporate strategy. These applications involved a number of major U.S., Japanese and Latin American firms. Given the sensitive nature of some of the applications, the discussion in this section will focus on the lessons learned from them, in particular; key conclusions from the applications, modifications made to the basic framework of Figure 1, areas requiring development.

KEY CONCLUSIONS FROM THE APPLICATIONS

Reflecting on the experience gained from six applications of the process described in Figure 1, the following conclusions can be reached:

- Top management teams have no trouble using the AHP

- Having a structure such as the one proposed in Figure 1 helps speed and facilitate the planning process

- The process as outlined in Figure 1 can be used both at the SBU and corporate levels

- The development of a mission statement is often a difficult task. The business definition component of the mission is often revised after completing a first run through the hierarchy.

- Regardless of management's initial evaluation of the tradeoff between short and long term, it is helpful to present them with the results of a sensitivity analysis that encompasses the entire range of options from 90/10 short versus long term to 10/90 short versus long term.

- The construction of scenarios is a task requiring significant staff input, especially if this step is used as a basis for situation analysis involving both internal and external forces. New competitive entries, dramatic technological developments, regulatory changes, and significant shifts in the demographic and lifestyle characteristics of the target markets offer useful starting points for the construction of key environmental scenarios.

• All the applications to date have involved multiple objectives. The most common ones are profit and sales levels and growth and reduction of downside risk. Other objectives tend to reflect idiosyncratic characteristics of management. In all cases the relative importance of specific objectives varies depending on the expected scenario. Typical relationships involved increased importance of profits as the scenario became less favorable.

• Most managers have difficulty directly evaluating market segments and businesses as they relate to their firm's objectives. The use of market attractiveness and business strength as intermediary composite criteria does not simplify the process. There is no agreement, however, across the various firms as to the specific components of each of the two criteria. The GE/McKenzie conceptualization offers a good starting point but is often modified by management. Managers also tend to vary in their evaluation of the relative importance of various components of these criteria as well as the relative importance of market attractiveness and business strength - some prefer to focus on attractive markets, while others prefer markets in which they have specific strengths.

• In most applications, synergy was viewed as a separate and significant criterion. Effective evaluation of positive and negative synergy among the segments and other portfolio operations requires, however, the identification of specific dimensions of synergy (e.g. distribution, manufacturing, procurement, etc.).

• The focus on the market segments to be served and their associated products is initially difficult, especially at the corporate level, but once explored, it greatly simplifies and focuses the remaining task of developing creative strategies to satisfy the needs of and benefits sought by the selected segments.

• The evaluation of the current and expanded portfolio of segments and products (on the selected criteria) is a relatively straightforward task. It is easily summarized in matrix form as segment/products by criteria, or on a market attractiveness business strength chart. It is much harder, however, to use the results of this evaluation as a guideline for the selection of innovative portfolio strategies (e.g. diversification, focus acquisitions etc.). Separate analysis should be undertaken focusing on the generation of portfolio strategies presented as a new level in the hierarchy. These portfolio operations reflect the results of the previous analysis and other considerations and should be evaluated on the objectives of the SBU or the firm.

• It has been helpful in all cases to augment the domestic portfolio of market segments and products with a global perspective focusing on segments by products by country by mode of operation. This is not an easy task, and lack of comparable information across countries has been one of the major obstacles. Such an implementation requires heavy reliance on the subjective judgments of experts.

• In a number of cases, management found it helpful to supplement the basic hierarchy with a direct evaluation of the segments and their associated products (and countries by mode of operation) on the requirements for success versus the firm's expected strengths under each of the expected scenarios.

• The generation of strategic options has greatly benefitted from the use of analogies and other approaches for enhancing creativity [4, Chap. 9].

• The focus on market segments and their associated strategic options helps in integrating the various functions (e.g. R&D, manufacturing, finance, marketing etc.) in a coherent, focused direction.

• All the participants in the various applications found the sensitivity analysis to be of great value and a useful input to the revision of previous decisions.

SPECIFIC MODIFICATIONS

In the course of six applications, a number of modifications of Figure 1 were employed. These included the following:

(a) Incorporating a dynamic analysis of the competitors and their likely responses to the firm's strategy. The basic model does not allow a dynamic competitive analysis and tends to view, as do most planning processes, the competition as part of the environment. To allow for the consideration of likely competitive reactions, the basic approach was supplemented by a parallel hierarchy for the key competitor(s). This involves role playing the competitor(s)' likely actions and reactions. This dynamic AHP framework is illustrated in Figure 2. It provides the framework for a series of iterations between the left- and right-hand-side hierarchies. The process starts by identifying the "best" strategy for the firm (say, segment/positioning A and strategic thrust 1). This strategy is now introduced as part of the scenario facing the key competitor (say, scenario 1) and the competitor's best strategy, reflecting our strategy as part of its environment, is now assessed. This strategy (segment/positioning D and strategy thrust 2) is now considered part of the scenario of our firm, and the previous strategy and other strategic options are examined against it to assure that the selected strategy is the best one. The series of iterations can continue until a "quasi optimal" strategy is found. In a number of applications of this procedure, about five iterations were required to select the best strategy.

	THE FIRM	KEY COMPETITORS
MISSION:	ACHIEVE LEADERSHIP OF THE XYZ MARKET WHILE MEETING CURRENT LEVEL OF PROFITABILITY AND GROWTH	ACHIEVE LEADERSHIP OF THE XYZ MARKET WHILE MEETING CURRENT LEVEL OF PROFITABILITY AND GROWTH
SCENARIO:	S1 S2 S3 S4	S1 S2 S3 S4
OBJECTIVES:	O1 O2 O3	O1 O2 O3
SEGMENT/ POSITIONING:	SEG/POS A, SEG/POS B, SEG/POS C	S/P A, S/P D, S/P E, S/P F
STRATEGIC	ST1 ST2 ST3	ST1 ST2 ST3 ST4

Figure 2. A Dynamic AHP approach to competitive strategy analysis.

(b) Developing supplemental hierarchies. In a number of cases, it was found that the basic hierarchy presented in Figure 1 had to be supplemented with a more specific hierarchy for the completion of specific tasks. For example, in deciding on an R&D/technology licensing strategy, it was found that the top six levels of the hierarchy in Figure 1 provide the basic structure but that the two new and interrelated hierarchies with additional Levels 7 and 8 should be developed. The product concepts most appropriate to reach each segment are placed in Level 7, and R&D project or technology licensing and acquisition options required to develop the product concept in Level 8. A second hierarchy was then developed in which the various R&D projects and technology, licensing and acquisition options (Level 8) were evaluated on a new set of criteria incorporating likelihood of success, expected cost and completion date, and synergy among the projects (as a new Level 7).

AREAS REQUIRING FURTHER DEVELOPMENT

The AHP using the market driven hierarchy outlined in Figure 1 works! It can, however, be further improved by:

- Simplifying the data collection task by reducing the number of required judgments.

- Integrating diverse data collection procedures such as the basic reciprocal matrix using a 9-point scale with 100 points constant sum allocation or ranking for the evaluation of a large number of options.

• Integrating other data sources, especially market response functions and environmental scanning and forecasting, with management subjective judgments.

• Incorporating management uncertainty in various judgments.

• Linking the resulting priorities with optimization programs leading to optimal allocation of resources.

5. CONCLUSIONS

The AHP offers a unique and valuable method for the generation and evaluation of marketing driven business and corporate strategy. The basic hierarchy presented in Figure 1 which focuses on a portfolio of target segments, assures that the planning process will be market driven.

The process has been successfully implemented in six diverse cases. The experience with these applications reinforces the favorable results obtained in many other applications conducted by Saaty and his colleagues. These results suggest that the process is easily implementable and offers a relatively quick and simple approach to business and corporate planning process.

The applications do support the need for further refinement of the data collection part of the process, its integration with other data sources and analytical procedures.

Another interesting future development is the linkage of AHP to a series of expert systems. Expert systems could facilitate the accumulation and synthesis of knowledge, in the discipline itself and in the participating firms, particularly for such processes as portfolio analysis and strategy. Such development can be modeled for advertising messages [1]. Yet, even without such a development the AHP greatly facilitates a marketing driven planning process and encourages the generation of creative solutions and their rigorous evaluation.

REFERENCES

1. Rangaswamy, A., R. Burke, Y. Wind and J. Eliashberg, "Expert Systems for Marketing", Wharton School Working Paper, Univ. Pennsylvania, Philadelphia, PA., 1986.
2. Saaty, T.L. "A Scaling Method for Priorities in Hierarchical Structures", *Journal of Mathematical Psychology* 15, 3 (1977) 234-281.
3. Saaty, T.L., *The Analytical Hierarchy Process*. McGraw-Hill, New York, 1980.
4. Wind, Y., *Product Policy: Concepts, Methods, and Strategies*. Addison-Wesley, Reading, Mass., 1983.

5. Wind, Y. and T. Saaty, "Marketing Applications of the Analytical Hierarchy Process", *Management Science* 26, 7 (1980) 641-658.
6. Wind, Y., "An Analytic Hierarchy Process Based Approach to the Design and Evaluation of a Marketing Driven Business and Corporate Strategy," *Mathematical Modeling* 9, 3-5 (1987) 285-291.

CHAPTER 11

NEW PRODUCT PRICING STRATEGY

1. INTRODUCTION

This chapter presents the development and application of a model for effective decision making in establishing strategies for the pricing of new products. The model developed evaluates all important criteria that need to be considered for the successful implementation of new products in the market. The formulation of the model was tailored for a specific new software product with unique marketing considerations in a well-defined, segmented market. The process used can easily be extended to include other products, provided that model changes and other appropriate parameters realistically describe the problem being analyzed. Such information needs to be established on a case by case basis by the user, for proper validation of the model.

The model has been applied to a case study involving an actual situation related to the introduction of a large new software product in the market place. The analysis performed considered potential sales and customer benefits covering both pessimistic and optimistic scenarios in an attempt to bound the impacts of this new product, and to support the decision on the best pricing strategy for the introduction of this product in the market. The product being marketed is an advanced high technology software program. Potential buyers will be identified by segmenting the market into groups. For example, market research indicates that the client base consists of electric utilities operating nuclear power plants. Due to the homogeneous nature of the client base, and as a result of extensive government regulations, multiple market mixes are not appropriate.

The product was developed to meet the customer's desire to accurately monitor reactor cores by providing advanced technology. The act of tailoring the product to the buyer's desires is consistent with demand-side marketing. Substitute products are not currently available to potential buyers of this new software. This is essential for changing the technological advantage currently present into a lasting commercial advantage.

The process of positioning allows the supplier to develop a broad range of uses or applications for the new product. It is essential that every effort be made to identify as many applications as possible, both current and future, for this software product's promotional campaign. As the product was designed to meet the demand for sophisticated reactor core monitoring capabilities, one of the primary sources for obtaining information concerning applications of the product will be the customer. The installation of a prototype at a customer's site has provided the opportunity to collect feedback concerning the customer's need for product modifications, enhancements as well as new applications. In addition, the foundation was laid for increasing customer loyalty to the product. Significant data was collected during the on-site demonstration of the software. This provided valuable marketing, research and development insight concerning potential applications in response to future customer needs.

The promotion of a new product encompasses advertising, personal selling, sales promotion and public relations. Brochures, pamphlets, catalogs and other print media, announcing the product, are produced by the in-house marketing department. The documents are periodically updated to reflect the new applications and enhancements that are identified as a result of marketing research and customer feedback. Supplies are given to the nuclear fuel vendor to be distributed during on-site visits to the plants. In addition, plans have been made to produce a video storyboard to be used in conjunction with more formal product presentations to senior management and regulatory agencies. Although the product will be sold by the nuclear fuel vendor, the marketing department provides follow-up assistance to potential buyers, attends trade shows and provides literature, and operated a speakers bureau service. The strategic marketing plan targets a very narrowly defined market segment. Marketing is essential due to the constant rate of change in a high-technology market and to ensure that potential buyers are fully informed of the software's capabilities. Following several years of development, the program is now available for customers.

Another dimension which is important in the development of a marketing strategy is product pricing. Classical economists in the eighteenth and nineteenth century viewed price as responding solely to market conditions. They believed that prices were a function of supply and demand alone. The economic system was supposed to automatically set the price of all products.

Just over 40 years ago, an economist, Gardiner C. Means, defined the term "administered prices" to describe goods which had rigid prices and did not fluctuate with a variation in demand. Today, "administered prices" are formulated in corporate offices of most companies as a matter of operating policy, financial planning, and marketing strategy. Nowhere is an "administered price" more a factor than with a new product. For a new product, there is a range of alternative pricing policies which can be adopted. Each alternative policy suits specific circumstances. The pricing policy alternatives relevant to our product are skimming, penetration, and strategic.

Skimming achieves the maximum profit in the shortest possible time by charging the highest price the market will bear. *Penetration* achieves the maximum market penetration by charging a low price to create a large sales volume. Penetration policies typically require that the company be convinced of the long-run demand elasticity of the product. Long-term cost recovery must be acceptable, and long-term profits desirable. Yet another alternative is *strategic pricing*. Strategic pricing is an extreme form of penetration pricing. No profit is generated; only fixed and variable costs are recovered. A few situations suggest strategic pricing.

Strategic pricing involves more than just the product being sold. It requires a long-term perspective on the part of the entire company.

Pricing is the major decision facing management during the birth of a new product because it determines the ultimate contribution to short, medium, and long-term profitability of both the product and the company.

2. THE ANALYTIC HIERARCHY MODEL

All the parameters included in the model developed have been tailored for the specific case of a new computer program software that provides sophisticated capabilities for the monitoring of nuclear reactor cores. As such, this product has targeted specific customers, which required unique considerations of the market and distribution channels. However, the considerations made in the model and the hierarchy can easily be extended for different situations, if appropriate criteria are identified and specific judgments are used in the analysis.

Several different scenarios were evaluated to consider the uncertainties in the planning scheme over the next 5 years; the time period of acceptance for this new product in the market.

The product considered is a sophisticated computer program for the support of operation in Nuclear Power Plants, with the capability to display margin to safety limits. However, it is not part of the plant automatic protection systems. This system provides information for operators, site engineers and designers on reactor core performance. The software operates on engineering workstations and integrates several independent functions at the power plant site.

This software has been under development for four years, and has resulted in a large computer program of approximately 70,000 lines of code. Considering the technical complexity and the interactive nature of its user interface, an extensive site demonstration was conducted during the past year, with the installation of the product at a host site for use in actual situations. This demonstration program was very successful, leading the Beta-Test customer to acquire the software for all its plants. It provided significant and valuable data on product modifications and enhancements that address future customer needs. This product introduces leading technologies in both software and hardware, with the potential of altering processes that can limit its acceptance.

The market for this software consists primarily of Electric Utilities that operate nuclear Power Plants. In addition, the product is more applicable to a specific class of reactors. This clearly identifies the potential participants in the market, thereby bounding clearly the potential demand for the product. The finite number of consumers involved and the highly technical nature of its application determine that an extremely focused marketing strategy should be employed.

At present there are no competitors who can offer products of similar technology and capabilities. However, there are strong indications that software is being developed that may match this product's functions, but such developments are at least two to three years from any practical implementation.

Since there is product exclusivity in the market, the model and economical considerations made in this paper are representative of a monopoly. However, initial market analysis has indicated that price is still an important parameter due to the approval of customers Operating & maintenance expenses by Public Utilities Commissions.

No specific considerations are required on distribution channels for the product as marketing, delivery and support will be provided by the nuclear fuel vendor. Commercial and technical relationships with potential customers are well established. These relationships provide an additional competitive advantage as competitors cannot offer the same level of support nor do they have the same leverage in packaging their product with other large contracts.

This software also provides other benefits to the supplier. In addition to sales, it strengthens existing supplier-customer relationships. The implementation of this product will act as a small barrier for competitors since they will be required to invest substantially supporting the system. It has a significant impact on the technical processes involved as it introduces new approaches that alter the technical interface between supplier-customer. These changes provide opportunities for additional businesses and differentiation in the market place, which are more significant than the technological leadership introduced by the product.

In sum, the objective of this model is:

To determine the best pricing strategy for a new software product that takes into account relevant considerations of market share and return on investment, and accounts for the overall uncertainties associated with product acceptance projections.

The hierarchy designed for this model (see Figure 1) evaluates the pricing strategies according to defined limits of relevant business criteria. Each needs to be considered for the particular problem in question, as well as for different scenarios that reflect uncertainties in the planning period.

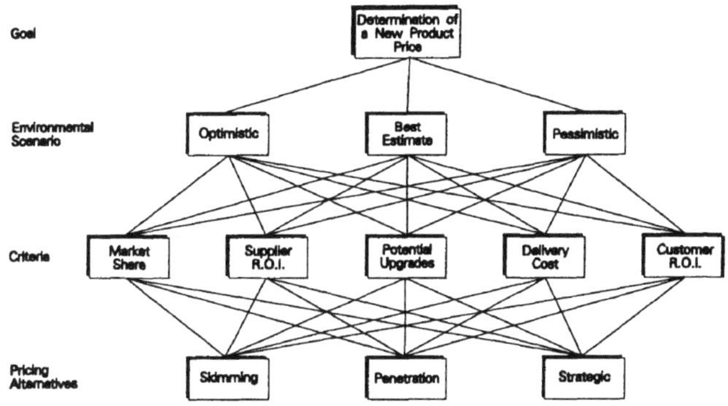

Figure 1. New Product Pricing Hierarchy

TIME HORIZON SCENARIOS

The Pricing Model described here has been established to guide pricing decisions of a new software product. It includes alternatives on time horizon uncertainties about the market behavior over the next five years. Three scenarios have been included in the hierarchy:

- The Optimist Market Scenario is the result of a set of circumstances that lead to the capture of the entire market, i.e., maximum market share,

- The Pessimistic Scenario establishes a set of potential situations that lead to a minimum market share, and

- The Best Estimate Scenario is the middle of the road, in which a realistic market potential will be possible for this product. Preliminary market research has indicated that this approach is the most realistic in the near term until the technology is fully approved by the licensing authorities.

These scenarios are described in detail in Table 1.

Table 1. Environmental Scenarios

Skimming	*Penetration*	*Strategic*
The product has a short life-cycle or has a high rate of innovation incidence, such as fashion.	For some products it is best to discourage competitive entry into the market, particularly if a high level of investment is required.	The company takes a very long-term view and wishes to preclude all competitors from the market. Profit can eventually be taken from enhancements later sold which will expand the capabilities of the product.
The product sells in quality markets where sales seem relatively inelastic to price but responsive to promotion.	The product may have a high degree of elasticity in demand resulting in increased revenue via price reduction.	The company sells related hardware or services and uses the software to secure the customer into its system. An example of this is the airline ticketing system, SABRE, developed and marketed by American Airlines.
The product is of a new concept for which the buyer has not means of comparison for value and utility.	Some section of the market may not currently be tapped by existing high-priced products.	
The product can incorporate improvements and modifications to meet changing consumer concepts of utility without price changes.	Economies of scale may dictate a high sales volume.	
The product is such that future price reductions will enable it to reach different consumers of a more elastic nature, thus widening the product's market.		
The company may have limited manufacturing facilities or sales force. In such circumstances, a small, but highly profitable segment of the market may be best.		

The potential pricing alternatives need to be evaluated according to the set of criteria relevant to the business parameters established for this product.

CRITERIA

Five criteria that influence the product price were identified. In the Analytic Hierarchy Process, each is compared against the others to determine their degree of influence on the goal:

Market - The potential market share achievable is an important parameter in defining the product price, as product development costs make a large contribution to the total product costs, and therefore, the profit. In addition, market share is important from the perspective of potential additional business through product upgrades and preempting the possibility of competitor entry into the market.

Supplier ROI - The Return on Investment is another important business consideration from the suppliers point of view, and product sales should meet minimum returns specified by Corporate guidelines. The ability to continue to develop new products depends on the success in the market, and to a great extent product acceptance is dependent upon price.

Product Upgrades - As described earlier, the initial installation of the product enables the deployment of a strategy of upgrades and enhancement that extend the product maturity cycle.

Delivery Cost - Product delivery is another component in the total product cost. Fixed costs will be large in proportion to market share, and variable costs basically steady and small in comparison to total costs.

Customer ROI - The success of the product in the marketplace is driven by the value that this product brings to customers. This software provides several areas of benefits, as discussed earlier, and the ultimate ROI from the Customer viewpoint is not particularly sensitive to price. However, due to limitations in operating budgets initial price is an important consideration in the decision to acquire the software.

ALTERNATIVE STRATEGIES

The pricing strategies developed for this model address the classical approach of marketing high technology products, and the seller's objectives (Figure 2):

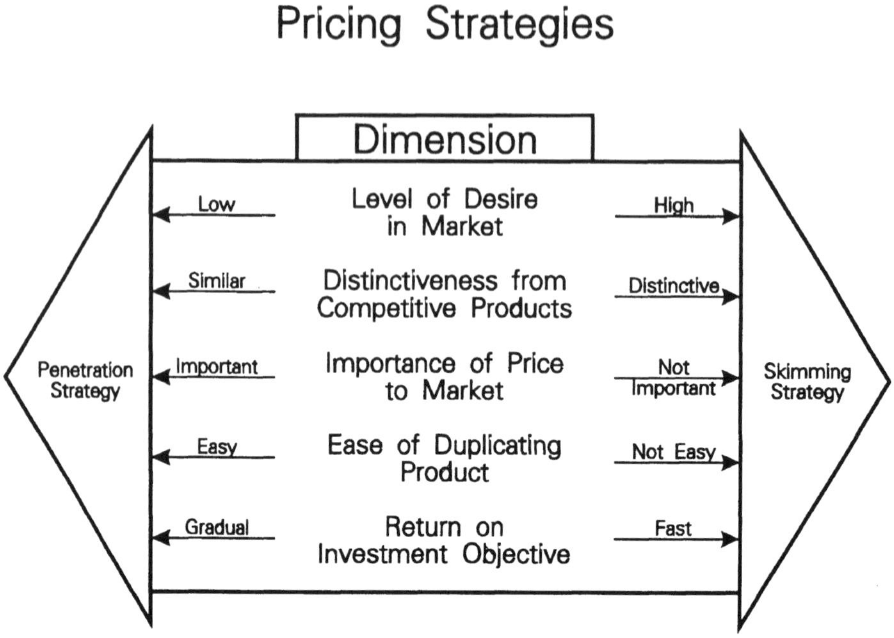

Figure 2. Pricing Strategies

Skimming Strategy - This strategy suggests to demand a premium for the product, which will result in a limited number of sales but with high overall ROI for the seller. This strategy could be justified in that the product provides significant benefits for customers, and the technology lead over competitors. However, it is the alternative with maximum risk, in that a high price makes the justification of the product purchase more difficult. There are several examples in product implementation that have adopted this approach with disastrous results.

Penetration Strategy - The Penetration Strategy proposes a pricing level that provides certain incentives for more customers to purchase the software, and at the same time, provide a good return to the supplier. This is a middle of the road approach that attempts to balance benefits for both the supplier and customer while ensuring a broad market for the seller.

Strategic Strategy - In the Strategic pricing strategy, the main consideration is to eliminate any barrier towards product acceptance, and price the product as near to cost as possible. Minimum price will capture the maximum market share possible, but will minimize supplier ROI. However, the market share position will permit the development of additional business through sale of product upgrades, and provide for the maximization of the total product related revenues in the long run.

3. MODEL APPLICATION

In this section, we discuss the results obtained with the model developed in Section 2. In addition to the reference model result, a sensitivity study was conducted to establish the reasonableness of the reference case and to identify the conditional parameters that would lead to a different course of action. The results of the sensitivity analysis provide insight into trigger points that could be established and monitored during the implementation of this product, and would indicate the need for reassessment of the initial pricing position.

REFERENCE CASE

The model was input into the "Expert Choice" AHP-based software program and run to define the base case pricing strategy for the new product introduction. As discussed in the previous section, fixed and variable cost structures and the required supplier return on investment were provided by corporate instruction. Pairwise comparison values of the elements within the model were designed by consensus within the group.

Based on the parameters discussed and the synthesis of the relevant criteria we conclude:

	Alternatives	Priorities
•	Skimming	10.8%
•	Penetration	42.8%
•	Strategic	46.4%

and hence, the overall best pricing strategy for the new product is the *Strategic* alternative

The strategic pricing approach incorporates the lowest price of the three strategies and facilitates product acceptance. In this case study, significant importance was placed on market share and provision for future profits through upgrades to the software; a long-term approach to economic performance of the product is used. Supplier's return on investment and delivery costs were the secondary concerns and customer return on investment was the least significant concern.

4. SENSITIVITY ANALYSIS

Sensitivity tests of the model to variations in the market demand were run to aid in the prediction of future changes in pricing strategy. In addition, the model's sensitivity to alternations in corporate strategy with respect to return on investment was tested.

Figure 3 illustrates the effect of the variations in the market strength on the pricing strategy employed in the reference case. For example, in a pessimistic market environment, *strategic* pricing is the most desirable approach. In a weak market environment, the supplier must be concerned with recouping sunk costs to a large extent and realize that a weak performance will bear on the viability of future projects.

As the estimate of market strength increases, a continued low price will provide maximization of market share and thus eliminate barriers to product acceptance. The *strategic* approach is the best alternative for this reason as well as the firm's continued emphasis on its long-term objective of additional business due to upgrades.

In an optimistic market environment, the *penetration* approach to pricing becomes increasingly more desirable than the *strategic* approach. More emphasis will be placed on the suppliers return on investment.

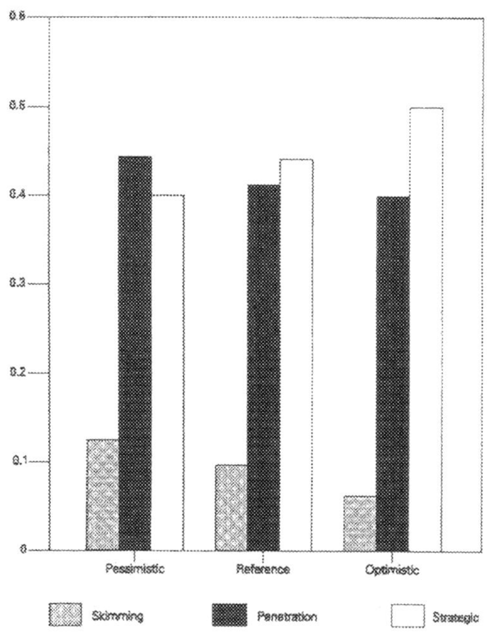

Figure 3. Strategy Sensitivity on Market - Base Case.

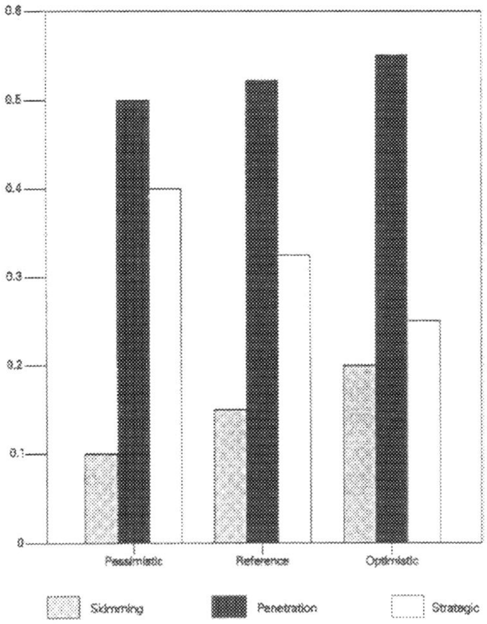

Figure 4. Strategy Sensitivity on Market - Aggressive.

Market Uncertainties - Variations in the demand for the new product results in a shift in the pricing strategy. As presented in Figure 4, an expanded (optimistic) market would strongly reinforce a continuation of strategic pricing. A shift in market demand to one worse than predicted also dictates a shift in pricing policy. The model is sensitive to reduced demand and indicates that a "soft" market would signal a switch to penetration pricing.

Corporate Objectives - Additional sensitivity tests were also run on this model to evaluate the effect of variations of corporate strategy on the pricing strategy. A shift in emphasis from long-run planning to short-run returns was tested. With the emphasis on short-run profits, the optimal strategy in all environmental scenarios, as defined by the model, is penetration strategy (Figure 4). A comparison of short-run vs. long-run pricing strategies in a best estimate environment is presented in Figure 5.

4. CONCLUSIONS

The decision as to how to price any product is a complex one. This process must be approached with a systematic methodology that accounts for all important criteria. The criteria used will vary with the product. In this study, the product being priced is an advanced software program that is used to monitor nuclear reactor cores. The market mix is limited due to the nature of the possible customers. This market can be thought of as a monopoly in that there is only one viable producer of this product.

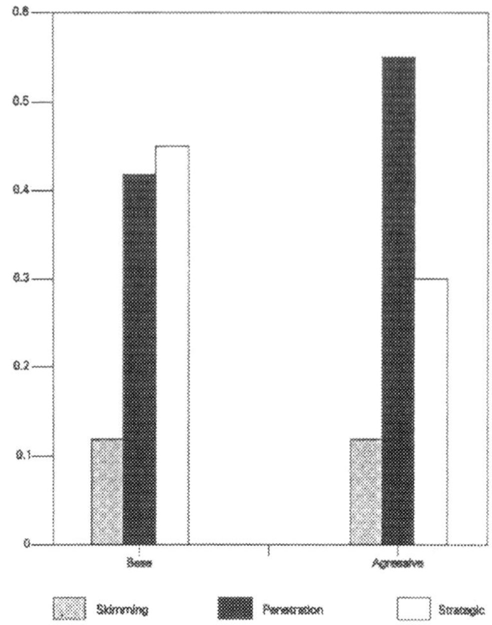

Figure 5. Strategy Sensitivity to Changes in Corporate Objectives.

A review of the market showed that there are three possible pricing strategies for this product. These include:

- Skimming - Maximum profit in the shortest amount of time.
- Penetration - Low price, high market share.
- Strategic - Extreme variation of penetration. Lowest price for the greatest market share.

It was from these three strategies that a best case must be selected. The results demonstrated that in the long-run, the *strategic pricing* approach would be best for this product. However, sensitivity analysis of the model showed that a switch to *penetration pricing* may be necessary if the market were to turn soft. In addition, if the emphasis of the company was to shift to short run profits, *penetration pricing* would become the strategy of choice regardless of the market strength.

A final conclusion is that the results of the sensitivity analysis could be further studied to precisely determine trigger points where a change in pricing strategy would be necessary. These trigger points would be the result of any change in company direction that altered the assessment of the model criteria or a significant change in the market conditions.

CHAPTER 12

INCORPORATING EXPERT JUDGMENT IN ECONOMIC FORECASTS: THE CASE OF THE U.S. ECONOMY IN 1992

1. INTRODUCTION

Professional and academic economists employ a variety of techniques and commit significant amounts of time and financial resources for the purpose of producing macroeconomic forecasts. This chapter illustrates the use of the Analytic Hierarchy Process in forecasting. It integrates macroeconomic theory, historical evidence (as reflected, for example, in formal forecasting models) and expert judgment. Importantly, in the context of current efforts to forecast the future course of the U.S. economy, expert judgment facilitates the incorporation of structural changes into such forecasts.

2. ON THE ROLE OF JUDGMENT IN ECONOMIC FORECASTING

Conventional approaches to macroeconomic forecasting tend to be constrained by the estimated values of the parameters and intercept terms imbedded in the multi-equation forecasting models which typically are employed to produce "first-cut" forecasts of relevant endogenous variables. Additionally, the values of a large number of "exogenous" variables (relating to the future course of monetary and fiscal policy, the value of exports, etc.) must be subjectively estimated on the basis of available evidence and consensus judgment. The initial forecasts produced by the raw models are then typically adjusted by the use of "add" or "fudge" factors, most commonly in the form of shifts in the values of previously estimated intercept terms. This procedure is employed in order to produce forecasts which are consistent with recent values of key endogenous variables when it is evident that a shift of some kind has occurred in portions of the underlying structure of the model ([1], pp. 108-110; [3], p. 256). Such exercises also provide ample opportunity for re-setting the values of exogenous variables.

Studies of "ex ante" forecasts produced by the builders of major models using add factors suggest that these forecasts have been more accurate than the "ex post" forecasts produced by the models themselves, even when the same add factors were employed. Fair ([3], p. 263) wrote:

> "In other words, the use of actual rather than guessed values of the exogenous variables decreased the accuracy of the forecasts.... This conclusion is consistent with the view that the add factors are (in a loose sense) more important than the model in determining the ex ante forecasts..."

All of this suggests that macroeconomic model builders/forecasters are well aware of the limitations of their underlying models and the need to incorporate subjective judgments, especially in the face of structural shifts in the models. However, these judgmental adjustments are necessarily non-systematic and ad hoc in nature.

Rather than further critiquing this approach, however, we instead provide an alternate which is both systematic and consistent in its ability to capture the impact of structural changes. While we have not illustrated this alternative by adapting a formal macroeconomic forecasting model, we do employ an eclectic conceptual framework grounded in modern macroeconomics. Our alternative, moreover, could also be readily employed to enrich forecasting exercises based on formal models (e.g. generating add factors more systematically and consistently; adjusting the values of exogenous variables). In this respect, the two forecasting approaches can be seen to converge quite compatibly.

3.THE SETTING: A SLUGGISH RECOVERY/STRUCTURAL CHANGE

The National Bureau of Economic Research (NBER), utilizing a panel of academic experts, has by consensus been given the responsibility for dating the actual turning points in the U.S. economic cycle. In addition to changes in real GNP or GDP[1] (New York Times, June 18, 1992), that organization arrives at its assessments by utilizing a variety of economic indicators. In December of 1992, the NBER announced (New York Times, December 23, 1992) that the trough of the current cycle occurred in the first quarter of 1991.

The severity of a recession as well as the strength of a recovery should be measured by both the cycle's amplitude and duration. With regard to its most recent cyclical phase, for example, the U.S. economy apparently peaked in the second quarter of 1990, and then proceeded to fall in terms of real GNP for the next three quarters at an annual rate of 2.6%. However, the economy had technically been expanding since second quarter of 1991, and was growing at an annual rate of about

---

[1] An alternative measure of U.S. aggregate economic activity is now used by the U.S. Department of Commerce: namely, gross domestic product (GDP), which nets out international factor payments and receipts. We will continue to cite GNP patterns in this chapter for historical purposes. Currently, real GNP is running slightly higher than real GDP.

1.69% from the first quarter of 1991 through the third quarter of 1992. The Annual rate of the expansion through the second quarter of 1993 is now stronger but still quite modest, about 2.7%. Thus, even if we agree with the NBER's dating of the most recent cyclical trough, the expansion's initial phase must be judged the weakest in recent history. Table 1 provides evidence for the first six quarters of the three previous expansions side by side with the most current expansion (using the NBER dates for the troughs):

Table 1. Recent Economic Expansions

REAL GNP GROWTH (average annual rates)				
Trough	Nov. 1970	March 1975	Nov. 1982	1st Quarter 1991
1st Six Quarters	5.9%	6.3%	6.8%	1.7%

Survey of Current Business, US Department of Commerce, various issues, NBER dates are used to identify troughs

Moreover, other general economic indicators have performed sluggishly. Most importantly, total employment failed to grow appreciably during this putative expansion, unlike the three previous expansions.

It needs to be emphasized that much of this information was unavailable to us when the authors convened in late-December 1991/early January 1992 to engage in an exercise aimed at forecasting the trough of the current cycle. At that point, we did not subscribe to the notion that a less than 1.0% rate of real GNP growth from the first quarter 1991 to the third quarter 1991 (the latest data then available) signified an economic expansion, especially when coupled with other economic data being reported at that time. When we reconvened in May 1992 to review our previous assessment and to engage in an exercise aimed at forecasting the strength of the eventual recovery, the annual rate of real GNP growth through the fourth quarter of 1991 (the latest then available) had apparently actually weakened marginally. The rate of real GNP growth between the last quarter of 1991 and the first quarter of 1992 subsequently rose to 3.5% on an annual basis, only to decelerate again in the second quarter to something of the order of 0.7%. The growth rate then grew substantially in the third quarter of 1992, perhaps signalling the onset of a stronger recovery. Again, this information was obviously not available to us in early May of 1992, though other negative economic portents certainly were.

It is also instructive to compare the forecasts produced in this chapter with those prepared at the time by professional economic forecasters. Blue Chip

Economic Indicators is a monthly publication which reports the consensus forecast of 50 major economic forecasters, including teams at universities, banks, corporations, forecast specialist firms, and professional and credit evaluation institutions.

In December of 1991, the Blue Chip CONSENSUS forecast for real GNP growth in 1992 was 2.2%. This represented a reduction of two-tenths of a percentage point from that projected in the previous month. However, the CONSENSUS reported that: "..., the seeds of growth have been planted and next spring should see a sustained economic recovery begin to sprout." Further, the CONSENSUS in March of 1992 indicated that the economy is "...perking up..." and suggests "...guarded optimism." for the expected recovery. More importantly, the CONSENSUS shifted to a "green" banner in April 1992, indicating that the economy was turning around and expanding above the long-range growth potential of 3%.

The foregoing provides the context for the forecasting exercises of December 1991 and May 1992 which are described in this paper. As noted, the NBER has now rendered its judgment concerning the date from which the economic recovery began. Ensuing events will also disclose the eventual strength of that recovery. However, as will be illustrated in a later section of this paper, our judgment in December 1991 was that a meaningful turning point in the current cycle was still a number of quarters in the future. Our judgment in May 1992, moreover, was that the strength of the eventual recovery was likely to be quite weak when compared to previous expansions, owing chiefly to the "braking" influence of major structural changes then taking place in the domestic and global economies (specifically, such factors as the de-emphasis of production based on national defense and the increasing integration of world financial markets).

4. APPLICATION OF AHP TO THE MACROECONOMIC FORECASTING PROBLEM

Our forecasting exercises employed the AHP to address two critical issues germane to forecasting: the timing and the strength of the expected recovery. The timing issue required us to incorporate into the forecasting exercise the sequence of global events of the previous two and a half years. In our view these events had been forging a restructuring of global resources and institutional arrangements. With regard to the strength of the recovery, our task was to think through the ways in which such restructuring acts as a moderating influence on the performance of the key macroeconomic variables most proximately connected to the U.S. economic cycle. Our first exercise thus sought to forecast the most likely period for the turnaround, while the second tried to predict the strength of the ensuing recovery.

DECOMPOSITION OF THE PROBLEM HIERARCHICALLY

As noted, the objective of the first exercise was to forecast the most likely date of a turnaround. The top level of both exercises consists of the factors representing the forces or major influences driving the economy. These forces are grouped into two categories: "conventional adjustment" and "economic restructuring." Both of these categories are decomposed into subfactors represented in the second level. For the timing forecast, the third level consists of time periods in which the recovery can occur. Figure 1 provides a schematic layout used to forecast the timing of the economic turnaround.

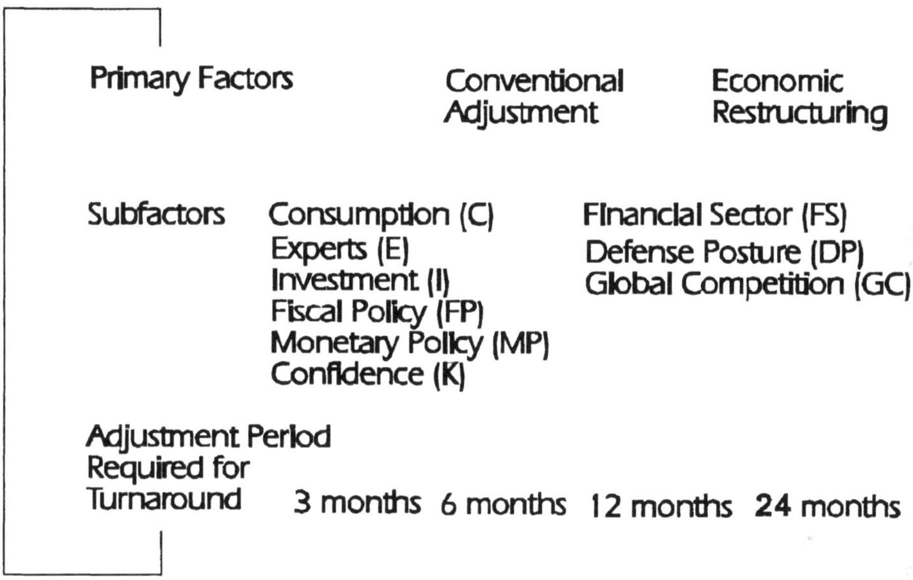

Figure 1. The U.S. holarchy of factors to forecast a turnaround in economic stagnation

Because conventional adjustment and restructuring are both time dependent factors, their relative importance had to be established in terms of each of the four contrasting time periods used to compose the forecast time frame. Thus, instead of establishing a single goal as one does for a conventional hierarchy, we used the bottom level time periods to compare the two factors at the top. This entailed the creation of a feedback hierarchy known as a "holarchy" in which the priorities of the elements at the top level are determined in terms of the elements at the bottom level, thus creating an interactive loop.

With regard to forecasting the strength of the recovery, we used a standard format for the hierarchy, beginning with the primary factors of conventional adjustment and economic restructuring. Their importance for this part of the exercise was established over a six month period after the turn around. Figure 2 is a standard hierarchy, and provides a representation of relevant factors.

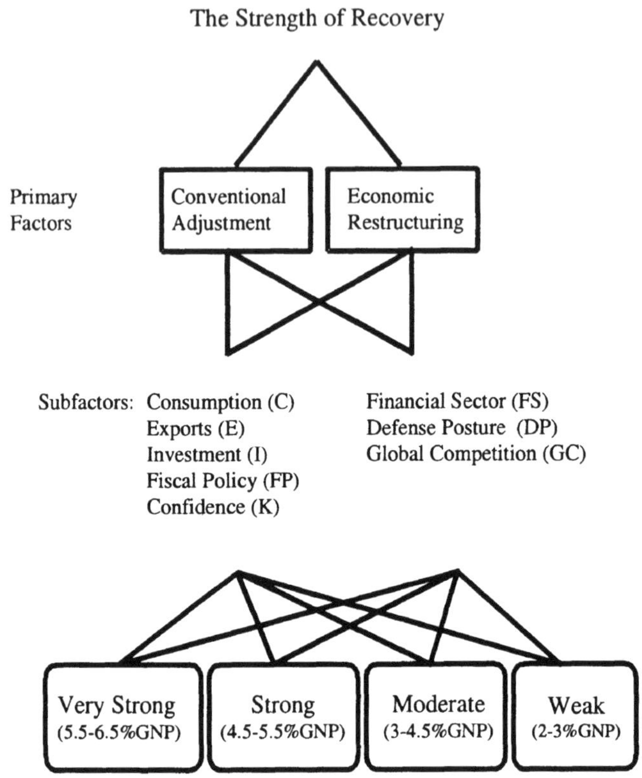

Figure 2. Strength of Recovery Hierarchy

Conventional adjustment assumes a status quo with regard to the system of causes and consequences in the economy. The presumption is that the underlying structure of the economy is stationary. Forecasting is possible within acceptable ranges of error. This is achieved by tracing the existing network of stimulus/response patterns initiated by a perturbation in a fundamental parameter of the economy. In our view, conventional adjustment can formally be divided into six macroeconomic subfactors that occupy the second level: consumer spending, investment spending, exports, indicators of confidence in the economy, fiscal policy, and monetary policy. We recognize that these subfactors are in some instances interdependent.

Viewed independently, for example, a lowering of interest rates by the Federal Reserve should induce portfolio rebalancing throughout the economy. In turn, this should reduce the cost of capital to firms and stimulate investment. Simultaneously, it should reduce financial costs to households and increase their disposable incomes. Any resulting increase in disposable income stimulates consumption and at the margin has a positive impact on employment and GNP. However, all of this assumes that the linkages of the economy are in place and are well understood.

Recent events in the global economy will exert fundamental changes in the way the U.S. economy will operate for the next several years and beyond by inducing an economic restructuring. The Gulf War, the demise of centrally planned economies in eastern Europe and the former Soviet Union, the integration of western Europe, the emergence of newly industrialized economies, and the quickening integration of financial sectors throughout the world are all events which suggest an economic structure that is not stationary but is undergoing dramatic change. Prudent recognition of these facts suggests that patience and monitoring of events are appropriate guidelines for public policy.

With regard to the nature of the current economic restructuring, we specifically recognized in this exercise the transformation of the financial sector, the reduction in the defense-based component of the economy, and the changing global competitiveness position of the U.S. economy as additional subfactors in the second level.

Changes in the domestic economic environment induced by these factors affect the economy in ways that are not well understood and are too complex to pursue here. We summarize these effects by estimating the impact of each subfactor on the expected length of time prior to a turnaround, as well as their impact on the relative strength of the ensuing expansion.

With respect to the timing of the turnaround, we considered four possible time periods of adjustment in the third level as a reasonable breakdown of time in periods long enough to discern change in making the comparisons, but short enough to consider all possible changes over the two year horizon of the forecast. These periods were: 3 months, 6 months, 1 year, and 2 or more years, dated from late December 1991.

With regard to the strength of the expansion, our May 1992 exercise employed ranges of average real GNP growth. Specifically, we considered the following possible outcomes: very strong (5.5% to 6.5%), strong (4.5% to 5.5%), moderate (3.0% to 4.5%), and weak (2.0% to 3.0%). These ranges represent annualized measures of percentage change in real gross national product for the first two years of the recovery. While the ranges are somewhat arbitrary, they generally reflect actual experiences during various post World War II cyclical expansions.

Pairwise Comparison

After decomposing the two problems hierarchically (i.e. the time period of the expected turnaround and the relative strength of the ensuing recovery), the second step in the process was to compare the factors as to their relative importance in affecting each of these questions in terms of their parent factor in the adjacent level above. Accordingly, comparisons were carried out using the AHP's nine point scale.

An illustration of the use of this scale to represent judgments proceeded in the following manner: if conventional adjustment factors were considered to be "strongly more important" than economic restructuring factors for an economic turnaround to occur within six months, the number five (5 times) would have been assigned to the pairwise comparison of conventional adjustment with economic restructuring.

The judgments with regard to the identification of factors as well as the comparisons of relative impact and strength of factors were conducted by the authors, who assumed the role of representative "experts". Obviously, the outcomes are heavily dependent on the quality of those judgments. As noted, the first exercise (timing of the turnaround) was conducted during the third week of December, 1991 and refined during first week of January, 1992. The estimation of the strength of the recovery was conducted during the second week of May, 1992.

Tables 2 through 7 provide the associated matrices of relative comparisons as well as a limiting and completed "supermatrix."

Table 2. Matrices for subfactor importance relative to primary factors influencing the Timing of Recovery

Panel A: Which subfactor has the greater potential to influence Conventional Adjustment and how strongly?

		C	E	I	K	F	M	Vector Weights
Consumption	(C)	1	7	5	1/5	1/2	1/5	0.118
Exports	(E)	1/7	1	1/5	1/5	1/5	1/7	0.029
Investment	(I)	1/5	5	1	1/5	1/3	1/5	0.058
Confidence	(K)	5	5	5	1	5	1	0.334
Fiscal Policy	(F)	2	5	3	1/5	1	1/5	0.118
Monetary Policy	(M)	5	7	5	1	5	1	0.343

Panel B: Which subfactor has the greater potential to influence Economic Restructuring and how strongly?

		FS	DP	GC	Vector Weights
Financial Sector	(FS)	1	3	3	0.584
Defense Posture	(DS)	1/3	1	3	0.281
Global Competition	(GC)	1/3	1/3	1	0.135

For example, in Table 2, when comparing consumption with investment as a means of conventional adjustment, consumption is thought to be strongly more important and a 5 is entered in the first row and third column (1,3). Its reciprocal value of 1/5 is entered in the (3,1) position. On the other hand, when compared with confidence, consumption is not more important but confidence is strongly more important and a 1/5 is entered in the (1,4) position and a 5 in the (4,1) position. All other judgments follow this procedure. The vector of weights is derived from the matrix as the principal eigenvector of the matrix as described in section 3.

Table 3. Matrices for relative influence of subfactors on periods of adjustment (months) (Conventional Adjustment)

For each panel below, which time period is more likely to indicate a turnaround if the relevant factor is the sole driving force?

Panel A: Relative importance of targeted time periods for **consumption** to drive a turnaround

	3	6	12	24	Wgts.
3 months	1	1/5	1/7	1/7	.043
6 months	5	1	1/5	1/5	.113
12 months	7	5	1	1/3	.310
24 months	7	5	3	1	.534

Panel B: Relative importance of targeted time periods for **exports** to drive a turnaround

	3	6	12	24	Wgts.
3 months	1	1	1/5	1/5	.083
6 months	1	1	1/5	1/5	.083
12 months	5	5	1	1	.417
24 months	5	5	1	1	.417

Panel C: Relative importance of targeted time **investment** to drive a turnaround

	3	6	12	24	Vec. Wts.
3 months	1	1	1/5	1/5	.078
6 months	1	1	1/5	1/5	.078
12 months	5	5	1	1/3	.305
24 months	5	5	3	1	.538

Panel D: Relative importance of targeted time for periods periods for **fiscal policy** to drive a turnaround

	3	6	12	24	Vec. Wts.
3 months	1	1	1/3	1/5	.099
6 months	1	1	1/5	1/5	.087
12 months	3	5	1	1	.382
24 months	5	5	1	1	.432

Panel E: Relative importance of targeted time periods for **monetary policy** to drive a turnaround

	3	6	12	24	Vec. Wts.
3 months	1	5	7	7	.605
6 months	1/5	1	5	7	.262
12 months	1/7	1/5	1	1/5	.042
24 months	1/7	1/7	5	1	.091

Panel F: Expected time for a change of confidence **indicators of consumer and investor activity** to support a turnaround in the economy

	3	6	12	24	Vec. Wts.
3 months	1	3	5	5	.517
6 months	1/3	1	5	5	.305
12 months	1/5	1/5	1	5	.124
24 months	1/5	1/5	1/5	1	.054

Table 4. Matrices for relative influence of subfactors on periods of adjustment (months) (Economic Restructuring)

For each panel below, which time period is more likely to indicate a turnaround if the relevant factor is the sole driving force?

Panel A: Most likely length of time for restructuring of financial system to support a turnaround

	3	6	12	24	Vec. Wts.
3 months	1	1/3	1/5	1/7	.049
6 months	3	1	1/5	1/7	.085
12 months	5	5	1	1/5	.236
24 months	7	7	5	1	.630

Panel B: Most likely time required for defense readjustment to affect a turnaround in economy

	3	6	12	24	Vec. Wts.
3 months	1	1/3	1/5	1/7	.049
6 months	3	1	1/5	1/7	.085
12 months	5	5	1	1/5	.236
24 months	7	7	5	1	.630

Panel C: Most likely time required for an adjustment to global competition can affect a turnaround in economy

	3	6	12	24	Vec. Wts.
3 months	1	1	1/3	1/5	.089
6 months	1	1	1/3	1/5	.089
12 months	3	3	1	1/5	.208
24 months	5	5	5	1	.613

Table 5. Most likely factor to dominate during a specified time period

Which factor is more likely to produce a turnaround during the specified time period?

Panel A: 3 Months

	CA	R	Vec. Wts.
CA	1	5	.833
R	1/5	1	.167

Panel B: 6 Months

	CA	R	Vec. Wts.
CA	1	5	.833
R	1/5	1	.167

Panel C: 1 Year

	CA	R	Vec. Wts.
CA	1	1	.500
R	1	1	.500

Panel D: 2 Years

	CA	R	Vec. Wts.
CA	1	1/5	.167
R	5	1	.833

Conventional Adjustment --> CA   Restructuring --> R

Table 6. The Completed Supermatrix

	C.A.	**E.R.**	**Con.**	**Exp.**	**Inv.**	**Con.**	**F.P.**	**M.P.**	**F.S.**	**D.P.**	**G.C.**	**3 mo.**	**6 mo.**	**1 yr.**	**≥ 2 years**
Conven. Adjust	0.0	0.0	0.0	0.0	0.0	0.0	0.0	0.0	0.0	0.0	0.0	0.833	0.833	0.500	0.167
Econ. Restruct.	0.0	0.0	0.0	0.0	0.0	0.0	0.0	0.0	0.0	0.0	0.0	0.167	0.167	0.500	0.833
Consum.	0.118	0.0	0.0	0.0	0.0	0.0	0.0	0.0	0.0	0.0	0.0	0.0	0.0	0.0	0.0
Exports	0.029	0.0	0.0	0.0	0.0	0.0	0.0	0.0	0.0	0.0	0.0	0.0	0.0	0.0	0.0
Invest.	0.058	0.0	0.0	0.0	0.0	0.0	0.0	0.0	0.0	0.0	0.0	0.0	0.0	0.0	0.0
Confid.	0.334	0.0	0.0	0.0	0.0	0.0	0.0	0.0	0.0	0.0	0.0	0.0	0.0	0.0	0.0
Fiscal Policy	0.118	0.0	0.0	0.0	0.0	0.0	0.0	0.0	0.0	0.0	0.0	0.0	0.0	0.0	0.0
Monetary Policy	0.343	0.0	0.0	0.0	0.0	0.0	0.0	0.0	0.0	0.0	0.0	0.0	0.0	0.0	0.0
Financ. Sector	0.0	0.584	0.0	0.0	0.0	0.0	0.0	0.0	0.0	0.0	0.0	0.0	0.0	0.0	0.0
Defense Posture	0.0	0.281	0.0	0.0	0.0	0.0	0.0	0.0	0.0	0.0	0.0	0.0	0.0	0.0	0.0
Global Compet.	0.0	0.135	0.0	0.0	0.0	0.0	0.0	0.0	0.0	0.0	0.0	0.0	0.0	0.0	0.0
3 months0.0	0.0		0.043	0.083	0.078	0.517	0.099	0.605	0.049	0.049	0.089	0.0	0.0	0.0	0.0
6 months0.0	0.0		0.113	0.083	0.078	0.305	0.086	0.262	0.085	0.085	0.089	0.0	0.0	0.0	0.0
1 year	0.0	0.0	0.310	0.417	0.305	0.124	0.383	0.042	0.236	0.236	0.209	0.0	0.0	0.0	0.0
≥ 2 years	0.0	0.0	0.534	0.417	0.539	0.054	0.432	0.091	0.630	0.630	0.613	0.0	0.0	0.0	0.0

Table 7. The Limiting Supermatrix

	C.A.	E.R.	Con.	Exp.	Inv.	Con.	F.P.	M.P.	F.S.	D.P.	G.C.	3 mo.	6 mo.	1 yr.	≥ 2 years
Conven. Adjust	0.0	0.0	0.484	0.484	0.484	0.484	0.484	0.484	0.484	0.484	0.484	0.0	0.0	0.0	0.0
Econ. Restruct.	0.0	0.0	0.516	0.516	0.516	0.516	0.516	0.516	0.516	0.516	0.516	0.0	0.0	0.0	0.0
Consum.	0.0	0.0	0.0	0.0	0.0	0.0	0.0	0.0	0.0	0.0	0.0	0.057	0.057	0.057	0.057
Exports	0.0	0.0	0.0	0.0	0.0	0.0	0.0	0.0	0.0	0.0	0.0	0.014	0.014	0.014	0.014
Invest.	0.0	0.0	0.0	0.0	0.0	0.0	0.0	0.0	0.0	0.0	0.0	0.028	0.028	0.028	0.028
Confid.	0.0	0.0	0.0	0.0	0.0	0.0	0.0	0.0	0.0	0.0	0.0	0.162	0.162	0.162	0.162
Fiscal Policy	0.0	0.0	0.0	0.0	0.0	0.0	0.0	0.0	0.0	0.0	0.0	0.057	0.057	0.057	0.057
Monetary Policy	0.0	0.0	0.0	0.0	0.0	0.0	0.0	0.0	0.0	0.0	0.0	0.166	0.166	0.166	0.166
Financ. Sector	0.0	0.0	0.0	0.0	0.0	0.0	0.0	0.0	0.0	0.0	0.0	0.301	0.301	0.301	0.301
Defense Posture	0.0	0.0	0.0	0.0	0.0	0.0	0.0	0.0	0.0	0.0	0.0	0.145	0.145	0.145	0.145
Global Compet.	0.0	0.0	0.0	0.0	0.0	0.0	0.0	0.0	0.0	0.0	0.0	0.070	0.070	0.070	0.070
3 months	0.224	0.224	0.0	0.0	0.0	0.0	0.0	0.0	0.0	0.0	0.0	0.0	0.0	0.0	0.0
6 months	0.151	0.151	0.0	0.0	0.0	0.0	0.0	0.0	0.0	0.0	0.0	0.0	0.0	0.0	0.0
1 year	0.201	0.201	0.0	0.0	0.0	0.0	0.0	0.0	0.0	0.0	0.0	0.0	0.0	0.0	0.0
≥ 2 years	0.424	0.424	0.0	0.0	0.0	0.0	0.0	0.0	0.0	0.0	0.0	0.0	0.0	0.0	0.0

NOTE TO TABLES 6 AND 7: Now we group all the derived vector weights as columns in the appropriate positions of a matrix of mutual influences known as the supermatrix. For example, the first vector we derived from the matrix of subfactors of conventional adjustment is placed in the first column next to the six subfactors and under conventional adjustment. The factors are listed systematically so that the right vectors are listed to indicate the impact of the relevant factors on the left on the factors at the top. The supermatrix, being stochastic (with columns adding to one) is then raised to limiting powers to capture all the interactions and obtain the steady state outcome in which all columns within each block of factors are the same. We are particularly interested in the two identical columns at the bottom left corner of the matrix of Table 7. Either one is given by (0.224, 0.141, 0.201, 0.424).

To obtain the forecast we multiply each value by the midpoint of its corresponding time interval and add (as one does when evaluating expected values). We have

$$.224 \times 1.5 + .151 \times 4.5 + .201 \times 9 + .424 \times 18 = 10.45 \text{ months}$$

from early Jan. 1, 1992. Note that at times the resulting supermatrix may not be stochastic which would then require weighting each cluster of factors as it impacts another cluster at the top.

SYNTHESIS/RESULTS

When the judgments were made, the software package known as "Expert Choice[4]," in which the AHP procedure is embedded, was used to perform a synthesis which produced the following results:

(1) A meaningful turnaround in the economy would likely require an additional ten to eleven months, occurring during the fourth quarter of 1992. This forecast was derived from weights generated in the first column of the limiting matrix in Table 7, coupled with the mid-points of the alternate time periods to provide unbiased estimates:

(2) At an annual percentage change in real gross national product of about 3.6%, the recovery would be "moderate" (using our range definition). Tables 8 through 11 provide the relevant comparison matrices. Specifically, Table 11 documents the judgments regarding the strength of the expansion.

Table 8. Matrices for Primary and Subfactors for Strength of Recovery

Panel A: Which primary factor will be more influential in determining the Strength of the Recovery?

		CA	R	Vector Weights
Conventional Adjustment	(CA)	1	1/5	0.167
Restructuring	(R)	5	1	0.833

Panel B: Which subfactor is more important in influencing Conventional Adjustment?

		C	E	I	K	F	M	Vector Weights
Consumption	(C)	1	7	3	1	7	3	0.3117
Exports	(E)	1/7	1	1/5	1/5	1	1/5	0.037
Investment	(I)	1/3	5	1	1/3	1/3	1/5	0.099
Confidence	(K)	1	5	3	1	7	3	0.305
Fiscal Policy	(F)	1/7	1	3	1/7	1	1/7	0.035
Monetary Policy	(M)	1/3	7	5	1/3	7	1	0.207

Panel C: Which subfactor is more important in influencing Economic Restructuring?

		FS	DP	GC	Vector Weights
Financial Sector	(FS)	1	1/5	1/3	0.105
Defense Posture	(DS)	5	1	3	0.637
Global Competition	(GC)	3	1/3	1	0.258

CI = 0.037

Table 9. Matrices for relative influence of subfactors on Strength of Recovery (Conventional Adjustment)

For each panel below, which intensity is more likely to obtain if the designated factor drives the recovery?

Panel A: Relative likelihood of the strength of recovery if consumption drives the expansion.

		V	S	M	W	Vec. Wts.
Very Strong	(V)	1	1	5	7	.423
Strong	(S)	1	1	5	7	.423
Moderate	(M)	1/5	1/5	1	3	.104
Weak	(W)	1/7	1/7	1/3	1	.051

C.I. = 0.028

Panel B: Relative likelihood of the strength of recovery if exports drives the expansion.

		V	S	M	W	Vec. Wts.
Very Strong	(V)	1	1	1/3	1/5	.095
Strong	(S)	1	1	1/3	1/5	.095
Moderate	(M)	3	3	1	1/3	.249
Weak	(W)	5	5	3	1	.560

C.I. = 0.016

Panel C: Relative likelihood of the strength of recovery if investment drives the expansion.

		V	S	M	W	Vec. Wts.
Very Strong	(V)	1	1	1/3	2	.182
Strong	(S)	1	1	1/3	2	.182
Moderate	(M)	3	3	1	6	.545
Weak	(W)	1/2	1/2	1/6	1	.091

CI = 0.0

Panel D: Relative likelihood of the strength of recovery if confidence drives the expansion.

		V	S	M	W	Vec. Wts.
Very Strong	(V)	1	1	3	5	.376
Strong	(S)	1	1	3	5	.376
Moderate	(M)	1/3	1/3	1	7	.193
Weak	(W)	1/5	1/5	1/7	1	.054

CI = 0.101

Panel E: Relative likelihood of the strength of recovery if fiscal policy drives the expansion.

		V	S	M	W	Vec. Wts.
Very Strong	(V)	1	1	1/5	1	.125
Strong	(S)	1	1	1/5	1	.125
Moderate	(M)	5	5	1	5	.625
Weak	(W)	1	1	1/5	1	.125

CI = 0.0

Panel F: Relative likelihood of the strength of recovery if monetary policy drives the expansion.

		V	S	M	W	Vec. Wts.
Very Strong	(V)	1	1	1/5	1/3	.084
Strong	(S)	1	1	1/5	1/3	.084
Moderate	(M)	5	5	1	7	.649
Weak	(W)	3	3	1/7	1	.183

CI = 0.101

Table 10. Matrices for relative influence of subfactors on Strength of Recovery (Restructuring)

For each panel below, which intensity is more likely to obtain if the designated factor drives the recovery?

Panel A : Relative likelihood of the strength of recovery if financial sector drives the expansion.

		V	S	M	W	Vec. Wts.
Very Strong	(V)	1	1	1/3	1/5	.095
Strong	(S)	1	1	1/3	1/5	.095
Moderate	(M)	3	3	1	1/3	.249
Weak	(W)	5	5	3	1	.560

CI = 0.016

Panel B: Relative likelihood of the strength of recovery if defense posture drives the expansion.

		V	S	M	W	Vec. Wts.
Very Strong	(V)	1	1/3	1/5	1/7	.055
Strong	(S)	3	1	1/3	1/5	.118
Moderate	(M)	5	3	1	1/3	.262
Weak	(W)	7	5	3	1	.565

CI = 0.044

Panel C : Relative likelihood of the strength of recovery if global competition drives the expansion.

		V	S	M	W	Vec. Wts
Very Strong	(V)	1	1	1/3	1/5	.101
Strong	(S)	1	1	1/3	1/5	.101
Moderate	(M)	3	3	1	1	.348
Weak	(W)	5	5	1	1	.449

CI = 0.012

Table 11. Overall Results for Strength of Recovery

	% GNP Growth	
Very strong	(5.5-6.5)	0.108
Strong	(4.5-5.5)	0.141
Moderate	(3-4.5)	0.290
Weak	(2-3)	0.461
% GNP Recovery Rate*		3.6

*% GNP Recovery rate calculated using the relative strength of conventional adjustment and restructuring (See Table 7, Panel A). Each used to multiply midpoints of % GNP Growth and then summed.

NOTE TO TABLES 8-11: The next example is a simple hierarchy as shown in Figure 2 in which the derived weights in each level starting at the top are weighted by the weight of the corresponding factor in the level above used to compare the elements. The results are then added for each element to obtain its overall weight. The process is continued to the bottom level of the hierarchy.

5. CONCLUSION

This chapter has demonstrated how the Analytic Hierarchy Process can serve as an additional tool for macroeconomic forecasts. We have used the highly interesting and relevant case of the U.S. economy during its current economic cycle (in which structural change has been particularly important) as the specific context for our analysis. As noted earlier, this approach could easily be adopted for use in forecasts based initially on formal macroeconometric models (e.g. to make judgments on shifts in intercepts and changes in the value of exogenous variables).

With regard to our forecasts, in addition to presenting the somewhat contrarian view that a meaningful turnaround in the present economic cycle was then still some months in the future, we concluded that the next recovery would be substantially less strong than those of the past three decades. We viewed this as being fundamentally attributable to the dramatic restructuring of important sectors of the global economy.

REFERENCES

1. Adams, F.G., *The Business Forecasting Revolution*, Oxford University Press, 1986.
2. Council of Economic Advisors, *Economic Report of the President*, 1993.
3. Fair, R.C., *Specification, Estimation, and Analysis of Macroeconometric Models*, Harvard University Press, 1984.
4. Forman, E. and T.L. Saaty, *Expert Choice Software*, produced by Expert Choice, Inc., 4922 Ellsworth Avenue, Pittsburgh, PA.
5. Hall, T.E., *Business Cycles - The Nature and Causes of Economic Fluctuation*, Praeger, New York, 1990.
6. Hershey, R.D., Jr., June 18, "Good Riddance to Recession?", *New York Times*, 1992.
7. Hershey, R.D., Jr., December 23, "This Just In: Recession Ended 21 Months Ago", *New York Times*, 1992.
8. Miller, G.A., "The Magical Number Seven Plus or Minus Two: Some Limits on our Capacity of Processing Information", *Psychological Review* 63 (1956) 81-97.
9. Saaty, T.L. and L.G. Vargas, *Prediction, Projection and Forecasting*, Kluwer Academic, Boston, 1991.
10. Saaty, T.L., *Multicriteria Decision Making: The Analytic Hierarchy Process*, RWS Publications, Pittsburgh, PA, 1990.
11. Saaty, T.L. and J.M. Alexander, *Conflict Resolution: The Analytic Hierarchy Approach*, Praeger, New York, 1989.
12. Saaty, T.L. and K.P. Kearns, *Analytical Planning: The Organization of Systems*, Pergamon Press, New York, 1985.
13. Sorkin, A.L., *Monetary and Fiscal Policy and Business Cycles in the Modern Era*, Lexington Books, Lexington, MA, 1988.
14. U.S. Department of Commerce, *Survey of Current Business*, various issues.

CHAPTER 13

A NEW MACROECONOMIC FORECASTING AND POLICY EVALUATION METHOD

1. INTRODUCTION

The economy is often faced with a turn that is not to our liking, and we sometimes think it ought to be controllable by macroeconomic policy. While the spectrum of policies ranges from Keynesian "fine tuning" to using monetarist "rules," every action (or inaction) of the government is a policy. Because of this it is important that government policy makers be guided by appropriate empirical models. Unfortunately, there is considerable variation in the large numbers of econometric models that have been developed thus far. Moreover, there are persistent problems, both technical and theoretical, with these models.

We will show that the Analytic Hierarchy Process (AHP) is an effective method for forecasting the end effects of a given policy or set of policies, and for determining the resulting impact on important variables such as unemployment and inflation. The forecasts could be made using the judgments of leading economists, congressmen, and personnel from major federal agencies such as OMB, CEA, commerce, the Federal Reserve and the Treasury. One side benefit would be a clearer understanding and appreciation of the problem under consideration as viewed from these different perspectives. The analysis in this chapter reflects the economic climate of the early 1980's.

2. A FEW WORDS ABOUT EXISTING ECONOMETRIC MODELS

There are problems with currently existing econometric models. Some problems are purely technical in nature and arise from the statistical approach. For example, there is a need to determine the proper estimation technique for equations with lagged dependent variables and serially correlated error terms when these equations are embedded in a simultaneous system of equations. There has been steady progress in the development of these statistical models but their formalism does not yield satisfactory solutions.

Other problems with the current crop of econometric models are more serious. For instance, the presence of so many models, all differing significantly in their structure, raises the question about how to specify the type of model and the parameters. There is a yet more serious question common to virtually all econometric models that use time series data to estimate historical correlations between variables. The estimated coefficients that represent peoples', firms', and governments' behavior are typically presumed to be "structural" in nature–that is, they are assumed to be invariant with respect to changes in the economic environment and, in particular, to changes brought about by policy actions. But, instead of being constant, these coefficients are unstable and may account for "sudden, unpredictable shifts in behavioral relationships..." [2]. Economists using these models have responded by developing statistical techniques that allow the estimated parameters to drift at random rather than forcing them to be constant ([6] and [4]). This has resulted in forecasts of somewhat increased accuracy [12].

However, allowing for random parameters in the estimation process is at best a statistical device for coping with a more basic problem. A fundamental observation is that on the part of consumers only the parameters of utility functions are truly invariant with respect to changes in policy, while for firms the same is true only for the parameters of their production functions. All "Behavioral" coefficients in an individual's demand and supply functions depend, in some fashion, on more primitive parameters in his utility function and his perceived budget constraint. After all, demand functions are the result of the individual maximizing his utility subject to the restraint given by the perceived economic environment as embodied in his budget constraint. Any change in government policy alters the economic environment and leads to a change in the structure of the demand function as the individual responds to the changed incentives. The same general conclusions are true for firms' (and individuals') supply functions. As a result, the assumptions made in most econometric models that the estimated coefficients of the demand and supply functions are stable with respect to changes in policy are hard to defend. Sargent [9] discusses in detail the econometric consequences of these observations (which originated with Lucas [5]) for standard econometric models.

These considerations have two immediate implications. The first is that the "sudden, unpredictable shifts...in the coefficients" are no longer a puzzle. The instability is a manifestation of the fact that a forecasting model's coefficients are not truly structural in nature and, because of this, shifts and changes are to be expected. The second, and more serious, weakness is that standard econometric models are particularly unable to forecast results of alternative policies because as different policies are instituted the parameters of the estimated demand and supply functions change due to people and firms altering their behavior. In virtually all econometric models, this effect is simply ignored because of technical difficulties.

These defects of existing models have led to widely differing reactions among economists. Equilibrium theorists tend to regard the objections sympathetically while disequilibrium (Keynesian) economists tend to dismiss them as minor. Some, such as Sims [10], concluded that all existing macroeconomic models are misspecified and that economists can predict virtually nothing about the effects of different policies. Robert Lucas [5] bluntly wrote, "features which lead to success in short term forecasting are unrelated to quantitative policy evaluation...The major macroeconomic models are (well) designed to perform the former task only, and these models can, in principle, provide no useful information as to the actual consequences of alternative economic policies." Others, such as Anderson [1], have attempted to manipulate existing models to avoid the problems mentioned above. Still others, mostly the designers, users and sellers of large econometric models have ignored these criticisms or else dismissed them as trivial. The AHP, however, enables us to take account of these points and to include effects of the policies being considered in our forecasts.

FIRST STAGE PROBLEM

We will consider the problem of finding the best macroeconomic policy package among a given set by considering the effect that each policy package has on national "welfare." The effect of each package on national welfare is, in turn, decomposed into the effects of the package on key criteria such as inflation, unemployment, and growth. In terms of the AHP, this problem formulation leads to a three level hierarchy. The goal of best policy for the national welfare is in the first level. The criteria occupy the second level and the policy packages occupy the third level. The hierarchy, corresponding to this problem from which the relative effectiveness of the different policies on the third level are determined, is illustrated later.

SECOND STAGE PROBLEM

In the second stage we incorporate both the uncertainty concerning the exogenous forces operating on the economy and the possibility that the effectiveness of the various policies may change over time. Uncontrollable forces that affect the economy are included in the hierarchy in another level that involves what we call "exogenous scenarios," or SE's. These SE's consist of elements beyond the control of the policymaker that are deemed to exert an important effect upon the economy. Examples of such elements are drastic changes in the real price of energy, or wars involving vital interests of the nation. Since these scenarios are by their nature uncertain, a number of potential scenarios are constructed. Moreover, time is intimately involved whenever a scenario is constructed, and the expected SE may change with the passing of time.

The hierarchy is a modification of that described above with a cycle between the projected scenarios and time appearing in level two and the rest of the hierarchy pushed down one level. Figure 1 presents the modified hierarchy. The cycles between the scenarios and the time periods are designed to give us the relative likelihoods of occurrence of the various SE's in the given time periods and also the relative importance of the time periods to the occurrence of the scenarios.

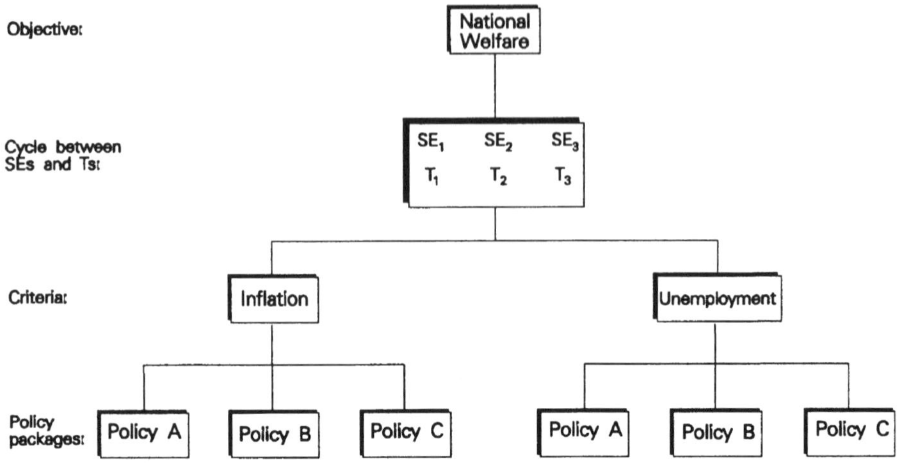

Figure 1. Illustrative Example, Stage Two Problem.

Using the AHP the likelihood of the occurrence of a given scenario in different time periods is calculated and for any given time period, the likelihood of each scenario actually occurring is obtained.

To find the priorities of both the time periods and the scenarios simultaneously a supermatrix is constructed (see [7]) for use of the supermatrix to solve cycling or feedback priority problems in the AHP). The two sets of eigenvectors which give the likelihood of the scenarios in each time period and the likelihood of occurrence of the scenarios across the time periods are used as the columns of two matrices. Each matrix occupies one of the two off-diagonal positions of a 2 x 2 super matrix which is column stochastic. The limiting power of the matrix yields the priorities of both the time periods and the scenarios. The priorities of the scenarios are used for subsequent weighting in the hierarchy.

Given these likelihoods, the next step in the procedure is to apply the familiar process of ranking the effectiveness of the policies with respect to the criteria. The only difference from the usual AHP composition concerns time. For each time period and exogenous scenario combination under consideration, the rankings are obtained from questions of the form: "Given exogenous scenario SE, how much more effective is policy P enacted at time T, than policy P, also enacted at time T, in lowering the unemployment rate at time T?" For each particular time period and exogenous scenario combination, the contribution of each policy toward the nation's welfare is computed precisely. For each particular time period, these welfare vectors are weighted by the likelihood of occurrence of the specific SE and the weighted vectors are summed to arrive at the overall expected relative contribution of the policies toward achieving the nation's welfare. Since each of these summed vectors applies to time periods somewhere in the future, they are discounted to the present to arrive at the overall effectiveness of the policies. One selects the policy with the largest priority.

QUANTITATIVE FORECASTS

After the policies have been qualitatively ranked, the next step is to obtain the quantitative forecasts. We will illustrate our forecasting procedure by using only the first stage, shortrun technique.

The forecasting procedure introduces a second hierarchy, which extends the first hierarchy further down, and adds a new element "non-controllable actors." Non-controllable actors are organizations, groups of individuals, or institutions who wield substantial influence over certain sectors or variables but who are not under the direct control of the policy maker. The noncontrollable actors will occupy the second level in this hierarchy, immediately beneath each criterion. The level under the non-controllable actors will contain the range of actions they can take to influence the criteria. Immediately beneath this will be the level containing the quantitative effect each possible action could have on the criteria.

An example of this type of hierarchy is given in Figure 2 for the criterion of inflation. The second row contains suggested non-controllable actors who exert direct influence on the inflation rate. It would be possible to include other groups who can influence the inflation rates but the three given in the figure will suffice for the purposes of this illustration. The first step would be to construct a comparison matrix between the three non-controllable actors and to calculate the relative influence each exerts upon the inflation rate.

The third level in Figure 2 illustrates a range of possible actions consumers could take that would affect the inflation rate. There would be other analogous entries in this level for the other non-controllable actors. We have omitted them to simplify things. These five actions are grouped in a comparison matrix and ranked according to the question: "Given that whatever specific policy we are quantifying has been adopted, what is the likelihood that one of the actions (e.g., increase demand with moderate intensity, "moderately") will occur relative to another action?" The weights obtained from this matrix will represent the relative likelihoods that consumers will change their demand for goods by the given intensity. The last level in the hierarchy lists the range of possible inflation rates. Again, each entry in the "possible actions" level of the hierarchy will have associated with it a range of possible inflation rates. Again, for simplicity, we do not show all the detail. This level is prioritized in a comparison matrix by answering the question: "Given that the specific possible action has occurred, (e.g., no change in demand) what is the likelihood that inflation will assume a certain value as compared to another?" The weights obtained from this exercise will be the priorities that the inflation rate will be equal to the given amounts.

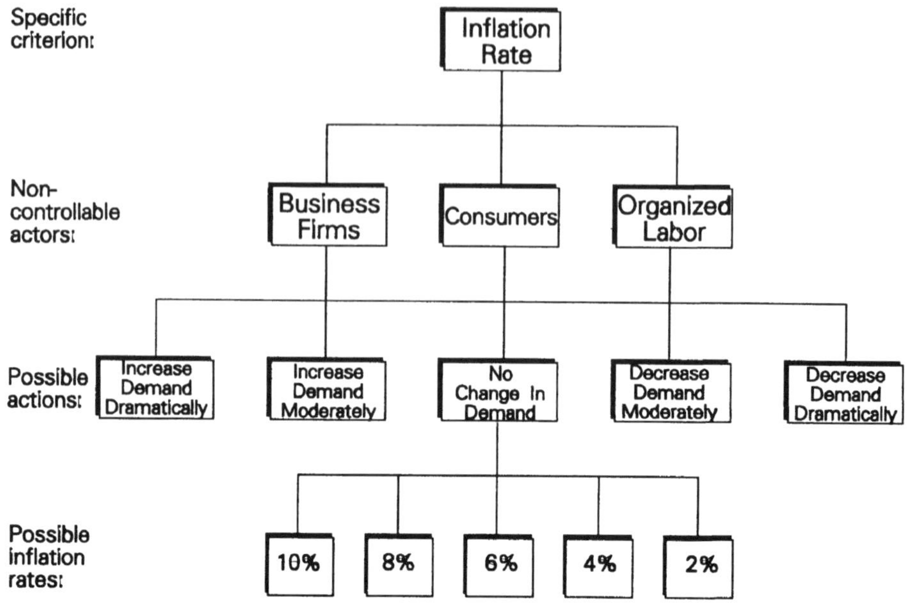

Figure 2. The Extended Hierarchy with Noncontrollable Actors.

The next step is to obtain the quantitative forecast. This is done by first weighting the possible inflation rates by the priority of their occurrence for each possible action. These expected inflation rates are then weighted by the likelihood that the possible action to which they pertain takes place. For example, the expected inflation rate, given that there is no change in demand by consumers, might be 7%. This figure is, in turn, weighted by the priority that there is no change in demand by consumers. When this has been done for each of the possible actions by consumers, the (five) weighted figures are summed to arrive at the expected value of the "consumer's contribution" to the inflation rate. This procedure is carried out for all other non-controllable actors being considered. The final step is to weight each non-controllable actor's expected contribution by the relative importance of the actor to arrive at the overall expected inflation rate. This procedure is implemented for all the criteria to be forecast for all the specific policies being considered.

There are several useful points to make about this approach. First, in other cases in which forecasting has actually been carried out, the results have proven to be accurate by other measures (See Zahedi [11] for forecasting applications). In addition, when forecasting, each comparison matrix is based on the specific policy considered. The question used to rank the possible actions refers directly to the policy package for which the forecast is being made. It is at this stage that we allow the non-controllable actors to react differently according to whatever policy we are considering. Thus we take into account the criticism of Lucas and others that the behavior of economic agents depends strongly upon the policies that are in force.

Finally, the use of the AHP, combined with judgment based comparisons eliminates the complaint levied against econometric models that the results of policy exercises are predetermined by the model's basic structure. The AHP is sufficiently general so that it is possible to include a variety of non-controllable actors in an effort to capture effects neglected by specific models and modelers. Economists belonging to the monetarist school tend to dismiss the effect that organized labor has on the inflation rate. If it were a monetarist economist using the AHP to forecast the inflation rate, it would still be possible to include labor unions in the series of non-controllable actors - the monetarist would simply give it a small weight.

3. APPLICATION OF THE AHP TO MACROECONOMIC POLICY

We examine the problem of selecting the best macroeconomic policy package in a given set of policy packages by considering the effect that each policy package has on national "welfare." In our example, we assume that national welfare is affected by five key criteria: the inflation rate, the unemployment rate, the economic growth rate, the level of domestic stability and the state of foreign relations. The economic criteria have the usual meanings. Inflation pertains to a general increase in prices as measured by, for example, the GNP deflator; unemployment refers to the percentage of the labor force unemployed; and economic growth refers to increased per capita real GNP. In our example, we define the reduction in inflation to be a four percentage point reduction; the reduction in unemployment meant a one percentage point reduction; and the increase in growth referred to a one half of a percentage point increase. The last two (noneconomic) criteria are not expressed quantitatively and could be defined at the start of the exercise to suit specific requirements. We also define domestic stability to include racial integration, political participation, and business-labor--government relations. The criterion of foreign relations included relations with allies, the Third World, the oil producing Middle East, and the Soviet/Communist nations.

Table 1. Contribution of the Criteria to the Overall Objective (National Welfare)

National Welfare	I	U	G	D	F	Weights
Inflation	1	3	5	4	6	.45
Unemployment	1/3	1	4	4	6	.30
Growth	1/5	1/4	1	2	2	.11
Domestic Stability	1/4	1/4	1/2	1	2	.09
Foreign Relations	1/6	1/6	1/2	1/2	1	.05

There are two features to note in the list of criteria. First, the set is not exhaustive. It would be possible to add or delete criteria depending on the views of the user. The indeterminancy resulting from what must be a normative listing of criteria for the objective function is not specific to the AHP but is common to all methods of evaluating alternative policies. The second feature is that the inclusion of domestic stability and foreign relations in the list of criteria serves to demonstrate the flexibility of the AHP to combine unlike factors in the decision-making process. Though the above two criteria are not immediately economic, it seems clear that the level of national welfare is influenced by the state of foreign relations and domestic stability. To this extent, the scope of this model is potentially much broader than conventional ones.

In the level below the criteria we have the policy packages. Thus this problem is a three level hierarchy. The overall objective, national welfare, is at the top of the hierarchy. The criteria occupy the second level and the policy packages, to be evaluated for how they affect each criterion, are in the bottom level.

In our example, we took the vantage point of a "representative" person in society to provide judgments for the pairwise comparisons of the criteria with respect to their importance to national welfare. It should be emphasized once again that any attempt through any model to develop economic policy must specify implicitly or explicitly an objective function for that policy. Either way such an objective function will rely on value judgments. Thus, establishing the relative importance of the criteria in level one for a "representative" person in society amounts to specifying explicitly the objective function and the value judgments leading to it. The result is the vector of relative weights, or the relative importance of the criteria to national welfare, given in Table l. Note that a reduction in the inflation rate is deemed the most important action to improve national welfare. A reduction in unemployment, while not as important as a reduction in the inflation rate, is still more important than the remaining criteria. The other criteria have very low priorities in comparison with inflation and unemployment. The values in this vector of relative weights can be interpreted either as the importance of one criterion over another, e.g., inflation is nine times (.45/.05) as important as foreign relations, or as the relative attention that should be paid a particular criterion (inflation = 45%) in attempting to improve national welfare.

The next level of the hierarchy involves specifying policy packages and forecasting their effect upon each of the five criteria. Various new and traditional macropolicies were selected, 20 in all. For simplicity, the policies were clustered into three sets "A", "B", and "C", corresponding to what is generally regarded as "conservative," "moderate" and "liberal" respectively. The policy packages were evaluated with respect to the economic criteria (inflation, unemployment and growth), three times--from the vantage point of a monetarist, from that of a Keynesian and, finally, from a "supply-side" viewpoint. For the criteria of domestic relations and foreign rela.tions we evaluated the impact of the policy packages from the point of view of a "representative" individual again; it was not necessary to distinguish among monetarist, Keynesian, and supply-sider opinions. We then selected the optimal policy from each set (A, B, and C) for each economic viewpoint, combined the optimal policies into a single set and selected the best overall policy for each school.

The policies were evaluated only for their presumed shortrun effect on the five criteria. And we took into consideration the constraint that the government's budget places on the use of various policy tools. For example, if the government lowers tax rates by 10% while leaving its total spending unchanged, there would be a potential shortfall of revenue. If this were the case, either bonds and/or money would have to be issued to finance the tax cut and to reconcile expenditures with revenues. Thus, in the following development, we specified complete policies (e.g., "lower tax rates by 10 percent and issue money to cover any shortfall"). The notation and symbols to describe the policies are given in Table 2.

Table 2. Symbols for the Description of Policies

G	Government spending
B	Issuance of Bonds
M	Issuance of Money
Tx	Total Tax Rates (Corporate and Personal)
Tc	Corporate Tax Rates
Gm	Military spending
Gtr	Transfer payments
↑	Increase
↓	Decrease

Examples of the notation:

1) Tx↓,B,M↑ implies a decrease in tax rates of 10% with any revenue shortfall made up by increasing, in the same proportion as they stood before the tax cut, the amount of bonds and money issued.

2) Gtr↑(10%) = G↓ implies a 10% increase in total Transfer payments that is offset by an equal decline in government spending on defense.

** In general, the given percentage change applies to the first item in the policy list. The only exception to this is the policy package denoted by G, Tx, M↓ where the percentage decrease applies to the first two entries in the string and the change in M is the balancing residual.

In Table 3, the evaluation of cluster B policies with respect to inflation from the monetarist viewpoint, we give an example of how we evaluated cluster policies through pairwise comparisons with respect to a criterion. Similar comparisons were carried out for every economic group and every cluster. The judgments were given in response to the following type of question: "From a monetarist viewpoint, how much more effective in reducing the inflation rate will be a policy of decreasing tax rates by 10% while balancing the budget using money and bonds (i.e., Tx↓, B, M↑ 10%) than will be a policy of cutting tax rates by 5 and issuing money and bonds to make up any revenue shortfall (i.e., Tx↓, B M↑ 5%)?" In this case, where the policies are ranked from a monetarist perspective, we judged the second policy to be between strongly and very strongly more effective (i.e., 6) than the first policy. Since the comparison is, by convention, between the first policy relative to the second policy, we placed the ranking (1/6) in the matrix. The remaining comparisons in this matrix were entered in a similar fashion. The extreme right column gives the vector of relative weights for these four policies to achieve a reduction in inflation.

Table 3. Evaluation of Cluster B Policies with Respect to Inflation (Monetarist Viewpoint)

Inflation .45	10% Tx↓,B,M↑	5% Tx↓,B,M↑	10% G,Tc↓	5% G,Tc↓	Relative Weights
Tx↓,B,M↑ 10%	1	1/6	1/7	1/5	0.044
Tx↓,B,M↑ 5%	6	1	1/7	1/5	0.115
G,Tc↓ 10%	7	7	1	3	0.560
G,Tc↓ 5%	5	5	1/3	1	0.281

Once the policy matrices are prioritized with respect to each of the five criteria, the overall efficacy of each policy is determined by multiplying the effectiveness of each policy with respect to a given criterion by the weight of the criterion toward affecting national welfare, and then adding over all the criteria.

An example of this procedure is given in Table 4. In this table we calculated the overall effectiveness of policy (G, Tx, M↓ 10%) when judged from a monetarist viewpoint. Column 2 gives the weights of the criteria we developed in Table 1. Column 3 reports how effective this particular policy is in satisfying the various criteria. The fourth column weights the effectiveness of the policy. These weighted contributions are summed and the overall effectiveness of the policy is given in the bottom row of the table.

Table 4. Determination of the Overall Effectiveness Of the Policy (G, Tx, M↓ 10%) (Monetarist Viewpoint)

Objective A	Weight of the Criterion B	Weight of The Policy With Respect to the Criterion C	Contribution to the Overall Criterion D = B x C
Inflation	450	.120	.05
Unemployment	.300	.103	.03
Growth	.110	.306	.03
Domestic Stability	.090	.240	.02
Foreign Relations	.050	.099	.01
Overall Effectiveness			.14

Now we have an initial sorting of the 20 policies. The next step is to select the most effective policies from each cluster and then rank them directly against each other to find the overall best policy. The technique of clustering the policies into 3 groups, calculating the rankings within the groups and then calculating the rankings between the most effective policies within the groups might appear to involve more work than directly comparing all 20 potential policies simultaneously. This is, however, not the case as a simple calculation will show. Each comparison matrix involves n(n-1)/2 judgments for the pairwise comparisons where n is the number of elements being compared. Our clustering method of evaluating policies required a total of 360 comparisons for each viewpoint. Directly comparing all the policies would have required 500 comparisons. Thus, the clustering technique requires only 72 percent of the comparison needed by the direct method. Professor Patrick Harker [3] of the Wharton School has developed a procedure for making an even smaller number of comparisons.

Table 5. Overall Effectiveness of Policies in Cluster A*

Policies	Overall Effectiveness Monetarist Viewpoint	Keynesian Viewpoint	Supply Side Viewpoint
G,Tx,M↓ 10%	.14	.10	.35
G,Tx,M↓ 5%	.11	.11	.19
G↓ 10%	.11	.11	.16
G↓ 5%	.09	.10	.11
G_M↑=G_{TR}↓ 10%	.08	.18	.04
G_M↑=G_{TR}↓ 5%	.08	.16	.04
M, G↓ 6%	.25	.14	.07
M, G↓ 3%	.16	.10	.05

	Inflation (.45)			Unemployment (.30)			Growth (.11)			Domestic (.09)	Foreign (.05)
	(1)	(2)	(3)	(1)	(2)	(3)	(1)	(2)	(3)		
G,Tx,M↓ 10%	.120	.107	.283	103	.030	.469	.306	.061	.487	.240	.099
G,Tx,M↓ 5%	.069	.119	.196	.185	.139	.225	.124	.117	.191	.103	.047
G↓ 10%	.072	.144	.171	136	.026	.155	.219	.064	.158	.177	.065
G↓ 5%	.034	.089	.134	.149	.110	.078	.124	.156	.077	.164	.033
G_M↑=G_{TR}↓ 10%	.014	.089	.021	.159	.299	.015	.026	.265	.018	.044	.351
G_M↑=G_{TR}↓ 5%	.014	.045	.022	.170	.299	.015	.023	.291	.014	.108	.188
M, G↓ 6%	.457	.254	.100	.033	.019	.026	.102	.017	.033	.087	.141
M, G↓ 3%	.220	.153	.072	.065	.078	.019	.058	.029	.022	.076	.078

(1): Monetarist Viewpoint, (2): Keynesian Viewpoint, (3): Supply Side Viewpoint.
(*) The top part of table lists the overall effectiveness of the policies in Cluster A. The bottom part lists the effectiveness of the policies with respect to the specific criteria.

For each school of thought we selected the two best policies from cluster A and cluster C and the single best policy from cluster B. We then used the AHP methodology to rank these policies to arrive at the "optimal" policy. Tables 8, 9, and 10 contain the results of this procedure for policies favored by monetarists, Keynesians, and supply-siders respectively.

4. CONCLUSION

Monetarists consider a policy to reduce the growth rate of the money supply by 6% matched by a decrease in government spending to be optimal. Keynesians find a policy of increasing government spending by 10% while financing the deficit by issuing bonds and money to be the best policy. Supply-side economists favor a policy to reduce government spending and tax rates by 10% and would allow change in the money supply to be a balancing factor in the government's budget constraint.

It is interesting to see what we can observe about this analysis from the hindsight of our early 1987 perspective. Probably the best we can say is that a mixed set of policies prevailed. There was a supply-sider in the White House (Ronald Reagan) and something of a monetarist (Paul Volcker) holding the reins at the Fed. Taxes were decreased; inflation has moderated significantly; growth in the economy has been modest but steady since late 1982. However, it has not been possible to restrain government spending, thought by both monetarists and supply-siders in 1981 to be a very desirable end to achieve. This was the result primarily of an impasse between Congress and the Administration as to where to make the cuts -- defense or social programs. (The recently enacted Gramm-Rudman legislation seeks to address this problem by annual across-the-board cuts if agreement is not forthcoming). There has accordingly been a tremendous rise in the budget deficit and in the trade deficit; unemployment, a goal though still high relative to the earlier post-war period, has been brought under control; interest rates are down significantly; the stock market has more than doubled from a Dow Jones Index of less than 1000 to over 2000. Whether this signifies a healthy economy remains to be seen and is probably dependent on one's point of view. The average U.S. citizen may consider himself to be better off than he was in 1981, but to those outside the U.S., we are living on borrowed money - to finance our trade and budget deficits.

In any event we have now shown how the AHP can be applied to the problem of selecting an optimal macroeconomic policy and estimating its impact. This approach to forecasting has some advantages over more conventional methods. For instance, it makes it possible to incorporate ideas or theories into forecasts that are difficult to include in quantitative econometric models. In addition, since the AHP procedure is essentially "structure free," it eliminates the criticism that the results obtained from its use are predetermined by its a priori specification. Our brief analysis shows that the optimal choices of the various schools can be predicted by this process. The AHP also shows how strongly each ranks alternative policies relative to their primary preferences.

Table 6. Overall Effectiveness of Policies in Cluster B*

Policies	Overall Effectiveness Monetarist Viewpoint	Keynesian Viewpoint	Supply Side Viewpoint
Tx↓, B, M↑ 10%	.20	.29	.41
Tx↓, B, M↑ 5%	.15	.19	.10
Tc, G↓ 10%	.40	.34	.38
Tc, G↓ 5%	.25	.19	.31

	Inflation (.45) (1)	(2)	(3)	Unemployment (.30) (1)	(2)	(3)	Growth (.11) (1)	(2)	(3)	Domestic (.09)	Foreign (.05)
Tx↓, B, M↑ 10%	.040	.073	.330	.509	.590	.602	.103	.583	.580	151	.109
Tx↓, B, M↑ 5%	.115	.129	.116	.245	.252	.068	.073	.261	.080	.076	.250
Tc, G↓ 10%	.560	.550	.421	.093	.050	.273	.544	.069	.287	.490	.418
Tc, G↓ 5%	.281	.247	.133	.154	.107	.057	.280	.087	.053	.283	.223

(1): Monetarist Viewpoint, (2): Keynesian Viewpoint, (3): Supply Side Viewpoint.

(*) The top part of table lists the overall effectiveness of the policies in Cluster B. The bottom part lists the effectiveness of the policies with respect to the specific criteria.

Table 7. Overall Effectiveness of Policies in Cluster C*

Policies	Overall Effectiveness: Monetarist Viewpoint	Keynesian Viewpoint	Supply Side Viewpoint
G, B, M$\uparrow$ 10%	.15	.20	.12
G, B, M$\uparrow$ 5%	.11	.11	.13
G, Tx, B M$\uparrow$ 10%	.07	.16	.05
G, Tx, B M$\uparrow$ 5%	.09	.12	.08
$G_{TR}\uparrow=G_M\downarrow$ 10%	.14	.07	.21
$G_{TR}\uparrow=G_M\downarrow$ 5%	.15	.12	.25
$G_{TR}\uparrow=Tc\uparrow$ 10%	.15	.07	.05
$G_{TR}\uparrow=Tc\uparrow$ 5%	.12	.12	.09

	Inflation (.45)			Unemployment (.30)			Growth (.11)			Domestic (.09)	Foreign (.05)
	(1)	(2)	(3)	(1)	(2)	(3)	(1)	(2)	(3)		
G,B,M$\uparrow$ 10%	.016	.028	.095	.410	.420	.158	.057	.329	.113	.176	.080
G,B,M$\uparrow$ 5%	.028	.043	.135	.225	.122	.114	.081	.231	.159	.131	.153
G,Tx,BM$\uparrow$ 10%	.052	.096	.041	.095	.282	.028	.057	.165	.039	.107	.088
G,Tx,BM$\uparrow$ 5%	.101	.170	.073	.082	.079	.064	.031	.119	.057	.054	.235
$G_{TR}\uparrow=G_M\downarrow$ 10%	.263	.141	.220	.035	.030	.272	.118	.043	.225	.052	.046
$G_{TR}\uparrow=G_M\downarrow$ 5%	.263	.232	.303	.039	.018	.249	.102	.043	.319	.073	.060
$G_{TR}\uparrow=Tc\uparrow$ 10%	.108	.076	.037	.055	.030	.033	.455	.023	.025	.264	.222
$G_{TR}\uparrow=Tc\uparrow$ 5%	.171	.208	.090	.066	.015	.082	.027	.027	.054	.144	.125

(1): Monetarist Viewpoint, (2): Keynesian Viewpoint, (3): Supply Side Viewpoint.

(*) The top part of table lists the overall effectiveness of the policies in Cluster C. The bottom part lists the effectiveness of the policies with respect to the specific criteria.

Table 8. Overall Effectiveness of Monetarist Policies*

Policy	Overall Effectiveness
M, G↓ 6%	.33
M, G↓ 3%	.18
Tc, G↓ 10%	.17
G, B, M↑ 10%	.18
G_{TR}↑=G_M↓ 5%	.14

	Inflation (.45)	Unemployment (.30)	Growth (.11)	Domestic (.09)	Foreign (.05)
M, G↓ 6%	.595	.063	.230	.075	.212
M, G↓ 3%	.240	.136	.147	.049	.153
Tc, G↓ 10%	.113	.159	.503	.184	.061
G, B, M↑ 10%	.026	.411	.061	.116	.543
G_{TR}↑=G_M↓ 5%	.025	.231	.059	.576	.030

(*) The top part of the table lists the overall effectiveness of the policies preferred by monetarists. The bottom part lists the effectiveness of the policies with respect to the specific criteria. Policies in this table were evaluated from a monetarist perspective.

Table 9. Overall Effectiveness of Keynesian Policies*

Policy	Overall Effectiveness
$G_M\uparrow=G_{TR}\downarrow$ 10%	.19
$G_M\uparrow=G_{TR}\downarrow$ 5%	.11
Tc, $G\downarrow$ 10%	.22
G, B, $M\uparrow$ 10%	.26
G, Tx, B, $M\uparrow$	.20

	Inflation (.45)	Unemployment (.30)	Growth (.11)	Domestic (.09)	Foreign (.05)
$G_M\uparrow=G_{TR}\downarrow$ 10%	.278	.068	.086	.100	.472
$G_M\uparrow=G_{TR}\downarrow$ 5%	.143	.093	.102	.223	.259
Tc, $G\downarrow$ 10%	.433	.037	.046	.107	.040
G, B, $M\uparrow$ 10%	.057	.522	.317	.365	.114
$G_{TR}\uparrow=G_M\downarrow$ 10%	.025	.231	.059	.576	.030

(*) The top part of the table lists the overall effectiveness of the policies preferred by Keynesians. The bottom part lists the effectiveness of the policies with respect to the specific criteria. Policies in this table were evaluated from a Keynesian perspective.

Table 10. Overall Effectiveness of Supply-Side Policies*

Policy	Overall Effectiveness
G, Tx, M↓ 10%	.33
G, Tx, M↓ 5%	.18
Tx↓, B, M↑ 10%	.17
G_{TR}↑=G_M↓ 10%	.18
G_{TR}↑=G_M↓ 5%	.14

	Inflation (.45)	Unemployment (.30)	Growth (.11)	Domestic (.09)	Foreign (.05)
G, Tx, M↓ 10%	.562	.536	.567	.116	.161
G, Tx, M↓ 5%	.232	.157	.156	.121	.261
Tx↓, B, M↑ 10%	.126	.239	.211	.193	.433
G_{TR}↑=G_M↓ 10%	.029	.040	.030	.346	.048
G_{TR}↑=G_M↓ 5%	.051	.028	.037	.224	.097

(*) The top part of the table lists the overall effectiveness of the policies preferred by supply-side economists. The bottom part lists the effectiveness of the policies with respect to the specific criteria. Policies in this table were evaluated from a supply-side perspective.

REFERENCES

1. Anderson, L.C. and J.L. Jordan, "Monetary and Fiscal Action: A Test of Their Relative Importance in Economic Stabilization," Federal Reserve Bank of St. Louis, *Review*, November, 1968.
2. Cuthbertson, K., *Macroeconomic Policy: The New Cambridge, Keynesian and Monetarist Controversies*, Wiley, New York, 1979.
3. Harker, P.T., "Alternative Modes of Questioning in the Analytic Hierarchy Process," *Mathematical Modelling* 9, 3-5 (1987) 353-360.
4. Hildreth, C., and J. Houck, "Some Estimators for a Linear Model with Random Coefficients," *Journal of the American Statistical Association* (1968) 584-595.
5. Lucas, R.E., "Econometric Policy Evaluation: A Critique," in The Phillips Curve and Labor Markets, eds. Karl Brunner and Allan H. Meltzer, *The Carnegie-Rochester Conferences on Public Policy, Volume* 1, p.20, Amsterdam: North Holland, 1976.
6. Maddala, G.S., *Econometrics*, McGraw Hill International, New York, 1977.

7. Saaty, T.L., *The Analytic Hierarchy Process*, McGraw Hill International, New York, 1980.
8. Saaty, T.L, "A New Macroeconomic Forecasting and Policy Evaluation Method Using the Analytic Hierarchy Process", *Mathematical Modelling* 9, 3-5 (1987) 219-232.
9. Sargent, T., "Interpreting Economic Time Series," *Journal of Political Economy*, 1981.
10. Sims, C.A., "Macroeconomics and Reality," *Econometrica*, 1980.
11. Zahedi, F., "The Analytic Hierarchy Process - A Survey of the Method and Its Applications," *Interfaces* 16, 4 (1986) 96-108.
12. Zarnowitz, V., 1978, "On the Accuracy and Properties of Recent Macroeconomic Forecasts," *American Economic Review* 68, 2 (1978) 313-321.

CHAPTER 14

FORECASTING THE FUTURE OF THE SOVIET UNION

1. INTRODUCTION

In this chapter we report on a study carried out in May of 1990 which uses the AHP to determine the future of the Soviet Union. This question has been of utmost importance to every person alive because of the Soviet Union's implicit and explicit influence on the future of the world. This work is an attempt to project the outcome of the various forces at work within and outside the Soviet Union that were thought to affect its destiny. Three different scenarios were formulated as possible outcomes. The purpose was not just to predict the future, but to develop a framework where variables involved in this complex problem could be identified, the effect of these variables on shaping the future could be evaluated, and the overall outcomes from these events could be derived. The hope is for identifying some actions to be taken to facilitate the way to peace, to avoid unnecessary violence, and to formulate intelligent and consistent policies.

The framework constructed for the analysis included a hierarchy with the most general factors at the top, with increasingly specific factors located further down the hierarchy. These factors, classified in a top-down fashion, are Time Horizons, Forces, Actors, Objectives, Policies and Outcomes (see Figure 1). The bottom level of the hierarchy contains the scenarios believed to be the possible alternative outcomes of the future of the Soviet Union. The analytical process includes making judgments on pairs of elements throughout the hierarchy, one level at a time beginning at the top, based on the analysts' knowledge and feelings of the relative importance of the factors involved. The most heavily weighted alternative outcome in the bottom level is the most likely one.

Time horizons, at the top level, were short-term (the next two years), mid-term (2-5 years), and long-term (over 5 years). Under these time horizons, in the second level, the main forces driving the actions were Technology, Religion, Nationalities, Economy, International Affairs and Internal Politics.

In the next level the significant actors affected by these forces were Communist Party, Mikhail Gorbachev, People of Baltic Republics, People of Russia, People of Islamic Republics, People of Other Republics, Western World Countries, and Rest of World.

Each actor has individual objectives. The objectives for the different actors were carefully defined based on specific research on each of them. The next step was to identify all the policies being currently implemented by the different actors in order to achieve their respective objectives. Also costs and benefits for each of the objectives were identified.

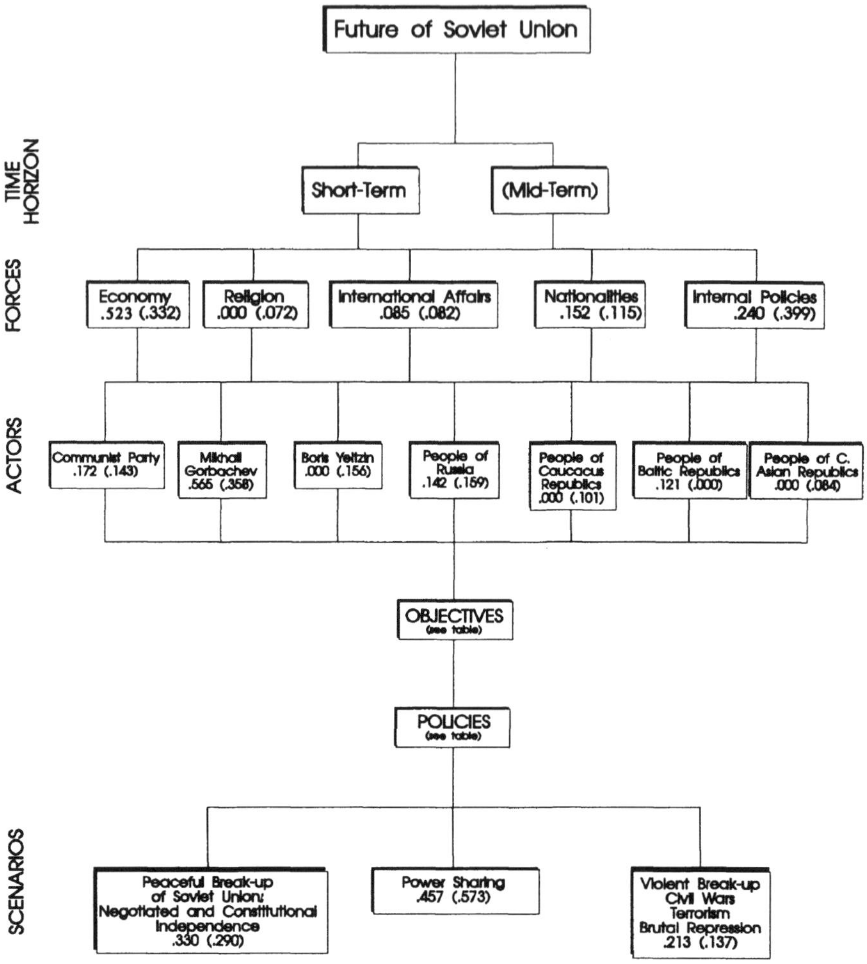

Figure 1. The Future of the Soviet Union Hierarchy

2. DEFINING THE FORECASTING MODEL

The evaluation of the future of the Soviet Union was focused toward three broadly defined potential outcome scenarios. The scenarios were called "Peaceful Breakup", "Power Sharing", and "Violent Breakup". Each of the scenarios was associated with a set of defining characteristics. Each of the proposed outcomes forecast a change in government and the power structure of the Soviet Union. The research team felt that change was an inherent aspect of progress and could not be avoided. The question to be answered with this analysis, based on the collective understanding of the team, was how the then current forces, actors, objectives, and policies for obtaining those objectives worked to shape the future of the Soviet Union.

The Analytic Hierarchy Process models complex sets of relationships between individual conceptual entities. It provides one with the ability to model "real world" situations in a manner that is fairly natural. Whenever we think about a complex problem, we tend to think of this problem in terms of its many aspects. For the construction of the prediction model for the Soviet future, the set of influences at work were defined as the interaction between two sets of entities, which were termed Forces and Actors. The value of AHP as a modeling method is that it allows one to account for all the interactions between the entities in the two sets. Comparisons of the different strength of Forces with each other, as well as comparisons between Forces and Actors were made. Further, it allows one to transmit the actors' influences on the outcomes through their own objectives and policies.

The general structure of the model relates the future of the Soviet Union in three different time frames. These Time Horizons were the prediction of the situation the Soviet Union may have found itself as a result of the circumstances and events at that time. It was further abstracted that the resulting situation would come from the interaction of the environmental conditions with the agents (Forces and Actors) which were modifying the environment.

3. FORCES

A Force is a macro-environmental condition that existed in the Soviet situation. There were several forces identified for use in the model: Economy, Technology, Religion, International Affairs, Nationalities, and Internal Politics. An Actor is a macro-environmental agent which works to transform the current Forces into future Outcomes for the Soviet Union. There were many actors identified as well: the Communist Party, Mikhail Gorbachev, Boris Yeltzin, the Western countries (NATO), the various peoples of the Soviet Republics grouped by region, and the various emerging political structures grouped by region.

It was not easy to define the Forces and actors. The Force labelled Economy was generally thought of as the set of all economic factors which describe the health of the national economy. Examples of such factors would be the availability and prices of raw materials for manufacturing, current prices and trends in food and essential goods; the gross national product, etc. Although no comprehensive list was composed to define this entity, it was taken to mean the degree of health of the national economy as a whole.

Technology was another abstract concept. The notion of technology as a force for change included the current distribution of technological resources among the Republics, the force of technological development as it affects economic change through innovation, and the relative desirability of technologies of neighboring republics threatening cessation.

Religion was a much more readily definable construct. Religion as a force for change was regarded as any religious influence which fostered a need for people to act. These influences were factors like an indoctrinated moral imperative, a need of religious solidarity, and nationalism born out of a common set of religious beliefs.

International Affairs were defined as the set of forces to which the Soviet Union was subjected to as a result of its position and strength in the world political arena. The scope of influence considered here relates to how internal policy was affected by international opinion.

Nationalities as a force were defined as the need experienced by a common ethnic group to express their identity; the need for expression being so strong that it fosters nationalism and a movement for nationalistic government. There did not seem to be any particular area within the Soviet Union that was exempt from this force.

The Internal Political environment within the Soviet Union was also seen to exert a collective force on the future of the Soviet Union. The scope of viable alternatives that would be acceptable to the interested parties stems from conditions which existed in this internal political arena.

4. ACTORS, OBJECTIVES, AND POLICIES

Caught up in this complex interplay of macro-environmental forces were the set of entities which were called actors. An actor was a definable individual or group which played a significant role in responding to forces that shaped current events and, therefore, future outcomes. Actors can be characterized in terms of their objectives and policies to carry out those objectives as attributes. These attributes help to define an actor's role and effectiveness in determining future outcomes. The structure of the model allows each actor to evaluate the importance of each objective under a particular circumstance (i.e. in light of a particular force) and vary the importance in a variety of situations. The relative effectiveness of the policies used to accomplish each of the defined objectives is also allowed to vary in accordance with the particular set of environmental parameters under consideration. The ability to express the relative importance of the objective depends on the Force under consideration at the time, is a particular strength of the AHP. This feature of the modeling technique allows one to give a situational context to the information in the model and to account for the overall meaning in a general context.

The Communist Party of the Soviet Union was certainly an actor in determining the future of the Soviet Union. Of particular concern within this group were the tendencies of the more traditionalist communists or staunch conservatives. They appeared to have three principal objectives: to maintain the Soviet constitution so that their legitimacy as the central authority was not undermined, to maintain the unity of the Soviet Union, and to retain the old form of strong central government. In support of its objective to maintain legitimacy and constitutionally support central authority, the Communist Party exercised policies of open opposition to "illegally declared" independence, tight restriction of centrally controlled raw materials and resources to the newly "independent" republics, and flagrant display of military strength in an act of intimidation. To further its objective of maintaining a cohesive Union, the Communist Party's policies focused public attention on the positive aspects of communism, opposed changes toward a more generally democratic multipartite system of election, and favored further isolation from the west. In order to advance its agenda on keeping the old form of strong central government, the Party's policy of recognizing only constitutionally ratified change as legitimate change was used. This policy was intended to maintain future authority through the party's current influence in the ratification process.

Another actor of significant impact was Mikhail Gorbachev. His objectives included keeping the Perestroika movement alive, maintaining the unity of the Soviet Republics, maintaining his personal political power and influence, and supporting a peaceful transition to the future. To keep Perestroika alive, Gorbachev adopted policies that elicited public support from the western world, attempted to enhance the level of domestic public support for his objectives, and accelerated the rate of change toward realizing the goals of Perestroika. The objective of unity is not so much concerned with maintaining a single political entity, such as the unity inferred from the objectives of the Communist Party, but rather to maintain a harmonious relationship regardless of the ultimate political configuration achieved. It seemed that Gorbachev intended to use his influence as president to forge new agreements between interested parties and to rewrite the constitution in order to derive the most mutually beneficial outcome for the Republics in the Union. The objective of maintaining personal political power was not considered to be an overwhelming concern of Gorbachev's, however, it was difficult to ignore the possibility that he would adopt policies that would enhance the likelihood of this objective. One visible policy was his opposition to the declared independence movement of the Baltic Republics. Although he was not officially opposed to independence, he was against the informal declaration process. That is to say, he wanted to uphold the Soviet constitution as the document that defined the Soviet Government since that was also the document which empowered the office of the president to act. His policy, which fostered the objective of peaceful change, was straight-forward. He was willing to negotiate and not to use force to accomplish his ends.

Boris Yeltzin became a new and powerful political actor. Yeltzin was riding a wave of public anti-Gorbachev sentiment to enhance his own political objectives. His strength came mainly from the popular support he received from the people of the Russian Federation. His specific objectives were to enhance his own political standing and power (at the expense of Gorbachev if possible or convenient), to realize a "free-market" economic structure, and to provide a greater degree of government autonomy for the Russian Federation. To achieve his objective of maintaining power, Yeltzin's policy focused on gaining the public support of his constituency - the Russian people, and weakening the power of his political rivals like Gorbachev. His policies regarding accelerated economic changes which were intended to result in a free market structure, and to increase international trade furthered his objective for the Russians to develop a free market structure in their economy. His objective of enhanced autonomy for the Russian Federation was supported by his policies of sovereignty and his vow to protect the self-interest of the Russian people.

The other actors that were identified as significant in shaping the future of the Soviet Union were the people of the various Soviet Republics. Specifically included in the analysis were the people of the Baltic Republics (Estonia, Latvia and Lithuania), the Caucasus Republics (Armenia, Azerbaijan, and Georgia), the Central Asian Republics (Kazakhstan, Kirgizia, Tadzhikistan, Turkmenistan, and Uzbekistan) and the people of the Russian Federation.

An objective of the people of the Baltic Republics was to increase the degree of liberalization as seen in their policies of a more liberalized economy and free speech. They also had an objective of independence from the Soviet Union. Policies that had furthered this objective were their respective declarations of independence, the election of new liberal political leadership, and their autonomous control of the communication channels.

The people of the Russian Federation had very different objectives. They felt that they had contributed disproportionately to the growth and development of the Soviet Union. Any future moves toward independence would have to take this strong sentiment into account. Indeed, the Russian people felt that they were due some type of compensation. They also held as an objective to rid themselves of their image of culpability for the social problems inside the Soviet Union. Another objective of the Russian Federation was to raise their individual standard of living. The masses were achieving these objectives through their open opposition to Gorbachev's reform policies and their support of more liberal reformers such as Yeltzin.

The people of the Caucasus Republics had highly interrelated and destabilizing objectives. The Georgians wanted independence and home rule, the Armenians wanted control of the territory up to and including Nagornokarabak, and the Azerbaijanis wanted control of Nagornokarabak so that they could expel the Armenians who live there. These people were considered not to be well organized and had few policies other than violence and demonstration to further their objective. This region was seen to have a high probability of contributing to general instability.

The People of Soviet Central Asia had a few minor objectives as well. They would have liked to upgrade their poor standard of living and they would have liked more equitable treatment and consideration from the central Soviet government. In general, they were a poorly organized group and had no formal policy short of protest and demonstration to help them realize their objectives. They had not yet awakened to their Islamic connection and the power they could wield by threatening alliance with the countries to their south, namely Iran, Turkey and Afghanistan.

5. OUTCOME SCENARIOS

The three outcome scenarios, "Peaceful Break-up", "Power Sharing", and "Violent Break-up" were all developed with the assumption that some change from the status quo was inevitable. Some time in the near future, the Soviet Union would become a very different political entity. A large impetus for this change would arise out of the vast cultural diversity of the Soviet people and the inability of a purely central authority to provide for the needs of these disparate groups. These scenarios all assumed some type of major shift in the make-up of the governing body of what was called the Soviet Union. Their principal differences stem from how closely aligned the resulting political entities are to each other and how the transformation process takes place.

The "Peaceful Break-up" scenario is the most utopian of the three. This scenario requires that all political change happen through the efforts of diplomacy under an umbrella of truce. No military force is used in order to secure a position for any of the interested actors.

The "Power Sharing" scenario also has room to accommodate peaceful change. Under this scenario, the governing interests of the Soviet Republics work together to form some type of coalition. The resulting structure could be as tightly defined and integrated as states are here in the United States or as loosely defined as the political and trade entities of NATO and the European Economic Community. It is believed that this scenario has the broadest appeal, since it accommodates such a wide spectrum of political and economic constructs for the betterment of the common good of all parties involved.

The "Violent Break-up" scenario implies that any final political and economic entity would be determined after some military conflict. The generally poor economic conditions and the relative strength of the economy as a force to shape destiny would rationally preclude this scenario. Unfortunately, other forces could conspire towards an irrational outcome.

6. PRUNING THE PROBLEM

The nature of the conflict in the Soviet Union was very complex. Many forces and actors were at work shaping the events impacting that nation's future. The forces exert pressure on the actors to shape policy, voice opinion, and produce action. In the initial model developed for forecasting the future of the Soviet Union, it was felt that there were too many force-actor relationships to accurately assess the effect of each of these interactions.

A decomposition of the problem was made for the purpose of clarification. All of the forces identified for the model had varying effects over time. A time horizon analysis was performed to determine if some of the forces and actors were more relevant in certain time frames than in others. Three time frames were used to test the time-relevance of each of the force/actor entities: the short term, 0-2 years; the mid-term, 2-5 years; and the long term, 5 years and over.

Two time series analyses were performed, one to get a time frame relevance of the forces at work and another to project the strength of an actor's influence over time. A hierarchy was developed for each of these analyses. Each of the forces and actors were compared to each other to determine their relative strength. Then each of the forces and actors were weighed against each of the time frames to determine what time frame held the greatest opportunity for the entity to influence events leading to the future. The results of the analysis are given in Tables 1 and 2.

The comparative model constructed to evaluate these forces and actors showed the extent to which each force or actor contributed to or influenced the future of the Soviet Union in each of the defined time frames. The percentages reflected the relative contribution of each of the elements compared to the comprehensive effect of all the elements.

This relative evaluation made it possible to select the most influential actors and forces from the above set of defined actors and forces. An actor was selected for use in the overall evaluation if the actor's individual contribution accounted for more than 5% of the overall effect of the actors in a given time frame. A force was selected if its relative contribution margin accounted for more than 10% of the overall effect.

Table 1. Contribution and Influence

Actors	ShortTerm Outcomes	Mid Term Outcomes	Long Term Outcomes
Mikhail Gorbachev	47.84%	35.85%	20.39%
People of the Russian Federation	13.15	9.85	9.60
People of the Baltic Republics	12.87	2.52	3.00
Communist Party	11.19	15.30	13.20
Western Nations	4.20	3.56	3.00
Boris Yeltzin	3.64	16.14	13.80
Government of the Russian Federation	2.24	2.31	1.20
Governments of the Baltic Republics	1.68	0.42	0.41
Emerging Govts. of the Central Asian Republics	0.84	5.03	6.00
People of the Caucasus Republics	0.84	5.03	6.00
Governments of the Central European Republics	0.56	1.26	9.00
Governments of the Caucasus Republics	0.28	0.63	3.00
People of the Central Asian Republics	0.11	0.21	1.80
Forces			
Economy	49.19%	22.83%	17.91%
Nationalism	16.34	29.21	24.69
Internal Politics	17.80	11.42	5.56
International Affairs	12.95	11.42	6.79
Religion	2.91	19.18	29.26
Technology	0.81	5.94	15.43

Table 2. Actors' Objectives and Policies
(short term priority/medium term priority)

	Objectives	Policies
Communist Party	Unity of the Soviet Union (.102/.114)	Opposition to Independence Movements (.021/.023) Tighten Economic Sanctions (.064/.068) Show Military Strength (.017/.023)
	Keep Old Government (.055/.028)	Focus on Positive Aspects of Communism (.018/.017) Opposition to Changes Toward Democracy (.026/.005) Favor Independence & Isolation from Western World (.009/.005)
	Maintain Constitution (.015/.000)	No Changes Outside the Constitution (.015/.000)
Mikhail Gorbachev	Keep Perestroika Alive (.292/.252)	Gain Support from Western World (.029/.012) Gain Popular Support (.173/.175) Accelerate Changes (.091/.063)
	Unity of Soviet Union (.021/.000)	Against Declared Independence Movements (.021/.000)
	Maintain Power (.106/.071)	Use New Position as President (.044/.036) Rewrite the Constitution (.060/.036)
	Peaceful Changes (.145/.037)	Willingness Not to Use Force (.145/.037)
People of Russia	Be Repaid (.048/.053) Improve Standard of Living (.075/.083) Change Image of Culpability (.020/.023)	Support Liberal Reformers (.105/.118) Opposition to Gorbachev's Reforms (..035/.039)

Table 2. (Cont.)
(short term priority/medium term priority)

	Objectives	Policies
People of Baltic Republics	Independence (.057/.000)	Declaration of Independence (.024/.000) Election of New Leaders (.019/.000) Control of Communication Channels (.014/.000)
	Liberalization (.065/.000)	Liberalize the Economy (.040/.000) Opening of Free Speech (.024/.000)
People of Caucasus Republics	Georgian Independence (.000/.034)	Peaceful Georgian Protest (.000/.034)
	Unification of Armenia (.000/.034)	Violence in Armenia
	Azerbajani Control of Nagornokarabak (.000/.034) and Azerbajan (.000/.068)	
People of Central Asian Republics	Equitable Treatment (.000/.043) Improve Standard of Living (.000/.043)	Protests and Demonstrations (.000/.086)
Boris Yeltzin	Political Power and Revenge (.000/.000)	Maintain Support of Russian People Weaken Gorbachev's Position in Power
	Free Market Economy (.000/.000)	Accelerate Shift to Free-Market Structure Increase Trade with the West
	Government AUtonomy (.000/.000)	Sovereignty for the Russian Federation Protect Self-Interest of Russia within Russia

7. CONSTRUCTION OF THE SHORT TERM MODEL

The forces that significantly contributed to the short term model were Economy, International Affairs, Nationalities, and Internal Politics. According to the time-frame analysis, it was determined that these forces contributed 85% of the net force effect in the future of the Soviet Union. The relative strength of each of these entities was weighted against each other. This resulted in a relative ranking among the four forces.

The actors that could have significant impact in the short term were the Communist Party, Mikhail Gorbachev, the People of the Russian Federation, and the People of the Baltic Republics. These actors contributed to 85% of the net actor effect on the future of the Soviet Union. The relative influence of the actors selected was also determined in a pairwise comparison fashion and their relative strength was calculated.

The situation in the Soviet Union was highly interdependent. As a result, all of the forces identified were seen to have relevance to the actors who were identified. Such a set of relationships was reflected in a hierarchy by comparing the relative strength of each actor in terms of each force. In the short term model, this established five sets of actor rankings; their relative strength in terms of each other and their relative strength when considering their ability to exert influence over one of the major macro-environmental forces. This feature of the modeling process allows a dynamic contextual definition of the effect of an actor on his environment. If the macro-environmental pressure can be represented by the effect of each of the identified forces, then each actor's ability to react to the components of this pressure are captured in the context of each force-actor relation. If the relative strength of a force changes over time, the model is well suited to reflect a similar shift in the ability of the actors to exert their own influence due to this context sensitivity.

The model defined an actor as an agent of change, responding to the forces in his environment. The actor accomplishes change by pursuing his individual objectives. The objectives are achieved to the extent of the effectiveness of the actor's policies as applied in a given situation. For example, if the People of the Baltic Republics exercise their policy to declare independence in order to achieve their objective of independence, this may be in solid response to pressures from Nationalism. However, it is questionable whether such a policy was useful in responding to the pressure of their Economic forces. A more influential policy to meet the needs of that force may come from exercising the policy of electing new, more liberal leadership.

The implication here is that although the set of interactions between an actor, his objectives and the policies used to obtain those objectives are fixed constructs, the distribution of importance is varied in each of the contexts in which the actor is situated. This makes the actor a dynamic entity within the model.

The mechanism which insures the context sensitivity of the definition of the actor's role in shaping the future comes from evaluating the actor's attributes, his policies and objectives, with regard to each of the forces presented in the hierarchy. This means that any path along the resulting hierarchy from the defined scenarios to the future of the Soviet Union, defines a perspective for the problem. This leads to a very rich definition of the problem, accommodating the many valid perspectives often found in such abstract decision making.

After constructing and evaluating a forecast for the future of the Soviet Union in a short term time frame, certain policies, objectives, and actors displayed a high degree of relative influence toward determining the potential outcomes for the future. The primary result of the analysis was that the forces and actors were focusing the forces for change toward a mutually beneficial outcome. Their strongest inclination was toward an outcome of shared power, followed closely by a peacefully negotiated independent existence.

Of all the actors considered in this time frame, clearly Mikhail Gorbachev emerged as the most influential. A high degree of his influence was channeled toward these peaceful ends by his objectives of keeping the Perestroika movement alive and by his desire for the peaceful evolution of his country's economic and political systems. The policies employed to accomplish these objectives also helped to direct his influence toward peaceful negotiation and coalition. He was actively pursuing the support of the people and must therefore have had their interests in mind. His desire to accelerate the rate of economic reform also favored the stability of a diplomatic resolution to the conflict.

The People of the Baltic Republics are non-violent in their approach to stimulating change. The people of the Russian Federation, although emphatic that their needs should be taken care of, are also supporting moves with stabilizing influence. This is not surprising since both peoples have suffered through long periods of war and destruction in this century. The policy of the Russian people to support liberal reformers for political office forces the hand of the Government to respond in kind or lose popular support, so essential in forcing cooperation.

Running slightly counter to this trend toward a peaceful resolution are the objectives and policies of the Communist Party. It would appear from our analysis that their objectives are slightly too self serving to accommodate the reform necessary to the people. Their policies tended toward repression and authoritarian response, not widely upheld by the people at large.

8. CONSTRUCTION OF THE MID-TERM MODEL

To test the consistency of the model in predicting future outcomes from current forces, the problem was also examined in the mid-term time frame. Additional forces and actors were added. The people of the Central Asian and Caucasus Republics were added to the set of actors and the people of the Baltic Republics were deleted. The common understanding which led to the introduction of the new actors was that these areas of the Soviet Union are rich in social problems and poor in developing an organized response. The People of the Baltic Republics were removed from consideration because of the belief that the Baltic conflict would have resolved itself in some manner consistent with the predicted outcomes of the short term model. This does not imply that they were no longer actors, but simply that they were no longer among the most significant in the mid-term time frame.

The increasing relative strength of the people of the Caucasus and Central Asian Republics in the mid-term also served to introduce another macro-environmental force, Religion. The inclusion of Religion as a force stems from the fact that the Central Asian Republics are largely composed of Islamic peoples. They are relatively fundamentalist in nature and take their religious beliefs seriously. In as much as religion is a strong force in the individual lives of these people, it must also be a macro-force for the collectivity.

Religion also figures prominently into the lives of the people of the Caucasus Republics. Here, however, religion is not so much a source of daily inspiration as it is a source of hatred and discrimination. Religious tension between the Armenians and the Azerbaijanis provided stimulus for action by other actors in the model.

Boris Yeltzin was also added as an actor in the mid-term. His influence primarily stems from the popular support provided by the people of the Russian Federation and his personal history of interaction with the Communist Party. Yeltzin is a reformer who wanted to speed economic reform.

This infusion of diversity into the prediction model stressed the need for negotiation in determining the future of the Soviet Union. With the addition of more disparate actors, the need for change was intensified. A greater number of disparate forces implied a greater number of perspectives to be accounted for and thus for a greater degree of compromise. Under these conditions, some type of coalitions were thought to be likely to emerge. In retrospect we believe that an error was made by Gorbachev in not being able to effect gradual change. The Soviet Union should have dissolved itself as a process rather than let loose to determine its destiny.

9. CONCLUSIONS

The forecast for the future of the Soviet Union strongly suggested an outcome scenario of peaceful negotiated change. The most beneficial and probable outcome was seen to be that of some type of coalition government or shared power. The needs of the Soviet people were varied. Any attempt to form a cohesive political or economic entity which could respond to those needs would have had to involve negotiation and compromise. The problem often encountered at the negotiating table is how to insure equitable compromise without unnecessary delay. Such compromise can be achieved and delay avoided through using the AHP in conflict resolution. The strength of the model in this arena is that it provides for a standard medium of discourse and allows for the expression of the normally unquantifiable components of such interactions, like individual emotion.

The outcome of the political upheavals in the former Soviet Union was not power sharing which many people, including some Americans wish had happened, but peaceful break up. There are two reasons for the difference between the exercise and what happened in reality. One is that the participants exaggerated Gorbachev's power and did not know enough about Yeltzin to accord him greater influence. The other is that in today's world, after the break up, strong efforts are being made by Yeltzin's Russia to get back to some form of sharing in trade, international relations and the like. Peaceful break up is leading to a modified form of power sharing among several of the republics of the former Soviet Union.

CHAPTER 15

ABORTION AND THE STATES: HOW WILL THE SUPREME COURT RULE ON THE UPCOMING PENNSYLVANIA ABORTION ISSUE

1. INTRODUCTION

In the Summer of 1992 the Supreme Court of the United States was supposed to rule on a controversial Pennsylvania statute [13] restricting the rights of women in obtaining an abortion. Included in this statute are provisions requiring that doctors provide women with state-prescribed information about pregnancy and abortion, that the procedure be delayed 24 hours after the recitation and that husbands be notified prior to the procedure. The lower court upheld the first two provisions but declared unconstitutional the husband notification requirement.

On January 22, 1973, the United States Supreme Court, in a landmark decision, ruled on the constitutionality of abortion by handing down judgments in two "test" cases: *Roe v. Wade* [10] and *Doe v. Bolton* [7]. The court replaced two states' statutes by declaring their restrictions on abortion unconstitutional. The court replaced the invalidated statutes with a uniform system clearly identifying the stages of pregnancy in trimesters and the "legal" enforcement one can expect during each trimester.

The Court used the "strict scrutiny" standard which applies to only a handful of constitutional rights that the Supreme Court has labeled "fundamental". They determined that the right to privacy, whether in the Fourteenth Amendment's definition of personal liberty, restricting government intrusion, or the Ninth Amendment's consignment of rights to the people, is broad enough to include the right to have an abortion. In denying a woman the choice of terminating an unwanted pregnancy, the state would create a hardship for the pregnant woman that could result in psychological harm ([8], p.11).

These rulings have come under close scrutiny since conservatives took office in 1980. Presidents Reagan and Bush have collectively appointed seven of the nine Supreme Court justices. Since the term of the president is four years and the term of a Supreme Court jurist is for life or until he or she voluntarily resigns, it is possible for the political philosophy of an ex-president to have a profound effect on Court decisions for many years after he leaves office.

This chapter examines, with the assistance of the Analytic Hierarchy Process (AHP), how these justices might rule on the pending Pennsylvania statute limiting abortion rights. We used the nine Supreme court justices as our criteria, giving each of them an equal weight. Beneath each justice we used five subcriteria that we determined to be the most important. These criteria are: 1) Women's issues, 2) Precedent, 3) Moral issues, 4) Political issues and 5) Biological issues. These are individually outlined and defined below. Finally, we concluded that there were three likely outcomes of the ruling: overturn *Roe v. Wade*, uphold *Roe v. Wade* in its present form and weaken *Roe v. Wade* by giving states more independent power to restrict abortions. These, too, are outlined and defined below. Figure 1 shows the hierarchic representation used in this analysis.

2. SUBCRITERIA

Women's Issues: We defined women's issues as those issues deemed important by the Pro-Choice movement. This would include the constitutional right of each woman to make her own decisions regarding her body. Although we have defined this as women's issues, we do not claim that all women agree with the Pro-Choice movement nor that all men are Pro-Lifers.

Precedent: By precedent we mean the numerous cases that have gone before the Supreme Court since the early 1970's. Included in this, but not restricted to it, is *Roe v. Wade*. Also of importance are the cases of *Webster v. Reproductive Health Services* which gave states more freedom to regulate abortions throughout the entire pregnancy, and *the City of Akron v. Akron Center for Reproductive Health* [5] which required parental consent, informed consent, a 24-hour waiting period and the proper disposal of fetal remains.

Moral Issues: We define moral issues as those issues deemed important by the Pro-Life movement. Included is the constitutional right of the fetus and the belief that abortion is murder and should be illegal.

Political Issues: To make the decision-making process easier, we loosely defined political issues as conservatism. Although, not always true, we determined that conservatives are much more pro-life than liberals. Along the same vein we linked Republicans with conservatism and Democrats with liberalism.

Biological Issues: Our broad definition of biological issues is *viability*. Viability is a medical concept that specifies a certain time within the gestation cycle when the fetus is capable of independent survival outside the mother's womb. This has been a difficult issue for the court to deal with because it is very closely related to the issue of "when life begins." In 1973, the court concluded ([8], p.1):

> "we need not resolve the difficult question of when life begins, when those trained in the respective fields of medicine, philosophy and theology are unable to arrive at any consensus. The judiciary, at this point in the development of man's knowledge, is not in a position to speculate as to the answer."

Also, in *Akron v. Akron Center for Reproductive Health* the Court ruled ([5], p.491):

"A State may not adopt one theory of when life begins to justify its regulation of abortion."

The Court has thus far ruled that viability should be determined by the attending physician. The current problem is that modern medicine has allowed for much earlier viability than existed in 1973. Current medicine has allowed pre-third trimester fetuses to survive outside the womb. This is an issue which has not yet, but will likely, be dealt with by the courts.

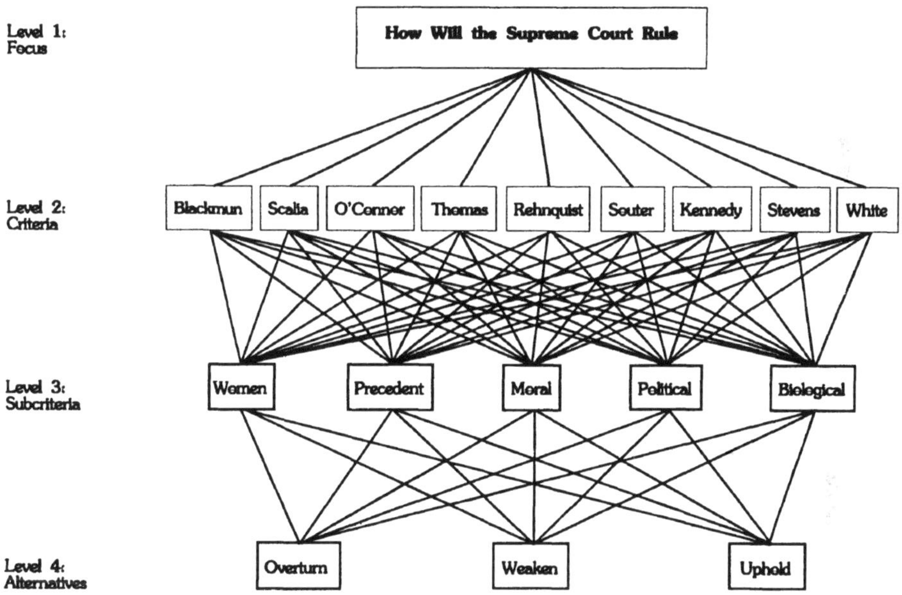

Figure 1. Judicial Decisions

3. ALTERNATIVES

We chose three alternatives that we felt were most likely to occur in the June ruling. In the past, including the very important case of *Webster v. Reproductive Health Services*, the Court has been averse to upholding or overruling *Roe v. Wade*. Whether or not this will be the case in the Pennsylvania ruling can only be determined by the Court.

First, we defined OVERTURN as disallowing abortion as a legal right in the United States. The court would rule that the right to an abortion is no longer a fundamental right protected by the Constitution. Basically, abortion would be legal only when the mother's life is in danger.

Second, we defined UPHOLD as allowing abortion to remain legal, without undue restrictions, in every state in the country. Basically, this would mean returning to the post-*Roe* era when there were no statutes limiting a woman's right to an abortion.

Finally, we defined WEAKEN as what is currently occurring in the United States with regard to abortion rights. Generally, this means granting individual states more power in controlling when and how an abortion can be received and who can receive it.

4. CRITERIA

As stated previously, we used as our criteria the nine justices currently sitting on the Supreme Court. Since each justice is allowed one "vote," we gave each equal weight. We used many experts' opinions from books and law journals to determine how each justice will weight each criterion and how each subcriterion will affect the alternative selected. Below we have outlined the major reasons for determining how each justice will vote:

William Rehnquist: As the most influential of the nine justices, Rehnquist's opinion is very important. Prior to his appointment as Chief Justice by President Reagan, Rehnquist ruled on many abortion cases as a regular jurist. He was one of two dissenting jurists in the *Roe v. Wade* decision. For this reason, we decided that PRECEDENT was not held in high regard by Justice Rehnquist, but that he would give it some weight (0.134) because of the recent cases limiting rights in which he concurred. We determined Rehnquist to be a conservative, and, therefore, we assumed that he would rank POLITICAL ISSUES about the same as precedent (0.118). In the area of WOMEN'S ISSUES we assumed that he would assign it a very low ranking (0.055); in fact, we ranked it lower than any of the criteria based on his ruling in *Roe v. Wade*. He opined ([8], p.15):

> "The fact that a majority of states have had restrictions on abortions for at least a century is a strong indication that the

> asserted right to an abortion is not so rooted in traditions and conscience of our people as to be ranked fundamental. Even today, when society's views are changing on abortion, the very existence of debates on the issue is evidence that the right to an abortion is not so universally accepted as one would have us believe."

In the area of BIOLOGICAL ISSUES, we thought that he would rank it low (0.086) because of *Webster v. Reproductive Health Services* in which he ruled that legislative determinations of when life begins are not per se unconstitutional. He ruled, in essence, that the Court permits a state to determine when life begins, but maintained that such determinations are not enough to save a statute if it is unconstitutional for other reasons ([4], p.513). Finally, we determined that Rehnquist would weight the area of MORAL ISSUES very high (0.608) based on his earlier rulings, his belief that the right to an abortion is not a fundamental individual right, and his belief that fetuses should have individual rights.

Byron White: In most cases which we have researched related to abortion rights, Justice White has ruled very closely with Justice Rehnquist. For this reason, and because of his written opinions, we have ranked White very closely with Rehnquist. In the area of WOMEN'S ISSUES, we ranked White slightly lower than Rehnquist (0.045). And we weighted MORAL ISSUES very high (0.529). These criteria were ranked based on his opinion in the *Doe v. Bolton* case ([8], p.28):

> "In a sensitive area such as this, involving as it does issues over which reasonable men may easily and heatedly differ, I cannot accept the Court's exercise of its clear power of choice by interposing a constitutional barrier to states efforts to protect human life and by investing mothers and doctors with the constitutionally protected right to exterminate it."

For the PRECEDENT criterion, we gave it a low ranking (0.097) for the same reason we did with Rehnquist: because he dissented in *Roe v. Wade*. For POLITICAL ISSUES, we rated it low (0.091) because, although he has voted conservative, he was appointed by a Democratic President. Finally, for BIOLOGICAL ISSUES, we gave it a fairly high ranking (0.237) because of his belief that life begins at conception and, therefore, fetuses have rights that should be protected.

Antonin Scalia: Although we have very little information on how Justice Scalia would vote in an abortion case, his extremely conservative rulings in matters such as law enforcement and capital punishment led us to believe that he would vote accordingly on abortion. For this reason, and because he was appointed by President Reagan whose views on abortion are well-known, we gave him a high ranking on POLITICAL ISSUES (0.230). Also, because he has been critical of earlier rulings, namely *Roe v. Wade*, we ranked PRECEDENT low (0.089) and WOMEN'S

ISSUES low (0.058). For BIOLOGICAL, we ranked it low (0.058) because we had little expert information. Finally, we ranked MORAL ISSUES high (0.565) because of his concurring viewpoint in *Webster v. Reproductive Health Services*: He never directly ruled on the issue of abortion, but made clear that he did not believe in the constitutional right of a woman to have an abortion. This led us to conclude that he believed in fetal rights and, therefore, moral issues should be ranked high.

Clarence Thomas: Because Justice Thomas was just recently appointed, we had no clear abortion rulings to use in our analysis. However, we do know that he has ruled very closely with Justice Scalia in almost all cases. In the Wall Street Journal it is stated that "...Justice Thomas continues to solidify his alliance with Justice Scalia. Not only do they nearly always vote on the same side of a case, but Justice Thomas's reasoning distinctly resembles that of Justice Scalia" ([3], p.B6). for this reason, we ranked each criterion identical to the rankings for Scalia: WOMEN'S ISSUES (0.058), PRECEDENT (0.089), MORAL (0.565), POLITICAL (0.230) and BIOLOGICAL (0.058).

John Paul Stevens: From our research, we found Stevens to hold individual rights and previous cases in high regard. Therefore, we gave PRECEDENT a high ranking (0.455). In a ruling in 1980, concerning state funding of abortions Stevens dissented with the majority seeing a "clear conflict with the decision in *Roe v. Wade*, which gave women the right to choose not to bear children. Here, government stacks the deck against this choice, at least for indigent women" ([11], p.160). Also, this ruling established his beliefs in women's individual freedom to choose, and, as a result, we also ranked WOMEN'S ISSUES high (0.220). Because these beliefs directly conflict with our definition of MORAL ISSUES we ranked it low (0.054). We also ranked political very low (0.049) since he is not considered to be a conservative jurist. Finally, we ranked biological high (0.223) because of his concurring with the trimester system of determining when, and if, women can have an abortion.

Sandra Day O'Connor: Although, Justice O'Connor has been on the court for many years, it is unclear how she would rule in an abortion case. She has ruled in a few cases involving abortion but has not clearly stated her opinion. We know, however, that Justice O'Connor does not believe abortion to be a fundamental right deserving "strict scrutiny." Instead she uses the "undue burden" standard saying that laws should not burden "unduly" a woman's right to choose an abortion. Therefore, our research has led us to believe that Justice O'Connor will vote to restrict women's rights by strengthening the rights of the states, but will not vote to overrule *Roe v. Wade.*

We ranked the issues that we deemed will weaken *Roe* high, including PRECEDENT (0.397) and BIOLOGICAL (0.397) and the other criteria low; including, WOMEN'S ISSUES (0.110), MORAL (0.048) and POLITICAL (0.048). In his book, Dan Drucker states ([8], p.164:

> "O'Connor, the only woman to sit on the Court, can be expected to play a crucial role in its deliberations. O'Connor is in the middle; she supports the right to abortion, but she may be willing to restrict it in some way."

David Souter: Because David Souter was appointed recently, we had very little expert information to incorporate into our model. We found, however, many people believing him to be a "fair and thoughtful jurist" who bases his rulings heavily on prior cases. For this reason, we ranked PRECEDENT extremely high (0.640). We also found him to have a high regard for individual rights and used this information to rank WOMEN'S ISSUES high (0.125). We had little information on his moral beliefs or his feelings related to viability, therefore, we ranked MORAL ISSUES low (0.069) and BIOLOGICAL ISSUES low (0.068). Finally, although he was appointed by President Bush and should be politically conservative his disparate rulings in numerous cases involving issues of individual freedoms caused us to rank POLITICAL ISSUES fairly low (0.098).

Anthony Kennedy: Anthony Kennedy is also a new justice who has no record regarding how he will rule on abortion issues. Because he was appointed by President Reagan and considered extremely conservative by many, we ranked POLITICAL ISSUES high (0.179). Also, he is known to follow closely prior rulings and, therefore, we ranked PRECEDENT very high (0.590). For WOMEN'S ISSUES we used a very low ranking (0.065) based on a statement by Eve Paul, general counsel for Planned Parenthood which stated ([8], p.164):

> "This is a new Court. Kennedy is new and has not previously expressed his views on the abortion issue."

Regarding the remaining criteria, we ranked each quite low because of the lack of available information. For MORAL ISSUES we gave it a ranking of 0.055 and for BIOLOGICAL ISSUES we ranked it 0.112.

Harry Blackmun: Justice Blackmun is the only justice that we believe will definitely rule in favor of upholding a woman's right to have an abortion. He concurred in the *Roe v. Wade* decision and has voted to uphold it in every decision since. He made it clear that a woman's right to receive an abortion should not be weakened in his *Webster v. Reproductive Health Services* decision ([8], p.180):

> "Although today, no less than yesterday, the Constitution and the decisions of this Court prohibit a state from enacting laws that inhibit women from the meaningful exercise of that right, a plurality of this Court implicitly invites every state legislature to enact more and more restrictive abortion regulation in order to provoke more and more test cases, in the hope that sometime down the line, the court will return the law of procreative

freedom to the severe limitations that generally prevailed in this country before January 22, 1973."

In fact, Justice Blackmun is very clear that the fundamental constitutional right of women to decide whether to terminate a pregnancy survives. He opined ([8], p. 161):

"I fear for the future. I fear for the liberty and equality of the millions of women who have lived and come of age in the 16 years since *Roe* was decided. I fear for the integrity of, and the public esteem for, this Court."

For obvious reasons, we ranked his criteria high that would uphold *Roe v. Wade* in its 1973 form. We ranked WOMEN'S ISSUES high (0.477), PRECEDENT high (0.292) and BIOLOGICAL ISSUES high (0.125). The criteria that would overturn or severely weaken *Roe v. Wade* we ranked low; MORAL ISSUES at 0.0252 and POLITICAL ISSUES at 0.054.

The priorities of the issues with respect to the judges are given in Table 1.

Next, we prioritized the alternatives with respect to each judge and each criterion. Table 2 summarizes the global priorities we obtained. The priorities of the alternatives are obtained by adding their weights (Table 2) for all the criteria and all the judges. We have: Overturn (0.376), Weaken (0.399) and Uphold (0.225). It is our belief, based on the AHP model, that the Supreme Court will uphold at least parts of the Pennsylvania statue and will, as a result, weaken the rights of women who choose to have an abortion in the state of Pennsylvania.

	Women	Precedent	Moral	Political	Biological
Blackmun	0.477	0.292	0.052	0.054	0.125
Kennedy	0.065	0.590	0.055	0.179	0.112
O'Connor	0.110	0.397	0.048	0.048	0.397
Rehnquist	0.055	0.134	0.608	0.118	0.086
Scalia	0.058	0.089	0.565	0.230	0.058
Souter	0.125	0.640	0.069	0.098	0.068
Stevens	0.220	0.455	0.054	0.049	0.223
Thomas	0.058	0.089	0.565	0.230	0.058
White	0.045	0.097	0.529	0.091	0.237

On June 30, 1992, The United States Law Week ([12], p.1201) reported the result of the U.S. Supreme decision:

"The U.S. Supreme Court yesterday reaffirmed the core principles of *Roe v. Wade*, 410 U.S. 113 (1973), but at the same time upheld most of a restrictive Pennsylvania abortion statute. Only a provision requiring a woman to notify her husband before obtaining an abortion was struck down. *(Planned Parenthood of Southeastern Pennsylvania v. Casey*, US SupCt, Nos. 91-744 & 91-902, 6/2/92)"

6. CONCLUSIONS

As shown in a recent poll conducted by Parade Magazine, abortion rights is a hot topic in the United States, one which is subject to fierce debate between Pro-choice advocates and Pro-lifers. Of the 2,538 people polled, 71 percent felt that abortion should remain legal and 61 percent believed *Roe v. Wade* should not be overturned ([6], p.4). How the Supreme Court rules in June will certainly have a serious impact on the people of Pennsylvania and, most likely, all citizens of the United States. This is a very complex problem without a clearcut solution. Certainly the type of problem suited for analysis by the Analytic Hierarchy Process.

	(1)	(2)	(3)	(4)	(5)	(6)	(7)	(8)	(9)
Women									
(A)	0.001	0.001	0.000	0.000	0.001	0.000	0.000	0.000	0.000
(B)	0.010	0.001	0.002	0.001	0.001	0.003	0.005	0.001	0.001
(C)	**0.042**	0.006	0.010	0.005	0.005	0.011	0.020	0.005	0.004
Precedent									
(A)	0.001	0.001	0.000	0.000	0.001	0.001	0.000	0.001	0.000
(B)	**0.023**	**0.046**	0.031	0.005	0.007	**0.050**	**0.035**	0.007	0.008
(C)	0.009	0.019	0.013	0.004	0.003	0.021	0.015	0.003	0.003
Moral									
(A)	0.004	0.005	0.005	**0.061**	**0.057**	0.007	0.005	**0.057**	**0.053**
(B)	0.001	0.001	0.000	0.006	0.006	0.001	0.001	0.006	0.005
(C)	0.001	0.000	0.000	0.001	0.001	0.000	0.000	0.000	0.001
Political									
(A)	0.005	0.016	0.004	**0.010**	**0.020**	0.009	0.004	**0.020**	0.008
(B)	0.001	0.003	0.001	0.002	0.004	0.002	0.001	0.004	0.002
(C)	0.000	0.000	0.000	0.001	0.001	0.000	0.000	0.001	0.000
Biological									
(A)	0.002	0.002	0.006	0.001	0.001	0.001	0.003	0.001	0.003
(B)	**0.010**	0.009	**0.033**	0.007	0.001	0.006	0.019	0.005	**0.020**
(C)	0.000	0.000	0.006	0.001	0.005	0.001	0.003	0.001	0.003

(1) Blackmun, (2) Kennedy, (3) O'Connor, (4) Rehnquist, (5) Scalia, (6) Souter, (7) Stevens, (8) Thomas, (9) White.
(A) Overturn, (B) Weaken, (C) Uphold.

* The bold priorities represent the most likely standing of each justice in each issue.

REFERENCES

1. Barret, Paul M., "Justices and two Lower Courts Face Confrontation Over Abortion, Taxes," *The Wall Street Journal,* p.B6: C2, January 24, 1992.
2. Barrett, Paul M., "Justices Agree to Rule on Abortion Law in Pennsylvania, but May Sidestep Roe," *The Wall Street Journal* p.A16: C1, January 22, 1992..
3. Barrett, Paul M., "Thomas Emerges as Bold New Justice With Strong Dissents in Criminal Cases," *The Wall Street Journal* p.B6: C2, May 28, 1992.
4. Brueschke, Erich and Jason Brueschke, 1990. "Constitutional Law: The Future of the Abortion Controversy and the Role of the Supreme Court After Webster v. Reproductive Health Services," *Oklahoma Law Review* 43, pp. 481-513.
5. *City of Akron v. Akron Center for Reproductive Health, Inc.* 462 United States Reports 416 (1983).
6. Clements, Mark, "Will They Make Abortion Illegal? What Voters Say," *The Pittsburgh Press, Parade Magazine*, pp.4-6, May 17, 1990.
7. *Doe v. Bolton*, 410 Unites States Reports 179 (1973).
8. Drucker, Dan, *Abortion Decisions of the Supreme Court, 1973 through 1989: A Comprehensive Review with Historical Commentary*, Jefferson, N.C.: McFarland & Co., 1990.
9. Gersh, Debra, "Press Lost a Friend on the Supreme Court," *Editor & Publisher* 124n1, p.18, 20, January 5, 1991.
10. *Roe v. Wade*, 410 United States Reports 113 (1973).
11. Rubin, Eva R., *Abortion, Politics, and the Courts*, Westports, CT: Greenwood Press, 1982.
12. "Roe v. Wade Is Reaffirmed But No Clear Standard Emerges," *The United States Law Week* 60, No. 51, p.1201, June 30, 1992.
13. *Planned Parenthood of Southeastern Pennsylvania v. Casey*, US SupCt, Nos. 91-704 & 91-902, June 2, 1992.

CHAPTER 16

THE BENEFITS AND COSTS OF AUTHORIZING RIVERBOAT GAMBLING

1. INTRODUCTION

On November 26, 1990, six months after the study on which this chapter is based was undertaken, the Pennsylvania House of Representatives rejected a bill to legalize riverboat gambling by a vote of 118-81.

Should riverboat gambling be permitted on Pennsylvania's rivers and lakes? What impact would this activity have on the state? What are the potential benefits? What are the possible costs? These are the questions that many are asking as a bill to authorized riverboat gambling is being considered by the Pennsylvania House of Representatives.

This chapter aims to determine the importance of the costs and benefits attributed to riverboat gambling and apply a sophisticated decision-making model to make a recommendation on the issue. First, the pending legislation is examined and the positions of those supporting and opposing the bill are delineated. Next, the Analytical Hierarchy Process (AHP) is applied to the riverboat gambling issue. Judgments acquired from individuals involved in the decision-making process or affected by the decision are then described. Finally, the synthesized results are interpreted, and a recommendation on riverboat gambling legislation is presented.

PENDING LEGISLATION ON RIVERBOAT GAMBLING

The Excursion Boat Gambling Bill, introduced by Representative Frank Gigliotti (D-Brookline), is expected to be brought up for vote in the House. It would authorize limited gambling on riverboats in Pennsylvania counties where the proposition is approved by voter referendum. The bill limits the maximum wager at $5 per hand or play and the maximum loss at $200 per person during each gambling excursion. The bill restricts gambling activity to 50% of a riverboat's square footage, requires gambling devices to pay out at least 80% of all wagers, and prohibits persons under 21 from engaging in gambling activities.

The Excursion Boat Gambling Commission, created under the bill, would license operators, adopt standards for the gambling operations, and regulate gambling activity. The commission would be funded through licensing and admissions fees. The initial license fee would be $50,000 with an annual fee of $25 per person-capacity on each riverboat. The admission fec, to be set by the EBG Commission, would be obtained for each person embarking on a riverboat gambling excursion. In addition, the municipality could adopt a local admission fee not to exceed 50 cents.

A wagering tax of 15% would be imposed on adjusted gross receipts from riverboat gambling. Twenty-five percent of the wagering tax would be distributed to each county having a home port or port of call, based on the ratio of the number of passengers embarking from that port to the total number of statewide embarkations. Another 25% would be allotted to the municipality, and the remaining amount would be credited to the General Fund of the state. Additionally, a recent amendment to the bill requires that $1,000,000 be allocated annually for the treatment of compulsive behaviors.

POSITIONS OF SUPPORTING AND OPPOSING PARTIES

Promoters of the bill claim ([6], [7], [9]) that riverboat gambling will stimulate local business, encourage economic development, and provide additional tax revenues for government. They cite examples of riverboat gambling operations in Mississippi, Iowa, and Illinois which have created new jobs and spawned tourism [8]. Supporters expect local economies to thrive as riverboat gambling patrons fill hotels, restaurants, and shops [2]. They also project that the legalized gambling operations will reduce illegal gambling [4], expand the tax base, and provide tax relief for citizens.

Opponents of the bill believe that legalization legitimizes gambling in the public mind and thus promotes gambling in both legal and illegal forms [1]. They expect serious social problems to result from an increase in the number of gamblers and compulsive gambling behavior [5]. They fear that riverboat gambling will lead to increased street crime, prostitution, and drug trafficking along with corruption, extortion, and bribery among public officials. Opponents claim that riverboat gambling will promote illegal gambling and attract organized crime to meet patrons' demands for credit betting, higher stakes, and avoidance of income taxes. It is also feared that legalized riverboat gambling will lead to pressures to allow gambling on Pennsylvania soil [3].

2. PROBLEM ANALYSIS

A team of three graduate students from the University of Pittsburgh applied the Analytical Hierarchy Process (AHP) to analyze Pennsylvania's pending legislation on riverboat gambling. A brief definition of the model and an explanation of the application are followed by a description of the judgments obtained from persons involved with the riverboat gambling issue (either as decision-makers or affected parties).

The goal of the model is to determine whether or not riverboat gambling should be authorized in Allegheny County. While the legislation encompasses the entire state of Pennsylvania, a more focused approach limited to Allegheny County provides more detail due to the team's familiarity with the area. Notably, the process can be applied to other local areas in Pennsylvania. Two similar hierarchies have been constructed, one identifying the benefits of the legislation (see Figure 1) and the other identifying the costs (see Figure 2). There are seven levels in each hierarchy identifying the goal, decision criteria, decision makers, factors, groups affected, objectives or issues, and alternatives.

Judgments obtained from decision makers and the groups affected were used to assign values of importance to the factors and objectives/issues. Those individuals in favor of the legislation were interviewed for the benefits hierarchy, and those against the legislation were interviewed for the costs hierarchy. Additional judgments were made regarding the importance of the decision criteria, decision makers, groups affected, and alternatives with respect to prior levels in the hierarchy.

Level 1: Goal	**Authorizing Riverboat Gambling in Allegheny County (benefits)**			
Level 2: Criteria	Economic	Political	Social	Environmental
Level 3: Decision Makers	State Government	Citizens	Lobbies	
Level 4: Factors	Social Opportunities	Economic Development	Revenue Gains	
Level 5: Groups Affected	Riverboat Operators	Citizens of Pittsburgh	Local Business	Government
Level 6: Objectives	-Increase Revenue	-Variety of Entertainment	-Development Opportunities & Increase Employment	-Increase Tax Revenues
	-Diversification of Services	-Potential Tax Relief	-Increase Tourism	-Reduce Illegal Gambling
		-Increase Job Opportunities	-Provide National Recognition	-Improve Image of Pgh & PA
Level 7: Alternatives		**AUTHORIZE**	**NOT AUTHORIZE**	

Figure 1. Benefits Hierarchy

Level 1: Goal	**Authorizing Riverboat Gambling in Allegheny County (costs)**					
Level 2: Criteria	Economic	Political	Social	Environmental		
Level 3: Decision Makers	State Government	Citizens	Lobbies			
Level 4: Factors	Damage to Environment	Potential/ Selective Economic Loss	Social Problems	Regulation Difficulties and Costs		
Level 5: Groups Affected	Riverboat Operators	Citizens of Pittsburgh	Local Gambling Businesses	Government	Other River Users	Environ- mentalists
Level 6: - Issues	- Regulation of Gambling Activities -Competition For Gambling Operations	-Safety & Crime Issues -Increase Traffic & Crowds -Moral Addiction	-Cannibalism of Other Legal Gambling Operations -Cannibalism of PA State Lottery -Govt Services - Law Enforcement & Waste Services	- Regulation of Gambling Operations	- Increase River & Need For Safety	-Increase Pollution
Level 7: **Alternatives**	**AUTHORIZE**	**NOT AUTHORIZE**				

Figure 2. Costs Hierarchy

JUDGMENTS OF DECISION-MAKERS

The relevant decision-makers in the model include the Pennsylvania State Government, voting citizens of Pennsylvania, and interest groups and lobbies. Telephone interviews were conducted in order to determine the importance of the primary cost and benefit factors with respect to their positive or negative influence on these decision-makers.

The three benefit factors in level 4 include:

- social opportunities (standard of living and variety of entertainment)
- economic development (employment and new business opportunities)
- revenue gain (for local businesses and the government)

The four cost factors in level 4 include:

- potential damage to the environment (pollution)
- potential/selective economic loss of individuals
- social problems (crime, corruption, and safety)
- regulation costs

State Government:

As a decision maker, State Representative Gigliotti feels that economic development and revenue gains are the most important factors influencing his decision to support the bill. He believes that the gambling activities would promote a new variety of entertainment for the area, thus creating additional economic development opportunities [9].

State Representative Clymer [1] strongly opposes the Excursion Boat Gambling Act. He believes that potential economic loss to individuals and social problems are the most important factors. He stated that gambling does not create any new wealth, rather, it only redistributes the wealth. By providing more access to gambling, Representative Clymer feels that riverboat gambling would create new gamblers and even lead to more illegal gambling. He also thinks that regulation would be an important factor to prevent private games from being held for "high rollers."

Citizen of Pittsburgh:

An unbiased citizen, who is completing his PhD in Public Affairs, rated increased social opportunities as the most important benefit and safety/crime issues as the most important cost impacting his decision on the legislation.

Lobbies/Interest Groups:

A local representative for a community organization, who is interested in preserving Pittsburgh's standard of living through economic development and increased employment, feels that the riverboat legislation will provide Pittsburgh with economic advantages which will benefit the whole city and the surrounding neighborhoods. Consequently, this individual rated economic development as the most highly rated factor, followed by revenue gains.

A representative from a local pro-family organization, who does not support the current legislation, is primarily concerned about social problems and potential financial loss to individuals that may result if riverboat gambling is legalized.

JUDGMENTS OF GROUPS AFFECTED

In addition to talking with the relevant decision-makers, the groups which would be impacted by the legislation were interviewed about the respective issues and objectives in level 6 of the hierarchies. The following groups were identified as having a stake in the outcome of the legislation: riverboat operators, citizens of Pittsburgh, local Pittsburgh businesses, state and local government, other river users, and environmentalists.

Riverboat Operator:

The local riverboat operator that was interviewed is strongly in favor of the legislation. The following two benefits are equally important to him: increased revenue and diversification of services. In terms of negative issues, he feels that increased costs of regulation are extremely more important than competition because regulation is not something that his operation has any control over.

Citizen of Pittsburgh:

The citizen of Pittsburgh, who is completing his PhD in Public Affairs, feels that an increase in the number of jobs in the city is the most important benefit that could result from the passing of the current legislation. Possible tax relief for the taxpayers is secondary in importance to this individual. This particular citizen also thinks that the safety of the Pittsburgh residents may be jeopardized due to the potential for crime and corruption to increase in the city and surrounding areas.

Local Business:

A representative from a large Pittsburgh hotel believes that the most important benefit that could result from the legislation is the potential for the number of tourists being drawn to the area to increase. He could not foresee any costs associated with riverboat gambling.

Local Gambling Business:

The team was unable to obtain the cooperation of a large local gambling operation, likely to be impacted by this legislation. The assumption has been made that increased competition for local gambling dollars could result and affect existing gambling operations in a negative way.

State and Local Government:

Representative Gigliotti envisioned the positive effects of increased tax revenues for local and state government to be the most important objective of having riverboat gambling in Pittsburgh and Pennsylvania. If the bill were to be passed, Representative Clymer felt that regulation would the most important issue for government. He said that he did not want to promote gambling, and he felt that the wagering and maximum loss limits would be increased in response to growing consumer demand.

Other River Users:

The two barge companies that were interviewed felt that any increase in the number of boats to be used for riverboat gambling would have no effect on their current operations in terms of increased traffic on the Pittsburgh waterways.

Environmentalist:

An interview with a representative from a local environmental group, who is concerned about having clean water and air, revealed that the legislation would not impact his organization significantly with respect to the issue of increased pollution.

The priorities derived from the judgments are given in Tables 1 and 2.

ADDITIONAL JUDGEMENTS

The decision criteria in level 2 of the hierarchies consist of economic, political, social, and environmental measures which were rated differently in the two hierarchies. In the benefit hierarchy, the economic criterion was rated most important, and in the cost hierarchy, the social criterion was considered most important. The political criterion was deemed more important in terms of costs than benefits. Environmental concerns were judged relatively unimportant in both hierarchies.

Since the bill requires passage in the state government and in individual counties by voter referendum, state government and citizens in level 3 of the hierarchies were rated equally important as decision-makers. The lobbies and special interest groups that influence the decisions were weighed with a lesser degree of importance.

Table 1. Priorities of Benefits

	Economic (.658)	Political (.085)	Social (.218)	Environmental (.040)
State Gov.	.444	.444	.444	.444
Citizens	.444	.444	.444	.444
Lobbies	.111	.111	.111	.111

	State Gov.	Citizens	Lobbies
Social Opportunities	.114	.637	.051
Economic Development	.481	.258	.367
Revenue Gains	.495	.105	.582

	Social Opportunities	Economic Development	Revenue Gains
Riverboat Operators	.049	.637	.051
Citizens of Pittsburgh	.551	.258	.367
Local Business	.104	.541	.376
Government	.296	.138	.211

	Riverboat Operators	Citizens of Pittsburgh	LocalGovt.	Business	Composite Priorities
Increase Revenue	.5				.115
Diversification of Services	.5				.115
Variety of Entertainment		.114			.024
Potential Tax Relief		.405			.087
Increas Job Opportunities		.481			.103
Dev. Opport. Increase Empl.			.113		.039
Increase Tourism			.709		.244
Provide Nat'l Recognition			.179		.062
Increase Tax Revenues				.773	.165
Reduce Illegal Gambling				.088	.019
Improve Image of Pgh & PA				.139	.030

Table 2. Priorities of Costs

	Economic (.045)	Political (.260)	Social (.611)	Environmental (.084)
State Gov.	.444	.444	.444	.444
Citizens	.444	.444	.444	.444
Lobbies	.111	.111	.111	.111

	State Gov.	Citizens	Lobbies
Damage to Environment	.037	.058	.045
Economic Loss	.313	.102	.296
Social Problems	.423	.549	.614
Regulations and Costs	.227	.297	.045

	Damage to Environment	Potential/Selective Economic Loss	Social Problems	Regulation Difficulties and Costs
Riverboat Operators	.034	.038	.049	.286
Citizens of Pittsburgh	.305	.496	.405	.132
Local Business	.030	.038	.049	.042
Government	.156	.302	.405	.478
Other River Users	.100	.056	.047	.032
Environmentalists	.375	.070	.047	.031

	Riverboat Operators	Citizens of Pittsburgh	Local Business	Govt.	Other River Users	Envornm.	Composite Priorities
Regulation of Gambling	.5						.054
Competition for Gambling Operations	.5						.054
Safety & Crime		.637					.220
Increase Traffic and Crowds		.105					.036
Moral Addiction		.258					.089
Cannibalism of other Legal Gambling			1				.049
Regulation of Gambling Operations				.600			.227
Cannibalism of PA State Lottery				.200			.076
Gov.Law Enforc./ Waste Services				.200			.076
Inc. River Traffic Need for Safety					1		.053
Increase Pollution						1	.068

Based on benefit and cost factors, the groups affected by riverboat gambling in level 5 of the hierarchies were weighted. Pittsburgh citizens were rated as the most important group affected by the social opportunities. Riverboat operators and local businesses were considered to be most affected by economic development and revenue gains. Government was also judged to be important in these areas. In terms of costs, Pittsburgh citizens and environmentalists were weighed heavily as groups affected by damage to the environment. The citizens of Pittsburgh were also considered to be most affected by potential economic loss and social problems. River boat operators and government were judged to be the most important groups affected by regulation costs.

The final set of judgments involved rating the two alternatives in level 7 in terms of each objective or issue. In the benefits hierarchy, the alternative to authorize riverboat gambling was weighted most heavily under increased tax revenues, diversification of services for riverboat operators, and variety of entertainment for citizens. In the costs hierarchy, the alternative to authorize riverboat gambling was considered most costly under moral addiction to gambling, government regulation, and government services.

3. FINDINGS AND DISCUSSION

The weighted judgments were synthesized to quantify the importance of the hierarchical elements (Table 3). This process produced a benefit/cost ratio of .851/.877 for authorizing riverboat gambling and a ratio of .149/.123 for not authorizing riverboat gambling. These results indicate that riverboat gambling should not be authorized in Allegheny County. In evaluating the sensitivity of the priorities, it should be noted that a reduction in the importance of the two highest weighted cost issues would still yield the same alternative. Furthermore, an increase in the importance of the three highest weighted benefit objectives does not alter the decision.

In evaluating the validity of this AHP application, limitations must be recognized. The biases of the individuals interviewed and of the team members may slant the judgments thus affecting the results. Interdependencies or commonalities among elements in the hierarchy possibly existed but were minimized by constructing two separate hierarchies. Additionally, imperfect preferences may lead to inconsistencies among the elements in the model. However, a certain degree of inconsistency in making judgments is acceptable in real world applications.

Benefits	Yes	No	Costs	Yes	No
Tourism	0.85	0.15	Gov't Reg.	0.90	0.10
Taxes	0.90	0.10	Safety	0.90	0.10
Revenue	0.85	0.15	Moral	0.95	0.05
Diverse	0.95	0.05	Lottery	0.90	0.10
Job Opport.	0.85	0.15	Services	0.95	0.05
Tax Relief	0.70	0.30	Pollution	0.50	0.50
Recognition	0.85	0.15	Regulation	1	0
Dev. Opport.	0.85	0.15	Competition	1	0
Image	0.85	0.15	Inc. Traffic	0.70	0.30
Variety	0.90	0.10	Cannibalism	0.85	0.15
Illegal	0.50	0.50	Traffic	0.85	0.15
COMPOSITE	0.851	0.149	COMPOSITE	0.877	0.123

REFERENCES

1. Clymer, P.I., "Making Waves: Riverboat Gambling Would Prompt Other Betting," *Harrisburg Patriot News,* May 13, 1991.
2. Guo, D., "Master Salesman Puts a New Spin on River Business," *Pittsburgh Post-Gazette,* May 28, 1990.
3. *Legalization of Gambling in Pennsylvania: A Study,* League of Women Voters of Pennsylvania, 1984.
4. Pagano, C. (Superintendent of New Jersey State Police), *Impact of Legalized Gambling on Illegal Gambling in New Jersey,* 16 October 1987.
5. Schroeder, M., "Talk About a Riverboat Gambler," *Business Week,* 72, July 23, 1990.
6. Shehan, A., "Gateway Fleet Charts Cautious Course on Gambling," *Pittsburgh Post-Gazette,* C5, November 22, 1990.
7. Sheehan, A. "Riverboat Gambling Seen Bonanza," *Pittsburgh Post-Gazette,* 4, May 14, 1990.
8. Siler, C. "Why are Las Vegas and Atlantic City Yawning?" *Forbes,* 140, April 30, 1990.
9. Wolf, D. "Riverboat Gambling Bill Founders," *The Pittsburgh Press,* B3, May 29, 1991.

CHAPTER 17

THE CASE OF THE SPOTTED OWL
VS.
THE LOGGING INDUSTRY

1. INTRODUCTION

In this chapter we analyze the controversy surrounding the Northern Spotted Owl. This debate has been raging in the United States for five years, particularly in the Pacific Northwest region of the country. On the surface it may appear that the problem is limited to deciding whether or not to fully protect a single species of bird, but in reality this issue has implications that extend much further.

Should the U.S. Government support the efforts of the environmentalist groups in saving the spotted owl from extinction? If so, the government will directly affect the logging industry in the Pacific Northwest part of the United States and restrict logging in over 7 million acres of old growth forests.

In developing the AHP model we decided to take a very macro, or "birds-eye," view of this current and prominent issue. Incorporated into the model are initial/immediate effects of the ultimate decision as well as indirect and longer term consequences of the outcome. Our final model is discussed in greater detail later in the chapter.

2. BACKGROUND/ISSUE DISCUSSION

The spotted owl debate first began in 1987 when an environmental group called Greenworld petitioned to have the owl listed as an endangered species. The U.S. Fish and Wildlife Service (FWS) decided the species was not in danger and therefore would not make the "list." This touched off a barrage of lawsuits from many different environmental groups.

The reason this turned into such a heated debate is because many environmental groups had a separate agenda - protecting old growth forests in the Northwest. In this debate "old growth" is defined as trees that are at least 200 years old and have never been exposed to cutting. These groups contend that the owl population cannot survive unless it maintains its habitat in the old growth forest lands, therefore moving the owls does not appear to be a viable solution. Recent estimates indicate that approximately twelve million acres of old growth forest remain in the U.S. Nine million of these acres are federally owned, six million of which are already protected from the logging industry. Estimates of the number of remaining owls range between 4,000 and 6,000. Environmentalists argue that we need to protect the spotted owl and the old growth simultaneously in order to preserve a species and a delicate ecological system for future generations to enjoy.

The environmentalists also contend that since we only have a limited supply of the old growth forest remaining, we should protect it despite short-term economic costs. One estimate of the remaining supply indicates that if the old growth were harvested at the rate it has been in the past, then these forests would disappear within 10-15 years. The argument is that since supply is limited, the value of protecting the spotted owl and forests today far outweigh the short-term economic costs associated with protection.

On the other side of this issue is the negative economic impact, the brunt of which is being felt by smaller logging operations in the Northwest. People living in towns directly affected by the controversy are now either unemployed or working in low-paying jobs elsewhere. In many small towns in Oregon local unemployment figures have reached 25% and higher. FWS projects 32,000 logging jobs will be lost due to the environmental stance. In addition to high unemployment rates, these areas are also experiencing increased cases of human depression and local crime, the costs of which are difficult to estimate.

The economic ripple effects are significant as well. Due to decreasing supply, domestic lumber prices have increased by over 35%. Estimates indicate that 65,000 more Americans cannot afford houses for every 20% increase in lumber prices. The high lumber prices in the U.S. have also aided foreign foresting companies who are keeping their prices steady and consequently are squeezing American firms. In addition to rising prices, the controversy has caused many local, non-timber firms to lose business due to increasing unemployment.

As part of our research we discussed the issue with two executives who run firms that are being affected by the owl controversy. One gentleman discussed forest management techniques being used in this country citing the fact that more trees are currently being planted than harvested. From an aesthetic perspective he feels that the forests will not suffer because we are continually planting new trees and clear cutting techniques have been greatly reduced. The strict regulation will cause his business, forest products, as well as other related industries to become less competitive in the global market. He also disputed the reported estimates that each owl needs 2,000 acres of old growth to maintain its habitat.

The other gentleman commented on the overall attention that all environmental issues are receiving in Washington. His company will spend $30 million per year over the next five years in order to comply with environmental regulations. He also believes that the economic tradeoffs associated with current regulations are far too great to enable American industries to remain competitive.

In developing our model we included a number of different criteria that are important to the outcome of this controversy. The specifics of our model are discussed later in the chapter. The issue is emotional and extremely important as it will set a precedent for handling future environmental and species problems. Questions to be pondered with this issue are as follows: Where do we draw the line of beautification? Are all species important? What is the ultimate purpose of trees in our world? Where do we place human beings in the grand scheme of this world? What is the value of demoralized people? Should economics play a large role in making these decisions? Attempting to answer these questions led to thoughtful development of a decision model.

3. AHP MODEL-ISSUE

This AHP project focuses on the macro issues and concerns surrounding the government's involvement in protecting the spotted owl from extinction and placing it on the endangered species list. Environmental lobbyists have asked the United States Government to give special consideration to the use of federally owned lands for the harvesting of old growth trees. The argument provided by the environmentalists states that the spotted owl can only exist in the old growth forest and it is unable to survive in any other habitat. The government consequently passed the National Forests Protection Act of 1991, which imposed controls on the use of federal land, much of which was used for harvesting trees for the logging industry.

The protection of the old growth forest may displace an estimated 200,000 individuals associated with the logging industry in the Pacific Northwest region. Generations of families have lived off the land and supported themselves through the logging of timber and fear that they will be displaced because of a bird. The issue of employment and livelihood are extremely important but are not the only issues involved.

How long will loggers be able to harvest some 170,000 acres a year without this resource being completely depleted? How much does the world rely on our exporting of lumber? And finally, how will the population demand for future housing and potential for substitute products affect the logging industry? These are just several of many questions and issues that we consider in the AHP model.

As mentioned earlier, we have focused on the macro issues and attempted to analyze them in a balanced manner so that no side would be unfairly represented. We also purposely listed general topics that encompass a number of stakeholders, so that we could better manage the model and the complex subject without having to spell out all stakeholders' interests.

4. AHP MODEL-STRUCTURE

We divided the criteria into factors that would presently affect the external environment, and those that would have consequential effects in the future. The first tier addresses those factors that would directly and presently be affected, while the second tier focuses on future effects.

The first tier is in turn divided into housing costs due to lumber price increase, the natural beauty of the country, the owl as an endangered species, the effect on the old growth forest and the effect on the employment situation in the United States. The second tier looks at the implications of the first level.

To assess this second tier, we referred to our own knowledge of the situation along with the research and discussions we had with business leaders in the forest related industries or sectors directly affected by this industry. Timber industry consolidation, export quotas, the ecological system and the rippling effect to other related industries are just several criteria on which we concentrated when considering this issue and the potential outcomes.

We considered three possible outcomes: (1) Save the owl and limit the harvesting on government lands, (2) Continue to harvest the forest, and (3) Gradually decrease harvesting and protect the spotted owl. The hierarchy summarizing all the factors and the alternatives is given in Figure 1.

5. PAIRWISE COMPARISONS

We analyzed and compared the data using our own personal judgments based on the interpretation of all the publications we read, and the thoughts of those business leaders and professors to whom we spoke. Consequently, this was a lengthy process which included a discussion of all three points of view and the implications of each. Before we actually undertook the exercise, we favored the combination outcome, which is positioned in the middle of all outcomes. The business leaders with whom we spoke favored the position of the logging industry, while most of the publications and articles that we read remained fairly neutral. When we finished pairwise comparing the criteria, the AHP decision was to save the owl and the old growth forests over gradually phasing out harvesting by a narrow margin (0.6 percent).

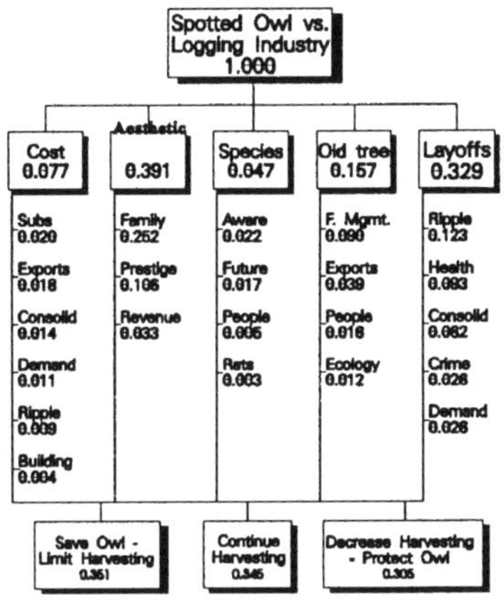

Aware	-	Level of Govt/Public attention devoted to end species issues
Building	-	Less new home construction
Consolid	-	Industry consolidation
Demand	-	The amount of individuals demanding housing
Ecology	-	Effect on the delicate ecological system in forests
Exports	-	The amount of U.S. lumber exports
F. Mgmt	-	The proper management of forests
Family	-	Future family enjoyment of nature
Future	-	Precedent setting decision for future endangered species issues
Health	-	Mental/physical health deterioration caused by layoffs
People	-	Mental health of forest lovers based on decision
Prestige	-	Reputation of U.S. as being naturally beautiful
Rats	-	Effect on rat population due to elimination of spotted owl
Revenue	-	Revenue rec'd by local parks and business economy from visitors
Ripple	-	The ripple effect on related industries in the building of houses
Subs	-	Substitute materials used in the construction of houses

Figure 1. The Spotted Owl v. the Logging Industry Hierarchy

The final priorities of the outcomes where: Save the Owl and the Forest - 35.1%, Continue Harvesting - 34.5% and Decrease Harvesting and Protect the Owl - 30.5%. We did not originally expect such a close margin between the alternatives, however, after we assessed the process, we felt that we compared the criteria in a fair and reasonable manner.

We weighted aesthetics and employment the heaviest in the first tier. Within the second tier, future family enjoyment, the reputation of the United States as being a beautiful country, and the rippling effect turned out to be the most important criteria. Unfortunately, we were unable to discuss this topic with environmental lobbyists and logging industry representatives. This could be a limitation of the validity of the final outcome because these individuals could perhaps have made us aware of other stakeholders who might have been considered.

6. DISCUSSION

As mentioned earlier, of the three alternatives examined, the AHP decision was to save the forest and the spotted owl. However, the final priorties of the three alternatives were relatively close, which suggests that any of the alternatives could have been recommended given slightly different criteria weights.

The topic analyzed in this chapter has far reaching implications in today's environment. The livelihood of people, the tenacity of lobbyists, and the control of the federal government, all impact the country and the global environment. Aesthetics, export quotas, ecological consequences, and the use of potential material substitutes in construction, are all affected and must be considered in the final decision. Given the complexity of the decision, it appears that the controversy will continue until world experts from the industry, from the sciences and from the environmental community convene in a summit meeting and lay out all possible alternatives and stakeholders.

REFERENCES

1. Fitzgerald, R., *Reader's Digest* 141, 91-95.
2. Yang, D., 1993, *Business Week*, 90, January 11.
3. Fisher, D. and C. Schubert, *The Progressive*, April 1992, 28-29.
4. McAdoo, M., *Scholastic Update* 124, 12-13.
5. Cook, J., *Forbes*, June 8, 1992, 109-110.
6. Yang, D., *Business Week*, October 29, 1990, 94-96.
7. Yang, D., *Business Week*, July 30, 1990, 64.
8. Yang, D., *Business Week*, July 16, 1990, 50-51.
9. Levine, J., *Business Week*, September 18, 1989, 94-95.

CHAPTER 18

SELECTION OF RECYCLING GOAL MOST LIKELY TO SUCCEED

1. INTRODUCTION

Americans throw out about 160 million tons of garbage a year - 3.5 pounds apiece each day. And, the volume of garbage keeps growing - up by 80% since 1960, and expected to increase by an additional 20 percent by the year 2000. Where we are going to put it all is becoming an item on the nation's agenda.

In this chapter we investigate methods of recycling municipal solid waste using the Analytical Hierarchy Process to identify which "mix" of recycling approaches and types of recyclable materials is most likely to succeed in minimizing landfill use. Within the past year public concern - and media attention - has been heightened significantly to the environmental issue of solid waste as municipalities and states are refusing to accept refuse being exported (by areas that no longer have the landfill space to store it) using "pooh pooh choo choos" .

As we debated the problem of how to handle the growing mass of municipal solid waste, we enumerated the following available courses of action.

1. Encourage separation and increase the number of recycling facilities.

2. Increase the number of landfills.

3. Increase the number of incinerators and convert more trash to energy.

4. Decrease the generation of solid waste at its source through a number of incentives and disincentives.

Although we could have examined each of these alternatives and established a hierarchy to find the most effective alternative, we decided to examine recycling alone for the following reasons:

1. Recycling is gaining popularity as people embrace a solution to a problem that they believe they can help solve. Unlike the greenhouse effect, toxic waste, industrial pollution and other critical concerns that cast a pall on the future of our economy and our society, recycling (technically separation) is a positive action that each person can take.
2. Governments are responding to the public enthusiasm by passing new recycling laws. Between January and September 1989, 38 states and the District of Columbia passed new recycling laws, according to the National Solid Waste Management Association. In fact, Pennsylvania Law 1988-101 is a protectionist measure passed to address the processing and disposal of municipal waste.

3. Recycling holds the edge in creating new jobs, protecting the environment, and conserving national resources.

4. The Environmental Protection Agency has set a goal of recycling 25 percent of the nation's waste by 1992.

2. BACKGROUND

Municipal solid waste is a heterogeneous mixture of discarded organic and inorganic material from residential homes and apartments, commercial facilities, and public offices, where composition varies according to the "point source generator" (the person producing the garbage), is cyclical with respect to the time of year, and may contain any commodity available for purchase. In addition, the volume of solid waste will vary by season depending on the type of point source generator.

Examination of a number of publications and articles yielded a profile of the typical composition of municipal solid waste (see Table 1).

Table 1. A Typical Composition of Municipal Solid Waste

	Percent
Material	35.1
Paper	7.0
Clear Glass	3.5
Colored Glass	1.4
Aluminum Cans	7.9
Ferrous Metals	5.5
Plastics	39.6
Yard Waste	100.00
Total	

APPROACH

We established three levels in the hierarchy, the Identification of the Goal, Categories of Municipal Solid Waste, and Criteria Influencing Recycling of Solid Waste. The hierarchy of the "Recycling Option Selection" is given in Figure 1.

Level 1 - Identification of the Goal

The goal of this investigation was to determine which approach to recycling would be the most likely to succeed in minimizing the amount of garbage trashed in a landfill. By defining success in this manner, two equally important sub-goals were satisfied. Minimizing the amount of material disposed of in a landfill automatically requires that the amount of recycling be maximized. This in turn leads to other desirable results:

1. Conservation of raw materials,
2. Promotion of environmental conservation,
3. Increase in non-environmentally degrading jobs.

The second and equally important sub-goal is the reduction of the amount of land required for landfills. Six states – Pennsylvania, Massachusetts, Connecticut, West Virginia, Virginia, and Kentucky – have less than five years remaining before all existing and potential landfill sites reach capacity. Another 5 states will reach capacity in the next 10 years. More than 14,000 landfills have shut down in the last decade; another 6,500 will close in the next five years - including Fresh Kills, the largest city dump in the world located in New York City.

The stories of states turning away imported garbage are legion. Governors are manning the barricades. In addition to PL 1988-101, Gov. Robert P. Casey issued an executive order freezing the amount of out-of-state garbage Pennsylvania landfills can accept at current levels. (An absolute ban was impractical, considering that Pennsylvania is an exporter as well.) New Mexico Gov. Garrey Carruthers declared a year-long moratorium on new landfills. (The target was a Maryland company's plan to build a 23,000 ton incinerator catering to out of state trash.) During his campaign, Gov.-elect L. Douglas Wilder pledged to keep out-of-state garbage out of Virginia.

In Indiana, meanwhile, environmental officials used a little-known state rule that out-of-state garbage cannot be dumped without a permit to send garbage-laden railroad cars back to Philadelphia. Echoing the beliefs of state officials everywhere, an Indiana official was quoted in the *Wall Street Journal* as saying, "Indiana doesn't want other states' garbage."

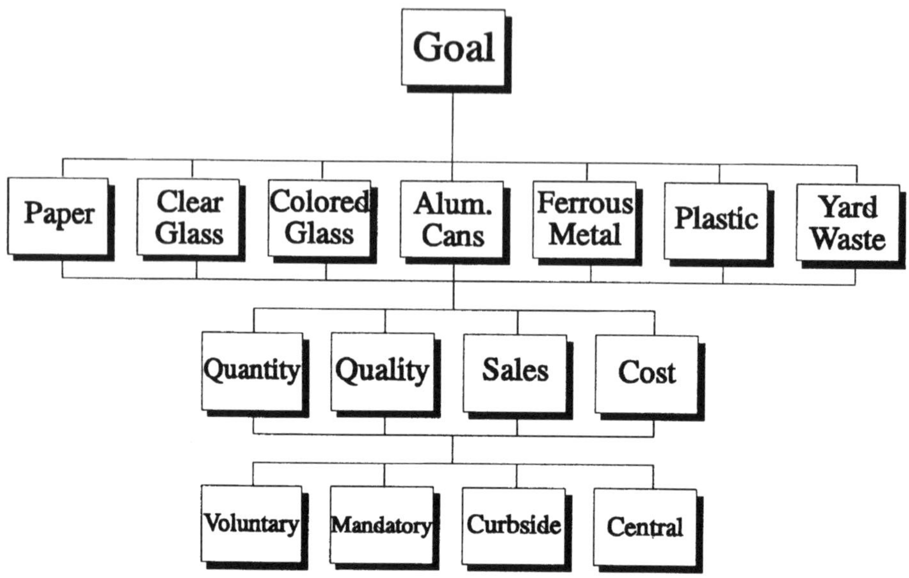

Pennsylvania senators Heinz and Spector introduced a bill to restrict the flow of interstate garbage, as well as to force states to reduce the amount of trash they generate. Exporting garbage is still at low levels, however. Only 12 to 14 million tons of the 160 million tons generated each year get buried out of state. Nevertheless, out-of-state waste has everyone's attention, even as the more serious problems of siting new landfills and incinerators are allowed to fester.

Siting of new landfills is a thorny issue for a number of reasons.

1. Geological, social, economic, commercial, and technical criteria must be met to establish a landfill. Geological criteria include topography, strata, sequence and competence, aquifers, and the potential for geologic disturbance due to natural processes (e.g., earthquakes, colluvial glaciers, floods, eolian disturbance). Another criterion is man-made processes, such as surface and subsurface mining, ground water depletion, and fires.

2. Social considerations seem to center mainly around the NIMBY Principle, or Not In My Back Yard.
3. Economic criteria include the location of sites which are within affordable distances to the source generators (although as the alternatives become more limited, this criterion diminishes in importance), the amount of funds required to upgrade a geologically

suitable site to conform with regulations, and the ability to use the site in a profitable manner.

4. Commercial factors include the desirability for a firm with sufficient resources to enter the garbage business, and whether or not the timing is appropriate for such an undertaking.

5. The list of technical criteria is almost endless, and involves selecting the materials of construction, scheduling execution of preliminary and on-going tasks, and solving unexpected problems all of which occur against the limitless backdrop of changing regulations.

3. CATEGORIES OF MUNICIPAL SOLID WASTE

A number of approaches were considered before selecting the appropriate criteria for the first level of analysis. We chose to concentrate on the composition of municipal solid waste. It was decided that all factors involved in maximizing recycled material and concurrently minimizing required landfill volume are dependent on the classes of material contained in the municipal solid waste. As a result, seven *Level 2* categories were developed which covered the types of materials found in municipal solid waste. These factors were weighted according to their relative percentages as found in municipal solid waste.

Here are some of the results of the research we conducted on the potential markets for some recyclable materials. We used this research to make the decision.

1. *Paper:* Nearly 30 percent of all paper products consumed in this country are recycled. This leaves more than 40 million tons clogging landfills and going up smokestacks annually. Expanding the market for recycled paper while increasing the reprocessing capacity will take time and coordination. With burgeoning collection efforts, "we have the potential in this country to increase the supply of wastepaper overnight," says Rodney Edward of the American Paper Institute in a recent *Newsweek* article. "But expanding the capacity to use it will take three to five years."

2. *Glass:* Reusing old glass also costs less than forging virgin materials. To date, only 10 percent of it is recycled, but markets are growing steadily. Glass bottles can live again as "glassphalt" (a combination of glass and asphalt) and, of course, as other food containers. A California firm, Encore!, grosses $3 million a year collecting and sterilizing 65,000 cases of empty bottles each month and selling them back to west coast wineries.

3. *Aluminum:* Turning bauxite into new aluminum is 10 times more expensive than reprocessing used cans. That is one key reason why more than half of all aluminum beverage cans are recycled today - 42.5 billion annually. Even so, Americans toss out enough aluminum every three months to rebuild the nation's entire airline fleet.

4. *Plastics:* The $140 billion plastics industry is finally addressing the recycling issue, but only one percent of plastics is recaptured. Manufacturers are scrambling to find new uses, from plastic "lumber" to stuffing for ski jackets. Proctor & Gamble is making new containers for Spic & Span entirely from recycled plastics, and hopes to turn even used Luvs and Pampers into plastic trash bags and park benches. Limitations include rules by the Food and Drug Administration that prohibit recycled plastic containers to be used to serve or store food (since it cannot be decontaminated), the presence of polymers in some plastics (like ketchup bottles) that complicate separating, and the "hang up" that no one wants something that looks like used plastic.

5. *Yard waste:* Composting America's fertile mounds of leaves and grass clippings could eliminate one-fifth of the nation's waste. Unfortunately there isn't much demand for mulch. Pesticides and lawn chemicals also pose toxicity problems in compost heaps. Still, Fairfield, CT offers a model: it opened a $3 million composting center to create topsoil for park, playground, and public landscaping.

4. CRITERIA INFLUENCING RECYCLING OF SOLID WASTE AND METHODOLOGIES FOR MUNICIPAL SOLID WASTE SEPARATION

We decided to base our evaluation of "success" of a given alternative recycling technique according to the following four criteria:

Quantity: The amount of material that would be recycled.

Quality: Whether the material that is recycled is of a quality that would be suitable for recycling, e.g., glass must be clean, aluminum and tin cans cannot be mixed.

Sales: The likelihood that the recycled material could be sold, i.e., markets for the recyclable material exist. If you cannot sell the material it will probably end up in the landfill anyway.

Cost: How much will the option cost everyone (consumer, local government) involved? (Less is preferable.)

The first step was to weight the criteria for each material. This was done by comparing the criteria in pairs and answering the question: What criterion is more important? The weighting of the four criteria was different for each material. Table 1 below shows the pairwise comparisons of quantity and quality for yard waste.

Four options by which solid waste may be separated were defined. These options and their definitions are listed below. The second step was to evaluate each option using each of the four criteria.

SQ - Status Quo/Voluntary Recycling: No change from whatever level of voluntary segregation of municipal solid waste is presently occurring.

Generator: The degree of separation imposed upon the point source generator of municipal solid waste as a result of the passage of laws.

Curbside: Separation of municipal solid waste at the pick-up point by sanitation workers.

Central Plant: Separating solid waste from the bulk of the garbage at a centralized plant.

The question we asked when evaluating each option with the criteria from above was: For a given criterion, which option is more preferred? For example, the first question for yard waste would have been whether, with respect to the quantity to be recycled, voluntary (SQ) or mandatory (GENERATOR) recycling would be preferable?

Table 1. Recycling Selection Priorities

	Paper (.350)	Clear Glass (.070)	Colored Glass (.035)	Alum. Cans (.014)	Ferrous Metal (.079)	Plastic (.055)	Yard Waste (.396)
Quantity	.515	.044	.059	.500	.063	.241	.241
Quality	.072	.227	.144	.039	.380	.073	.046
Sales	.079	.414	.494	.134	.392	.347	.050
Cost	.333	.315	.303	.326	.164	.339	.662

	Quantity	Quality	Sales	Cost	Composite Priorities
PAPER	Quantity	Quality	Sales	Cost	Priorities
Voluntary	.094	.529	.251	.627	.315
Mandatory	.419	.292	.126	.261	.334
Curbside	.040	.092	.051	.040	.044
Central	.448	.088	.572	.072	.306
CLEAR GLASS	Quantity	Quality	Sales	Cost	Priorities
Voluntary	.083	.222	.511	.644	.502
Mandatory	.317	.466	.243	.247	.425
Curbside	.174	.254	.144	.072	.217
Central	.426	.058	.102	.037	.256
COLORED GLASS	Quantity	Quality	Sales	Cost	Priorities
Voluntary	.066	.287	.250	.572	.342
Mandatory	.288	.346	.250	.306	.283
Curbside	.130	.276	.250	.075	.194
Central	.515	.091	.250	.047	.181
ALUM. CANS	Quantity	Quality	Sales	Cost	Priorities
Voluntary	.150	.483	.529	.632	.371
Mandatory	.620	.315	.281	.258	.444
Curbside	.106	.136	.147	.077	.103
Central	.124	.066	.043	.033	.081
FERROUS METALS	Quantity	Quality	Sales	Cost	Priorities
Voluntary	.049	.183	.359	.542	.302
Mandatory	.209	.221	.200	.309	.226
Curbside	.087	.119	.082	.059	.093
Central	.655	.477	.359	.090	.378
PLASTIC	Quantity	Quality	Sales	Cost	Priorities
Voluntary	.072	.323	.156	.325	.205
Mandatory	.253	.290	.229	.345	.279
Curbside	.105	.081	.303	.167	.193
Central	.570	.306	.312	.162	.323
YARD WASTE	Quantity	Quality	Sales	Cost	Priorities
Voluntary	.128	.409	.422	.541	.429
Mandatory	.484	.136	.141	.278	.314
Curbside	.341	.409	.388	.126	.204
Central	.047	.045	.049	.055	.052

5. CONCLUSIONS

Based on the results of the pairwise comparisons, we have concluded that the following mix of recycling approaches would be likely to succeed in minimizing landfill requirements.

Voluntary Recycling (.284)
1. Clear Glass
2. Colored Glass
3. Yard Waste

Mandatory Recycling (.303)
1. Paper
2. Aluminum Cans

Separation at the pick-up point (.128)
1. Nothing

Separation at a Centralized Processing Facility (.311)
1. Ferrous Metal
2. Plastic

Note that this recycling alternative may not be in complete agreement with current practices in many cities where, for example, glass is mandatorily recycled in addition to aluminum cans and paper. The final recycling policy is obviously location dependent and statistics such as those given in Table 1 will be needed to decide the optimal alternative. Here we have provided a framework to analyze the problem and develop a mix of recycling strategies.

REFERENCES

1. "The Garbage Glut is Everyone's Business", *USA Today*, November 17, 1989.
2. "The Garbage Glut is None of My Business", *USA Today*, November 17, 1989.
3. "How Can We Solve Our Trash Problems?", *USA Today*, November 17, 1989.
4. "Pay for What you Throw Away", *USA Today*, November 17, 1989.
5. "Waste Spurs Uncivil Was Between States", *Wall Street Journal*, November 20, 1989.
6. "125 New Recycling Laws Passed in U.S. between January and September 1989," *Inside EPA*, November 24, 1989.
7. "Buried Alive," *Newsweek*, November 27, 1989.
8. Act 1988-101, *Laws of Pennsylvania.*
9. *Small-Scale Municipal Solid Waste Energy Recovery Systems,* Gersham, Brickner, and Bratton, Inc., Van Nostrand Reinhold Co., New York, 1986.
10. *Energy from Municipal Wastes: Opportunities for an Emerging Market*, U.S. Department of Energy, Washington, D.C., 1985.

11. *Municipal and Industrial Waste*, Third Annual Conference, University of Wisconsin-Extension, 1980.
12. *Resource Recovery Technology,* Urban Technology Center, Columbia University, New York, 1976.
13. *Solid Wastes-II*, American Chemical Society, Washington, D.C., 1973.
14. *Recovery and Utilization of Municipal Solid Waste,* Environmental Protection Agency, U.S. Department of the Interior, Washington, D.C., 1971.
15. *A Plan for Solid Waste Management in Pennsylvania,* Commonwealth of Pennsylvania, Harrisburg, 1970.

CHAPTER 19

TO DRILL OR NOT TO DRILL: A SYNTHESIS OF EXPERT JUDGMENTS

1. INTRODUCTION

Petroleum exploration is a costly venture which always involves a great deal of uncertainties and unknown factors. A decision to drill could result in a giant discovery, a modest discovery, or a dry hole. The factors influencing drilling decisions could be of geologic, economic and personal nature. When making a decision based on geologic factors alone, geologists and geophysicists will try to find answers to the following questions [2].

(a) Are there any hydrocarbons present in the geographical area under consideration?

(b) If hydrocarbons are present, what are the chances of finding them?

(c) What is the probable size of the reserves?

If the size of the reserves is known the concern includes how fast and at what cost could oil be produced. Most of these decisions must be made without adequate statistical data.

There are numerous methods of estimating oil and gas resources in a reservoir. Some of the more popular methods are Geologic Analogy [1], Delphi Technique [3], Areal Yield [3], and Volumetric Yield [6] in which the Monte Carlo method is used to simulate the probability distribution of the factors that determine the volume of hydrocarbon to be expected. Each method has its own advantages and limitations.

In this chapter we introduce a new approach which provides a framework for a systematic analysis of crucial geologic factors determining recoverable oil and estimating the probable size of the reserves.

2. MODEL FOR ESTIMATING THE VOLUME OF RECOVERABLE OIL

The pre-condition for petroleum accumulation is the existence of a source rock, where oil and gas originate. Once formed, the oil and gas must migrate from the source rock into more porous and permeable rock called reservoir rock. The reservoir rock acts as a container for the fluids. A reservoir rock must have enough room to store a significant volume of hydrocarbons and must discharge oil or gas readily when the reservoir is penetrated by a well. In order to accumulate oil or gas, the reservoir rock must be deformed either by folding or faulting to form structural or stratigraphic traps.

In the structural type, the traps are the result of movements of the Earth's crust: folding, faulting, fracturing, or intrusion of a salt dome. A stratigraphic trap occurs when a porous rock layer is tilted and eroded. The eroded end is then sealed off by a tight rock layer. Also, to get the petroleum out, there must be some natural driving force within the reservoir, usually gas and/or water.

Figure 1 illustrates the interrelationships of the key factors determining the volume of recoverable oil in a reservoir and Figure 2 is the hierarchy for estimating effective porosity (φ), oil saturation (S_o), effective permeability, recovery factor (RF), and bottom hole pressure (BHP). A brief explanation of each factor is given below.

DEFINITIONS OF GEOLOGIC TERMS

Petroleum trap. Petroleum trap is a geologic setting conducive to concentration and preservation of hydrocarbon. Petroleum traps are generally classified as structural and stratigraphic traps. A structural trap is a geologic setting resulting from deformation of crystal rock to an upward arch-shape (Anticline), to a downward trough-shape (Syncline), and fracturing and displacement (fault). A stratigraphic trap is a geologic setting resulting from termination of a reservoir rock against an impermeable formation.

Effective porosity (φ). Porosity is the volume of empty spaces in a rock which determines its capacity to store fluids (oil, gas or water). Effective porosity is the portion of pore spaces which are connected with channels large enough for fluids to circulate through them. The rest of the pores will not yield their fluids.

Effective permeability (K). Permeability is the property that permits the flow of fluids through the interconnected pores of a formation. Permeability is reported in millidarcies (MD). Absolute permeability is the ability of a rock to transmit a single fluid when it is 100% saturated with it. Effective permeability is permeability with more than one fluid present in the rock. Effective permeability is less than absolute permeability.

Saturation (S_o). Saturation is the percent of pore volume in a rock filled with a fluid (i.e. oil). Generally, a formation will produce oil if its oil saturation is more than 50%. Oil saturation ranges between 0 and 90%.

Bottom-hole pressure (reservoir pressure). The fluids in the pores of reservoir rock are under pressure which approximates the hydrostatic pressure of a column of salt water to that depth. The hydrostatic pressure gradient ranges between 0.43 and 0.47 psi ft^{-1}.

Recovery factor (RF). Recovery factor is the percent of recoverable oil or gas stored in the pore spaces of reservoir rock. The primary recovery factor for oil ranges between 20 and 40%.

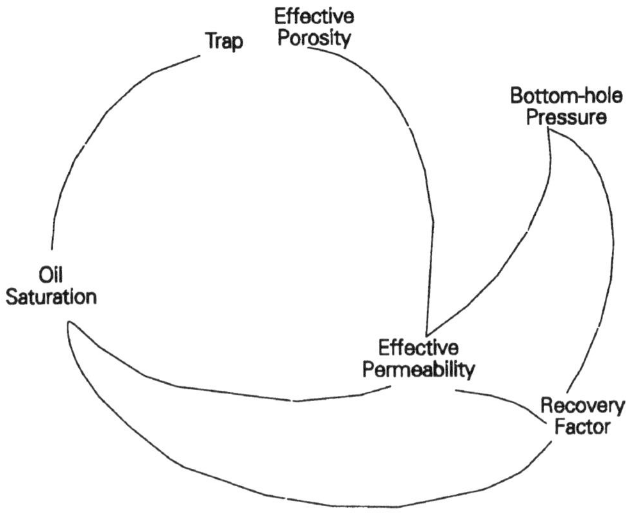

Figure 1. Interrelationships of factors determining the quantity of recoverable oil in a reservoir.

3. COMPUTATION PROCESS

The Analytic Hierarchy Process is used to determine the probability distribution for each element in the hierarchy of Figure 2. To demonstrate the application of the model, the Aux Vases formation in Jasper County in the Illinois Basin was selected. Judgments on the relative importance of the factors and the relative likelihood of the outcomes were made by the second author of the original paper (see acknowledgements at the end of the chapter), who is a geologist, based on the available information on the field under study and his experience in this area. The computation process involves the following steps:

Step 1: Determine relative weights of the factors and relative likelihood of the outcomes using pairwise comparison matrices.

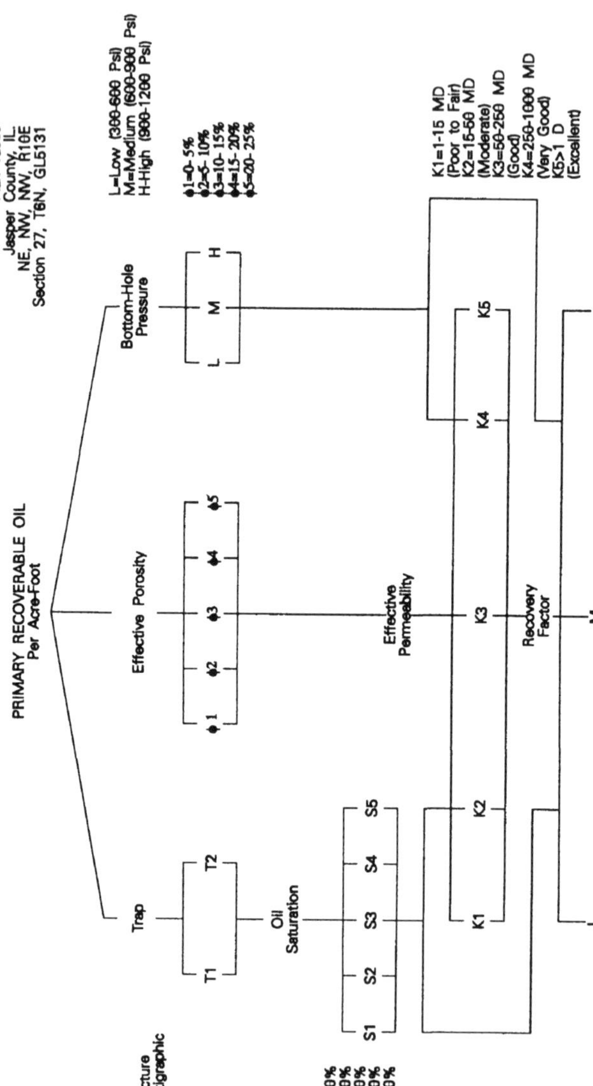
PRIMARY RECOVERABLE OIL
Per Acre-Foot
Aux Vases
Jasper County, IL
NE, NW, NW, R10E
Section 27, T6N, GL5131
Trap
Effective Porosity
Bottom-Hole Pressure
T1
T2
φ1
φ2
φ3
φ4
φ5
L
M
H
T1 = Structure
T2 = Stratigraphic
L=Low (300-600 Psi)
M=Medium (600-900 Psi)
H-High (900-1200 Psi)
φ1=0-5%
φ2=5-10%
φ3=10-15%
φ4=15-20%
φ5=20-25%
Oil Saturation
S1
S2
S3
S4
S5
S1 = 40-50%
S2 = 50-60%
S3 = 60-70%
S4 = 70-80%
S5 = 80-90%
Effective Permeability
K1
K2
K3
K4
K5
K1=1-15 MD
(Poor to Fair)
K2=15-50 MD
(Moderate)
K3=50-250 MD
(Good)
K4=250-1000 MD
(Very Good)
K5>1 D
(Excellent)
Recovery Factor
L
10-20%
M
20-30%
H
30-40%

For demonstration purposes, the pairwise comparison matrix of effective porosity (φ), its largest eigenvalue, eigenvectors, and consistencies are shown below.

The question asked in the matrix of Table 1 is: which range of effective porosity is more probable for the area under study? For example, when comparing φ_1 to φ_4, we assigned a value of 1/5 which means, in our judgment, φ_4 is 'strongly' more probable than φ_1. When comparing φ_2 to φ_3 we assigned a value of 3 which means φ_2 is 'slightly' more probable than φ_3. However, in comparing φ_1 to φ_5 we assigned a value of 1 which means they are equally probable.

Table 1. Effective porosity.

		φ_1	φ_2	φ_3	φ_4	φ_5	Weights(w)	Midrange(φ)	w×φ
0 - 5%	φ_1	1	1/8	1/6	1/5	1	0.043	0.025	0.001
5 - 10%	φ_2	8	1	3	5	8	0.521	0.075	0.039
10 - 15%	φ_3	6	1/3	1	2	6	0.238	0.125	0.029
15 - 20%	φ_4	5	1/5	1/2	1	5	0.156	0.175	0.027
20 - 25%	φ_5	1	1/8	1/6	1/5	1	0.043	0.225	0.009

EV = 0.105 or 10.5%

$\lambda_{max} = 5.182$, CI = 0.045, CR = 0.040.

The numbers in the lower triangular part of the matrix are simply the reciprocals of the numbers in the upper triangular part. For example, $\varphi_1/\varphi_2 = 1/8$, whereas $\varphi_2/\varphi_1 = 8$. Both of these numbers show the dominance of φ_2 over φ_1 as well as the intensity of this dominance. Since the consistency ratio (CR) is 0.04, it means that we are very consistent in making judgments about the relative probability of effective porosity.

The principal right eigenvector (weights) of the matrix clearly shows the relative likelihood of each range of effective porosity. The most likely range of effective porosity for the area under study is φ_2 (5-10%) with a probability of 0.521; and the least likely ranges are φ_1 (0-5%) and φ_5 (20-25%) with equal probability of 0.043.

Step 2: Determining the expected value of each variable.

(a) Expected value of effective porosity(φ). To determine the expected value of effective porosity we use the following equation:

$$EV(\phi) = \sum_{i=1}^{5} \phi_i P(\phi_i)$$

where φ is the midpoint of each range of porosity and P(φ) is the probability of each range represented by W in Table 1. According to this table, EV(φ) = 0.105 or 10.5%.

(b) Expected value of bottom-hole pressure (BHP). A similar procedure is used to determine the expected value of the bottom-hole pressure as shown in Table 2.

Table 2. Bottom-hole pressure (BHP)

		_range (W)	midrange (M)	W × M
300 - 600 psi	L	0.226	450	101.7
600 - 900 psi	M	0.674	750	505.5
900 - 1200 psi	H	0.101	1050	106.0
				EV = 713.25

(c) Expected value of oil saturation (S_o). Figure 2 shows that oil saturation range depends on the type of trap. Thus, to compute the expected value of oil saturation we must first determine the relative likelihood of each kind of trap, structure and stratigraphic and probability distribution of oil saturation for each type of trap. We then compute the overall probabilities of the saturation ranges by multiplying the probability distributions of the oil saturation by the probability of their corresponding trap as shown in Table 3.

Table 3. Probability distribution for the type of trap and oil saturation.

		Trap				
	Oil saturation	T1 (0.167)	T2 (0.833)	Composite weights (W)	Midrange (S)	W×S
40-50%	S_1	0.124	0.129	0.128	0.45	5.76
50-60%	S_2	0.310	0.153	0.479	0.55	26.345
60-70%	S_3	0.469	0.261	0.296	0.65	19.24
70-80%	S_4	0.064	0.063	0.063	0.75	4.725
80-90%	S_5	0.032	0.033	0.033	0.85	2.805
						EV = 58.875

(d) Expected value of effect permeability (K). Relative permeability depends on effective porosity (φ), bottom-hole pressure (BHP), and oil saturation (S_o). Thus, to compute the expected value of the relative permeability for each range of values for the above variables, we compute the composite weights of each range of relative permeability as described in [5] (see Tables 4-7).

(e) Expected value of recovery factor (RF). Recovery factor depends on oil saturation (S_o), relative permeability (K) and bottom-hole pressure (BHP). The computation process for determining the expected value of the recovery factor is similar to (d) (see Tables 8-11).

(f) Volume of primary recoverable oil. The volume of primary recoverable oil from one zone can be determined using the following equation:

$$V_{(STB)} = \frac{B \, x \, h \, x \, \phi \, x \, S_o \, x \, A \, x \, RF}{1.05 + \left(\frac{5 \, x \, D}{100{,}000} \right)}$$

where

$V_{(STB)}$	is the volume of recoverable oil reserves in stock tank barrels (STB),
B	is a constant equal to 7,758 when the volume is measured in barrels and 43,560 when it is measured in cubic feet,
h	is the thickness of the reservoir rock in feet,
φ	is the porosity of the reservoir rock,
S_o	is the oil saturation,
A	is the drainage area in acres based on well spacing of 40, 80, 160, or even 640 acres,
RF	is the recovery factor, and
D	is the depth of the reservoir rock in feet.

For the field under study we have:

h = 10 ft
φ = 10.5% (from Table 1)
S_o = 59% (from Table 3)
A = 40 acres
RF = 22% (from Table 11)
D = 2750 ft

Thus, we obtain:

$$V_{(STB)} = \frac{(7758)(10)(0.105)(0.59)(40)(0.22)}{1.05 + \frac{(5)(2750)}{100{,}000}} = 35{,}615 barrels.$$

Considering the large number of variables in the model and uncertainties associated with these variables, this is a good estimate. Based on the current rate of production from a well, the actual volume of primary recoverable oil from Aux Vases formation is estimated to be between 40,000 to 50,000 barrels of oil.

Table 4. Probability distribution for effective porosity and relative permeability.

Relative permeability	Effective Porosity φ_1 0.043	φ_2 0.521	φ_3 0.238	φ_4 0.156	φ_5 0.043	Composite weights (W)
K_1	0.513	0.328	0.295	0.059	0.031	0.274
K_2	0.261	0.485	0.526	0.305	0.095	0.441
K_3	0.129	0.104	0.099	0.430	0.226	0.160
K_4	0.063	0.054	0.051	0.147	0.507	0.088
K_5	0.033	0.030	0.029	0.059	0.140	0.039

Table 5. Probability distribution for bottom-hole pressure and relative permeability.

Relative permeability	Bottom-hole pressure L 0.226	M 0.674	H 0.101	Composite Weights (W)
K_1	0.513	0.102	0.029	0.188
K_2	0.261	0.504	0.102	0.409
K_3	0.129	0.245	0.287	0.223
K_4	0.063	0.102	0.428	0.126
K_5	0.033	0.046	0.153	0.054

Table 6. Probability distribution for oil saturation and relative permeability.

Relative permeability	Oil Saturation S_1 0.128	S_2 0.479	S_3 0.296	S_4 0.063	S_5 0.033	Composite weights
K1	0.513	0.081	0.060	0.034	0.030	0.125
K2	0.261	0.428	0.257	0.201	0.183	0.333
K3	0.129	0.275	0.488	0.420	0.263	0.328
K4	0.063	0.176	0.149	0.270	0.432	0.168
K5	0.033	0.041	0.047	0.076	0.092	0.046
						EV = 175.47

Table 7. Probability distribution for relative permeability.

Relative permeability	Oil saturation	Effective porosity	Bottom-hole pressure	Composite weights (W)	Midrange (K)	WxK
K_1	0.125	0.274	0.188	0.196	7.5	1.47
K_2	0.333	0.441	0.409	0.394	32.5	12.18
K_3	0.328	0.160	0.223	0.237	150	35.6
K_4	0.168	0.088	0.126	0.127	625	79.4
K_5	0.046	0.039	0.054	0.046	1005	46.2

Table 8. Probability distribution for oil saturation and recovery factor.

Recovery factor	Oil saturation S_1 0.128	S_2 0.479	S_3 0.296	S_4 0.063	S_5 0.033	Composite weights
L	0.785	0.731	0.333	0.218	0.167	0.568
M	0.149	0.188	0.592	0.691	0.740	0.352
H	0.066	0.081	0.075	0.091	0.094	0.078

Table 9. Distribution for bottom-hole pressure and recovery factor.

Recovery factor	Bottom-hole pressure L 0.226	M 0.674	H 0.101	Composite weights
L	0.785	0.333	0.167	0.419
M	0.149	0.592	0.740	0.507
H	0.066	0.075	0.094	0.074

Table 10. Distribution for relative permeability and recovery factor.

Recovery factor	Relative permeability K_1 0.196	K_2 0.394	K_3 0.237	K_4 0.127	K_5 0.046	Composite weights
L	0.785	0.309	0.200	0.072	0.061	0.335
M	0.149	0.582	0.683	0.649	0.353	0.519
H	0.066	0.109	0.117	0.279	0.586	0.146

EV = 0.216.

Table 11. Probability distribution for recovery factor.

Composite Recovery factor	Oil saturation	Relative permeability	Bottom-hole pressure	weights (W)	Midrange (K)	W × RF
L	0.568	0.335	0.419	0.440	0.15	0.066
M	0.382	0.519	0.507	0.459	0.25	0.115
H	0.038	0.146	0.074	0.099	0.35	0.035

4. CONCLUSIONS

In this chapter we have shown a simple way of solving a complex geologic problem. The advantage of the Analytic Hierarchy Process over more conventional methods for estimating oil and gas resources are as follows:

(a) It provides a framework for breaking down a large and complex decision problem into smaller and more manageable decisions.

(b) It leaves a permanent record of all the factors and assumptions from more 'fuzzy' elements at the top to very small and 'crisp' elements at the bottom of the hierarchy.

(c) It enhances our understanding of the problem by going through it step by step.

(d) It considers interactions and interdependence among all the factors influencing our decisions.

(e) It incorporates data and judgments of experts into the model in a logical way.

(f) One can obtain an excellent estimate of the volume of recoverable oil in a reservoir in a very short time and with the least amount of physical and financial resources.

REFERENCES

1. Gess, G., and Bois, C., Study of Petroleum Zones--a Contribution to the Appraisal of Hydrocarbon Resources, *The Future Supply of Nature-made Petroleum and Gas*, edited by R. F. Meyer (New York: Pergamon Press) , 1977, 155-178.
2. Megill, R.E., *Introduction to Risk Analysis*, Petroleum Publishing Company, Tusla, OK, 1977.

3. Miller, B. M., et al., *Geological Estimates of Undiscovered Recoverable Oil and Gas Resources in the United States*, U.S. Geologic Survey Circ. 725, 1975.
4. Miller, G. A., *Psychol. Rev.* 63, 81 (1956).
5. Newendorp, P. D., *Decision Analysis for Petroleum Exploration*, Petroleum Publishing Company, Tusla, OK, 1975.
6. Nezhad, H. G., *How to Make Decisions in a Complex World* GINN Press, Massachusetts, 1989.
7. Nezhad, H. G. and A. Baharlou, "To Drill or Not to Drill: A Synthesis of Experts' Judgments", *International Journal of Systems Science* 22, 9 (1991) 1613-1624.

CHAPTER 20

MODELING THE GRADUATE BUSINESS SCHOOL ADMISSIONS PROCESS

1. INTRODUCTION

Each year thousands of individuals seek admission to graduate schools of business in order to pursue courses leading to a master's degree such as the MBA. From late autumn through early spring, graduate admissions committees within schools of business expend enormous amounts of effort and resources to select an appropriate mix of entering students [1]. The overall decision-making process is usually complex and time consuming. Quantitative and qualitative selection criteria must be agreed upon. Thousands of pieces of application materials must be collected and evaluated. Prospective candidates must be interviewed and their performance judged. Final selections must be made [7]. The entire process must be thorough, fair, and carefully executed.

During the course of the process, difficult questions that focus on "measurables" and "intangibles" are frequently posed. Is the applicant a dependable person with high moral integrity and dedication? How difficult and challenging was the applicant's program of study? How does the committee trade off a high grade point average (GPA) against a low Graduate Management Admission Test (GMAT) score [3]? The answers to these questions depend on the judgments, preferences, and goals of the admissions committee which, in turn, reflect those of the school's faculty and administration.

In this chapter, we try to capture the overall decision-making process in the form of an admissions selection model that is based upon the Analytic Hierarchy Process (AHP) [4, 5]. Our model provides an explicit, unambiguous, and replicable way of evaluating applicants. It should help to increase the efficiency, objectivity, and fairness of the admissions process.

We recognize that many individuals involved in the admissions process may be reluctant to abdicate their own way of making selections in favor of decision making guided by a model. Indeed, they may find it difficult to incorporate their years of experience and idiosyncratic behavior into a more formalized framework. However, we regard this model as an aid to facilitate admissions. Although our model is based upon our experiences at the University of Pittsburgh and is tailored to meet the university's current selection process, we believe that admissions committees in other schools of business around the country, and in other graduate schools as well, will find our model appealing, insightful, and useful. We think that it can help improve communication among committee members, as well as foster better understanding of the process that is used to evaluate applicants.

2. THE SELECTION PROCESS AT THE UNIVERSITY OF PITTSBURGH

In order to provide the reader with some background concerning graduate business admissions, we describe the current selection process that is in place at the Joseph M. Katz Graduate School of Business, University of Pittsburgh [7].

The director of admissions at the Katz School is responsible for the recruitment, evaluation, and selection of applicants. The director and her staff first collect and organize all relevant application materials (such as transcripts and recommendations) from each candidate. The amount of paper work is substantial. In recent years, over 3,000 individuals have applied to the school per year. Once a candidate's information file is complete, the admissions staff evaluates and classifies the application into one of six categories: Automatic accept, Accept, Marginal accept – accept on recommendation of director, Marginal reject – reject on recommendation of director, Reject, or Conditional accept – pending satisfaction of a condition (such as completion of a mathematics requirement). To facilitate the discussion and selection process, this classification is done prior to submitting the files to the admissions committee.

In past years, this broad classification was accomplished by comparing an applicant's undergraduate GPA and GMAT score to scales that had been developed by admissions staff members. To preserve the confidentiality of the school's admission process, these scales will not be given in detail. For example, we would automatically accept a student with a GMAT score above 625 and with GPA above 3.30 with other supporting qualifications. Each scale was divided into categories indicating levels of acceptability which helps in identifying marginal candidates or candidates who do not qualify. For those candidates who would qualify or fall in a marginal category, other criteria (such as letters of recommendation, community services, activities, essays, and work experience) would be examined further in order to ascertain if there is sufficient cause to continue the evaluation process. In addition, an interview may be requested of a candidate to obtain more information or to provide a clarification of the application materials. After all application information has been reviewed and the initial classification has been made, the application file is then submitted to the admissions committee for final review and decision.

3. ADMISSIONS SELECTION MODEL

In the current selection process, we see that, for a single applicant, the admissions director and her staff and the admissions committee itself are confronted with a large number of tradeoffs over a diverse set of criteria. When there are several thousand applicants to evaluate, the number of tradeoffs that must be considered is nearly intractable [1]. We believe that the current process could be made more efficient if all applicants were scored as to their performance on the same set of criteria. Scores could then be compared to "cutoff values" established by the admissions committee.

To model the process, we use a ratings hierarchy [2, 5]. With the input of the admissions director at the Katz School of Business (she is the third author of this paper) and her staff, we constructed the hierarchy shown in Figure 1. In this figure, the local and global weights assigned to each criterion and each subcriterion are shown inside each box.

At the top level, we see that the goal of the process is to select the best applicants for admission to graduate school. At the second level, the goal is broken down using Quantitative and Qualitative criteria.

At level three, the Quantitative criterion is divided into two subcriteria: Undergraduate information and GMAT results. Undergraduate information is further divided into School, Major, and GPA. The School criterion measures the competitiveness of the applicant's undergraduate educational institution. Based on the university quotient index determined by the Educational Testing Service (ETS), a school is rated as Extremely competitive, Very competitive, Competitive, Average, or Below average. These rating are shown in the fifth level of the hierarchy. The Major criterion is used to evaluate applicants on the basis of their previous course of study. It was broken down into broad rating categories: Business and related majors (such as economics), Engineering, Liberal arts (for example, English, history, or political science), and Sciences (for example, chemistry, biology, or nursing). GPA is the actual average from all previous college-level work that is shown on an applicant's official transcript. The ratings for GPA are divided into five categories that range from Over 3.6 to Under 2.75 points.

The other level 3 criterion under Quantitative is GMAT scores. This criterion is subdivided into three scores: Verbal, Math, and Total. The ETS scores the verbal and mathematical parts of the GMAT are evaluated on a scale from 0 to 60 (scores below 10 or above 46 are rare). An applicant's total score on the GMAT is not calculated by summing the verbal and mathematics scores. Rather, the total score lies between 200 and 800. To account for this, we have subdivided the Verbal and Math criteria into four ratings that range from 30 and Over to Below 20. The Total criterion is broken down into five ratings that range from 600 and Up to Under 480.

Also at the third level, the Qualitative criterion is divided into two subcriteria: Application Information and Work Experience. Application Information covers all of the data submitted by an applicant and is broken down into four subcriteria: Essays, Letters of Recommendation, Academic Awards, and Activities. Applicants are required to submit two essays and can also submit an optional third essay. These essays are read by the admissions office staff and critiqued for content, grammar, style, and general writing ability. The entire set of essays are then rated as Outstanding, Very good, Average, Below average, and Poor.

The second subcriterion under Application Information is Letters of Recommendation. Applicants are required to submit two recommendation forms that have been completed by employers, professors, or other non-related superiors. On these forms, respondents rank applicants on several questions and answer several open-ended questions. The admissions staff then rates the letters as Outstanding, Very good, Average, Below average, and Poor.

The third subcriterion under Application Information is Academic Awards. This takes into account an applicant's university awards, fellowships, membership in honor societies, and other forms of recognition for academic excellence. The overall number of awards and prestige of the awards are determined by the admissions staff and a rating from Outstanding to Poor is then assigned to the applicant. The final subcriterion, namely Activities, is handled in a similar way. An applicant's community and extracurricular activities are rated from Outstanding to Poor.

The Work Experience subcriterion is broken down into Years of Experience and Type of Work Experience. Years of Experience is a straightforward category with applicants rated as having experience of 5 Years or More, 3 to 5 Years, 1 to 2 Years, and Less Than 1 Year. The Type of Work Experience subcriterion classifies applicants into four work categories: 1) a business-related job in which the applicant is considered a professional or management level employee (for example, staff accountant, credit analyst, bank manager); 2) a business-related job in which the applicant is an hourly or clerical-level worker (for example, bank teller, secretary, receptionist); 3) a non-business job in which the candidate is considered a professional (for example, doctor, nurse, dentist); 4) a non-business job in which the applicant is not considered a professional or manager (for example, janitor, construction worker, waitress).

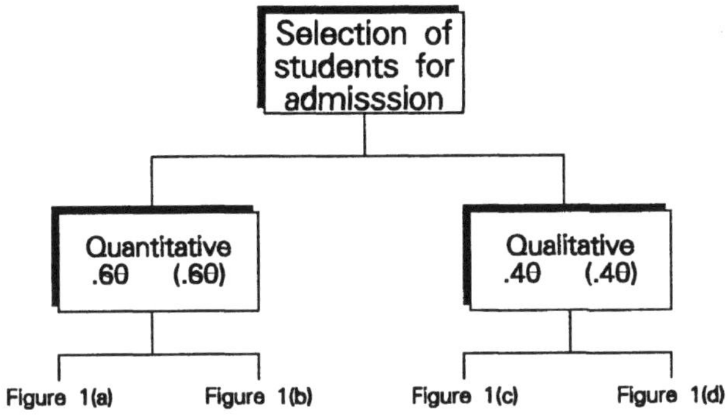

Figure 1. Admissions Hierarchy

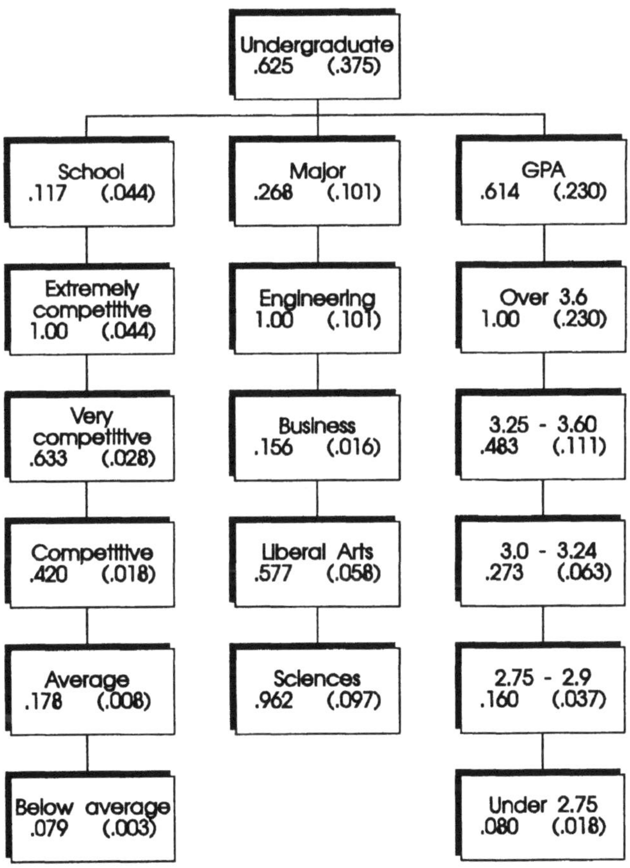

Figure 1(a). Undergraduate Component of Admissions Hierarchy

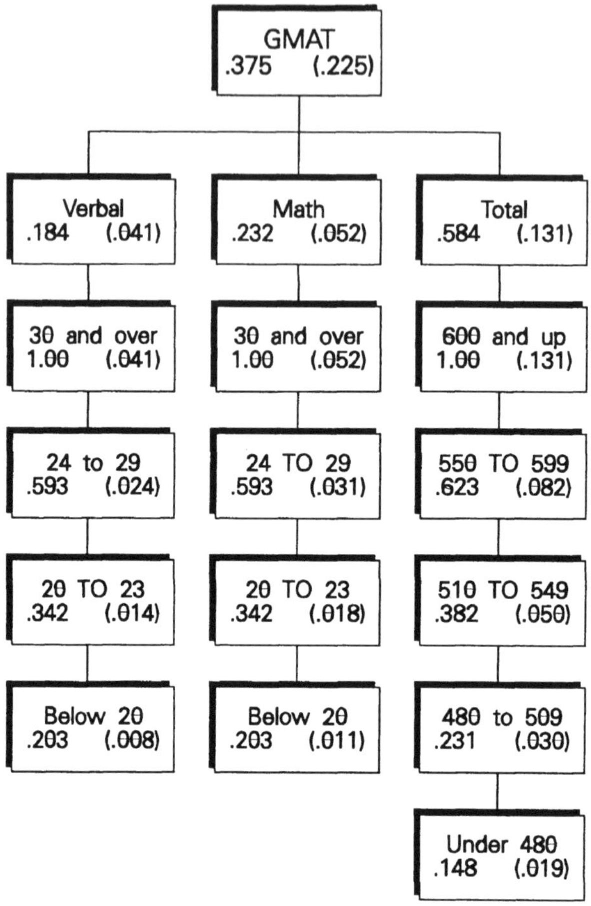

Figure 1(b). GMAT Component of Admissions Hierarchy

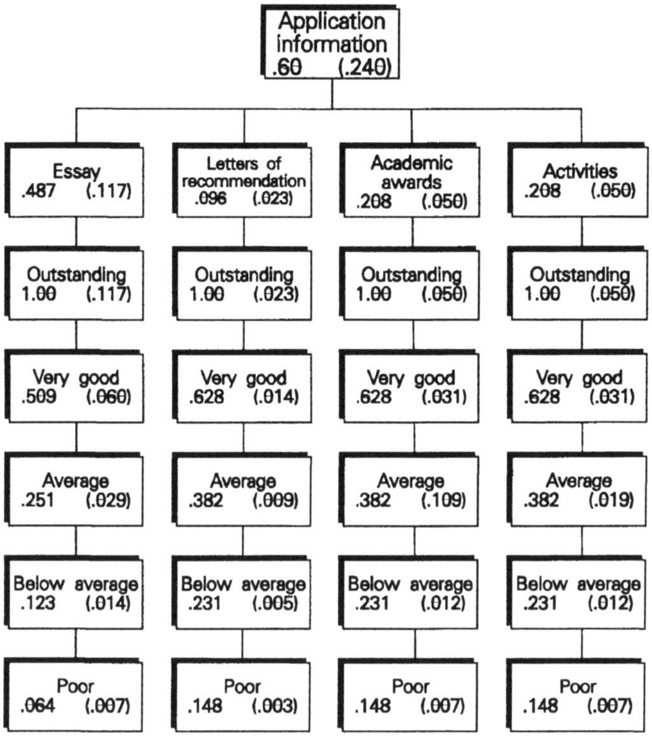

Figure 1(c). Admission Information Component

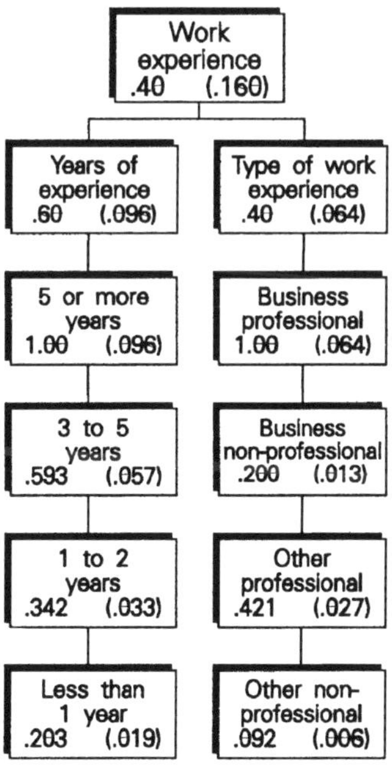

Figure 1(d). Work Experience Component of Admissions Hierarchy

Table 1. Set of scores for a hypothetical set of applicants

Quantitative									Qualitative			
Undergraduate			GMAT			Application Information				Work Experience		
Total	School	Major	GPA	Verbal	Math	Total	Essay Recomm.	Letters of	Academic Awards	Activities	Years of Experience	Type of Work Experience
High Score (1.00)	**Ext. Competitive** (.044)	**Eng.** (.101)	**Over 3.6** (.230)	**30 and over** (.041)	**30 and over** (.052)	**600 and up** (.131)	**Outstanding** (.117)	**Outstanding** (.023)	**Outstanding** (.050)	**Outstanding** (.050)	**5 or more years** (.096)	**Business Professional** (.064)
J. Smith (.442)	**Very Competitive** (.028)	**Business** (.016)	**2.75-2.9** (.037)	**30 and over** (.041)	**30 and over** (.052)	**600 and up** (.131)	**Below Average** (.014)	**Average** (.009)	**Below Average** (.012)	**Average** (.019)	**Less than 1 year** (.019)	**Business Professional** (.064)
F. Davis (.557)	**Very Competitive** (.028)	**Lib'l Art** (.058)	**Over 3.6** (.230)	**24 to 29** (.024)	**below 20** (.011)	**510 to 549** (.050)	**Very Good** (.060)	**Very Good** (.014)	**Average** (.019)	**Very Good** (.031)	**Less than 1 year** (.019)	**Business Non-Professional** (.013)
C. Jones (.417)	**Comp.** (.018)	**t.Eng.** (.101)	**3.0 to 3.24** (.063)	**below 20** (.008)	**below 20** (.011)	**under 480** (.019)	**Very Good** (.060)	**Average** (.009)	**Below Average** (.012)	**Poor** (.007)	**5 or more years** (.096)	**Business Non-Professional** (.013)
K. Baker (.471)	**Below Average** (.003)	**Sciences** (.097)	**3.0 to 3.24** (.063)	**24 to 29** (.024)	**30 and over** (.052)	**550 to 559** (.082)	**Average** (.029)	**Below Average** (.005)	**Poor** (.007)	**Below Average** (.012)	**1 to 2 years** (.033)	**Business Professional** (.064)
Low Score (.124)	**Below Average** (.003)	**Business** (.016)	**Under 2.75** (.018)	**below 20** (.008)	**below 20** (.011)	**under 480** (.019)	**Poor** (.007)	**Poor** (.003)	**Poor** (.007)	**Poor** (.007)	**Less than 1 year** (.019)	**Other Non-Professional** (.006)

Remark - Earlier applications of the absolute mode of Expert Choice simply weighted subcriteria weights by criteria weights, then intensities by subcriteria weights to obtain the overall weights of the intensities. In this model we have modified the former approach. To produce a ratio scale that is part of the unit priority of the top level goal would be to divide the intensities with respect to each criterion by the maximum intensity under it thus producing a unit for the intensities with respect to each criterion. The overall rating of the alternatives would then belong to a ratio scale which when normalized becomes a proportionate allocation of the unit weight of the goal to each alternative.

4. IMPLEMENTING THE MODEL

We envision that our AHP model would be used in the following way. At the beginning of each application period, the admissions committee would meet as a group to review the overall appropriateness of the model. The model would be updated: new criteria might be added or old criteria might be deleted in accordance with the "qualities" that committee members are looking for in a prospective student. The group would then judge the importance of criteria and subcriteria for that particular year. In our experience, using the Expert Choice computerized package [2] greatly facilitates this process. Next, the committee would compare the performance ratings at the bottom level of the hierarchy. For example, the relative importance of intensities such as outstanding, very good, average, below average, and poor for each criterion would be determined via the expert judgment of the committee.

To demonstrate this process, the current director of admissions at the Katz School of Business used Expert Choice to generate the weights shown in each box of Figure 1. (Of course, the actual judgments necessary to produce the weights would be made by the admissions committee.) From this figure, we see that the Quantitative criterion with a weight of 0.60 is slightly favored over the Qualitative criterion with a weight of 0.40.

Once the overall weights have been generated, individual applicants are then rated. We recommend using a spreadsheet with table lookup functions to carry out this part of the process. We illustrate this in Table 1 with a hypothetical set of applicants. From this figure, we see that J. Smith is rated as to her performance in each of the 12 categories. For example, in the School category, she received a Very Competitive rating. This contributed a weight of 0.028 to her overall score of 0.442. Smith's score could then be compared with a predetermined threshold; if the score fell above this value, J. Smith would be admitted. We point out that, with our model, the maximum score an applicant could achieve is 1.00 and the minimum score is 0.124.

5. CONCLUSIONS

Using the AHP, we have constructed a model that can provide admissions committees with help in making complex admissions decisions. We believe that our modeling process ensures that committee members are in general agreement on admission goals. Our approach is systematic and thorough: it effectively uses all information supplied by an applicant. The most obvious advantage of using our model for admissions selection is that it provides for consistent decision making. All applicants are evaluated on a single set of weighted criteria. This should help to reduce the subjectivity of the process. Again, we wish to emphasize that our model does not replace directors of admissions, staff personnel, and committees. Rather, it should be used as an aid in the overall decision-making process.

Early in the spring of 1991, we formally presented our model to the graduate admissions committee of the Katz School. The committee viewed our model favorably and believes that it is a tool that can be incorporated into the evaluation and selection process.

The committee plans to refine the hierarchy, modify the judgments, and generate a new set of weights. Through use of the model, the hierarchy will no doubt be expanded to accommodate other factors such as graduate education and part-time work experience that need to be considered in the admissions process.

REFERENCES

1. Dickason, Donald G., "Identification, Recruitment and Admissions of Graduate Students." Council of Graduate Schools, Proceedings of the 27th Annual Meeting, Washington, D.C., 1987.
2. Forman, Ernest H. and Thomas L. Saaty, Expert Choice Manual, McLean, Virginia: Decision Support Software Inc., 1983.
3. Messick, Samuel J., "Ethical Issues in Selection." *Selections* Autumn (1985) 27-29.
4. Saaty, Thomas L., *Decision Making for Leaders*, RWS Publications, 4922 Ellsworth Ave., Pittsburgh, 1986; Original version published by Lifetime Learning Publications, Belmont, California, 1982.
5. Saaty, Thomas L., *Decision Making, The Analytic Hierarchy Process*, RWS Publications, 4922 Ellsworth Ave., Pittsburgh, 1988; Original version published by McGraw-Hill, New York, 1980.
6. Saaty, T.L., J.W. France and K.R. Valentine, "Modeling the Graduate Business School Admissions Process", *Socio-Economic Planning Sciences* 25, 2 (1991) 155-162.
7. Swanberg, Carol, William Moody, and Kevin Duffy, "KGSB Admissions Decision Advisor", Submitted in Partial Fulfillment of Course Requirements BA AIM 211.
8. Turcotte, Robert B., "Enrollment Management at the Graduate Level." *Journal of College Admissions* April (1983) 24-28.

CHAPTER 21

INFERTILITY DECISION MAKING

1. INTRODUCTION

Infertility is perceived as a major crisis in life. There are strong religious, cultural and societal pressures to have children. The most commonly accepted definition of infertility is the continued inability of a couple to conceive after a year. The high level of interest in the problems associated with infertility has led to the rapid development of medical technology in this area. It is one of the few specialty fields that have given rise to many emotional, ethical and legal considerations.

It is estimated that 11 per cent of all married couples with the woman between the ages of 15 and 44 had problems with conception. An increasing number of infertile couples are seeking help. It has become more socially acceptable to seek fertility care. The number of US infertility clinics performing high-technology procedures increased from 84 in 1985 to 270 in 1992. The procedures are quite costly. Infertility has become an industry with revenues of $2 billion a year [1].

Confronted with the reality of infertility, couples have several options: remain childless, adoption, undergo in vitro fertilization (IVF) or artificial insemination, or become parents with the cooperation of a surrogate mother. The effects of childlessness and its alternatives on peoples' quality of life and on their self-perceptions provide many challenges for modern mental health professionals. Not only do we need to know what alternatives exist and their potential benefits, but also the costs and risks involved with each. Related psychological and legal issues have increasingly come to the fore. The feelings of frustration, self-doubt and negative self image are real and as painful as the medical procedures themselves. In addition to these considerations, there is another major factor – the financial cost inherent in adoption, biotechnological procedures and surrogacy. The extensive medical efforts vary from hundreds to thousands of dollars per procedure or attempt. Adoption agencies as well as "brokers" charge for their services. Surrogate mothers frequently assume that status from around $10,000 to $15,000. Attorneys charge anywhere from their normal hourly rate for the paper work to $10,000 or more for their "matchmaking" role.

2. THE ALTERNATIVES

The complex problem of arriving at the best option for having a baby when it is not possible by natural process is analyzed by the Analytical Hierarchy Process (AHP). The AHP is a process of solving complex problems by logic and systemic rationality. It incorporates both the qualitative and quantitative aspects of human thought in the decision making process. The problem is defined and the hierarchy constructed in a qualitative manner and the judgments made qualitatively. It enables one to study the problem as a whole while taking into consideration the interactions between the components within the hierarchy. Six alternatives were chosen for consideration as a possible solution to the problem. A description of each alternative follows.

ADOPTION

Adoption is defined as "the overall legal process by which a parent who is not the natural parent of a child becomes legally recognized as that child's parent". It is often the last resort of infertile couples in trying to establish a family. Many of the couples have pursued medical therapies and most have rejected the legally and emotionally risky option of surrogate motherhood. In 1986 it was estimated that there were 60,000 nonrelative adoptions [2]. Until the 1970s, the most common form of nonrelative child placement was through public agencies. The most common criticism of agency adoption was that prospective parents had to sometimes wait for as long as 7 years to receive a child placement. Private or independent agencies were established in the following years. They charged ten times the fees charged by public agencies, $10,000 compared to $1,000 by the public agencies. However, they became successful as the wait period was only 12 to 18 months and couples were willing to pay the price for that. This form of adoption still has an intermediary, but it is more likely to be an attorney or physician rather than a state agency. The legal documents are still drawn in court and the judge must grant the adoption.

A number of court cases have considered the constitutionality of racial matching in adoption. The standard commonly used in making an assessment of whether a particular home would benefit the child is that the placement be in the "best interest of the child". Several federal courts have reviewed statutes that make racial matching a factor in adoption. In all of these rulings, the courts have held that race may be a factor, if it is in the best interest of the child, but it cannot be the automatic factor in determining placement of the child.

The changes in adoption practice and laws have made this a somewhat more hazardous alternative to childlessness than was true one or two generations ago. Yet there is no question that the majority of adoptions go through the courts without problems and result in happy families. Today, more than in previous years, there may be a need for mental health counseling and effective legal advice at the initial stage when adoption is considered and then throughout the adoption process.

ARTIFICIAL INSEMINATION (AIH & AID)

Artificial insemination, practiced successfully for almost a century, is a relatively straight forward and simple procedure compared to some of the other techniques developed in more recent years. There are two types in this procedure – artificial insemination by husband's sperm (AIH) and artificial insemination using donor sperm (AID). AIH is the least controversial procedure and has been widely applied in the management of infertility. The success rates for AIH depends on the clinic and varies between 0 and 50 per cent. Benefit/cost ratios are unavailable due to inadequate data.

AID is one of the oldest and most successful therapies in infertility treatment. According to a survey published by the Office of Technology Assessment of the US Congress. over 170,000 women undergo AID and about 30,000 babies are born each year. Yet, despite the widespread practice and success of AID, there are numerous controversies regarding clinical strategies, techniques, and ethical concepts. The process should be initiated only after a thorough review of the indications, comprehensive discussion of the nature of donor screening and selection, and sensitive consideration of the emotional, social and legal implications of the process.

IN VITRO FERTILIZATION (IVF)

In vitro fertilization, also known as the creation of "test tube babies", has been performed since the late 1970s. It involves extracting ova from the woman, fertilizing with the husband's sperm in a glass petri dish, and then after several days of growth reimplanting it in the woman's womb. One of the striking features of this procedure is the wide variation of success rates due to the complex nature of the technique and consequently the numerous variables which may impact the success. Some clinics have established a higher success rate and couples gravitate toward them. Even then the success rate is at most only 12 or 13 per cent. It is a rather expensive procedure, costing between $6,000 and $10,000 per cycle including medication. The high cost is due to tight quality control and individual care which produce good results [3]. IVF has spawned a burgeoning industry that is almost devoid of regulation. As a result, over 200 clinics have sprung up across the country. Yet, approximately 1/3 of these clinics have not produced successful births. The current IVF market is estimated at $30 million to $40 million per year [4].

At present there are no specific federal statutes concerning assisted reproduction. Two bills may be introduced in the near future in Congress that could have an effect of the practice of IVF. The greatest controversy concerns the legal standing of embryos. The two sides of the controversy are that the embryos are property and, conversely, that they are humans.

SURROGACY

Surrogate motherhood is a method in which a contract with the surrogate is entered, usually for a fee, to bear a baby. Conception could be achieved two ways - (1) through artificial insemination of the husband's sperm and using the surrogate's egg, or, (2) implanting an embryo belonging to the couple created by IVF. The contract usually includes, in addition to the fee, the medical expenses of prenatal care and also a fee paid to the attorney who draws the contract. The surrogate's fee is about $10,000 and the attorney's fee ranges from $10,000 to $15,000 [5]. The ethics of surrogacy have been the subject of much debate because it resembles the outlawed practice of baby selling. The overall monetary, emotional and legal implications surrounding surrogacy is very high.

3. PROCEDURE

The Analytical Hierarchy Process was applied to benefit/cost analysis to obtain the overall best solution for the problem. The benefit (success) of each alternative was weighed against the cost and risk involved and a ratio of benefit/cost × risk was calculated. Three separate hierarchies were constructed for the three parameters, viz., benefit, cost and risk. The results were then integrated to obtain the best solution. The three hierarchies are discussed below:

I. <u>BENEFIT (SUCCESS)</u>

In order to achieve maximum benefits with the alternatives, the criteria considered most important were (1) genetic identity, (2) legality, and (3) gender selection (Figure 1).

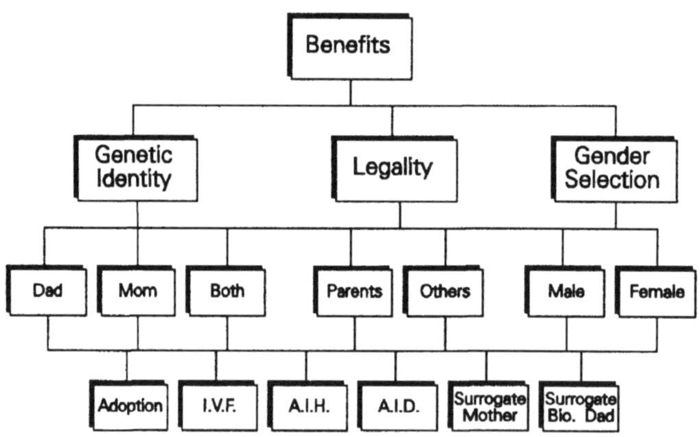

Figure 1. Benefits Hierarchy

<u>Genetic Identity</u>: With advances in biomedical technology it is now possible to screen a potential mother or father for congenital defects. The probabilities of passing on a trait to an offspring can be calculated and in many instances corrective or preventative measures can be taken to avoid their occurrence in the offspring.

<u>Legality</u>: The development of effective therapies to treat infertility has given rise to legal implications. More medical malpractice suits were filed in the past decade than in the entire previous history of American tort law. In the last several years,

Congress has taken an active interest in infertility practice. The state governments regulate infertility practice by licensure of clinics, hospitals and personnel. Law suits could arise from high-risk and invasive procedures requiring surgery. In the case of a law suit, the issue of liability must be assessed early on so that the proper defense can be pursued. Legal issues that are likely to arise should be considered by both the parents as well as others involved, like the surrogate mother.

Gender Selection: This criterion gains consideration only in the case of adoption. Having made the decision to adopt, the couple is in a position to select a boy or a girl for adoption. Amniocentesis is a procedure performed during pregnancy to detect congenital defects and fetal-maternal incompatibility. However, the procedure also determines the gender of the fetus. The procedure has been criticized when, in some instances, the results have been used for the unethical purpose of choosing a baby of preferred gender.

II. COSTS

There are three types of costs that were taken into consideration in determining the best alternative: (1) monetary, (2) physical, and (3) emotional costs. Monetary cost is tangible and physical and emotional costs are intangible costs. One of the characteristics of AHP is that it allows one to measure such intangible costs.

Monetary cost: In addition to considerable physical and psychological costs and time away from work, infertility treatment is expensive [6, 7]. According to Office of Technology Assessment estimates [8], the total cost to treat infertile couples ranges from $3,660 for the simplest problem to $22,200 for the whole treatment if the couple goes all the way through IVF. Not all insurance companies will cover infertility as part of the benefit package; therefore, monetary cost may affect the patient's choice of treatment. In evaluating the costs involved in the entire process, three factors contributed to the expenses. These constitute the subcriteria in the hierarchy. The first expense a couple encounter is the cost of evaluating the various alternatives. These are the fees paid for medical screening in IVF and artificial insemination procedures and initial consultation fees paid to attorney or adoption agency for surrogacy and adoption.

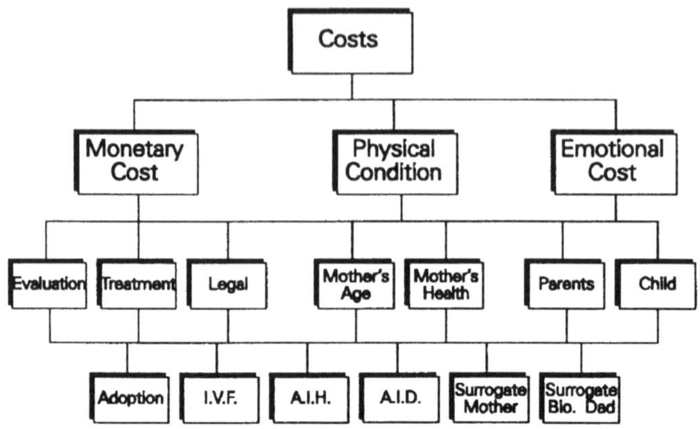

Figure 2. Costs Hierarchy

The next expense is the cost of the actual procedure. This includes expenses incurred with the surgical procedure in IVF and artificial insemination. Payment to the surrogate mother and her prenatal care and childbirth are incurred in the case of surrogacy. Fees paid to the adoption agency may be considered as the adoption expense.

The third expense is the legal fee paid to the attorney. Adoption requires a legal contract to be drawn. It also requires filing a petition with the court and obtaining a ruling. Laws allowing surrogacy vary from state to state. Of the states allowing surrogacy, no state has set a detailed regulatory scheme to establish the legal rights and obligation between the parties and the child. If allowed, a surrogacy arrangement would require a legal contract drawn by an attorney and court approval prior to initiation of a pregnancy.

Physical cost: Fertility rate in women is highly dependent on age. Late teen and early twenties is the most fertile period in a woman's life. Infertility increases with age and significantly so after the age of 35. The infertility rate for women between the ages of 35 and 39 is 24.6 per cent and for women between the ages of 40 to 44 is 27.2 per cent [9]. Hence success in medical procedures to overcome infertility is highly dependent on the age of the person carrying the baby. In the case of surrogacy where the biological mother's egg is used, the age of both the biological mother and surrogate become important. Another physical factor equally important is the state of health of the person carrying the baby.

Emotional cost: Infertility creates psychological distress in itself. In addition, they are faced with a confusing array of options, as well as uncharted ethical and legal implications that are very stressful. Support groups have proved to be valuable. Infertility makes couples more vulnerable to depression. The emotional stress experienced during the process of adoption or any other alternative is considerable and is further enhanced by the previous status of infertility.

Emotional cost to the child also needs consideration. A child adopted at a very young age is curious to know about the birth parents and the reason why he/she was given up for adoption. In some instances the child seeks to find the birth parents and goes through emotional turmoil in coming to terms with the situation. Children adopted by a stepparent in "their best interest" often experiences emotional distress in adjusting to the new family created by the state statute.

III. RISK

All surgical procedures involve physiological risk to various degrees depending upon the type of procedure. Except adoption, all other alternatives being considered in this case require surgical procedures. The risk for all the individuals involved is considered in the risk hierarchy (Figure 3).

4. RESULTS

The decision reached by the AHP is discussed for each hierarchy followed by benefit/(cost×risk) analysis. Note that risk is in the denominator multiplied by the cost because one asks: which person is more at risk and which alternative has greater risk? The weighted judgments for each hierarchy were synthesized. Of the three criteria for the benefits of the process, genetic identity was the most important. IVF was found to be the most beneficial solution, but at the same time the riskiest procedure and also one of the most expensive. Surrogate mother using biological egg and sperm was found to be the least beneficial and at the same time most expensive. Artificial insemination was the most cost effective.

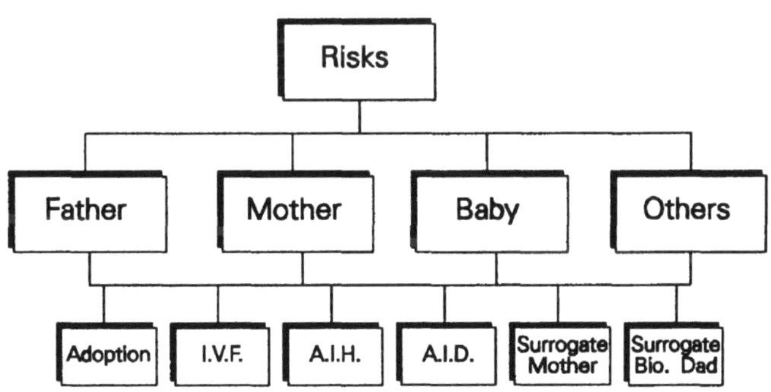

Figure 3. Risks Hierarchy

Benefits were weighed against cost and risk taken together. A benefit/cost ratio by AHP showed AIH as the best solution for a couple who are unable to have a baby naturally (Table 1).

Table 1. Benefit to Cost × Risk Ratios

	Benefits (B)	Costs (C)	Risks (R)	C×R	B/(C×R)	%
Adoption	0.112	0.154	0.044	0.007	16.47	26.92
I.V.F.	0.234	0.212	0.323	0.069	3.09	5.06
A.I.H.	0.220	0.087	0.108	0.009	23.40	38.26
A.I.D.	0.145	0.104	0.117	0.012	11.88	19.46
Surrogate Mother	0.201	0.220	0.277	0.061	3.30	5.40
Surrogate Biol. Father	0.088	0.223	0.131	0.029	3.01	4.92

In evaluating the validity of AHP in the problem, the limitations of the model must be recognized. The results depend upon the criteria chosen to evaluate the benefits and costs and also the weights given to the judgments by the individual or individuals conducting the study. However, consistency is checked to maintain coherence among the judgments. While perfect consistency is not always possible, and often not even desirable, inconsistency of up to 10 per cent is tolerated. If inconsistency exceeds 10 per cent, the AHP model allows one to retrace the steps and revisit the judgments.

Given the complexity of the issues in this problem and the rapid technological advances in this area, the decision may change in the future. However, under the present circumstances, we feel that we have considered all the important and relevant criteria in the study to offer the best solution to the problem.

REFERENCES

1. Dewitt, P.M., "In pursuit of pregnancy," *American Demographics* 15, 5 (1993) 48.
2. Gibbs, N., "The baby chase," *Time*, Oct. 9 (1989) 86.
3. Meldrum, D.R., "In vitro fertilization." In *Decision making in reproductive endocrinology*. Eds. Schlaff, W.D. and Rock, J.A. Blackwell Scientific Publication, Boston, 1993.
4. Cosco, J., "Baby boom," *Public Relations Journal* 44, 2 (1988) 28.
5. Yeh, J. and M.U. Yeh, *Legal aspects of infertility*, Blackwell Scientific Publications, 1991.
6. Cooper, G.S., "An analysis of the costs of infertility treatment," *Am. J. Public Health* 76 (1986) 1018.

7. Fuchs, V.R. and L. Perrault, "Expenditures for reproduction related health care." *JAMA* 255 (1986) 76.
8. Congress of the United States, Office of Technology Assessment. *Infertility : medical and social choices*, 1988.
9. Pratt, W.F., W.D. Mosher, C.A. Bachrach, and M.C. Horn, "Understanding US fertility: findings from the National Survey of Family Growth, Cycle III." *Population Bulletin* 39, 5 (1984) 1.

CHAPTER 22

THE DECISION BY THE US CONGRESS ON CHINA'S TRADE STATUS: A MULTICRITERIA ANALYSIS

1. INTRODUCTION

In this paper, we used a decision making tool, the Analytic Hierarchy Process (AHP), to analyze a decision to select a trade status for China that is in the best interest of the United States before that decision came before Congress for a vote.

Since 1986, China has been trying to join the multilateral trade system, the General Agreement on Tariffs and Trade (GATT) and its successor, the World Trade Organization (WTO)[1]. According to the rules of the 135-member nation WTO, a candidate member must reach a trade agreement with any existing member country that wishes to trade with it [2]. By the time this analysis was done, China signed bilateral agreements with 30 countries-including the US (November 1999) - out of 37 members that had requested a trade deal with it [3].

As part of its negotiation deal with the US, China asked the US to remove its annual review of China's Normal Trade Relations (NTR) status, until 1998 called the Most Favored Nation (MFN) status [4]. In March 2000, President Clinton sent a bill to Congress requesting a Permanent Normal Trade Relations (PNTR) status for China [5]. The analysis was done and copies were sent to leaders and some members in both houses of Congress before the House of the Representative voted on the bill, May 24, 2000. The decision by the US Congress on China's trade relations status will have an influence on US interests, in both direct and indirect ways, with China. The direct impact will include changes in economic, security and political relations between the US and China as the trade deal is actualized. The indirect impact will occur when China becomes a WTO member nation and adheres to WTO rules and principles. China has said that it would join the WTO only if the US gives it permanent normal trade relations status.

It is likely that Congress will consider four options. The least likely option is that the US will deny China both PNTR and annual extension of NTR status. The other three options are:

- **Passage of a clean PNTR bill:** Congress grants China permanent normal trade relations status with no conditions attached. This option would allow implementation of the November 1999 WTO trade deal between China and the Clinton administration. China will also carry out other WTO principles and trade conditions.

- **Amendment of the current NTR status bill:** This option would give China the same trade position as other countries and disassociate trade from other issues. As a supplement, a separate bill may be enacted and address other matters, such as human rights, labor rights, and environmental issues.
- **Annual Extension of NTR status:** Congress extends China's normal trade relations status for one more year, and, thus, maintains the status quo.

There have been many debates as to whether Congress should grant China PNTR status. The debate has reflected the different attitudes about this subject. Proponents of the China trade bill emphasize only the benefits, and opportunities (mostly economic), to be derived from passage of the PNTR bill. Opponents are against the bill because of the costs and risks it involves, such as potential loss of jobs in the US. Moreover China's PNTR status eventually could increase its expenditures on military modernization and increase threats to Taiwan.

The following is a summary of the main criteria in the hierarchies of the benefits, costs, opportunities and risks to the US from acting on this decision.

2. BENEFITS TO US

A. Increase US Exports to China

China's PNTR will increase US exports by $3.1 billion per year in the short-term and could increase them by $12.7 billion to $13.9 billion a year by 2005 [6]. China promised to lower overall tariffs from an average of about 25% to 9% [7]. US firms will have broader accessibility to the Chinese market, particularly in the agriculture, service and financial sectors. For example, there are currently only 25 foreign banks in China that are permitted to take deposits and lend money in China's currency, the renminbi, and there are only seven foreign insurers doing business in China. These foreign companies' operations are restricted to a few cities, such as Shanghai, Shenzen and Guangzhou [8]. These geographical restrictions will be dropped in five years [9]. Foreign banks are not allowed to take deposits from Chinese enterprises or individuals [10]. However, once China joins the WTO, immense changes will come to the financial market. Foreign banks will be allowed to do business with Chinese enterprises in renminbi within two years of WTO accession, and with Chinese individuals within five years [11].

B. Improved Rule of Law

Improved Rule of Law will be guaranteed and could reduce China's infringement of intellectual property rights (IPR), which is a large source of profits. IPR has been a serious cause of trade dispute between the US and China, and has caused a loss of US profits [12]. One of the most important differences between the WTO and its precursor, the GATT, is that the WTO not only deals with trade issues but also covers services and intellectual property rights, according to the Trade-Related Aspects of Intellectual Property rights (TRIPs) [13]. All WTO member nations are required to abide by TRIPs. Moreover China agreed to US demands that upon its accession to the WTO it would implement TRIPs without a transition period. Accordingly, China's accession to the WTO should increase profits of US businesses particularly in software, music recording, and other high-tech and cultural industries [14].

Once China joins the WTO, it has to follow the rule of law in accordance with WTO principles [15]. As China becomes more law-abiding, the resulting transparency and predictability in China's actions would lead to an improved investment environment in China.

C. China's Promise to Respect US Provisions

China agreed to adhere to US demands to continue two powerful US provisions to protect its domestic industries [16].

1) Anti-dumping measures for 15 years after China joins the WTO. If the US International Trade Commission and the US Department of Commerce conclude that dumping is occurring, and if the dumping practice by foreign exporters injures the domestic industry, the government can impose an anti-dumping duty, an import tariff equal to the dumping margin. The US uses antidumping policies much more extensively than other countries [17].

2) Section 201 Law of the 1974 Trade Act, also called the escape clause or the safeguard, stipulates that the president can impose severe restrictions up to five years to reduce imports of a foreign product [18].

D. Increased Employment

Increased exports can create more jobs, particularly in areas where the US is highly competitive such as in high-technology, telecommunication, and farm industries.

E. Benefits to Lower Income Consumers

If the US imposes higher tariffs on Chinese products, as a consequence of any trade dispute between the two countries, US consumers may pay higher prices for consumer goods, such as apparel, toys, and electronic appliances. This would become a burden for lower income households [19].

3. COSTS TO US

A. Loss of US Access to China's Market

Competition among nations over China's market is high. If China does not obtain Normal Trade Relations status, it is likely to blame the US. In that case, China would be less inclined to offer US businesses the opportunities given to other competitors in Chinese markets.

B. Possible Job Losses in the US

Labor unions have expressed their concern that jobs will be at risk if Congress passes the bill, because some US firms would move to China in pursuit of its low-wage labor [20].

4. OPPORTUNITIES FOR US

A. US–Sino Relations

Congress' decision could result in a breakthrough in US-Sino relations in the economic, political, social, cultural, and security arenas. Congress can help draw China, which was isolated until Deng Xiaoping began an extensive economic reform, closer to the rest of the world, and open wider arenas for US-China exchange.

B. Improve the Environment

China's large population and fast economic growth generate high-energy consumption and exhaust other natural resources, thus causing environmental concerns. There are two reasons why the US can expect better environmental policies in China with PNTR. First, many developing countries, such as China, cannot afford environment-friendly equipment. When China's economy develops further, it is more likely that China would take measures against environmental degradation. Second, as the US-China Forum on Environment and Development has demonstrated, close relations between China and the US can enhance US' ability to influence China's behavior regarding environmental protection [21].

C. Promote Democracy, D. Improve Human and Labor Rights

The more China is exposed to the rest of the world through the flow of goods, finance, technology and ideas, the more it is likely to become a democratic nation. Labor and human rights are also more likely to be improved through China's exposure to standards adhered to by developed nations [22].

5. RISKS FOR US

A. Loss of Trade as Leverage over Other Issues

Some believe that the annual review process of China's trade status gives the US an economic leverage over other issues such as human rights, labor rights, and security issues. Consequently, granting China Permanent Trade Relations is perceived by some as sacrificing US leverage over China [23].

B. US-China Conflict

Denying China PNTR can lead to conflicts between the US and China. Some analysts have suggested that China may become a major rival for the US, replacing the former Soviet Union. Thus, the potential friction with China could be a serious cause for risk.

C. China Violating Regional Stability

Failure of engagement with China can yield regional instability, particularly across the Taiwan Strait. Isolating China from the WTO may also lead to a withdrawal of China's commitment to alleviate potential conflict around the Korean Peninsula, and between Pakistan and India [24].

D. China's Reform Retreat

China's leaders, primarily Premier Zhu Rongji, are attempting to reform China's economic system and politics. If the US does not cooperate with this effort, China's reactionary forces, including officials of the Communist Party of China and other privileged groups [25], would try to pressure the current leaders to diminish their desire to reform China.

6. PULLING IT ALL TOGETHER

The two-sided debate and the imminent decision on China's trade status have motivated us to use a powerful modern multi-criteria decision approach, the Analytical Hierarchy Process, to examine the positives and negatives of the options. This approach will allow us to cull the most promising of the three positive alternatives.

This analysis brings two strengths to the debate. It is comprehensive by identifying all the issues bearing on the three factors of the decision: economic, security, and political. It is also an objective examination of the problem strictly based on criteria and priorities that anyone might consider in the decision.

Our analysis involves four steps. First, we prioritize the criteria in the benefits, costs, opportunities and risks hierarchies. Figure 1 shows the resulting prioritization of these criteria. The alternatives and their priorities are shown under each criterion. The syntheses of the priorities of the alternatives are shown beneath each hierarchy.

The priorities shown in Figure 1 were derived methodically from judgments which compared the elements involved in pairs. The judgment of preference of one element over another expresses the strength of that preference. This strength can be represented numerically. For the readers to estimate our original pairwise judgments which are not shown here, form the ratio of the corresponding two priorities shown and then take the closest whole number or its reciprocal if it is less than one.

It is likely that in a particular decision, the benefits, costs, opportunities and risks are not equally important, so we must also prioritize them. This is shown in Table 1. We established priorities for the economic, security and political factors themselves as shown in Figure 2 and Table 1 and used them to rate the importance of the benefits, costs, opportunities and risks. Finally, we used the priorities of the latter to combine the synthesized priorities of the alternatives in the four hierarchies to obtain their final ranking shown at the bottom of Table 2. It turns out that PNTR is by far the preferred outcome.

Note that in Figure 1 we have used the normalized reciprocal values of the synthesized priorities for the criteria and the alternatives with respect to the costs and the risks. The reason for this is that in making pairwise comparisons for example under costs, we asked which is the more important cost criterion and which is the more costly alternative. We do this first and identify the less costly element of a pair in each comparison as the unit, and estimate how many multiples of that unit, the more costly element is. We cannot directly compare the elements as to which is less costly because now the more less-costly element is larger than the less less-costly one is. Thus we must resort to inversion. For that purpose we used the transpose of the matrix of "which is more costly" matrix to calculate the priorities for what is less costly. Similarly, we calculated for the risks "which is less risky". If the consistency of the matrices is high, one can use the reciprocals of the derived priorities (in bold numbers) without resorting to transpose, as we did here because in fact the two sets of priorities are reciprocal when the matrix is consistent. For example, with respect to "Loss of US Access to China's Market," under costs, the priorities of the alternatives are 0.10, 0.30, and 0.60 whose reciprocals are respectively 10, 3.33, and 1.67. We normalized these values by dividing by their sum, 15 to obtain **0.67, 0.22,** and **0.11**. It is such reciprocal values for all the criteria and the alternatives with respect to each criterion that we used to obtain the synthesis of the alternatives under costs and did the same for the risks. For completeness, we have listed all the priorities for the benefits, and opportunities, and the reciprocal priorities for the costs and risks and obtain the overall synthesis of the alternatives. The purpose of the complete listing is to enable us to do a sensitivity analysis for the alternatives with respect both the criteria and also the merits of the benefits, costs, opportunities, and risks which we must determine first.

The assessment criteria we used to determine the priorities of the merits are shown in Figure 2.

The primary goal of any economic policy is to spur economic development. A trade policy always creates the inequity of "winners" and "losers," and this is why equity needs to be considered. **Economic growth** and **equity** should be used as the economic criteria. The security criterion has three sub-criteria. They are: **regional security** in Asia, particularly between China and Taiwan, **non-proliferation** efforts to diminish nuclear and conventional military competitions, and the direct **threat to US security.** Two sub-criteria are considered under the political criterion: the impact that the decision has on the **American voters** and the spread of **American values** such as democracy, human rights and labor rights.

How to derive the priority shown next to the goal of each of the four hierarchies in Figure 1 is shown in Table 1. We rated each of the four merits: benefits, costs, opportunities and risks, in terms of intensities for each assessment criterion. These intensities were themselves prioritized in a matrix as to how much each is preferred over each of the other intensities. We then assigned the appropriate intensity for each merit on all the assessment criteria. The outcome is given in Table 1.

Table 1. Priority Ratings for the Importance of Benefits, Costs, Opportunities, and Risks

	Very High (0.42)	High) (0.26)	Medium) (0.16)	Low (0.1)	Very Low (0.06)
		Benefits	**Costs**	**Opportunities**	**Risks**
Economic (0.56)	Growth (0.19)	High	Very Low	Medium	Very Low
	Equity (0.37)	Medium	High	Low	Low
Security (0.32)	Regional (0.03)	Low	Medium	Medium	High
	Non-Proliferation (0.08)	Medium	Medium	High	High
	Threat to US (0.21)	High	Very High	High	Very High
Political (0.12)	Constituencies (0.1)	High	Very High	Medium	High
	American Values (0.02)	Very Low	Low	Low	Medium
Priorities		**0.25**	**0.31**	**0.20**	**0.24**

Figure 1. The Four Decision Hierarchies for Benefits, Costs, Opportunities, and Risks

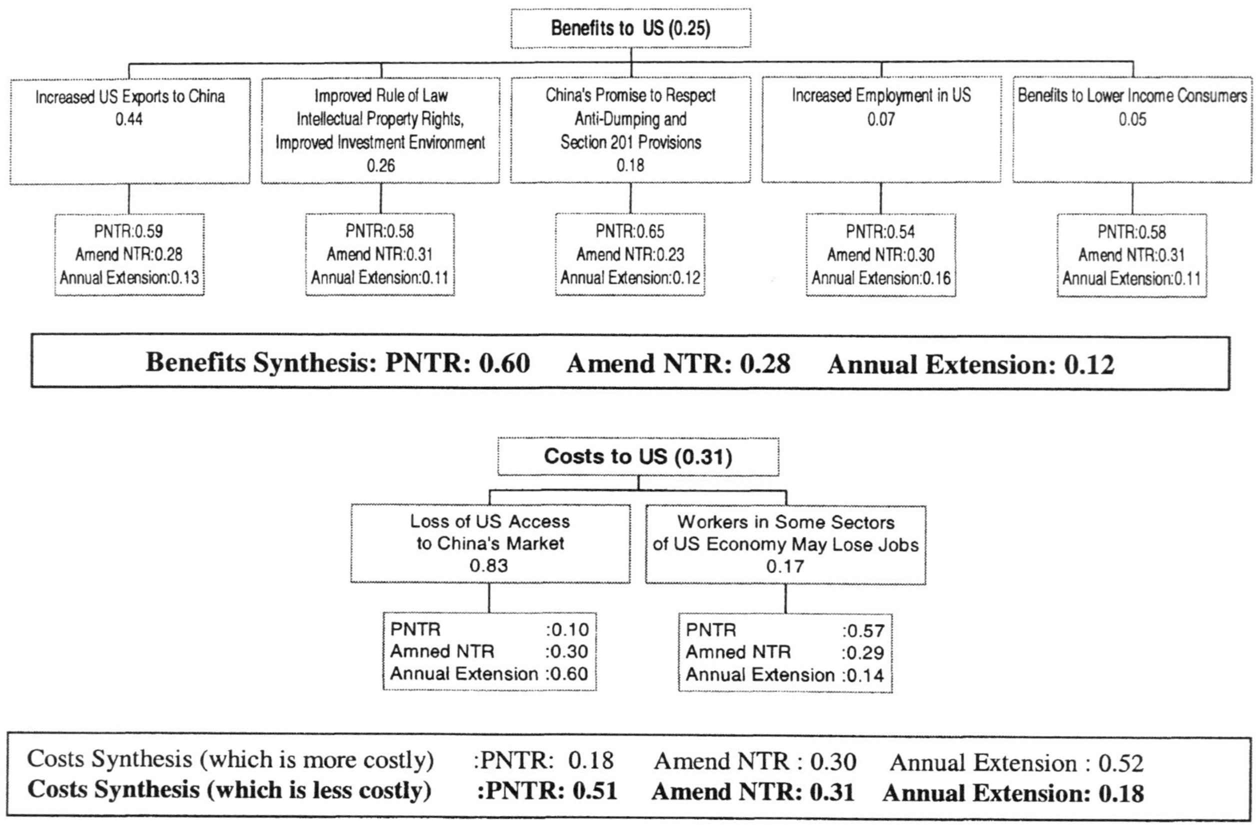

Figure 1. (cont'd.)

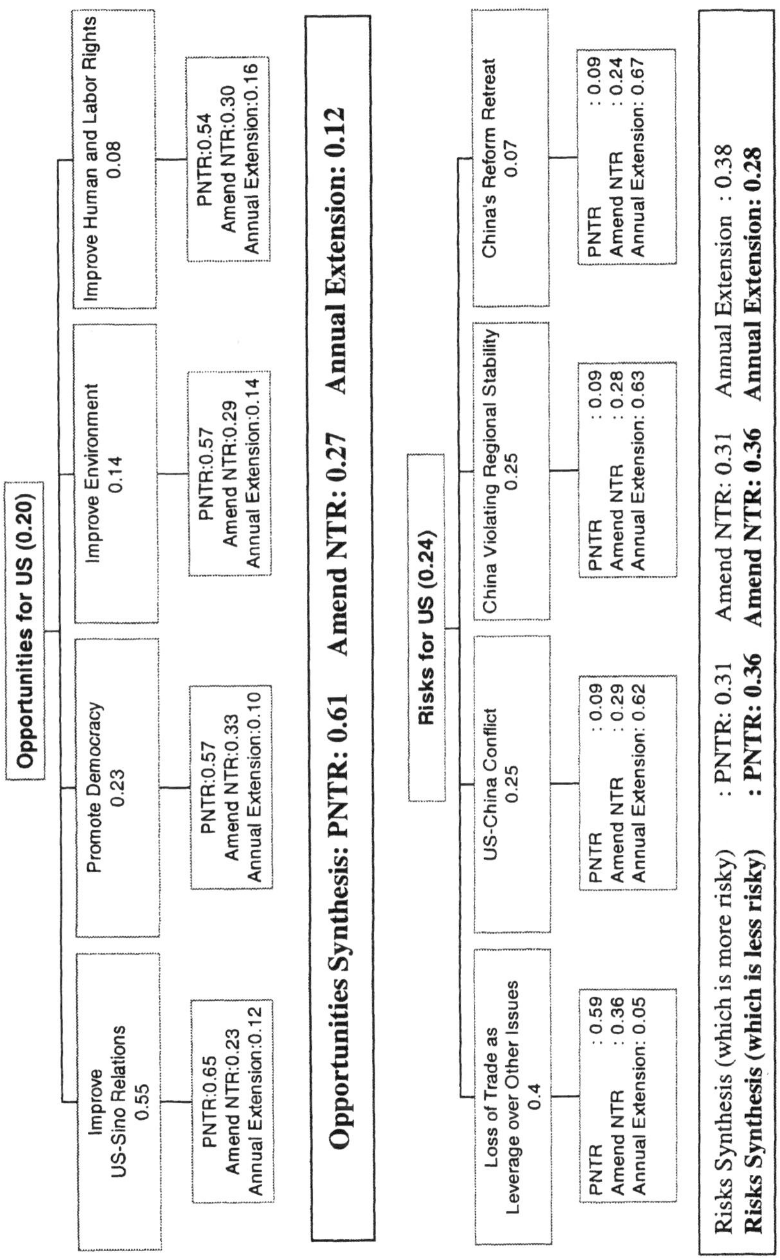

Figure 2. Hierarchy for Rating Benefits, Costs, Opportunities, and Risks

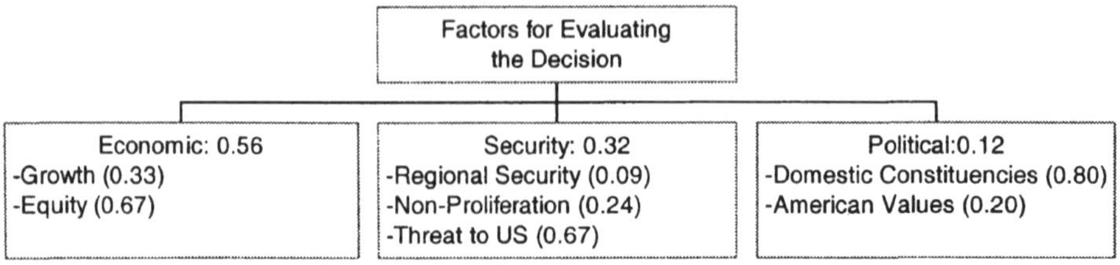

The overall priorities of the three decision alternatives as to what to do about China are given in Table 2.

Table2. Final Synthesis of Alternatives' Priorities

	PNTR	Amend NTR	Annual Extension
Benefits to US (0.25)	0.60	0.28	0.12
Costs to US (0.31)	0.51	0.31	0.18
Opportunities for US (0.20)	0.61	0.27	0.12
Risks for US (0.24)	0.36	0.36	0.28
Final Analysis	**0.51**	**0.31**	**0.18**

7. STABILITY OF THE OUTCOME WITH CHANGING PRIORITIES

Our analysis indicates that granting China Permanent Normal Trade Relations status is the best alternative (0.51) followed by Amend NTR by normalizing trade relations with China, while enacting a separate bill (0.31). The status quo, extension of the NTR status with China, is the least favorable option (0.18).

Comprehensive sensitivity analysis involves perturbing the priorities of the benefits, costs, opportunities, and risks and also jointly perturbing the priorities of the criteria and finally also perturbing the priorities of the alternatives. We would then note what happens to the rank order of the alternatives to determine if the most preferred one remains the same for all or at least for a preponderance of the perturbations. That would be a formidable task for anyone to do. There are two shortcuts in doing sensitivity. The first is to assume that the priorities of the alternatives with respect to the criteria are well understood and do not need to be perturbed. That leaves open the perturbations of the two higher level sets of criteria. Here we have one possible shortcut and that is to delimit the range of perturbation of the criteria with the assumption that very large perturbations would carry their priorities into unreasonable ranges no one would think is feasible. In that case, one would take the existing priorities and perturb them by small values up and down in combinations and note the resulting stability of the priorities of the alternatives. Even then, stability may not obtain in all the cases and one must decide on a way to justify adopting the leading alternative for the decision. The number of possibilities to try here can be very large. What we have done is to determine the stability of the outcome with respect to changes in the criteria with a fixed priority for the benefits, costs, opportunities, and risks. We then performed sensitivity by fixing the priorities of both the alternatives and criteria at their present values and perturbed the priorities of the benefits, costs, opportunities, and risks. This effort leads to the following abridged conclusions.

With the original priorities of the benefits, costs, opportunities, and risks, sensitivity analysis with the software Expert Choice shows that the best alternative is insensitive to thirteen out of the fifteen criteria in Figure 1. Only two criteria, "Workers in Some Sectors of US Economy May Lose Jobs," and "Loss of Trade as Leverage over Other Issues," substantial change in whose priorities individually and together, can make the top ranked alternative PNTR, less desirable. That would happen, if the importance of the first of the two criteria increases by more than twice its current value or if the importance of the second increases several times more than the current value. In both these cases, Annual Extension becomes the preferred alternative. There are numerous combinations of the priorities of the two criteria that can lead to rank reversal. However, reversal begins to occur only when the priorities of both criteria are simultaneously increased to twice their current value which, given the present circumstances, is highly unlikely. Thus, sensitivity analysis shows that the final outcome derived in Table 2 is very stable.

When we assumed that the priorities of the alternatives and of those of the criteria were fixed and varied the weights of the benefits, costs, opportunities and risks up and down by five percent in all possible combinations, we found that the priorities of the alternatives remained stable in all the cases.

Our sensitivity analysis indicates that overall, it is in the best interest of the United States to grant China PNTR status.

REFERENCES

[1] *Economist*, "China and the WTO," April 3, 1999, v351 i8113.

[2] Lorien Holland, and Shada Islam, "Call waiting," *The Far Eastern Economic Review*, March 9, 2000.

[3] *China daily*, "China concludes WTO accession talks with Poland, Kyrgyz Republic", March 25, 2000, http://www.chinadaily.com.cn/highlights/wto/wtoframe.html

[4] Sue Kirchhoff, "WTO, after 5 years, still getting its balance," *The Congressional Quarterly,* November 27, 1999.
[5] Michael Phillips, and Helene Cooper, "Clinton to send China-Trade bill to Congress," *The Wall Street Journal,* March 8, 2000.
[6] China trade relations working group, "The US-China WTO accession agreement: effects on trade flows," The White House, March 30, 2000, http://www.Chinapntr.gov/factsh
[7] US Department of Commerce, "Oral Testimony by Commerce Secretary William M. Daley," before the Senate Commerce, Science and Transportation Committee, April 11, 2000, http://204.193.246.62/public.ns
[8] *Economist,* "China and the WTO," April 3, 1999, v351 i8113.

[9] *Economist,* "The real leap forward," November 20, 1999, v353 i8146.
[10] *Wall Street Journal,* "Foreign banks in China fear loan limits curbing growth," March 2, 2000.
[11] *Economist,* "The real leap forward," November 20, 1999, v353 i8146.
[12] Yarbrough, V. Beth, and Yarbrough, M. Robert, "Case Three: Intellectual Property and Piracy in China," The World Economy, 1997, P330.
[13] WTO, "General Agreement on Trade in Services," http://www.wto.org/services/services/htm
[14] China trade relations working group, "The US-China WTO Accession Deal: A Clear Win for U.S. High Technology, Greater Openness and U.S. Interests, April 6, 2000, http://www.Chinapntr.gov/factsh
[15] *Economist*, "China opens up," November 20, 1999, v353 i8146.
[16] China trade relations working group, "The US-China WTO Accession Deal: A Clear Win for U.S. High Technology, Greater Openness and U.S. `Interests, April 6, 2000, http://www.Chinapntr.gov/factsh
[17] Yarbrough, V. Beth, and Yarbrough, M. Robert, "Case Four, Hard Choices: China, MFN Status, and the WTO," The World Economy, 1997, p247.
[18]Beth V. Yarbrough , and Robert M. Yarbrough, The World Economy, 1997, P330.
[19] China trade relations working group, "The US-China WTO Accession Agreement: Effects on Trade Flows," The White House, March 30, 2000, http://www.Chinapntr.gov/factsh
[20] Lori Nitschkei, "Buttonholing the Undeclared: China NTR Foes Hit the Hill," *The Congressional Quarterly,* April 15, 2000.
[21] China trade relations working group, "China PNTR and the Environment," The White House, April 5, 2000, http://www.chinapntr.gov/factsh
[22] *New York Times,* "Clintons' Words on China: Trade Is the Smart Thing," March 9, 2000.
[23] Lori Nitschke, and Miles Pomper, " With Date Set for China Trade Vote, Battle for Public Opinion Heats UP," *The Congressional Quarterly,* April 8, 2000.

[24] China trade relations working group, "China and Regional Security," White House, April 6, 2000, http://www.chinapntr.gov/factsh

[25] *Economist,* "China's worried boss," November 13, 1999, v353 i8145.

CHAPTER 23

DECIDING BETWEEN ANGIOPLASTY AND CORONARY ARTERY BYPASS SURGERY

1. PROBLEM

This chapter is an effort to create a decision process for patients and physicians to decide between open-heart bypass surgery or the less intrusive angioplasty procedure. The model was developed with "Expert Choice for Windows vs. 9.0," including pairwise comparisons of benefits, of risks and of both procedures. The overall result slightly favors angioplasty because it indicates a lower risk potential and in addition seems to be more beneficial for the patient. The results that we determined with the AHP model, support some of the research in the medical community, but not all evidence favors angioplasty.

More than two decades ago, medical scientists discovered a new procedure to treat heart disease (see Figure 1) besides using the conventional bypass surgery.

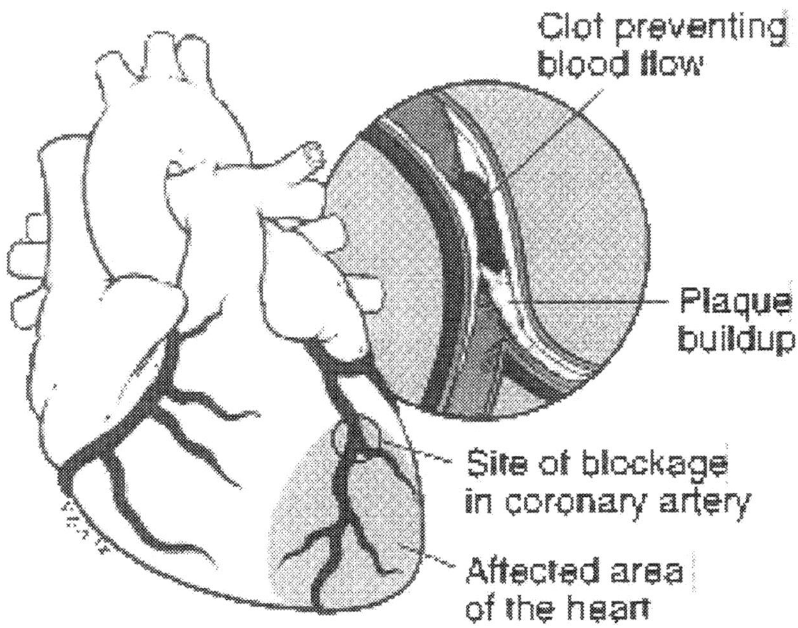

Figure 1

The bypass technique required a vein from elsewhere in the patients' body be taken and used to bypass the blocked artery (See Figure 2)

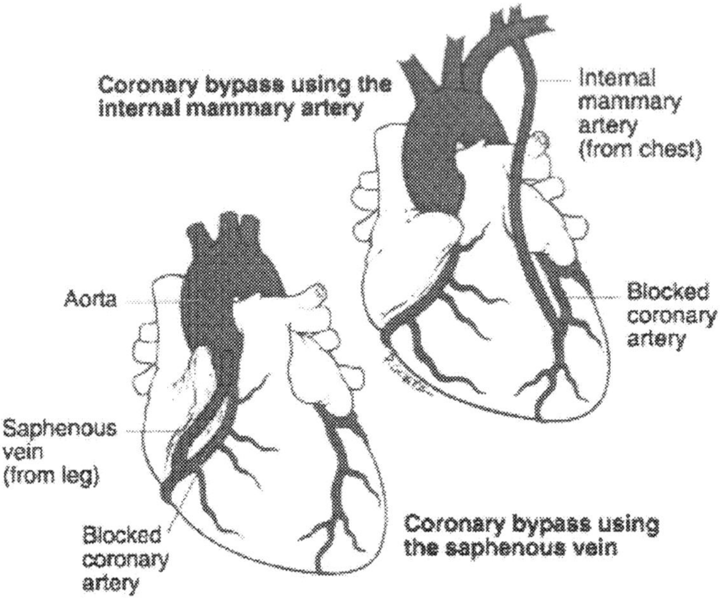

Figure 2

Angioplasty is a newer procedure in which a balloon is expanded in a narrowed blood vessel, stretching the walls of the vessel to restore normal blood flow. In 1996, 666,000 (452,000 men and 214,000 women) angioplasties were performed in the U.S. Angioplasty is mainly used if a patient has coronary artery disease (CAD), which is the most common form of heart disease in the U.S. CAD means that blood vessels that feed the patients' heart are narrowed or blocked (See Figure 3).

Figure 3

During angioplasty, a catheter (a thin, flexible tube) with a balloon at the tip is inserted into the patients' artery to widen the passageway (see Figure 4). Then, the catheter is removed. After the procedure, the patient may need to stay in the hospital for a day or more.

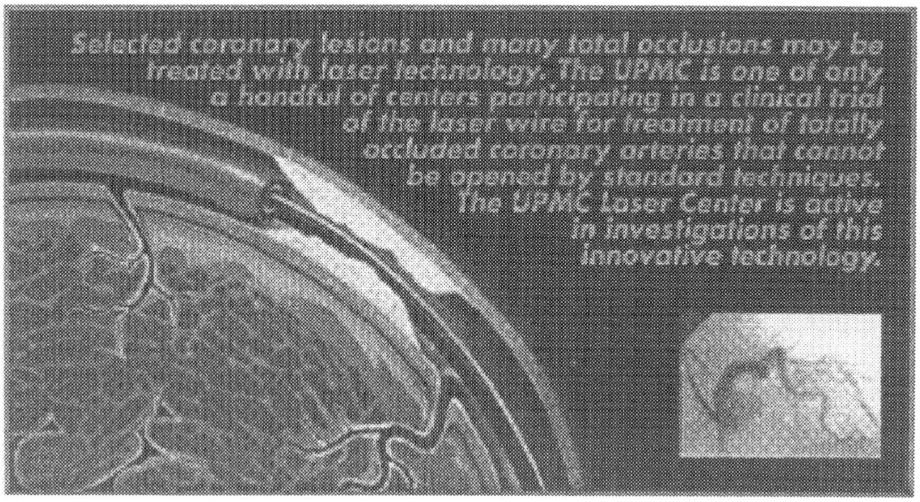

Figure 4

If a patient needs treatment for serious CAD, he/she and the doctor face one of the above-described prospects. Consequently, the central question the physician seeks to answer is whether to recommend bypass surgery or angioplasty. By using the AHP, the following discussion examines the various risks and benefits that are inherent in the two methods.

2. THE MODEL

Two models were built to answer the question of whether angioplasty is preferable to the more traditional bypass operation. The first model weighs the "benefits" of the angioplasty when it is compared to the bypass; several factors were taken into consideration and weighed accordingly. The second model did the same but weighed the most important "risks" of the angioplasty when compared to the bypass procedure. The following sections will detail each level of the model and attempt to explain its importance to the decision making process and why it is included in the analysis.

1. Benefit Analysis

Under the "Benefits" model there are two sub-headings, technical and patient benefits. Each is detailed in the following synopsis. The major benefit of the angioplasty procedure is that actual surgery is not required and it is less invasive to the patient. In addition, a single angioplasty procedure is less expensive then a bypass operation.

a. Technical Benefits

Age: For this model, age is the most important factor (see Table 1). With advancing patient age, angioplasty is a more suitable option since its higher recurrence rate is less likely to matter given shorter life expectancy.

Medical Comorbidities: The following comorbidities are included:

- Hypertension
- Diabetes
- Renal Failure
- Hepatic Failure
- Systemic Cancer
- High general risk for general anesthesia
- Poor rehabilitation candidate

The presence of any of these conditions would tend to favor angioplasty to varying degrees. For example, a bypass surgery for diabetics is better in comparison to an angioplasty because there is greater tendency for their arteries to reclog after angioplasty.

Patient Symptoms: Patient symptoms in the model include acute chest pain and congestive heart failure. Patient symptoms is one of the less important factors in the model. Patients with ongoing chest pain or congestive heart failure are better candidates for angioplasty, which can often relieve these symptoms quickly without the need for prolonged recovery following bypass.

Cardiac History: The most important factors of a patient's prior cardiac history in this model are:

- Lack of prior angioplasty and/or stenting
- Presence of prior bypass
- Lack of need for valve repair

Patients who have not had either prior angioplasty or stenting procedures are better candidates for angioplasty compared to those who have. In addition, patients who have had, and failed, a prior bypass are increasingly considered better candidates for angioplasty. Patients who need an open operation for valve repair would not be good candidates for angioplasty since they need an open procedure anyway.

Cardiac Pathology: This factor is rather important in our model (see Table 1). The following three elements are included in this factor:

- single vessel stenosis
- lack of complete occlusions
- less than 50% blockage of the left main coronary artery

Patients with stenosis (narrowing of a vessel) of only a single blood vessel are the best candidates for angioplasty; this is in contrast to patients who have had complete blockages of all three major arteries to the heart. If more than 50% of the left main coronary artery is blocked, it is better to have an open bypass operation.

Patient Preference: A rather less important factor is a patient's preference. The patient can have religious reasons for not allowing blood transfusions (e.g. Jehovah witnesses). In addition, it is necessary to pay attention to a patient's fear of general anesthesia and his/her refusal of surgical incision. Patients with a stronger preference for minimally invasive procedures or inability to have blood products transfused would be more strongly considered for angioplasty.

Physician Factors: The physician factors in the model are rather unimportant. They include experience, skill, and personal preference. Physicians with more experience and greater skill with angioplasty would tend to recommend angioplasty. Experience matters, especially in complex procedures like angioplasty. Standards recommend that a physician perform at least 75 angioplasties per year and that an institution perform at least 200 of these procedures annually.

b. Patient Benefits

Pain: Compared to open-heart bypass surgery, angioplasty is less painful. The general consensus among patients is that this is a sometimes uncomfortable, but not painful, procedure. The patient may feel some twinges in his/her chest when the balloon is inflated, but once the blockage is compressed, the pain should disappear. Additionally, the patient may also feel nauseous, feels his/her heart "skip" or have a headache during the procedure; these are all normal, brief side effects. Afterwards, the patient will probably feel some discomfort for the day of, and following, the procedure. Pain medication is available, and he/she should let his/her doctor or nurse know if he/she is experiencing additional discomfort.

Scars: Incisions and scars are almost invisible when the patient undergoes angioplasty. As described in the introduction, an angioplasty does not need opening the body of the patient. Instead, the catheter fed into the body only needs a tiny hole in the leg, near the patients' groin.

Recovery time: Patients recover faster from an angioplasty. A major benefit of using angioplasty is that this procedure is a less invasive approach compared to bypass surgery because it is carried out through a tiny catheter inside the artery. Since the surgery itself takes only a few hours, patients return to a normal lifestyle (e.g. work) much faster. In addition, angioplasty involves only insertion of a thin, balloon-tipped plastic tube (the catheter), through a small incision in the leg. Therefore, it is less traumatic than open-heart surgery. The patient is able to leave the hospital considerably earlier than those who undergo bypass surgery. However, in the long-term, because of repeating the procedure, angioplasty patients are more likely to spend more time in the hospital than bypass patients do. Nowadays, the procedure of angioplasty using a stent diminishes the total days a patient has to stay in the hospital.

Definitiveness of procedure: Although the first angioplasty was conducted more than twenty years ago, there is still a degree of insecurity using this method. A recurring blockage (restenosis) occurs in about one-third to one-half of the successful angioplasty procedures performed. A doctor may choose to do additional angioplasty, incorporating the stenting procedure to minimize the chance of restenosis. Sometimes bypass surgery is warranted. If a patient has received a stent, they will be on an anti-clotting medication for several weeks. A stent is a tiny mesh tube that is left at the blockage site to help the artery stay open. They may also receive special medication to help the arteries to heal. Following the angioplasty, a patient will need to see the doctor for a stress EKG to measure how effectively the blockage was eliminated. Also the patient would be put on an exercise program and his/her doctor would likely to see him/her several times a year to make sure no more blockages have occurred.

Expense: This analysis does not outline the quantifiable costs explicitly because these costs are about the same for both procedures. The angioplasty treatment costs less originally, but clots form so often that it has to be repeated, which increases the total costs.

2. Risk Analysis

Angioplasty blocks the artery briefly when the balloon is inflated and consequently the artery collapses immediately, which can trigger a heart attack if the blood supply to the heart muscle is already too severely restricted. The procedure can also damage or puncture an artery. In addition, the risk of blood clots increases slightly (as the catheter touches the artery wall). Another disadvantage of the method is that the artery frequently becomes blocked again, requiring another angioplasty or surgery.

There are in fact some potential negative side effects, which can occur after the angioplasty, e.g. the arm or leg (at the insertion site) may feel numb or cold, there may be signs of infection (redness or oozing) appearing at the insertion site or there may be chest pain and discomfort.

In addition, angioplasty patients have a higher likelihood of experiencing angina (chest and arm pain) and exercise-induced ischemia (insufficient supply of blood to a particular organ or tissue). In order to become angina-free over time, patients must undergo repeat procedures of revascularization (through either angioplasty and/or bypass surgery). This in turn increases all the other mentioned risks connected to both techniques. However, a new method of angioplasty using a stent can decrease repeated revascularizations.

The preceding factors along with others were considered in the model. As in the "Benefit" model, the "Risk" model also has two sub-headings, patient and technical risks. The technical risks include five equally weighted factors. However, the patient risks include eight separate factors with varying weights according to their importance.

Technical Risks

Medical Comorbidities: The first heading under the technical risks is comorbidities, which includes the anethesia risk and the rehabilitation risk for this procedure. The anethesia risk is weighted much higher because although it is an often practiced technique, and one can never be sure of a patient's reaction to it (see Table 2).

Cardiac Pathology: The next technical consideration is the pathology of the procedure. Under this heading there are three equally weighted factors. These factors are: single vessel stenosis, lack of total vessel occlusion and total vessel blockage.

Physician Factors: This technical consideration is rather arbitrary and depends on luck of the draw more than anything else. Under this heading there are three factors. The most important is the skill of the physician performing the procedure. This is closely followed by a related factor, the experience of the surgeon. Both are followed by the personal preference about what he/she believes is the most effective procedure.

Cardiac History: The cardiac history of the patient to receive the treatment is one that cannot be forgotten when considering a choice between the two procedures. The risks under cardiac history are equally weighted between three factors. The first is whether the patient has ever had an angioplasty performed before. The next factor is similar and that is whether the patient has any prior stenting. The final historical factor is if the patient has ever undergone a bypass procedure.

Age: The final technical consideration when weighting the risks of the two procedures is the age of the patient at the time of the procedure. Obviously, due to its less intrusive nature, angioplasty is preferred for older patients and for the same reason for younger patients who hope to avoid the bypass procedure.

Patient Risks

Death: With any type of medical procedure there is always the chance of death. This factor is weighted very heavily in the model, because it is a very significant risk factor for the patient.

Blood Loss: The risk of blood loss is very low in angioplasty, therefore it has the lowest weight in the model (see Table 2). Two types of blood loss are considered; the most important is loss that would require transfusion.

Infection: Even in today's pristine operating conditions, there is always a chance of infection when a surgical procedure is performed. The most common in these two procedures is the sternal infection that can result from a bypass procedure. With the angioplasty one associates groin infection where the incision is made during the procedure.

Lung: Difficulties can arise in a patient's lung when the bypass procedure is performed. Pulmonary edema is the problem that has the largest weight in the model, closely followed by pneumothorax.

Sudden Occlusion: Sometimes, following angioplasty or bypass surgery, one of the major coronary arteries can become suddenly blocked. This can lead to death of the cardiac muscle that it supplies, which is more common with angioplasty.

Arrhythmia: This is a condition that occurs when the heart muscle is irritated and its electrical activity altered. The more common form is atrial arrhythmia followed by ventricular arrhythmia, with the latter being much more dangerous to the patient. Atrial arrhythmia is not uncommon after bypass surgery and is less common after angioplasty. Fortunately, ventricular arrhythmia is rare following both procedures.

Disease recurrence: There always exists the danger of recurrence of the symptoms. The model lists the two most common: myocardial infarction and chest pain. In general, disease recurrence is much more common following angioplasty.

Vascular Complications: The final factor in patient risks is vascular complications, or injury to various blood vessels in the body. The two factors included under this injury are femoral pseudoaneurysm and venous insufficiency. The former is more common after angioplasty, while the latter is more common after bypass. Unfortunately a femoral pseudoaneurysm often requires an additional surgical procedure to repair it.

3. PATIENTS FOR MODEL

To test the model, it was appropriate to use it on two actual cases for which the decision as to whether to proceed with bypass or instead use angioplasty was known. The first patient was a 52-year-old man with all the symptoms associated with the onset of heart disease. He is a smoker, asthenic, with high cholesterol and most importantly a strong family history of coronary artery disease. This patient had a history of mild chest pain when he exerted himself, such as when shoveling snow. One day he experienced severe chest pain and subsequently had a heart attack. Imaging at the hospital indicated severe triple vessel disease with complete occlusion of two to three vessels. Clinically this patient would be selected for the bypass procedure because of the high risk of recurrence, the severity of his disease and because he had complete occlusions. When this patient's characteristics were put through the AHP model, it also favored the bypass procedure.

The second clinical case was an 87-year-old woman, who remained an active non-smoker and had no family history of heart disease. She was a diabetic who experienced mild renal failure. With no prior history of chest pain, she developed severe chest pain while walking. Imaging at the hospital indicated 85% stenosis of the left main coronary artery, the other three vessels showed no damage. Clinically this patient would be selected for angioplasty due to her low risk of recurrence, high risk for surgery given her age and diabetes. The AHP model also favored angioplasty for her.

In general, angioplasty has slightly greater benefits (0.528 versus 0.472) and slightly lower risks (o.445 versus 0.555) (see Tables 1 and 2).

4. CONCLUSION

As pointed out in the previous sections, angioplasty appears to be a more effective and successful treatment if a patient suffers from coronary artery heart disease. Nevertheless, it is not a cure. The patient needs to change any unhealthy habit (also called risk factor) that helped create his/her heart problems in the first place. Some risk factors are smoking, eating too much fat and salt, and not getting enough exercise. Making changes to reduce the risk factors can help keep the patients' heart condition from getting worse and may even improve the health of his/her heart.

Table 1. Benefits Hierarchy

Benefits

					Angioplasty	Bypass
Technical	Age		0.34		0.5	0.5
0.5	Medical Comorbities		0.21			
		Hypertension		0.027	0.5	0.5
		Diabetes		0.027	0.624	0.376
		Renal failure		0.233	0.76	0.24
		Hepatic failure		0.245	0.93	0.07
		Systemic cancer		0.214	0.932	0.068
		High risk for Anes.		0.171	0.832	0.168
		Poor rehab. Cand.		0.084	0.849	0.151
	Patient symptoms		0.032			
		Chest pain		0.5	0.749	0.251
		Congenital Heart failure		0.5	0.251	0.749
	Cardiac history		0.174			
		Prior Angioplasty		0.089	0.406	0.594
		Prior stenting		0.121	0.395	0.605
		Prior bypass		0.606	0.653	0.347
		Lack of need for valve repair		0.184	0.101	0.899
	Cardiac pathology		0.183			
		Single vessel stenoses		0.33333	0.81	0.19
		No complete occlusions		0.33333	0.683	0.317
		<50% block of main coronary artery		0.33333	0.107	0.893
	Patient preference		0.03			
		Religious		0.455	0.885	0.115
		Anesthesia		0.09	0.708	0.292
		Surgery		0.0455	0.974	0.026
	Physician factors		0.031			
		Experience		0.455	0.5	0.5
		Skill		0.455	0.5	0.5
		Personal preference		0.09	0.5	0.5
Patient						
0.5	Pain		0.171			
		Narcotic use		0.5	0.86	0.14
		Depression & anxiety		0.5	0.638	0.362
	Scars		0.046		0.941	0.059
	Recovery time		0.208			
		Length of hospital stay		0.33333	0.877	0.123
		Off work		0.33333	0.877	0.123
		Length of ICU stay		0.33333	0.541	0.459
	Definitiveness of Procedure		0.487			
		Addt'l test & monitoring		0.162	0.32	0.68
		Addt'l procedures & surgery		0.838	0.12	0.88
	Expense		0.088			
		Insurance		0.33333	0.685	0.315
		Hospital		0.33333	0.655	0.345
		Society		0.33333	0.624	0.376
	Composite Priorities				**0.528**	**0.472**

Table 2. Risks Hierarchy

	Risks			Angioplasty	Bypass
Technical					
0.5	Medical comorbidities	0.2			
	Anesthesia risk		0.885	0.093	0.907
	Rehabilitation risk		0.115	0.245	0.755
	Cardiac pathology	0.2			
	Single vessel stenoses		0.33333	0.5	0.5
	Lack of total vessel occlusion		0.33333	0.208	0.792
	Total vessel blockage		0.33333	0.863	0.137
	Physician factors	0.2			
	Experience		0.364	0.5	0.5
	Skill		0.493	0.5	0.5
	Personal preference		0.143	0.5	0.5
	Cardiac history	0.2			
	Prior angioplasty		0.326	0.658	0.342
	Prior stenting		0.326	0.033	0.967
	Prior bypass		0.348	0.5	0.5
	Age	0.2		0.5	0.5
Patient					
0.5	Death	0.438		0.1	0.9
	Blood loss	0.02			
	Anemia		0.246	0.086	0.914
	Transfusion		0.754	0.097	0.903
	Infection	0.07			
	Sternal wound infection		0.923	0.016	0.984
	Groin wound infection		0.077	0.274	0.726
	Lung	0.059			
	Pulmonary edema		0.626	0.136	0.864
	Pneumothorax		0.374	0.105	0.895
	Sudden Occlusion	0.218		0.887	0.113
	Arrhythmia	0.059			
	Atrial		0.079	0.31	0.69
	Ventricular		0.921	0.684	0.316
	Disease recurrence	0.1			
	Chest pain		0.104	0.942	0.058
	Myocardial Infarction		0.896	0.928	0.072
	Vascular complications	0.037			
	Femoral Pseudoaneurysm		0.64	0.906	0.094
	Venous insufficiency in lower extremeties		0.36	0.039	0.961
	Composite Priorities			**0.445**	**0.555**

The outcome of the analysis using the AHP indicates only a very slight tendency to rather do an angioplasty instead of the traditional and more definitive open-heart bypass surgery. This outcome appears to be a consequence of the great similarities in the effects of the two surgical techniques (e.g. long-term survival rates and quality of life measures).

However, the decision whether to do an angioplasty or an open-heart bypass surgery should consider each patient on an individual basis. Doing either procedure itself must be considered on an individual basis as well.

INDEX

FSC
www.fsc.org
MIX
Papier | Fördert
gute Waldnutzung
FSC® C083411

Kolibri 360 GmbH
Ferdinand-Jühlke-Straße 7
99095 Erfurt, Deutschland
produktsicherheit@kolibri360.de